SAP S/4HANA Systems in Hyperscaler Clouds

Deploying SAP S/4HANA in AWS, Google Cloud, and Azure

André Bögelsack
Utpal Chakraborty
Dhiraj Kumar
Johannes Rank
Jessica Tischbierek
Elena Wolz

Foreword by Alexander Zeier

Apress®

SAP S/4HANA Systems in Hyperscaler Clouds: Deploying SAP S/4HANA in AWS, Google Cloud, and Azure

André Bögelsack
Bern, Switzerland

Johannes Rank
Irschenberg, Germany

Utpal Chakraborty
Kolkata, India

Jessica Tischbierek
München, Germany

Dhiraj Kumar
Kolkata, India

Elena Wolz
Ismaning, Germany

ISBN-13 (pbk): 978-1-4842-8157-4
https://doi.org/10.1007/978-1-4842-8158-1

ISBN-13 (electronic): 978-1-4842-8158-1

Managing Director, Apress Media LLC: Welmoed Spahr
Acquisitions Editor: Jonathan Gennick
Development Editor: Laura Berendson
Coordinating Editor: Gryffin Winkler

Cover image designed by Freepik (www.freepik.com)

Distributed to the book trade worldwide by Springer Science+Business Media LLC, 1 New York Plaza, Suite 4600, New York, NY 10004. Phone 1-800-SPRINGER, fax (201) 348-4505, e-mail orders-ny@springer-sbm.com, or visit www.springeronline.com. Apress Media, LLC is a California LLC and the sole member (owner) is Springer Science + Business Media Finance Inc (SSBM Finance Inc). SSBM Finance Inc is a **Delaware** corporation.

For information on translations, please e-mail booktranslations@springernature.com; for reprint, paperback, or audio rights, please e-mail bookpermissions@springernature.com.

Apress titles may be purchased in bulk for academic, corporate, or promotional use. eBook versions and licenses are also available for most titles. For more information, reference our Print and eBook Bulk Sales web page at http://www.apress.com/bulk-sales.

Any source code or other supplementary material referenced by the author in this book is available to readers on GitHub.

Printed on acid-free paper

To our families, colleagues, and friends.

Table of Contents

About the Authors

 **André Bögelsack** works as Managing Director for Accenture in Switzerland and supports customers of all industries in moving their SAP systems into the cloud and operating those systems in a cost-efficient way on Hyperscaler Cloud platforms. He received a PhD from Technische Universität München in the area of SAP.

 **Utpal Chakraborty** works as Manager for Accenture in India and serves multiple clients across the industries. His main focus is migrating and operating SAP S/4 systems in the Hyperscaler Cloud. He combines a strong understanding of the technology of public clouds as well as SAP technology, which helps to mitigate common risks to such projects.

Dhiraj Kumar works as Senior Manager for Accenture India, and, together with his team, he managed the move of SAP systems of several customers into the public cloud. He has a strong focus on the automation of SAP migrations and new ways of provisioning SAP in the cloud.

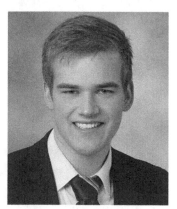

Johannes Rank is Head of the SAP Basis team at the SAP University Competence Center at Technische Universität München. He is a certified SAP HANA Technology Associate and oversees the operations of all the SAP S/4HANA systems with a strong focus on migration and automation. He holds a Master of Science in Business Informatics from Technische Universität München.

Jessica Tischbierek is Specialist Customer Engineer for SAP on Google Cloud at Google Deutschland in Munich. Before starting at Google, she was in the SAP consulting business for a long time. She holds a Bachelor of Science and a Master of Science in Business Informatics and an extensive experience in SAP technology and public clouds.

Elena Wolz works as SAP Basis Administrator for the SAP University Competence Center at Technische Universität München. She is the Product Owner for SAP S/4HANA and is responsible for all the deployments of S/4 systems in Hyperscaler Clouds as well as traditional hosting scenarios. She holds a Master of Science in Business Informatics from Technische Universität München.

Foreword

The constant technological change and the compulsion to digitize have never been more evident than in the past two years when the Corona pandemic changed work habits drastically. It was at this point that Chief Information Officers (CIOs) became Chief Digitization Officers with new challenges and new demands from the wider world of work.

All those CIOs who had already consistently focused on digitization before Corona and had understood the technical change not as a challenge, but as an opportunity, could consider themselves lucky. The companies that had already focused on high flexibility and scaling before the pandemic and had already moved their IT systems to the public cloud were well prepared. They were able to pass on the full potential of the public cloud to their employees.

With the same speed that the Corona pandemic drove cloud adoption, CIOs must now address the second major IT challenge: SAP S/4HANA. The shift from traditional SAP ERP systems to a digital core based on SAP S/4HANA is a daunting task in many organizations and requires close collaboration between business and IT departments.

By combining the use of public cloud services with the transformation to SAP S/4HANA, companies open up new possibilities. Business processes can be redesigned and made more flexible, and companies create a new, highly flexible technological platform for the continued success of the company.

This book shows how companies can easily build a new technical platform for future SAP S/4HANA systems in the public cloud. However, the book does not limit itself to just one of the major public clouds but describes the three most important market players: Microsoft Azure, Amazon Web Services, and Google Cloud. The reader thus receives a comprehensive overview of the individual public clouds and learns how those can best be used for SAP S/4HANA systems.

The book is a must-read before implementation for all companies that are not yet using SAP S/4HANA and are yet to create this technical platform. It is also suitable for all those companies that are already in a public cloud but still want to gain inspiration and see how other companies are making this transition.

FOREWORD

I am pleased that the authors have summarized the topic so comprehensively but succinctly in one book. The technical depth is remarkable and reflects the importance of the topic. The book will help you, dear reader, to answer the important questions regarding the deployment, migration, and operation of SAP S/4HANA systems in the public clouds. I hope you enjoy it!

Prof. Dr. Alexander Zeier

1. Cloud Fellow

CTO ASBG

Global Managing Director

Accenture GmbH

Appreciations

Book projects are always a great challenge for the authors and require a lot of time and energy, which is not available for other things. Therefore, the authors would like to take this opportunity to thank their families, colleagues, as well as project partners and customers.

Individual Appreciations

André Bögelsack

I would like to thank my wife Kathrin and my two children for their understanding when I sat at the laptop on weekends or in the evenings rather than spending time with them. A special thanks goes to **Niklas Feil**, who provided a lot of content for the book. Many thanks for this! Another special thanks goes to Samiksha Munjal for keeping my back free, when I was too much focused on writing the book. For inspiring me to write another book, I would like to thank Debolina Banerjee – thank you!

My thanks also go to all the co-authors, without whose expert knowledge and time commitment we would never have written the book. I am very happy that we were able to do this together.

Utpal Chakraborty

First of all, I would like to express my gratitude to Dr. André Bögelsack, who gave me the opportunity to share my knowledge and experience with a wider audience through this book, which would not have been possible without him. I would also like to thank my family who supported me in this pandemic situation, and I dedicate my achievement to my daughter Sreejani.

Last but not least, a big thank you to my co-authors, without whose support this would not have been possible.

Dhiraj Kumar

My thanks to my wife Shikha for her constant motivation and understanding and to my son Agastya for giving me the time to write this book. My special thanks to my friends Ravi Kumar and Ravi Surana, Kunal, Misal, and Sushobhit for keeping me alive (and grounded) with their weekend calls.

APPRECIATIONS

A special thanks to Dr. André Bögelsack, who believed in me more than I believed in myself. Thank you André for always being there for me. This book has taken its shape through the great collaboration with my co-authors. To all of them, my very special thanks for their time and expertise.

Last but not least, thank you to my brother Manoj Kumar, who always inspires and encourages me in whatever I do. Thank you Bhaiya.

Elena Wolz

I would like to thank my family and friends for their support and understanding when I spent evenings in the company with load balancing modules and availability groups instead of with them. I would also like to thank the SAP UCC TU Munich for their support during the project, as well as my colleagues at the SAP UCC TU Munich for their everlasting encouragement. I would also like to thank my co-authors, whose contributions and collaborative exchanges helped to provide new perspectives. A special thanks goes to Johannes Rank; I appreciated the close collaboration very much.

Johannes Rank

A big thank you goes to my co-authors of this book, especially to Andrè who made it possible for me to contribute my expertise in the first place and without whose help this book would probably not have been possible. I would also like to say a special thank you to my family. To my daughter, who had to do without her dad many weekends and evenings, and to my wife, who always had my back.

Jessica Tischbierek

First, I would like to thank my co-authors for the exchange of experiences and especially Dr. André Bögelsack for the request, ideas, and opportunity to contribute to this book project.

A huge thank you goes to all my colleagues who supported this book with their ideas, motivation, and especially their review of the content: Hasmig Samurkashian, Thorsten Staerk, Benjamin Schuler, Alexander Schmid, Abdelkader Sellami, Alison Hettrick, and to my manager Ian Moria.

Finally, a very special thank you goes to my partner Mike for his ongoing support, critical questions, as well as his understanding of the intense book project.

Joint Acknowledgments
Accenture

The author team would like to thank all those who contributed to the success of this book and who supported the book during its creation. In particular, this includes Tobias

Regenfuss, Alan Mohr, Veronica Wolters, Bernhard Schulzki, and the entire Accenture Cloud First leadership team. Without their dedication and support, this book would not have been written.

SAP

We would also like to thank SAP and the SAP University Alliances (SAP UA) program, which has supported universities worldwide for many years and helped make book publications possible in this way.

Partners and customers

Writing a book about multiple Hyperscalers can only succeed with the support of Microsoft, Amazon, and Google. Without this support on technical issues, the book would not have come to fruition. For this, the entire author team would like to thank – especially the Alliances teams of the vendors.

To make the book more exciting with the many examples from the customers, we also need the support of the respective companies. We would like to thank LANXESS and especially Tobias Greskamp for their support.

Technische Universität München

In addition, we would like to thank the Technische Universität München, the Chair of Information Systems (i17), and the SAP University Competence Center (SAP UCC), which provide an excellent basis for research and development in the field of SAP and cloud computing. Special thanks go to the Head of the SAP UCC, Dr. Holger Wittges, and to the Chair Holder Prof. Dr. Helmut Krcmar.

Google

We would like to thank Google Cloud and all teams working around SAP on Google Cloud: Solution and Sales Specialists, Product Engineering, the Center of Excellence, SAP Management, the SAP Partnership Team, and many more. A very special thank you to the global SAP Marketing team and the Accenture Partner Alliances team.

Apress

Last but not least, we would like to thank our lectors, who helped us and guided us during the whole time. Many thanks to Jonathan and Jill for their guidance and patience.

André Bögelsack, Utpal Chakraborty, Dhiraj Kumar, Elena Wolz, Johannes Rank, and **Jessica Tischbierek**

Introduction

The public cloud has existed for more than ten years, and it is impossible to imagine the current IT landscape without it. Many well-known companies rely on services from the public cloud to strengthen their IT, and Hyperscalers now form the backbone of many companies from a wide range of industries. Millions of customers and consumers of the companies use websites or order portals, which are operated on one of the large public clouds, in their daily operations.

SAP systems represent the neuralgic points in the IT operations of companies. Production lines come to a standstill or trucks can no longer leave the warehouses if SAP systems fail. Hardly any other IT system has this importance in today's world. Nevertheless, more and more companies are moving SAP systems to the public clouds. This is done due to cost pressure, pressure to innovate, or simply to expand capacity.

Goal of the Book

With the current pressure among all SAP customers to jump to the new generation of SAP S/4HANA systems, the topic of public clouds is also gaining momentum. Companies are taking advantage of this S/4 momentum to migrate to a public cloud in addition to transforming to SAP S/4HANA.

This book will introduce you to several points of public clouds and SAP S/4HANA systems. Here, in addition to the theoretical constructs, the practical implementations are also shown. The book enables you to directly implement and provision a new SAP S/4HANA system on one of the three big public clouds: Azure, AWS, and Google. The chapters are structured identically, and thus the necessary steps for setting up and operating SAP S/4HANA systems can be compared between the public clouds.

In all chapters, the authors provide real-world examples to make the content tangible and applicable. The book will detail the following aspects:

- The emergence of public clouds and the three largest Hyperscalers: Microsoft Azure, Amazon Web Services, and Google Cloud

- The offerings available from SAP for the use of cloud services

- The architecture of SAP S/4HANA systems

- The key drivers and use cases for SAP S/4HANA systems on a public cloud

- The provisioning and operations of SAP S/4HANA systems on the three main public clouds: Microsoft Azure, Amazon Web Services, and Google Cloud

After completing all chapters, you will know what to look for when deploying public clouds and how to efficiently run SAP S/4HANA systems on public clouds without getting out of line with the effort required to run them or, alternatively, the cost of running them on public clouds.

Organization and Structure

The book guides you through the typical life cycle of an SAP S/4HANA system, highlighting the important aspects of selecting a public cloud, provisioning SAP S/4HANA systems, and operating them on the public clouds:

- Chapter 1 provides an overview of the most important terms, such as private, public, and hybrid clouds. It also presents the three most important public clouds in detail and outlines the current market of cloud providers with, for example, the IBM Cloud. Chapter 1 then sheds light on SAP's cloud strategy, the SAP RISE program, as well as the SAP HANA Enterprise Cloud, which is present in the market as a private cloud.

- Chapter 2 describes the architecture of the SAP S/4HANA systems, which will later be taken up again and again in the following chapters. It also contains the important aspects for operating SAP S/4HANA systems on the public cloud, such as sizing, backup, high availability, and automation. The following chapters on the respective public clouds show the implementations of these points.

- Chapter 3 describes the general procedures for deploying and migrating SAP S/4HANA systems and explains, for example, points such as greenfield and brownfield deployments, but also shows possible migration scenarios for the systems. It also discusses the most important factors when selecting a new Hyperscaler.

- Chapter 4 is the first part of the book to describe the deployment of Amazon Web Services. To this end, the chapter first explains the most important terminology, which is AWS specific. It goes into the types of machines available, but also explains the basic concepts of networking and storage.

- Chapter 5 is the practical part on AWS and shows how to create and control an SAP S/4HANA system on AWS. For this purpose, the chapter shows the system to be implemented and then describes the steps that can be taken to build the system on AWS. The important typical use cases, such as recovery after a disaster case, are described successively.

- Chapter 6 is the first chapter on Microsoft Azure and describes how Azure can be used as a public cloud solution and which important basic concepts exist for the operation and provisioning of SAP S/4HANA systems.

- Chapter 7 builds on the foundation previously established in Chapter 6 on Microsoft Azure and illustrates the provisioning of a new SAP S/4HANA system and shows the implementation of the important use cases from Chapter 2.

- Chapter 8 highlights the important concepts and architectures of Google Cloud and describes how SAP S/4HANA systems are scheduled in Google Cloud.

- Chapter 9 uses the previously described concepts of the Google Cloud to show the concrete implementation of an SAP S/4HANA system in the Google Cloud.

- In the concluding chapter, Chapter 10, all the important points from the previous chapters are summarized, and an outlook is given on developments in the coming years.

After completing all chapters, you, dear reader, will have a comprehensive overview of all aspects of the topic "SAP S/4HANA systems on Hyperscaler clouds" and will know how to plan, conceptualize, implement, and control these systems on public clouds.

CHAPTER 1

Introduction to Public Cloud and Hyperscalers

Before entering the world of SAP S/4HANA systems on the public cloud, this chapter first describes the basic features of cloud computing and introduces the most important terms. This makes it easier to understand the rest of the book.

Important Features of Public Cloud

Cloud computing emerged in the mid-2000s and was developed on the basis of excess capacity in data centers. Originally, the approach was to allocate excess computing capacity to other customers. The goal was to achieve consistently high utilization throughout the year.

Cloud computing is, on the one hand, about a new way of delivering services to customers and businesses. For example, cloud services and services from the cloud can be used *without major prior contract negotiations*. Only the general terms and conditions (GTCs) have to be accepted and a valid payment option has to be deposited, and then the services can already be used.

On the other hand, cloud computing is an important factor in *innovations* and the introduction of completely new services. In the meantime, not very much has remained of the original idea of making surplus capacities available. Cloud providers are constantly making new services available and regularly also new versions of the services. Customers benefit from this because new services do not have to be explicitly requested but come automatically with the use of the cloud.

In addition to the *simplicity* of using the services and the very high level of innovation, another point is in focus. In principle, the cloud knows no limits, and so customers and companies can assume limitless capacities in a cloud. This distinguishes clouds from conventional providers, where resources are usually limited.

© André Bögelsack, Utpal Chakraborty, Dhiraj Kumar, Johannes Rank, Jessica Tischbierek, Elena Wolz 2022
A. Bögelsack et al., *SAP S/4HANA Systems in Hyperscaler Clouds*, https://doi.org/10.1007/978-1-4842-8158-1_1

The *high scaling* of the clouds, that is, the large number of customers, means that the economy of scales applies in full. Here, customers benefit from providing the same services to other customers and achieving a very low price.

If the most important features of a cloud are summarized, the following characteristics are the key points of clouds:

- Simplicity of use and access

- High level of innovation through new services

- Very large capacities/infinite capacities

- Very high price attractiveness

In the context of Hyperscalers, such as Amazon, Microsoft, and Google, the preceding criteria apply, and companies can take advantage of the benefits. However, the many advantages are also paired with some disadvantages when using the clouds. Here, it is not so much technical, but rather organizational and process-related points that can be interpreted as disadvantages.

Although the use of clouds is very simple, the use must also be constantly and continuously controlled. Very often, a "shadow IT" exists alongside the actual IT, in which specialist departments have provided themselves with IT services from the cloud. This contradicts central IT and efficient control of the entire IT.

Although the prices of the cloud are very good, the use of the cloud in a first step can become more expensive than if a company had continued to work without a cloud. So, to a certain extent, the use of the cloud must be accompanied by a transformation of IT. Simply transferring IT services to the cloud without transformation usually does not bring the hoped-for effects.

Unlimited resources in a cloud were a reality for a very long time. There were never any reports of bottlenecks or unavailability of resources. Since the Corona crisis, however, it has become clear that clouds are also "just" data centers with conventional capacities. At the latest since the Microsoft Azure Cloud ran out of spare capacity for certain SAP workloads in March 2020, the myth of infinite resources has been disproved.

Companies have to do a lot themselves when using clouds. This is very different from using services from a service provider. Here, the provider does a lot of tasks and takes responsibility for the tasks and results. A cloud provider will only do this for the services that are their responsibility. In contrast to a service provider, however, these are much fewer. Therefore, the customers have to take over tasks or commission another provider with them.

When operating SAP systems on a cloud, the difference to the service providers must be taken into account. This is illustrated in Table 1-1.

Table 1-1. *Responsibilities in the Public Cloud*

Component	Responsibility with Customer	Responsibility with Cloud Provider	Responsibility with Service Provider
Data center			
Compute/storage/ network			
Security and compliance			
Operations of infrastructure			
Stack design			
Operating system			
Operations of SAP basis			
Operations of non-SAP applications			

All dark fields in the table show the responsibilities of the respective parties. It is clear that the typical service provider can map the complete stack and provide all services in a traditional hosting. When using the cloud, customers must provide services themselves, as the cloud provider does not.

Public, Private, and Hybrid Cloud

The cloud computing market is very heterogeneous and permeated by many trends. Three main clouds are used for SAP workloads and operations in a cloud: the public cloud, the private cloud, and the hybrid cloud.

The **public cloud** is a cloud that most companies are familiar with. It is the type of cloud which is offered by all Hyperscalers (i.e., Amazon, Microsoft, and Google). The name public already implies the most important feature of the cloud – it is public and equally accessible to every customer. However, this does not mean that all companies can see all workloads and all data of all other companies. It simply means that the cloud is available to all companies equally and that the cloud has not been built dedicatedly for just one company. The providers of the public cloud have implemented mechanisms for this, which also make access to the resources of a company possible only for the actual company.

In contrast to a public cloud, the **private cloud** is set up exclusively for one company. All resources of this private cloud are only available to one company and can also only be used by the company. However, the private cloud has a decisive disadvantage. The built-up resources of the private cloud can be used until the capacities are reached and must then be expanded. Private cloud operators implement such expansions in a similar way to normal service providers: hardware resources are acquired exclusively for the customer and therefore also invoiced. Another disadvantage of private clouds is the strong focus on the intended use. The providers of private clouds do not enrich the clouds with new services, but leave them as they are.

In addition to the public cloud and the private cloud, there is also the *hybrid cloud*. This is not so much a cloud but a merger of a public cloud with a private cloud or with an existing data center of a company. This already shows that the majority of companies are directly in a hybrid cloud scenario as soon as the first services from the public cloud are consumed.

Many companies still operate SAP systems in their own data centers. These data centers often reach their capacity limits or are heading to end of support because they have become too old. This also happened at a large German manufacturing company. The data centers on the same campus were to be demolished to make room for new office buildings.

The company had several options open to it. It could use an external service provider with data center capacity, it could buy temporary data center capacity and operate it itself, or it could use the public cloud. The company strategically opted for the public cloud. Due to many projects and project activities, various numbers of SAP systems were required. When the company started provisioning these systems in the public cloud, it moved into the hybrid cloud scenario. Many systems still exist in the two data centers to be demolished, but the new systems are in the public cloud. This scenario is a hybrid one.

The preceding example shows that by simply using the first service from the public cloud, a company goes into the hybrid cloud scenario. This is what happens to all companies that go to the cloud with the first service.

Companies that combine two public clouds, for example, Google and Amazon, can also create a hybrid cloud. For example, some companies decide to move SAP workloads to one public cloud and the non-SAP workloads to another public cloud. In this way, two public clouds are combined with each other, and a large hybrid cloud is created.

Overview of the Clouds of the Major Market Players

Currently, the public cloud market is dominated by three Hyperscalers. These are Amazon Web Services, Google Cloud, and Microsoft Azure. All three Hyperscalers are presented in this chapter. In addition, the other cloud providers, which currently have small footprints such as IBM or Oracle, are also described.

Amazon Web Services
History

Amazon Web Services was the first real cloud provider on the market and is still one of the leading providers of cloud computing services. There are several versions to the reasons why Amazon Web Services started.

One version is based on a situation of excess capacity. In the early 2000s, Amazon's business was developing steadily, and due to the strong sales activities on Amazon's platform, the demands for computing power to provide the platform and its services became enormous. Particularly due to seasonal effects, such as Black Friday in the United States, demand increased dramatically and then dropped rapidly back to normal levels. Amazon reacted to this and built the platform accordingly in such a way that the load peaks were cushioned by the seasonal events and the platform ran in a performant and stable manner. This focus on maximum performance led to a steady overcapacity in Amazon's data centers during the rest of the year – outside of the seasonal effects. This excess capacity was made available as resources for customers. Then, in 2006, Amazon launched its Amazon Web Services subsidiary, which made capacity from Amazon's data center available externally through an open access portal.

Another version of the emergence of cloud computing at AWS is based on the internal processes and workflows within Amazon. Here, Amazon faced recurring issues due to the steady growth of its platform, where web developers had to repeatedly coordinate with data center teams on network, capacity, and availability. To eliminate this dependency, a type of commodity IT was introduced (AWS) that allowed web developers to assemble the necessary resources themselves. In other words, they became independent of data center teams. Amazon realized that any web developer would appreciate such capabilities and decided to make these new services available as Amazon Web Services.

Regardless of the version to emerge, the launch of Amazon Web Services was a resounding success. Within a few years, AWS managed to create a large customer base and thus achieve high usage of the platform – even if it was initially relatively complicated to get your own SAP systems up and running on AWS.

Current Market Position

AWS is the market leader and serves a very large number of customers from global corporations, as well as small- and medium-sized businesses and home users. AWS serves this broad abundance of customers by offering a very wide range of products.

AWS stands out among customers because of the following:

- High density of AWS data centers in many different countries with availability zones

- Continuous updates of the cloud services with new features on a regular basis

- High availability of services with no major impact on a large number of customers so far

- Very large ecosystem with many third-party providers offering additional services

- Ease of adoption

However, AWS' clientele also sees some negative points:

- All services are paid, and in some cases the prices for cloud services are very high. This can lead to very high bills for using AWS.

- Strict contracts between customers and AWS with no flexibility to customize for businesses.

- Complexity in integrating services within AWS and with third-party providers.

- Very steep learning curve required and AWS support can't always assist – especially with third-party software (like SAP!).

In general, AWS can continue to defend its first place among cloud providers, and its high level of innovation and very strong customer base means this will not change in the foreseeable future. However, potential customers should keep an eye on costs and contractual arrangements.

Collaboration with SAP

Amazon began realizing the potential of hosting and operating SAP on AWS early on, as SAP systems are among the most important IT systems used by companies. As such, the systems are always in use and must achieve high availability. As early as 2011, SAP and AWS began working together to enable customers to host SAP systems on the public cloud.

AWS quickly focused on providing customers of HANA-based systems, a new platform. In the year 2016, the first large SAP HANA certified systems were made available (*r1.32xlarge*). The catalog of servers to host SAP HANA databases kept on growing over years offering customers a range to choose from to suit their workload, thus keeping the performance on top and price in check. AWS set the pace with this, and other cloud providers often followed.

AWS expanded the portfolio of supported SAP systems and now also tries to support the somewhat older SAP systems. Support for old R/3 systems, for example, still looks very limited. In fact, however, all companies still have to deal with R/3 or even R/2 systems, some of which have to be kept for regulatory reasons.

Microsoft Azure

History

Microsoft recognized the enormous benefits and potential of cloud computing very early on and launched the first version of Microsoft Azure in 2008 – just two years later than AWS. As of 2010, Microsoft's cloud computing platform became General Available; it was previously restricted to developers only. Microsoft changed the name of the platform a few times: from the introduction of the Azure platform as "Windows Cloud" to

"Windows Azure" to "Microsoft Azure" in 2014. Since 2014, the name has been constant and has established itself as an important brand in the cloud computing market.

Microsoft continued to steadily build Azure and expand the portfolio of services offered in Azure. Parallel to the expansion of the portfolio, Microsoft expanded into new regions. For example, Azure initially started in the United States and Europe, but very quickly expanded its offering. Currently, Azure includes 54 regions on all continents. Not every region offers the same services, but the most important infrastructure services can be accessed in all regions. The available regions can be viewed on Microsoft's website:

```
https://azure.microsoft.com/en-us/global-infrastructure/
geographies/#geographies
```

Microsoft bases the expansion of the Azure regions very much on the most important markets and countries, which have some strict specifications and regulations. For example, in Asia, the regions in India were built to address the rapidly growing market and to meet the legal requirements according to the data storage. With the same thought, Microsoft has built the regions in Switzerland and Germany to meet the industry norms of the Swiss banking industry and the EU directives according to DSGVO. The regions in the United States are the most developed regions, and this is also where new services will be made available first.

Current Market Position

Microsoft Azure is considered one of the leading providers of cloud computing in the current market studies (such as by Gartner), but usually takes second place behind Amazon Web Services. From a customer perspective, both providers set the pace in the individual categories. For example, Microsoft was the first cloud computing provider to be able to offer very large SAP HANA machines at the time, while AWS was only able to do so a short time later. Both providers keep taking turns from the customers' point of view.

In fact, Microsoft has a decisive advantage with its large market dominance in the Office area. Due to the wide distribution of Office products, Microsoft always has a starting point for negotiating additional cloud products. In addition, companies are currently making a strong shift from traditional Office products to Office365 products, which are offered in the cloud. This will allow Microsoft to expand its share of cloud computing. In addition, this keeps the hurdle for the use of further Azure services very low.

Microsoft Azure stands out among customers in particular due to the following points:

- Simple integration of existing infrastructure into MS Azure services (such as Active Directory or SharePoint)

- High compatibility with Linux

- Very high similarity with other Microsoft products, which makes it easier to switch to them

- Ease of use of new services

There are also points with Microsoft Azure which customers consider critical:

- High speed of new features causes interfaces and documentation to diverge with existing services.

- Support for Azure from Microsoft needs improvement, especially for specific questions and problems.

- Complex pricing of services and partly high, unexpected, costs during usage.

Microsoft can and will defend second place and has ambitions to challenge AWS for first place. Due to the high penetration of Microsoft products in enterprises, Microsoft is in an excellent position to further penetrate the market.

Collaboration with SAP

Microsoft and SAP have been working together for quite some time; in fact, their technological partnership goes back by 25 years. Microsoft entered the world of hosting for ERP systems with the introduction of SAP R/3 on the Microsoft Windows Server platform. Microsoft and SAP started their cooperation as early as 1989 and accelerated it in 1993. Microsoft, which itself offers an ERP system with Navision, also uses SAP as its ERP system with over 100,000 users.

SAP and Microsoft jointly develop the Microsoft platforms in Redmond and Walldorf. The Azure platform has been released for SAP for several years, although there are also some limitations in supporting older versions of SAP. However, this applies to all Hyperscalers.

Microsoft and SAP have announced an intensified partnership in 2021. This will be about collaboration on three important sectors: collaboration between people and employees, collaboration on the migration to SAP S/4HANA on the Azure platform, and collaboration on the technology level:

- Collaboration between employees: Here, SAP and Microsoft are planning very tight and high integration between Microsoft Teams (as the core collaboration platform) and SAP services. Against the backdrop of the COVID-19 pandemic and the need to change the way people work on a daily basis, both partners decided to drive the integration. This should not only apply to the employees of the same company but also to the business partners of a company.

- Collaboration during migration to SAP S/4HANA on Azure: Both partners want to simplify the migration from the traditional infrastructure and non-HANA systems to a new S/4HANA system on the Azure platform. This is to be done through simpler migration methodologies and high automation. In addition, the topics of automation, monitoring, provisioning, and security are to be pushed further.

- Collaboration at the technology level: SAP and Microsoft each have a great deal of experience in operating application landscapes, and both partners want to work more closely together to advance the topics of integration, availability, connectivity, and security. The goal is to technically upgrade the SAP Business Technology Platform (see the later section on SAP RISE).

The extent to which the planned collaboration between Microsoft and SAP will be decisive for customers is difficult to assess. However, two technology giants are entering the market here, and it can be assumed that they will have a positive influence on the market and customers.

Google Cloud
History

The Google Cloud Platform (GCP) is part of the larger Google Cloud, which Google uses to deliver its own services (such as YouTube or Google Maps) and makes them available to its customers. In 2008, the Google Cloud Platform was announced, which was supposed to enable the use of cloud computing, as in terms of AWS and Azure.

At that time, the "App Engine" was first introduced, which primarily addressed developers of web applications.

A few years later, Google added quite a few new services and thus also made the Compute Engine available to the public in 2013. This was the starting point for the Infrastructure-as-a-Service services in the Google Cloud, even if the Cloud Storage was already made available in 2010.

Compared to AWS and Azure, Google is considered the pioneer in the areas of big data and the newer technologies such as machine learning and artificial intelligence. This is where the company's origins come into full play, which are not in the areas of Infrastructure-as-a-Service like AWS and Azure, but rather in the development of cloud-native and highly complex applications.

Before the introduction of Google products, some customers and companies were still unsure whether it would be a reliable platform. The background to this is often experience from the private customer sector, where customers would have to deal with discontinued, no longer supported products. This should not happen in the corporate environment and should be avoided. However, Google has ensured strong continuity here by strengthening the cloud area in terms of personnel and has allayed customers' fears of a discontinuation of the Google Cloud.

Current Market Position

Google is established as one of the leading cloud providers worldwide but can only achieve third place behind AWS and Azure in most market analyst reports. The analysts assume a market share in the low double-digit percentage range, while the top dog AWS dominates a good third of the market. Nevertheless, Google has managed to win some lighthouse projects. These are particularly in the retail, financial services, and healthcare/pharma industries.

Despite the fact that Google does not have a huge market share compared to AWS and Azure, the Google Cloud can score with a significant footprint of data centers and regions worldwide. Currently, Google Cloud has 24 regions with more than 77 data centers and is present on all continents of the world. Google also manages to cover specific markets, such as Switzerland, Germany, or India.

Through the placement of G Suite, the Google Workplace product, Google has already been able to build a broad customer base. In addition to acquiring new customers, the goal is to jump customers from an existing contract with Google

Workplace to full use of the Google Cloud Platform. Microsoft is pursuing a similar strategy, trying to bundle its products.

Customers like to highlight the following key benefits with Google:

- A very high level of integrity among cloud services (rated higher than AWS and Azure)

- The simplicity of the Google Command Line Interface, which greatly simplifies the creation and management of cloud services and allows for a high level of automation

- The very advanced and partly cost-efficient services

In addition to the many advantages, however, there are also points that could be improved from the customer's point of view:

- The actual portal is, compared to Azure and AWS, not yet as advanced and partly still very complicated.

- The danger of rapidly increasing costs.

Google still has plenty of room to grow as the third Hyperscaler. The market for cloud computing is far from being completely served. Google has good opportunities to further increase its market shares and to further place its cloud services with customers. However, in some innovative areas, which are less relevant for hosting SAP S/4HANA systems, Google is the market leader and will remain so for the foreseeable future.

Collaboration with SAP

In 2017, Google officially announced a partnership with SAP at Next'17 and presented initial progress at SAPPHIRE, which took place later. As the first steps in the partnership, Google focused on certifying Google Cloud Platform for SAP workloads. Initially, Google focused on SAP's newest products – currently HANA-based workloads – and then had Google Cloud Platform certified for NetWeaver products as well. As early as 2017, Google began offering big data services related to SAP in addition to its basic Infrastructure-as-a-Service offerings. Goggle did not want to appear as just another player in the virtual hardware segment, but to offer added value to customers.

Over the next few years, Google's portfolio for SAP systems was steadily expanded. In 2018, new and larger machine types were announced, as well as the integration of SAP Smart Data Access to Google's BigQuery. With the acquisition of Stackdriver in 2014,

Google was now able to leverage these features to implement monitoring of SAP systems on GCP and implement initial automation. SAP, in turn, also relied on the Google Cloud Platform and supported it from the SAP Cloud Application Library.

Gradually, Google was able to expand its customer base and in 2019 was able to celebrate its first major successes together with its customers. This certainly includes the customer example of Metro, a very large retailer. Starting this year, the extensions for SAP C/4HANA systems were also brought into focus and customers were helped with the development of the extensions. Google also managed to integrate G Suite into SAP products, enabling a barrier-free exchange of data between the two worlds.

Google and SAP also deepened their partnership on RISE. Shortly after the announcement by SAP, Google was able to win over some key customers and SAP offered RISE based on Google Cloud.

After a few years of collaboration and cooperation between SAP and Google, it is clear that Google's business with large enterprises is important, and here it is on a par with Microsoft and Amazon Web Services at the Infrastructure-as-a-Service level. If, on the other hand, we look at the topics of big data, analytics, and machine learning, Google offers the leading services in cloud computing for SAP.

Other Market Participants

In addition to the three major Hyperscalers, there are other providers of cloud services which should also be mentioned here. These providers either rely on private clouds or provide public cloud services in specific countries.

Alibaba Cloud

Alibaba is an Internet company from China, which started its own cloud provider with Alibaba Cloud in 2009. Alibaba Cloud initially concentrated on business in China, as it saw the most important market for itself here. Since the Chinese market is now highly regulated and companies have to pay attention to many specifications when operating the IT infrastructure, Alibaba Cloud has established itself as the most important market player in China. After entering the Chinese market, Alibaba is opening up more and more to the global market. New regions are being opened up, and currently Alibaba operates 24 regions worldwide, with a few in the US region, but primarily in Asian.

Alibaba Cloud offers several certifications for SAP workloads. The latest versions of SAP S/4HANA systems are fully supported. Alibaba Cloud consistently relies on Intel's popular processor technology with the latest architectures of Cascade Lake, Skylake, and Broadwell. However, support for older SAP systems is very limited.

Oracle Cloud

The Oracle Cloud has found a strong presence on radio and television through promotion in motion pictures. The first version of Oracle Public Cloud (OPC) was not very successful but offered all the features and services of a public cloud. At that time, SAP workloads could already be installed and operated on the OPC. In 2018, the new generation of the cloud was announced as "Oracle Cloud Infrastructure." This was a new development of the cloud without reference to the previous platform. Currently, regions of the OCI exist on all continents.

Although Oracle is losing more and more weight as a manufacturer of databases in the environment of SAP systems and very many companies are turning away from Oracle as a database platform, Oracle is nevertheless succeeding in expanding its business with the cloud services. Oracle also manages to position its cloud services in the environment of SAP workloads. SAP continues to support the Oracle Cloud as a target platform, albeit only to a limited extent. In particular, for SAP systems that operate on the basis of Oracle Exadata, Oracle can offer a migration to the cloud that does not work in this way for other Hyperscalers. Support for SAP S/4HANA systems on the Oracle Cloud, on the other hand, is not given, and thus the latest SAP systems cannot be operated on the OCI.

IBM Cloud

The beginning of the IBM Cloud can be dated to 2010. In this year, IBM opened two cloud computing data centers in the United States and in Germany (Ehningen near Stuttgart). At that time, this was to be regarded more as a private cloud and not as a real public cloud, since it was not accessible from the Internet and did not have a general portal. IBM itself dates the beginning of cloud computing to the 1950s, as this was when resource sharing of the expensive mainframes first began, leading to the development of virtualization. This is the cornerstone of cloud computing.

IBM launched various cloud services for IBM customers, but for a long time could not break out of the area of private clouds. In the meantime, IBM also offers a public cloud, which as IBM Cloud offers customers a wide range of cloud services. The IBM Cloud has a variety of regions, with a strong focus on the markets in the United States and Europe. In Asia, IBM Cloud is also present, but with very few locations.

SAP systems of the traditional kind (i.e., non-HANA), as well as newer SAP systems based on SAP HANA, have long been certified for IBM hardware, and many customers use IBM's systems to host SAP. The IBM Cloud per se is also certified for SAP systems, and thus the new SAP S/4HANA systems can be hosted on the IBM Cloud.

Private Clouds

In addition to the larger public cloud providers, there are also providers of private clouds, as well as the traditional hardware manufacturers, who want to motivate customers to set up private clouds with their hardware. These include manufacturers such as Cisco, HPE, and the software manufacturer VMware. All manufacturers either try to build their own clouds or to make their specific products available in the clouds of the Hyperscaler.

SAP's Cloud Strategy

Since 2021, SAP has made the cloud its top priority since the cloud is considered to be the most important growth driver for SAP. It is possible to speak of a new SAP. Although the monolithic SAP systems still exist in enterprise environments, SAP's success will be derived from the capabilities of SAP software as "cloud-ready." In addition, SAP relies on strong partners in the adoption and enforcement of the cloud strategy (adaptation, implementation, value generation). This section shows the evolution of SAP cloud approaches.

SAP RISE Program

The SAP RISE program is the implementation of SAP's strategy to generate more and more revenue through cloud services and SAP systems from the cloud. This section describes the basic components of RISE and how the program can be used by customers.

History and Features

SAP RISE was announced in 2021 by Christian Klein; however, basic pillars of SAP RISE have already been mentioned by him in 2020. This includes the idea of integration, which is a central element in SAP RISE. In 2021, Christian Klein reflected the strong ambition to make the company more focused through the cloud and through business in the cloud, thus generating strong growth. The growth target is set at $22 Bio. by 2025. The company will have to measure itself against this. In doing so, the cloud is expected to act as a factor, but this will be accompanied by the following key themes:

- New business models

- Investments in products and platforms

- Focus on industries

All three themes are to be achieved through the following three products, although the products are not separable:

- SAP RISE

- SAP Business Technology Platform (BTP)

- Industry Cloud

SAP RISE is therefore a product that SAP offers to many customers and is also a complex construct. Although there is only one contract between SAP and the customer, the contract can map several points from SAP RISE and is advertised by SAP as "Business Transformation as a Service." SAP offers the following items through RISE:

- SAP S/4HANA Cloud: This is the ability to transform SAP systems to S/4HANA systems and have them run in a cloud via subscription.

- Infrastructure provider of choice: The customer can choose the provider of the infrastructure for the SAP S/4HANA systems. This can be a private cloud, but also a public cloud.

- Business Process Intelligence: SAP has made an acquisition with the company Signavio, which enables SAP to offer a product in the area of process mining. This is offered under the name Business Process Intelligence as part of SAP RISE.

- Custom Code Analyzer, SAP Readiness Check, and SAP Learning Hub: These tools, which already existed before SAP RISE, are delivered as important onboarding tools for the transformation toward SAP S/4HANA with SAP RISE.

- SAP Business Network Starter Pack: This is a network of partners of SAP, as well as customers who can and want to collaborate with other customers in a network controlled by SAP. The aim is to make the processes between the companies as simple as possible.

- SAP Business Technology Platform: The SAP BTP is effectively the conglomerate of all the most important SAP technology products and thus represents a new technology stack. Customers can assemble a custom-fit solution from the multitude of applications and processes. In the following section, SAP BTP is explained in more detail.

All the preceding points can be contracted by the customers in one contract only. The contract then exists between the customer and SAP and its partners. More than one partner can come into play here.

An important core element in SAP RISE is the change of the license model. Here, SAP adapts the common practice of clouds, which makes a move away from tied licenses to subscriptions. This means that customers can determine their use of SAP RISE relatively simply and flexibly and do not have to go through lengthy process steps. However, this is only of interest to customers who no longer have SAP licenses on their books and no longer need to amortize them.

In order not to increase the confusion about the new product RISE, we will say in the following what RISE is not:

- RISE is not a new technology or a completely new technology platform.

- RISE is not the only way for customers to obtain SAP S/4HANA licenses.

- RISE does not include the migration of non-SAP systems to the public cloud.

The last point in particular does not really seem relevant, but when strategically moving an SAP environment to a public cloud, in addition to the SAP systems, the non-SAP systems must also be considered.

Most Important Core Processes

SAP RISE was not announced until 2021; however, many of the products already exist, and the key point of integration and expansion of the products is moving forward. SAP has set up road maps for this – but this time not for the individual products, but for the core processes of a company. The move away from road maps for products is strategically important for SAP, as it would like to focus on the functions from the cloud and place less emphasis on the products.

The four defined core processes in SAP RISE are as follows:

- Lead to cash: This is the process for capturing purchase interest, through ordering, to invoicing and payment processing.

- Recruit to retire: This is the process for handling all activities and steps in the environment with the company's employees including all key career steps.

- Design to operate: This is the process of designing, manufacturing, distributing, and delivering a company's products. It is very much aligned with the supply chain.

- Source to pay: This is the process of sourcing and ordering of services and products and payment.

It is obvious that all these four processes apply to every company in the world, and therefore every customer can benefit from SAP RISE. The "lead to cash" process here is fulfilled by not just one product, but two fundamental products from SAP: SAP C/4HANA for all tasks up to the creation of the purchase order and SAP S/4HANA for invoicing and invoice processing (including payment). This already shows the complexity in SAP's product portfolio and in SAP RISE. The complexity becomes very clear when the "lead to cash" process is further detailed. This consists of the following most important process steps, which are implemented by the products listed behind them:

- Contact to lead: SAP S/4HANA, SAP Customer Data Cloud, SAP Marketing Cloud, SAP Commerce Cloud

- Lead to opportunity: SAP Marketing Cloud, SAP Sales Cloud

- Opportunity to quote: SAP Sales Cloud, SAP Commerce Cloud, SAP CPQ

- Quote to order: SAP CPQ, SAP Qualtrics, SAP Commerce Cloud

- Order to cash: SAP Commerce Cloud, SAP S/4HANA, SAP Service Cloud

In Table 1-2, the complexity is shown again. Between all the products, SAP BTP creates the interfaces and the possibilities to exchange the data.

Table 1-2. *SAP BTP Process Coverage*

SAP BTP Components	Contact to Lead	Lead to Opportunity	Opportunity to Quote	Quote to Order	Order to Cash
SAP S/4HANA	X				X
SAP Customer Data Cloud	X				
SAP Marketing Cloud	X	X			
SAP Commerce Cloud	X		X		
SAP Sales Cloud		X	X		
SAP CPQ			X	X	
SAP Qualtrics				X	
SAP Commerce Cloud				X	X
SAP Service Cloud					X

Table 1-2 shows how many and which products from the SAP RISE portfolio must be used for a core process. This clearly shows how much effort has to be put into such an implementation. It also shows that SAP RISE is not just an offer for the adoption of the public cloud but stands behind a very complex transformation of business processes. This transformation must be considered and evaluated individually for each company.

For all core processes, SAP provides road maps on the current status of implementation, functionalities, and integration. This gives the customer a good overview of the current status.

Current Situation

SAP RISE is considered by many customers as a possible scenario for a move to the public cloud. There are various reasons for this, which make SAP RISE attractive for customers:

- Simpler licensing and pricing model
- Outsourcing of SAP operations and migration to the public cloud in one step

- Simpler transformation to SAP S/4HANA thanks to the tools supplied with the solution

- Flexible and easy booking of additional options

SAP is working hard to provide all customers with an appropriate SAP RISE offer and thus realize the goal of generating $22 million in cloud revenue by 2025. However, customers are still hesitant to adopt SAP RISE. This is partly because SAP RISE is still very fresh to the market and consequently has a moderate maturity. The road maps for implementing the core processes clearly show this.

For many customers, the shift of SAP systems and the transformation to SAP S/4HANA goes hand in hand with a migration to the cloud. However, SAP only offers this together with a coupling with the future operation of the SAP systems by SAP or its partners. Customers who are currently with a reliable provider see little incentive to make a complete change of provider.

Ultimately, SAP RISE is still very young, but SAP has built an important tool here that will be important and elementary for many customers in the coming years. It is not just a technical offer, but a holistic offer for the transformation of the company.

SAP HANA Enterprise Cloud

The SAP HANA Enterprise Cloud (HEC) has been around for a long time and offers customers of SAP a way to host SAP systems on hardware controlled and operated by SAP in SAP's data centers (or co-locations). This section will provide an overview of the SAP HEC and describe how customers can use the HEC.

History

SAP HANA Enterprise Cloud, or SAP HEC, was launched by SAP in 2013 as an alternative to other cloud providers. It was intended to offer customers a way to switch to SAP HANA quickly and easily and to complete the associated platform change in one step. SAP signed contracts with many partners for this purpose in order to offer customers worldwide a platform. At that time, customers were faced with the challenge that new, certified hardware had to be purchased for a switch to SAP HANA and that this was only available to a limited extent from established providers. SAP HEC filled this gap.

When SAP launched HEC, many customers were still on their way to SAP HANA and were transforming SAP systems for it. At that time, there was specialized hardware for SAP HANA and very precise plus high requirements for the hardware. Few customers could meet these requirements in their own data centers, and so many customers looked for alternatives to avoid high investments.

SAP HEC is considered a cloud, which is completely maintained and administered by SAP (fully managed). SAP addressed two points by launching the offering:

- Providing new SAP HANA hardware as a cloud

- Offering a fully managed service including patching, security, and SAP Basis plus SAP application management.

The combination of the preceding points was not new on the market and had already been offered by other providers, such as Fujitsu or IBM. What was new at the time, however, was that SAP, as a vendor, was in the unique situation of operating SAP-created software for customers in SAP-operated data centers. Customers followed the idea that "the manufacturer of the software will know best how to operate the software" and migrated the SAP systems into the SAP HEC. SAP HEC was thus able to create a very solid customer base, from which it continued to draw for a long time.

After the transformation to SAP HANA, the transformation to SAP S/4HANA is on the horizon for many customers. SAP has positioned SAP HEC as the bridge to the new transformation. SAP RISE can be seen as a successor program that supports customers on their way to the public cloud.

Features of the SAP HANA Enterprise Cloud

SAP HEC was launched as a fully managed cloud and, following the criteria, was not a true cloud. It did not have unlimited resources and was not readily accessible from anywhere in the world. Rather, it was and is a managed services approach, but for some many customers, that is exactly what they need.

SAP HANA Enterprise Cloud still offers some interesting features to its customers today:

- Operation of SAP systems by SAP with a flexible pricing structure as the workload grows

- Professional operation by SAP hosting within SAP's data centers or data centers leased by SAP, respectively

- Market-compliant service-level agreements for the availability of
  SAP systems

- Operation of SAP systems up to application management
  (application maintenance)

- Support for industry solutions (e.g., IS-U)

The SAP HEC is primarily created for SAP systems, and thus the support of the SAP
HEC for all non-SAP systems is very limited. For example, common non-SAP systems,
such as archiving systems, can be included in a contract, but the support provided by the
SAP HEC is very limited.

SAP HEC competes directly with Hyperscalers on the one hand by bundling services.
On the other hand, SAP competes with managed service providers for customers. In
both cases, SAP HEC uses a flexible pricing model based on the respective competitors.
Thus, customers can expect either prices based on volumes (i.e., the number of systems)
or fixed prices. The SAP systems are offered as a bundle with the hardware and billed in
this way. This gives customers a very fine-grained breakdown of the costs incurred.

Customers cannot simply use the SAP HEC, but are guided by SAP through a
supported, accompanied process. At the end of this process, the SAP HEC is used. The
process consists of the following steps:

- Assessment: Through a review of the current system environment,
  as well as a detailed examination of the systems, SAP gains an
  overview of what will later be operated in the SAP HEC. The results
  of the initial assessment are then incorporated into the contract. In
  principle, this step is the most important, as it forms the basis for the
  subsequent collaboration between the customer and SAP.

- Onboarding: The onboarding process is the creation of the
  contractual basis and the creation of the initial structures for
  the support of the systems and the customer. Here, processes,
  communication, collaboration, escalations, etc. are coordinated.
  Since SAP has created a highly standardized platform with the HEC,
  customers can agree individual solutions here, but there is a clear
  preference to leave the processes as they are offered by SAP. This is
  also in line with the basic idea of the cloud.

- Migration: Once the customer's onboarding has been completed, the SAP and non-SAP systems are migrated successively by SAP to the SAP HEC. During this process, customers naturally support and sometimes have to support the coordination with the old provider. SAP uses established procedures for the migration. Particularly in the case of combined migrations and upgrades to HANA, SAP was able to fully exploit the advantages and use procedures such as DMO (Data Migration Option).

- Operation: After the successful migration of the systems, they are taken over into operation and operated by SAP with the assured SLAs. If the systems are extended (e.g., additional SAP systems), there are established processes and a service catalogue from which customers can obtain the respective services.

- The preceding process is not fundamentally different from the processes of other manufacturers and does not represent a distinguishing criterion.

The preceding process exists for entering the SAP HEC, and to the same extent, the process for leaving the SAP HEC also exists. Here, SAP usually agrees on an individual approach with precisely defined services and scopes ("Exit Out").

Current Situation

SAP HEC has lost its uniqueness over time. The most important argument was the availability of SAP HANA–certified hardware, which, however, is now available in all common Hyperscaler clouds and is also very easy to access.

Furthermore, SAP HEC still shows a very complex pricing structure for different numbers of services and options. The contract structure is complex and leads to a rethinking by the customers, as well as by SAP, due to the commitment to the higher prices. SAP launched RISE to capitalize on the growth of Hyperscalers. Many customers are now no longer riding the wave of SAP HANA transformation but have already moved past it and are looking at SAP S/4HANA.

It is certainly questionable how long SAP HEC will continue to exist and when it will ultimately be replaced by SAP RISE.

Additional SAP Services from the Cloud

In addition to the SAP solutions already mentioned, the portfolio consists of many other cloud-based services. With these additional services, SAP covers several technological as well as process-related areas. Through the diverse combination of different cloud services from the SAP portfolio, an SAP S/4HANA landscape can be transformed into an innovative and effective environment for the execution of business processes. SAP also refers to an optimized and automated environment as "Intelligent Enterprise." The term describes a holistic approach whose technological foundation is S/4HANA. Based on this, various cloud services from the SAP portfolio are connected to the S/4HANA architecture and thus integrated into the business processes. Figure 1-1 shows a schematic overview of the best-known cloud solutions.

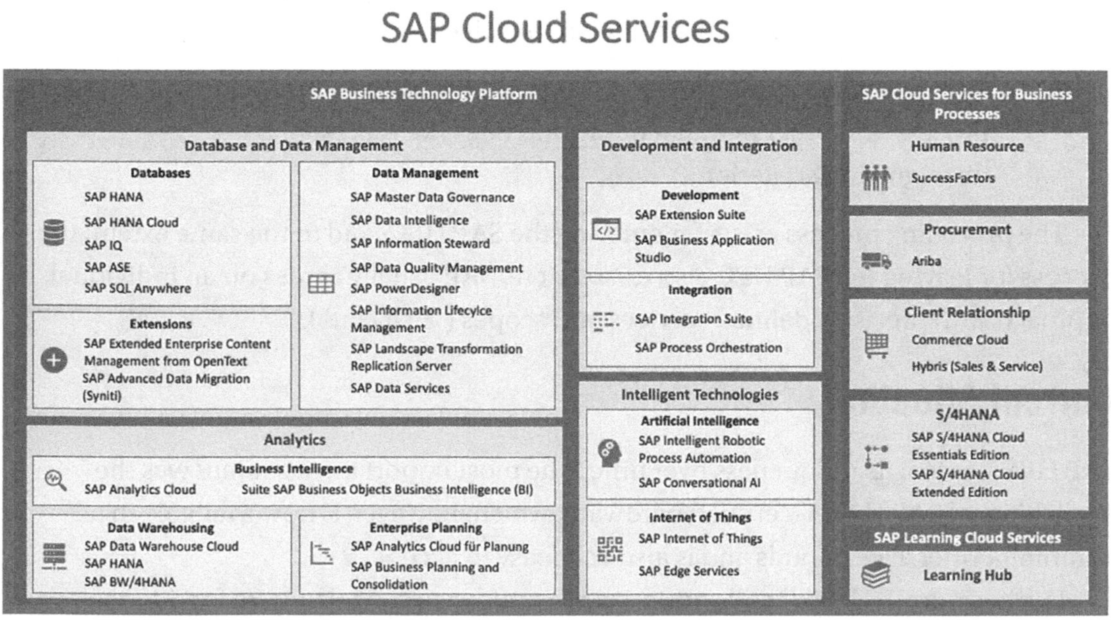

Figure 1-1. SAP Cloud canvas

SAP Business Technology Platform

A central component of the cloud service offering is the SAP Business Technology Platform (SAP BTP). This is a cloud-based platform that groups and categorizes multiple services based on technical or business commonalities. With the help of these services assigned to the Business Technology Platform, companies have the option of extending the S/4HANA landscape in order to network and optimize business processes. The networking of processes can be carried out across several company divisions with the help of cloud technology. The Business Technology Platform uses a multicloud strategy, which allows the SAP customer to make an individual selection via the Hyperscaler provider. As a result, the sourced services of the platform are executed in the selected Hyperscaler cloud. However, before deciding on a Hyperscaler provider, it is advisable to check the availability of the respective cloud services, as some services are only available from certain cloud providers and in selected regions.

The cloud services in SAP Business Technology are divided into different categories from a technological perspective. Within a category, the respective services are grouped based on their technological application environment.

The "Database and Data Management" category is made up of cloud services that deal with the storage and processing of data. For example, SAP HANA Cloud is an in-memory database offered as a service in the cloud. This model is also known as Database-as-a-Service (DBaaS). As a consumer of this service, a cloud-based HANA database is provided that enables real-time data queries, among other things.

Building on the storage of data, it can be analyzed with the help of cloud services from the "analytics solutions" category. One of the most frequently used services in this category is the SAP Analytics Cloud. This Software-as-a-Service (SaaS) enables extensive and individual evaluations using business intelligence. The analyses can also be consulted for forecasting and planning purposes in a company. SAP Analytics Cloud offers a wide range of functions to optimize and automate reporting processes.

The application development and integration area was originally known as "SAP Cloud Platform" and was replaced as part of a portfolio restructuring at SAP. The services of the former SAP Cloud Platform can be found again as "SAP Extension Suite" and "SAP Integration Suite." Both solutions form a Platform-as-a-Service in which applications can be developed and deployed as an extension to an S/4HANA instance. The applications can be built on the basis of various Software-as-a-Service, such as workflow management.

The fourth category of the SAP Business Technology Platform comprises intelligent technologies, such as artificial intelligence and the Internet of Things. The services located in this area support the automation of business processes. With the help of SAP Conversational AI, for example, it is possible to integrate a chatbot into the Fiori launchpad of the S/4HANA system. Based on this, the respective transactions can be automated in the background by SAP Intelligent Robotic Process Automation.

In summary, the SAP Business Technology Platform consequently stands for a collection of innovative cloud services that can be integrated into an S/4HANA landscape for extension and optimization. The cloud solutions of SAP BTP can be used in almost all business processes.

SAP Cloud Services for Business Processes

In addition to the technological perspective, SAP's cloud service portfolio consists of specific solutions that focus on particular business processes or areas. SuccessFactors is often used for the execution of human resources processes. SuccessFactors can be used to handle processes related to payroll, talent management, feedback, and workforce planning.

With Ariba, SAP offers a cloud service for digitizing and automating the ordering process. The service supports companies in the purchasing process in the areas of supplier management, logistics chain management, procurement, and sales and order processing.

In the "Customer Relationship Management" category, SAP provides both Commerce Cloud and SAP Hybris. SAP Commerce Cloud focuses on optimizing ecommerce processes. For example, this service can be used to set up an online store in which business partners and customers can place orders that are processed in the Commerce Cloud. Over and above the specific cloud services, it is possible to obtain SAP S/4HANA as a Software-as-a-Service across all business processes.

SAP Learning Cloud Services

The third category of the service portfolio contains the SAP Learning Cloud Services. Specifically, this refers to the SAP Learning Hub. With the help of this cloud solution, a company can promote the further education and training of its employees, as it is a central learning platform. The trainings and learning materials available there enable the deepening of knowledge around SAP and support companies in how SAP can be used in the best possible way in their daily processes.

Summary

The first section gave an overview of the beginnings of cloud computing and the three main types of cloud (private, public, hybrid). Here, it was shown what characterizes cloud computing and how companies can benefit from cloud computing.

The three most important providers of public clouds, Amazon Web Services, Microsoft Azure, and Google Cloud, were introduced, and a brief summary of the history of their development was provided in each case. Since the current product portfolios are very complex, a deliberate decision was made not to list all the possible services of the Hyperscalers and rather to focus on the advantages and disadvantages of the respective Hyperscalers from the customer's point of view.

Another large section is devoted to SAP as a provider of the world's most important ERP software and as a provider of new methodologies for operating SAP systems. In addition to SAP HEC and RISE, SAP also offers other services from the cloud, which have also been described.

Thus, dear reader, you have a very solid basis for the further chapters of the book, which build on the important basics from the first chapter.

CHAPTER 2

SAP S/4HANA Systems on Public Cloud

SAP S/4HANA systems are based on a consistent evolution of SAP systems from R/3 versions to HANA-based SAP products. They support all important business processes of a company and thus represent the backbone of business operations.

Development of SAP S/4HANA

In 1979, the SAP R/2 system was introduced on mainframes and became one of the standard ERP systems worldwide. The architecture was kept stable for a long time, and only in 1992 SAP introduced a significant evolutionary step: the SAP R/3 system. For the first time, business transactions were performed in real time, and the system combined all major business processes within one large SAP system.

SAP then followed the path of ERP Central Components, or ECC for short. Here, customers could activate and use the most important functions that were important for the companies. There were also specific systems, such as Supplier Relationship Management, which could be installed in addition to the SAP ECC systems. From 2004 onward, there was a renewal in the system landscapes of the customers, and the older SAP R/3 systems were successively replaced by the SAP ECC systems. The duration of 12 years from R/3 to ECC shows the complexity and intricacy of the transformation of such ERP systems.

In 2010, the new database HANA was announced by SAP. The new platform HANA was placed by SAP not only as a new database but also as a development platform for OLAP (Online Analytical Processing) applications. Through this, many steps in evaluation of large amounts of data could simply be done in the HANA database, instead of within the application layer as before. As of 2013, SAP's most important applications

29

© André Bögelsack, Utpal Chakraborty, Dhiraj Kumar, Johannes Rank, Jessica Tischbierek, Elena Wolz 2022
A. Bögelsack et al., *SAP S/4HANA Systems in Hyperscaler Clouds*, https://doi.org/10.1007/978-1-4842-8158-1_2

were then available on HANA – previously, only a few applications had been released for HANA. The "Suite on HANA" introduced additional features, such as access from mobile devices. This already worked before but was significantly simplified by the new platform.

In 2015, SAP introduced the S/4HANA system. This is a simplified (S) system for (4) HANA-based systems. It is at its core a completely redesigned system, still based on the ABAP (Advanced Business Application Programming) programming language, but completely rebuilt. With this announcement, SAP also made a shift away from supporting all common relational database systems to exclusively supporting SAP's own database HANA.

SAP S/4HANA in the Cloud

With the development of the new SAP S/4HANA platform, SAP also focused on the cloud. The new products should no longer be able to be operated only in the data centers of customers or partners but also in the cloud in particular. The basic idea of Software-as-a-Service came more and more to the fore. This was certainly due to the enormous growth of cloud services, but also due to the acquisitions of, for example, SAP Ariba or SuccessFactors, which were sold as pure SaaS solutions. SAP saw the future in the cloud business, and this is still one of the fundamental strategies in 2021.

As one of the first products based on the new S/4HANA architecture, S/4 Public Cloud Multi Tenant Edition (MTE) was launched in 2017. The offering is an SAP S/4HANA system delivered as SaaS. Customers could and can use the new S/4 functionalities based on it. In principle, the offer is aimed at customers who aim for a very high level of standardization and require little customizing. In return, customers then receive a system that undergoes regular upgrades per year and thus always contains the latest codebase. In 2019, the Multi Tenant Edition was renamed to Essentials.

Opposite the MTE, an S/4 Public Cloud Single Tenant Edition (STE) was also launched in 2018 – also as a pure SaaS solution. Through this, customers could obtain a new S/4HANA system and could perform more customizing here than with the MTE. In addition, STE also supported more industry-specific business processes. However, changes to the actual ABAP code were not possible here either. STE was renamed Extended in 2019.

In 2020, SAP launched the S/4 Private Cloud Edition in pilot operation, and from 2021, this edition was also available to all customers. This is an SAP S/4HANA system that is operated and supported by SAP for customers. The customers have the complete S/4HANA codebase at their disposal and can completely adapt the system (customizing). SAP performs an upgrade once a year. In contrast to the Essentials Edition, the Private Cloud Edition supports 25 industry-specific processes.

In addition to the cloud-based offerings, customers can still keep the traditional SAP system in the data center world (on premise). Here, the systems can be operated in the traditional data centers or also in the Hyperscaler clouds.

SAP S/4HANA Architecture

The architecture of SAP S/4HANA can be described from different perspectives, and the different use cases require different components. Thus, the structure of a BW/4HANA system is different from the architecture of an S/4HANA system. Nevertheless, there are basic components which are the same in all SAP systems.

Overview

The architecture of SAP S/4HANA systems is not fundamentally different from the architecture of SAP ECC systems. The same components still exist, which are summarized in an overview in Figure 2-1.

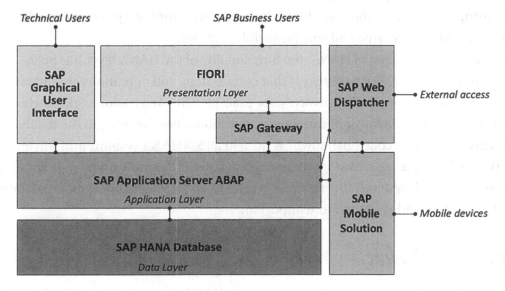

Figure 2-1. *SAP S/4HANA architecture*

The different layers of the SAP S/4HANA system are as follows:

- Data storage layer: This layer is fulfilled by the column-oriented HANA database.

- Application layer: This layer is formed by the application server ABAP.

- Presentation layer: This layer is formed by the SAP GUI and Fiori.

- Communication layer: This layer is formed by the SAP Gateway, SAP Web Dispatcher, and SAP Mobile Solution.

All the preceding layers are explained in a bit more detail in the following.

Data Layer

Data storage and processing take place in the database. In all SAP S/4HANA systems, it is a HANA database. The HANA database holds all data in relational tables in the main memory, which are connected to each other via key relationships. This basic functionality is the same in all SAP systems. The HANA database is a column-oriented database, which stores relations in a column-oriented manner. By storing data in main memory, the database gains very high speed compared to traditional databases, such as Microsoft SQL Server. However, this high speed also comes at a price: the HANA database requires very large and very powerful hardware.

Since the introduction of HANA, the functionality of the HANA layer has been successively extended. SAP's strategy is that certain steps and operations should take place in the database layer. This involves, for example, the preparation of data, which often used to happen in the application layer but should now be done in the database layer. This concept of "code pushdown" is lived in all S/4HANA systems and will also be incorporated into the new ABAP programs. Thus, there is a significant change compared to the previous SAP systems: the database is used as an intelligent component of the SAP S/4HANA system and is all the more important.

Application Layer

The application layer processes the data from the HANA database. In the SAP S/4HANA systems, this is the application server ABAP. In the previous SAP systems (such as ECC), there was still the application server Java, but this is no longer used strategically.

The ABAP programming language (Advanced Business Application Programming) is SAP's own language and has been used by SAP since time immemorial.

The ABAP application server not only processes the transactional data and programs of the S/4HANA system but also provides the functionalities for analytical tasks and search queries. This makes the application server one of the central components alongside the HANA database. The ABAP application server consists of some very important processes, which become very important in the chapters on implementations on the public clouds. These include the following processes:

- Dispatcher: The process distributes all incoming requests to the work processes.

- Work processes: The work processes process the user requests, run the ABAP programs, and access the data in the HANA database.

- Gateway: The gateway serves incoming and outgoing requests to the SAP S/4HANA system.

- Update: The processes update the results of transactions.

- Enqueue: The processes lock records to prevent parallel changes or changes in the background.

- Background: The processes are used for long-running programs (jobs) that need to change or evaluate a lot of data.

- Message server: The message server is used for communication between individual processes of the SAP system.

- Spool process: The spool processes serve print jobs, among other things, also for mass printing.

All processes can also be found in this form in older SAP systems and play the same important role there.

Presentation Layer

Over time, SAP has released a wide variety of programs that served as the central interface between users and SAP systems. Probably the best-known program is SAP GUI, which has been the central operating element of SAP for many years and many development steps. In addition, however, there were and are other products, such as for BusinessObjects.

33

For the SAP S/4HANA systems, there is a new component, Fiori, which is the central layer that takes over the tasks of representing data and providing functions. Fiori is no longer an optional component, as it was a few years ago, but is essential for the full use of SAP S/4HANA systems. Thus, Fiori also provides applications (apps), which are used for robotics or analytics, for example. Access via SAP GUI is still possible, but end users should ideally access via Fiori.

The three components Fiori plus the SAP HANA database plus the application server ABAP make up the SAP S/4HANA system. There are additional, optional components, which are needed to extend the functionalities or the integration.

Communication Layer

There are three important technical components that are installed in SAP system environments: the SAP Gateway, an SAP Web Dispatcher, and the SAP Mobile Platform.

The SAP Gateway should not be confused with the normal gateway of the ABAP application server. It is a new component, which can also be installed as a stand-alone component. The gateway offers SAP and non-SAP applications the connection to the SAP S/4HANA system. This allows non-SAP applications to access SAP system data via OData services (Open Data).

The SAP Web Dispatcher acts as a proxy for connections to the Internet in all system environments. The Web Dispatcher is not installed in parallel with the SAP system, but in a DMZ (demilitarized zone) where access to and from the Internet is secure. The SAP S/4HANA systems are never directly accessible from the Internet.

The SAP Mobile Platform is a third component that enables direct access to the SAP S/4HANA system from mobile devices. This way, users can access the SAP system natively (i.e., without having to use a web interface) from the mobile devices running Android or iOS. The SAP Mobile Platform is also a separate small SAP system, for which an appropriate architecture must be defined and implemented.

Although the elements of the communication layer are to be seen as optional, the components can be encountered in almost all environments.

Additional Components

Depending on the area of application of the SAP S/4HANA systems, additional applications/interfaces/infrastructure components can be provisioned in the customer environments. This depends very much on the requirements of the companies.

Very often, components for communication with other non-SAP systems, such as warehousing systems or archiving systems, can be found. These components must also be considered and taken into account when thinking about the architecture.

Use Cases of SAP S/4HANA on Public Clouds

This section will describe the important technical use cases for SAP S/4HANA systems on the public clouds. This is not yet about the concrete implementation, but about the importance of the use cases, such as correct sizing or the right selection of availability. These points must be addressed before provisioning the SAP S/4HANA systems.

Sizing

Importance of Right Sizing

Sizing provides the basis for subsequent stable system operation. An SAP S/4HANA system that is too small runs the risk of not being able to process user requests quickly enough. An SAP S/4HANA system that is too large may be able to process user requests well, but will incur high costs, which will be reflected in the public cloud. Therefore, it is important to find a good target value for the size of the new system/the system to be migrated. It is important to avoid unnecessary costs, but also to ensure stable system operation. In addition to the selection of the future size of the virtual machine(s), the sizing also includes the necessary memory requirements, as well as backup and other resources (such as load balancers). An SAP S/4HANA system that is sized too small can cause various problems. The key is to avoid them:

1. Stability problems: A sizing that is chosen too small can lead to significant problems in the stability of an SAP system. For example, a very high utilization of the main memory (greater than 98%) can lead to serious stability problems. In addition to the main memory, storage that is too small or an incorrect storage connection can lead to noticeable performance bottlenecks, which can have a major impact on users and business processes.

2. Low performance: The performance of SAP systems is critical in the execution of companies' business processes. For example, a lot of data needs to be processed in as little time as possible, and you can find industries, such as retail, where SAP systems need to process many small transactions in as little time as possible. Low performance can not only impact users but disrupt entire supply chains and cause delays that can cost customers a lot of money.

3. Frequent maintenance: If systems are not built to meet requirements, there is a risk that frequent maintenance will have to be performed. Such maintenance often requires downtime of SAP systems, which ultimately results in a severe impact on users and processes.

4. Downtime: Probably, the worst-case scenario, due to incorrect sizing, is the downtime of a system. This can be caused by an overload of the virtual machine and/or the memory and thus lead to a complete crash. Especially systems in high availability clusters show such patterns and should be sized with much care.

The data resulting from the sizing are the clues for the later sizing of the system and the design of the system. The next section describes how the process of sizing is performed for SAP S/4HANA systems.

Sizing Process

The process for sizing a system is usually based on the known framework parameters for a new system or for migrating a system. In both cases, however, the following steps are performed:

> *Step 1: Transparency to data volume.* The size of a new system is first derived from the size of the current system or from the expected size. For this, it is important that existing systems are not taken over 1:1 in this way. For example, business warehouse systems often contain a lot of data that is no longer needed. The same applies to SAP ERP systems. Often, no archiving runs are carried out, and thus the systems grow day by day. It is therefore necessary to prepare the systems and perform an archiving/

selection of data to be deleted. In addition, a strategy should already be defined now on how to deal with future data growth. Nearline storage or data aging via SAP HANA can be used here, for example.

Step 2: Execute sizing. For the actual sizing, SAP offers sizing reports that can be executed within an SAP ERP system. For brownfield transformations/migrations, SAP OSS Note 18721170 applies to estimate the future size for a transformed system. After running the sizing reports in the system, a target size can be defined based on this. For greenfield implementations, the Quick Sizer should be used. Based on a few input factors, it can determine a first sizing for the future systems.

Step 3: Adjusting the results. After the first sizing is done, it is important to adjust the results. Two factors should be considered: future growth and specific usage scenarios.

- Growth: The general growth of SAP S/4HANA systems is assumed to be 10% per year. This growth primarily refers to the additional data that is created in a year. If a sizing of 3 TB is assumed for year 1, a target size of 3.3 TB must be expected in year 2. During the time when there were no HANA databases, growth played a role in storage sizing. After the introduction of HANA and in-memory technology, growth must be seen against the background of the main storage size of the virtual machines. Growth makes regular resizing of machines necessary.

- Special usage scenarios: Short performance peaks in the use of SAP S/4HANA systems can have a brief impact on users, but are usually tolerable. For longer performance peaks or even overloads due to long month-end/year-end closings, sizing should be adjusted based on the experience of the previous systems.

Step 4: Transfer sizing to hardware. For all new systems or systems to be migrated, an approximate new hardware size is specified with the number of CPUs and RAM, etc. The CPU-RAM ratio is fixed for SAP HANA-based systems in the public clouds. Thus, in the Hyperscaler Cloud, only the sizes of virtual machines are offered that correspond to the ratio and are therefore also approved by SAP. After an initial sizing has been created, a suitable virtual machine must be selected from the list of supported virtual machines. While mapping CPU and RAM to the available sizes is easy, there are further dependencies with the storage.

Step 5: Verification of the sizing. The final step in sizing is to verify the target size through a test installation or a sandbox installation including a migration of the data from the legacy system. After the system has been set up, it should always be subjected to a stress test or performance test. Only through a test can the actual performance be checked.

HANA Sizing

The sizing of HANA-based systems is based on the size of the main memory. This is done in Gigabytes or Terabytes. For all HANA-based systems, there are certified solutions from Hyperscalers as well as from traditional hardware manufacturers. A detailed list of certified solutions exists on the SAP website at the following link:

```
https://www.sap.com/dmc/exp/2014-09-02-hana-hardware/
enEN/#/solutions?filters=v:deCertified
```

The sizing of HANA systems is determined by the ratio of CPU and main memory (RAM). This ratio is different for OLTP and OLAP workloads. OLTP stands for Online Transactional Processing, while OLAP stands for Online Analytical Processing. OLTP systems are the normal SAP S/4HANA systems, and BW/4HANA systems, for example, belong to the OLAP systems.

Many of the Hyperscalers use Intel-based hardware for SAP S/4HANA systems, which is effectively Intel Xeon processor based. For an Intel Xeon E7-8890 v4, the following ratios would apply to both workloads:

- OLTP: 1 TB per socket

- OLAP: 0.5 TB per socket

A lower memory ratio is therefore assumed for OLAP workloads. The background for this is the high use of memory in the OLAP environment for the intermediate storage of data, for example, during large load processes into SAP BW. These load processes can often require a lot of temporary memory. Therefore, a lower ratio is assumed when sizing.

It is important to note that sizing for OLTP and OLAP can only be indicative at the beginning and must be refined again later by other usage patterns (use cases). Nevertheless, the main memory remains the important criterion for HANA sizing in order to arrive at an initial sizing.

SAPS – SAP Application Performance Standard

The SAP Application Performance Standard Benchmark is an application benchmark that is executed within SAP systems. It therefore differs from synthetic benchmarks, such as iobench, which only test a specific aspect of performance. The SAPS benchmark was published by SAP and is still the standard benchmark used to measure and also certify the performance of hardware.

The SAPS primarily consists of simple transactions that are executed within the SAP system. These transactions are still available in the newer SAP S/4HANA systems and will continue to exist. These include, for example, the creation of a material master record via MM01 or the creation of bills of materials. The benchmark aims to allow as many parallel users as possible to process the predefined sequence of steps.

While the SAPS benchmark used to be primarily used as a means to measure the performance of hardware and certification of new platforms, it is still used today in sizing to achieve a simpler comparison. For projects migrating from a traditional, on-premise, data center to the cloud, the difficulty of comparing hardware performance arises. Therefore, the SAPS value of the old hardware is always considered a good guide for sizing the new virtual machine in the cloud.

Example: Replacing old hardware with the cloud

A customer was in the process of having its two older data centers on the company's premises demolished. The hardware inside had already depreciated and had not been renewed for several years. Among them were many SAP systems that had not yet been migrated to S/4HANA.

After an initial analysis of the situation, a first indicative schedule for a data center exit was created and sizing was started. Since the old hardware was already several years old, a number of SAPS was first defined for each server type based on historical data. There was very powerful hardware as well as less powerful hardware, some of which only reached 10,000 SAPS.

Then, based on the SAPS, the new target size of the virtual machines, such as DS3v2, was mapped, and the new VM was defined machine by machine. Since the hardware in the data centers was already very old, the customer was able to benefit from the very powerful hardware in the public cloud, and so only very small virtual machines had to be used. These small VMs have a very low price (even in the pay-as-you-go model). This meant that the customer was able to avoid having to renew the hardware and also benefited from a saving in operating costs. The return on investment (ROI) of the actual migration was achieved in less than a year.

The SAP benchmark provides added value as supplementary information, especially for older hardware and systems. Here, mapping based on CPU and main memory can lead to excessive sizing and thus additional costs. This can be prevented by using the SAPS value.

I/O Sizing

The SAP benchmark is also used as an indicator for calculating the storage throughput. The performance of the storage is indicated by IOPS. IOPS stands for "input/output operations per second" and indicates the maximum performance/current throughput of the I/O operations. While SAPS primarily shows the size of the CPU and main memory, the SAPS value cannot make any statement with regard to IO. However, this is very important because HANA databases have specific storage requirements.

In general, the SAPS value can be converted into IOPS as follows:

1 SAPS = 0.6 IOPS (example: 200,000 SAP = 120,000 IOPS).

Depending on the future SAP S/4HANA system and the usage of the system, the value for IOPS can still increase. There are S/4HANA systems that have been created with a ratio of 1 SAPS = 0.9 IOPS.

Now, the SAP HANA database is an in-memory database, but even with a HANA database, the data must be stored consistently on storage. For this purpose, different data areas are required, which should also be separated from each other:

- Redo Log Volumes: All changes to the HANA database and the data are logged in the Redo Log Volumes, so that even after a database failure, all changes can be restored (block size 4 KB up to 1 MB).

- Data Volumes: The data of the HANA database is stored on the Data Volumes. A change of the data occurs at the savepoints every 5 min by default (block size from 4 KB up to 16 MB, maximum 64 MB for super blocks).

- Backup Volume: All created backup data is stored in blocks (size up to 64 MB) on the Backup Volume.

The respective volumes differ in the requirements according to IO performance. The Redo Log Volumes have the highest requirements, since all transactions must be permanently written to the storage as quickly as possible. The Data Volumes have equally high requirements for performance, since no further changes are made to the data when a savepoint is created. The Backup Volume has the lowest requirements. Here, the data is stored asynchronously from the database.

The storage type within the cloud can also be selected according to the requirements:

- Redo Log Volume: Fastest storage

- Data Volume: Fastest storage

- Backup Volume: Normal Storage

The size of the respective volumes depends on many factors, but can be determined with the following "rules of thumb":

- Redo Log Volume: The rule states that the size is selected as follows: Redo Log Volume = 0.5 x RAM.

- Data Volume: The simplest rule for sizing an SAP S/4HANA system is as follows: Size of Data Volume = 1x RAM.

- Backup Volume: The rule is to size the Backup Volume as follows: Backup Volume = 1x Data Volume + 1x Log Volume.

These calculations are only valid as a first reference point for the initial sizing and also only as a calculation of the size of the volumes, but not for their layout. The size of the volumes can be addressed very easily by the offered sizes of the different storage classes. However, the performance must not be neglected. The larger a volume becomes, the more IOPS are offered by the Hyperscalers. This can be easily illustrated with Microsoft Azure:

- The smallest Premium Disk P1 with 4 GiB can achieve up to 120 IOPS.

- The largest Premium Disk P80 with 32,767 GiB can achieve up to 20,000 IOPS.

It follows that to achieve a high IOPS number, several disks must be connected to each other in stripping.

Example Sizing I/O: SAP S/4HANA System in Azure

The following example is intended to show I/O sizing for a new SAP S/4HANA system in the Microsoft Azure Cloud.

Through the initial sizing, the following key data has been determined:

- RAM requirement: 3.5 TB

- SAPS requirement: 152,000

- IOPS requirement: 91,200

Based on the key data, the following instance type can be used in the Microsoft Azure Cloud:

- Target instance: M128ms with 128 vCPUs and 3892 GB RAM

This instance type is offered without further storage, so that the storage still has to be dimensioned for the Data Volumes and Redo Log Volumes.

- Size of Redo Log Volume: 2 TB

- Size of Data Volume: 4 TB

- Size of Backup Volume: 6 TB

However, the target size of the storage is only one parameter. The necessary IOPS are achieved by stripping the disks:

- Redo Log Volume: 2x P30 with 1024 GiB each and 5000 IOPS each = 10,000 IOPS

- Data Volume: 2x P40 with 2048 GiB each and 7500 IOPS each = 15,000 IOPS

- Backup Volume: 3x E40 with 2048 GiB each and 500 IOPS each = 1500 IOPS

This results in a target sizing with the following data:

Compute and RAM:

- 1x M128ms with 128 vCPUs and 3892 GB RAM

Storage:

- 2x P30

- 2x P40

- 3x E40

Costs

When using public cloud technologies, many companies pursue the goal of reducing the costs of the IT landscape in particular. Often, the migration of the complete IT landscape to the public cloud is aimed at very high cost savings, which are to be realized in the shortest possible period of time. The Hyperscaler providers of public cloud technologies offer a variety of cost reduction measures for this purpose. When applying these methods, business viability must still be ensured, and the impact on existing processes in the company must be taken into account. In practice, a step-by-step approach is therefore recommended, as the price optimization measures usually have an impact on the IT architecture and are accompanied by corresponding changes.

The costs of an IT infrastructure are made up of operating expenses (OpEx) and investment costs (capital expenditure, CapEx). Operating expenses are the ongoing costs of maintaining and ensuring the availability of the IT landscape. These are, for example, the electricity costs for operating a company's own on-premise data center, but also personnel costs incurred for maintaining and keeping the IT infrastructure up and running. Investment costs refer to one-off costs incurred as part of setting up an IT architecture. These are, for example, the procurement costs for physical components required in the infrastructure of the IT landscape, such as servers and data center premises. The total costs incurred for a company's IT environment are referred to as the "total cost of ownership" (TCO for short).

The advantage of using a public cloud is that the investment costs in particular are eliminated, as the Hyperscaler provider makes the physical components available. As a result, the responsibilities for the individual levels of the IT architecture are divided between the provider and the company. The public cloud offers the following models in which responsibilities are divided differently: Infrastructure-as-a-Service (IaaS), Platform-as-a-Service (PaaS), Software-as-a-Service (SaaS). Depending on the model, an organization has the opportunity to reduce operating costs by reducing responsibilities. An overview of the distribution of elements in the different models is provided by the so-called "Shared Responsibility Matrix" shown in Table 2-1.

Table 2-1. *Shared Responsibilities*

Local (On-Premise)	Infrastructure-as-a-Service (IaaS)	Platform-as-a-Service (PaaS)	Software-as-a-Service (SaaS)
Data and Access - C	Data and Access - C	Data and Access - C	Data and Access - C
Application - C	Application - C	Application - C	Application - V
Runtime - C	Runtime - C	Runtime - V	Runtime - V
Operating System - C	Operating System - C	Operating System - V	Operating System - V
Virtual Hardware - C	Virtual Hardware - C	Virtual Hardware - V	Virtual Hardware - V
Compute - C	Compute - V	Compute - V	Compute - V
Network - C	Network - V	Network - V	Network - V
Storage - C	Storage - V	Storage - V	Storage - V
Responsibility of Customer - C		Responsibility of Vendor - V	

In addition to the model of distributed responsibilities for individual levels of an IT architecture, Hyperscaler providers offer pricing models that help companies to reduce costs. In connection with public cloud technologies, consumption-based pricing has become established. With this pricing model, the Hyperscaler provider only charges the company for the actual usage time of the resources and instances used. For example, if a virtual machine is only used during regular business hours and remains switched off during other times of the day, only the period of business hours during which the VM is switched on is charged. This model is also known as "pay-as-you-go" (PAYG for short). As soon as an instance is not needed continuously (24*7), there is the option to apply the usage-based pricing model.

Since all systems and applications are often continuously available in an on-premise environment, the decision on applicability with the PAYG model faces some challenges in practice during the migration of the IT architecture to the public cloud. Since the change from continuous availability to limited availability of selected applications is accompanied by a certain need for adaptation of internal processes, a selective analysis of usage is required before any adaptation takes place. One example of such a process adaptation is the way globally distributed development teams work. Due to the different time zones, the availability of a development system must also be ensured outside the business hours applicable to a specific country. Since the actual useful life of components of an IT architecture can only be determined during ongoing operation, it is suitable to establish the usage-based pricing model gradually after migration to the public cloud. All Hyperscaler providers provide various, fully integrable monitoring options for usage monitoring. In addition, the usage period of an instance can also be adjusted retrospectively for deployment in the public cloud.

In contrast to usage-based billing, Hyperscaler providers support a long-term commitment of a company to the public cloud resources offered. The billing model is offered as reservation of the cloud instances ("reserved instances"). Depending on the duration, the Hyperscaler provider grants a discount, which can be up to 70%. Through the commitment, the company makes a binding commitment to use the respective resource or service for a certain minimum duration, but in return receives a discount from the Hyperscaler provider.

In a practical enterprise environment, usage-based billing is usually not applicable to all components in an IT architecture. In particular, business-critical applications are usually subject to the requirement of 24*7 availability in order not to interrupt essential processes and thus possibly jeopardize the ability to do business. For productive workloads, the reserved instance model is therefore often suitable, since these are also usually used for longer periods.

For non-productive components, the decision is consequently made between the pay-as-you-go model and reserved instances. In order to make this decision as cost-effectively as possible, it is advisable to first determine the minimum required availability of each instance concerned. Using the pricing calculators provided by each Hyperscaler vendor, the monthly usage price for the usage-based model and for the commitment model can be calculated based on the instance type. The break-even amount of the respective instance type serves as the basis for deciding on the billing model. This can also be determined using the price calculators by comparing the two billing models and approximating the useful life. The amounts of the useful life are alternately approximated until the monthly price for both billing models is identical. The useful life that applies in this case represents the break-even for the particular instance type. The break-even represents the value of the useful life at which identical costs are incurred for both the usage-based pricing model and the commitment. From the break-even useful life onward, the reserved instance model is therefore suitable from an economic point of view, since the workloads are available for longer at the same price, in contrast to PAYG. The diagram in Figure 2-2 provides an example of the comparison between the ratio of the useful life and the monthly costs incurred in relation to the respective pricing model based on a virtual machine of type D4 v3 (4 vCPUs, 16 GB RAM, 100 GB temporary storage) in the Microsoft Azure Cloud.

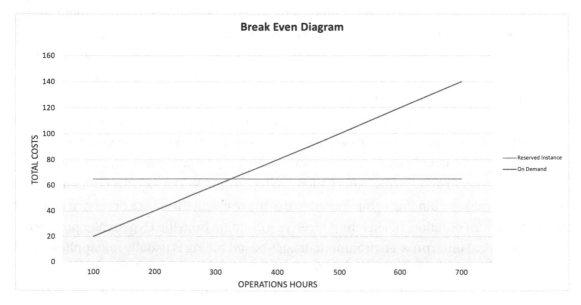

Figure 2-2. *Break-even after 300 hours of operations*

To determine the break-even value, the following assumptions were used as the basis for the calculation in the Microsoft Azure price calculator:

- Region: West Europe

- Operating system: Linux (Ubuntu)

- Tariff: Standard

- Instance: D4 v3 (4 vCPUs, 16 GB RAM, 100 GB temporary storage)

- Virtual machines: 1

- For the comparison between usage-based payment and reserved instances, a useful life of three years was added for the long-term commitment.

Figure 2-2 shows that the costs for usage-based billing are higher than for reserved instances from an operational, monthly usage period of more than 320 hours. This value corresponds to the break-even.

With the help of the break-even of the usage time of an instance, the decision process is initiated. The determined break-even is compared with the actual usage time. This comparison distinguishes between the following cases, which serve as decision-making aids:

- Break-even is lower than the actual usage period: In this case, the reserved instance model is economically more efficient because the instance or service can be operated continuously (24*7) for a lower price in contrast to the usage-based billing model. In summary, the Hyperscaler provider's customer gets a higher utilization rate at a lower price.

- Break-even corresponds to the actual utilization period: The assessment of this scenario is analogous to the first scenario. If break-even matches the useful life, the user has a longer useful life of the instance at an identical price as with usage-based billing.

- Break-even is higher than the real useful life: If the break-even is significantly higher than the real useful life of the instance, the use of the usage-based pricing model is suitable. It is not possible to make a blanket decision recommendation for this case, as the size of the difference between the two amounts is particularly decisive.

For example, if the break-even is only a few cents higher than the comparative value, the reserved instance model would be a more efficient option despite the minimally higher costs, since the instance would be continuously available in this case for a minimal increase in costs. Therefore, it is recommended to make an individual decision for each instance.

With reference to the exemplary comparison of the two billing models, the decision depends on the planned, monthly usage period of the virtual machine. If this should be higher than 320 hours, it is recommended to use the reserved instance model for economic reasons and cost efficiency. At this point, however, it must be taken into account that this is a long-term commitment.

In addition to the described pricing models to reduce costs, Amazon Web Services offers a volume discount for selected services. With an increase in usage and an associated, higher storage requirement, the costs decrease if more storage is consumed.

Another method for optimization is sizing the cloud infrastructure, which has already been described in more detail in the previous section. With the aid of resizing and right sizing, the components used in the architecture are checked for their actual utilization. The aim is to optimize the resources within the IT architecture, for example, to identify unused computing or storage capacities. Adjusting the resources used to the capacities actually used can support the reduction of costs in a company.

Example Calculation SAP S/4HANA System in Azure

The following example uses a productive SAP S/4HANA system in the Microsoft Azure public cloud to determine the break-even. The first step is to define the requirements and prerequisite needed to run an S/4HANA system in the Azure Cloud. The central business processes are carried out in the productive SAP S/4HANA system. Consequently, the system is continuously required to maintain the business capability. We use the following assumptions:

- No high availability or disaster recovery is considered in the first calculation approach.

- The second calculation approach provides for high availability via the provision of an additional availability zone.

- Initially, only the buildup of the resources required for operation is to be taken into account. Therefore, **no additional** Azure Native Services or other integration points are added in the calculation.

- The SAP S/4HANA system is composed of the ERP application with the associated **HANA database**, as well as the **Fiori environment**. To accommodate high performance and the principle of modularity, both environments are built in **separate VM instances**.

In the Azure price calculator, the following characteristics were assumed to calculate the total costs:

- Region: Western Europe.

- Licenses: The licenses for the operating systems are already in place, so the Azure hybrid benefit can be applied (bring-your-own-license).

- Reservation: The instances are reserved for three years.

- Storage: An SSD Premium Edition was assumed as the managed disk of the virtual machines for each instance.

Table 2-2 summarizes these components and their costs.

Table 2-2. *Components and Costs*

Environment	Workload	Type	Operating System	Storage	Instances	Costs
ERP	SAP	D16s v3	Windows	650	1	$384.63
	DB	M64ms	Linux	4096	1	$2945.36
Fiori	SAP	D8s v3	Windows	250	1	$164.89
	DB	M32ts	Linux	896	1	$648.87

The total monthly cost in this approach is $4143.75, and annually the total cost is $49,725.00. Due to the commitment for the reservation of the instances over three years, the complete sum for this period is $149,175.00.

Table 2-3 shows the cost for a high availability (HA) architecture.

Table 2-3. *Costs for Components for an HA Architecture*

Environment	Workload	Type	Operating System	Storage	Instances	Costs
ERP	SAP	D16s v3	Windows	650	1	$384.63
	DB	M64ms	Linux	4096	2	$5890.71
Fiori	SAP	D8s v3	Windows	250	1	$164.89
	DB	M32ts	Linux	896	2	$1369.73
Azure Site Recovery					2	$42.17

The total monthly cost in this approach is $7852.13, and annually the total cost is $94,225.56. Due to the commitment for the reservation of the instances over three years, the full amount for this period is $282,676.68.

High Availability

SAP S/4HANA systems must ideally be available 24 hours a day, 7 days a week. This also applies if there are problems in the data center or in the SAP systems. There are several ways to keep the systems highly available, which are described here.

Overview High Availability

SAP S/4HANA systems form the backbone of the companies' business and are an integral part of all business processes. Therefore, SAP S/4HANA systems are designed in the architecture to be as highly available as possible and to remain available and provide services even if a component fails.

The availability of an SAP system is measured in percent, and the architecture of a system is based on the importance/criticality of the system. For example, systems such as sandbox or test system are not very critical and therefore do not require high availability. However, production systems are very critical and are protected from component failure via high availability. Companies must evaluate the criticality of the systems in the architecture and align the technical architectures accordingly.

The availability of an SAP S/4HANA system is given as a percentage. The calculation basis is the maximum theoretical, calculated availability of the SAP system in the month in minutes. The maximum availability is 31 days * 24 hours * 60 minutes = 44,460 minutes.

Availability = (Max. availability - unavailability)/(Max. availability)*100

Based on the formula, an SAP system downtime of 700 minutes in a month, for example, can be said to have an availability of 98.43%:

Availability = (44,460-700)/44,460*100 = 98.43%

The overall availability of an SAP system results from the combination of the availabilities of the individual components. In the Hyperscaler Clouds, for example, customers are offered a possible availability of up to 99.99% for a virtual machine. However, it is important to understand that the virtual machine is only one component. It is important to consider the other components of an SAP system for overall availability. This includes the operating system, the network, the storage, and the file system, as well as the individual components of the SAP system. When these availabilities are all combined, the result is a different overall availability of a system. In the following, the total availability is calculated as a result of the availabilities of the other components:

$$Availability = 99.99\%(VM) * 99.9\%(Storage) * 100\%(OS) * 99.9\%(Network)$$
$$* 99.9\%(SAP) = \mathbf{99.69\%}$$

The preceding calculation example shows how the overall availability of the SAP system falls, although the availability of the individual components is very high. This must be taken into account when discussing the availability of SAP systems. Even if only one small component in the overall S/4HANA system network is not available, it can directly affect availability. To rule out these possibilities, various high availability solutions can be used.

Availability Classes

The importance of S/4HANA systems for the companies can be derived from the criticality of the systems and a possible influence on the business processes. There are systems which are not important for the continuation of the companies. In addition, there are S/4HANA systems that are existential for the continuation of the business.

Companies categorize S/4HANA systems according to criticality and assign a corresponding necessary availability to each criticality. This availability should then be translated into a corresponding architecture in SAP systems. The architecture must be able to ensure the availability of the SAP systems and protect against failures. A categorization can be very different and can be named after, for example, metals:

- Gold class: Systems of the highest criticality level, which have a major impact on business processes due to a failure and as a result of which a company would no longer be able to operate. These are often the productive S/4HANA systems.

- Silver class: Systems of the medium criticality level, which have a limited impact on the company's business processes due to a failure (e.g., on only one area of the company). These are often quality assurance systems or productive business warehouse systems.

- Bronze class: Systems of the lowest criticality level, which have a very small impact due to a failure (e.g., a very small group of employees affected). These are often the development or even some quality assurance systems.

In addition to naming based on metals, it is also possible to simply work with numbers, which also reflect the criticality. Table 2-4 gives an overview.

Table 2-4. *Availability Classes*

Category	Gold	Silver	Bronze
Availability	99.5%	98%	95%
Max outage	4 hrs	14 hrs	37 hrs

The availability classes must be realized by a corresponding architecture. There are various options for this for the SAP S/4HANA systems in the Hyperscaler Clouds:

- Cloud native: Since the Hyperscaler Clouds all rely on virtualization, the S/4HANA systems also benefit from higher availability, which is given by the availability of the virtual machines in the cloud. For example, Microsoft Azure puts the target availability of the simplest virtual machines at up to 95%. If the availability turns out to be lower, service credits can already go back to the customer.

- Availability zones: In all large Hyperscalers, there is the option of additionally securing a virtual machine. This additional protection is provided by availability zones (availability zones, availability sets, etc.) and can increase availability up to 99.99%.

- High availability clusters: The availability of an SAP system is determined by the availability of its components. Since Hyperscaler Clouds only secure the virtual machines, high availability clusters are used to secure the other availabilities.

By using Hyperscaler Clouds, a basic availability of SAP S/4HANA systems can already be ensured.

High Availability of SAP S/4HANA Architecture

In recent years, SAP has worked continuously to eliminate the so-called single points of failure in SAP systems through redundancies. The architecture of an SAP system essentially consists of the following components, which can also be seen in Figure 2-3:

- SAP Central Services: SAP Central Services (SCS) provide the most important central services of the SAP system. These include the Enqueue Server and the Message Server. Without these two components, users can still work on the SAP system, but only with limitations.

- Application server: The application servers of an S/4HANA system handle user requests and hold the disp+work processes of an SAP system. Since an S/4 system can have multiple application servers, these servers can also fail without having an impact on the overall availability of an SAP system.

- HANA database: The HANA database stores the business data of the SAP system and can therefore be seen as a single point of failure. If the database is unavailable, the entire SAP system is unavailable.

- File shares: Typically, SAP S/4HANA systems need the files from the global mount point and the files from the transport directory accessible to all components of the SAP system and system line (i.e., development, quality assurance, and production system).

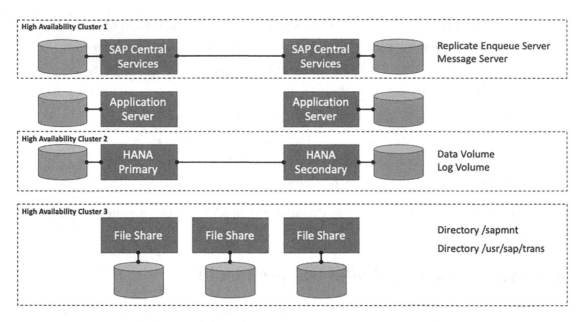

Figure 2-3. *Components of the SAP system*

Figure 2-3 shows the components of an S/4HANA system that should ideally be kept highly available. A virtual machine with connected storage is used for each component. The figure shows how the individual components are secured against failure:

- SAP Central Services: The central services of the S/4HANA system are secured by a high availability cluster. For this purpose, a Linux Pacemaker can be used, for example, which monitors the services and can restart the processes on the second node if necessary.

- Application servers: The application servers are normally not further secured against failure. Since there are usually several application servers in an S/4HANA system, the end users can continue to work even if one server fails.

- HANA database: The HANA databases of the S/4HANA systems are interconnected by HANA System Replication. Again, a high availability cluster is required to monitor the HANA services (such as the hdbindexserver).

- File share: The file shares are usually kept highly available as well. This can happen either through the clouds' native NFS means (e.g.,

Azure Share) or can be done through other clustering technologies (e.g., Gluster).

So, for very critical S/4HANA systems, the architecture required to achieve high availability can become very complex.

Example:

Looking at the exemplary architecture for a highly available SAP S/4HANA system, the question naturally arises as to the costs of such an architecture. It is therefore important that such architectures are only used for the critical systems, as otherwise the cost trap threatens and a very high invoice amount would be due from the cloud provider.

To ensure that this does not happen, an exemplary customer has subdivided its SAP system landscape as follows:

Highest criticality: Only two of the ten productive SAP systems were classified as so critical that they were given a highly available architecture. These were two ERP systems that were operated for two divisions of the customer. These two systems were built on the basis of the architecture shown before. These two systems were also equipped with active disaster recovery, which is described in the following subsection.

High criticality: All other productive SAP systems fell into this category. These included, for example, the business warehouse systems, the PI/PO systems, and other systems (such as Fiori Gateway, Solution Manager, and GRC). In the event of a failure of these systems, the customer would be impacted, but the customer's business would be able to continue. Therefore, the customer decided against a complex architecture for this.

Low criticality: All other systems (quality assurance, development, and sandbox systems) were given a very simple architecture with no further safeguards or complex architecture.

The customer worked with the business department to determine the criticality of the systems. This is not and cannot be a decision made by the IT department alone.

Disaster Recovery

Disaster Overall

While the high availability of S/4HANA systems protects against the failure of a component, it cannot protect against the failure of an entire data center and thus the entire system. The failure of a data center can be triggered by various factors:

- Airplane crash: The crash of an airplane on the data center can trigger the disaster and lead to a total failure of the data center. However, since plane crashes are very unlikely, this reason can be used more as a theoretical reason.

- Fire: In fact, there have been fires in data centers or even outside data centers in the past, which have led to an outage. The most recent example of a data center operator in France shows the possible extent of a fire. Huge amounts of customer data were lost.

- Power failure: Data centers are protected against power failures by uninterruptible power supplies (UPSs) or emergency power generators. Nevertheless, a failure can occur if, for example, maintenance work is carried out incorrectly or there is a problem with the UPSs.

- Cooling failure: A failure of the central cooling system is rarely possible, but can lead to a successive shutdown of the servers due to overheating.

- Connectivity failure: Data centers are connected to the outside world through multiple, redundant connections. Nevertheless, the famous example of the excavator (i.e., earthworks outside the data center) can lead to a loss of connectivity and thus affect SAP systems.

- Lightning strike: A lightning strike in a data center should not lead to an outage in any case for the large cloud providers, but it should for smaller cloud providers.

- Terrorist act: A bomb attack on a data center can lead to an outage, but must be classified as very unlikely. The data centers of the cloud providers are secured and monitored several times.

- Hacker attack: A hacker attack is a very likely event, but it cannot affect the entire data center.

- Emergency patching: Emergency patching cannot be seen as a disaster, but it can certainly be seen as a situation that can lead to a failure of the SAP system. This situation occurred, for example, after the discovery of the Heartbleed vulnerability.

- Earthquake: Although the probability of occurrence is rather low, earthquakes are considered a possible scenario for a data center failure.

In the event of a disaster, customers must either expect the SAP S/4HANA system to fail or there are precautions in place to keep the SAP system available. This is the goal of a disaster recovery.

Important Parameters in a Disaster Case

Although the failure of a data center is an unlikely event, it can nevertheless occur due to the reasons mentioned in the previous section. The disaster recovery mechanisms, which can be implemented in different forms, protect against the failure of a data center. The two most important parameters for implementing the mechanisms are RTO and RPO. RTO describes the Recovery Time Objective and indicates the time period in which a system should be available again after a disaster. The Recovery Point Objective (RPO) describes the maximum data loss after a disaster. Based on RTO and RPO, different mechanisms are implemented depending on the criticality of the SAP S/4HANA systems.

If a data center or an entire region fails (e.g., all data centers in Amsterdam), this is referred to as a disaster. Provided SAP systems are secured for this eventuality, there is an automatic switch to the second region. The time required to make the SAP system available to end users in the second region is defined as the RTO – Recovery Time Objective.

If a data center or an entire region fails (e.g., all data centers in Amsterdam), this is referred to as a disaster. SAP systems are basically protected against a disaster, but there are systems where no difference in data between the primary region and the secondary region (or primary data center and secondary data center) may occur. The RPO (Recovery Point Objective) refers to the maximum loss of data between the two regions and is expressed in minutes/hours.

Since not all SAP S/4HANA systems need to be immediately operational and available again after a disaster, the importance of the SAP systems is also taken into account to decide which mechanisms are implemented. Table 2-5 shows the different RTO and RPO of SAP systems.

Table 2-5. *Availability Classes*

Category	Gold	Silver	Bronze
Availability	99.5%	98%	95%
Max Outage	4 hrs	14 hrs	37 hrs
RTO	< 30 min	< 4 hrs	< 24 hrs
RPO	< 15 min	< 1 hr	< 4 hrs

For highly critical systems (gold category), a maximum data loss of 15 min is thus assumed and a maximum recovery time of 30 min. This means that critical production systems must be available again immediately after a disaster. Less critical systems (silver category) can also be restarted later, and systems in the bronze category can be available up to one day later. The following section shows how these goals can be achieved via technical mechanisms.

Possible Implementations

Various mechanisms can be used to protect SAP systems against the failure of a complete data center. For this purpose, a distinction is first made according to the type of mechanism. Each of the mechanisms has certain advantages and disadvantages:

- Hot standby: If, in the event of an SAP system failure, the DR (disaster recovery) data center is to have as short a period as possible until the system is available again, mechanisms are used for a hot standby. In this case, parts of the SAP system are synchronized (e.g., the database).

- Cold standby: Replication mechanisms are often used for a cold standby, which leads to an increased RTO.

- Backup and restore: For less critical systems, it is recommended to implement a pure backup and restore strategy in case of a disaster. This allows systems to be restored in a limited amount of time.

Each component of the SAP system can be secured against a disaster in different ways, and these are listed in Table 2-6. For SAP S/4HANA systems, for very critical systems, synchronizations are used via the onboard means of the HANA databases. This includes HANA System Replication, which brings the options of replication and full synchronization. Cloud onboard means can be used for the application server and SAP Central Services components. One example is Azure Site Replication, which replicates the Central Services virtual servers to a DR data center.

Table 2-6. *Comparison of DR Implementations*

Mechanism	Hot Standby	Cold Standby	Backup and Restore
Character	Synchronous – Primary and secondary sides are kept synchronous; there is no time offset between the primary and secondary sides	Asynchronous – There is a small time offset between the primary and secondary sides	Asynchronous – There is a large time offset between the primary and secondary sides
RTO	< 30 min	< 4 hrs	< 24 hrs
RPO	< 15 min	< 1 hr	< 4 hrs
Investment	High effort for initial setup	High effort for initial setup	Low effort
Operations	High costs due to active components in the secondary side	High costs due to active components in the secondary side	Very low costs due to storage of backups
Disaster recovery tests	Simple DR tests by simply switching to the secondary side	Simple DR tests by simply switching to the secondary side	High effort due to full restore tests

To secure S/4HANA systems against disaster, the mechanisms are considered and implemented at the beginning of the deployment. The implementation of an active DR mechanism, via HANA System Replication, for example, requires some effort and time. In addition, HANA systems must be operated on both the primary and secondary sides. This results in costs for the Hyperscalers, which can be significant.

The lower the RTO and RPO, the higher the costs for a DR mechanism during implementation and operation. In addition to the initial implementation, there are also high costs for the operation of synchronous and asynchronous solutions, since the components in the secondary side must be constantly available here.

Especially with HANA databases, the running costs can be very significant. For example, a virtual machine for a 3.8 TB HANA database in Western Europe (Amsterdam) in Microsoft Azure costs up to $22,000 (as of mid-2021) per month. These costs can be reduced by commitments, etc., but are incurred monthly for synchronous and asynchronous implementations. With a solution based on backup and restore, hardly any resources are required on the secondary side, and in principle only the costs for storing the backups are incurred.

In addition to the costs of implementation and operation, costs also arise from the actual DR tests. Here, testing is rather simple for synchronous and asynchronous solutions. There is a switch from the primary side to the secondary side and a final test:

1. Check of the synchronization between primary and secondary sides

2. Checking of the current data status by simple tests (e.g., number of currently existing users in the client)

3. Change from the primary to the secondary side

4. Switching off the primary side

5. Check of the secondary side and adjustment of connectivity

6. Check of the data status

7. Synchronization from the secondary to the primary side

8. Change from the secondary to the primary side and adjustment of connectivity

Performing a DR test for backup and restore involves more effort in this respect. For this, new virtual infrastructure must first be created, and then a restore must be performed. Performing these tests usually takes much longer and can include the following steps for a restore based on a database backup:

1. Checking the available backups in the secondary side.

2. Provisioning of the new virtual hardware (virtual machine, storage, network, resource groups, etc.).

3.   Provisioning of the operating system and file system.

4.   Provisioning of the empty S/4HANA system (without data).

5.   Installation and configuration of the backup agent.

6.   Execution of the restore of the database.

7.   Testing of the S/4HANA system after successful restore.

8.   Testing of the data status.

9.   Deprovisioning of the virtual machine.

10. Regular testing of DR mechanisms is important for any organization and should be performed annually for all SAP systems.

Backup and Restore

In the previous section, the topic of disaster recovery was discussed, which is an elementary topic for modern SAP S/4HANA systems. Here, backup and restore was a way to restore the SAP systems in the event of a disaster. In general, however, backup and restore should not be missing in any environment, because only in this way can the data of the SAP systems be backed up, and the availability of the data in the event of an error can also be ensured.

Important Components for Backup and Restore

SAP S/4HANA systems consist of a number of components and important parts that must be included in a data backup. Depending on the criticality of the SAP systems, the data and configurations are backed up with different frequency. The following components are important for a backup:

1.   Virtual machine: When backing up the virtual machine, the configuration of the VM is important. This includes the name of the VM, which virtual disks are attached to the VM, which VM template was used (e.g., in Azure M128), and which virtual network ports were configured. It is important that this information is backed up at regular intervals for a possible restore. However, it is not likely that the configuration will change too frequently.

2. Operating system: The operating system is the foundation of the SAP S/4HANA system. It contains the basic virtual machine configurations, file systems, and SAP system configuration files. Since it does not change frequently, operating systems are backed up at regular but not too frequent intervals.

3. File system: An SAP S/4HANA system usually does not have only one file system, but it includes quite a few file systems. It contains all important configuration files of the operating system, as well as the SAP system and the kernels of the database and the SAP system.

4. Database: The database contains all the important data of the SAP system, and regular backup is essential. For a backup of HANA databases, the backups of redo logs and data volumes are important. Backup can be done in different ways (full and incremental).

5. SAP-specific directories: SAP S/4HANA systems store various files in the file systems. These include the SAP kernel, database kernel, sapmnt and global mount file system directories, and the transport directory. All of these important directories are important for a backup.

In addition to the most important components listed earlier, there are often other directories and data that are important for a backup. These include, for example, interface and audit directories or directories for the exchange of files. However, since these are very individual, they are not considered further here.

Backup Classes

Not all SAP systems in a company are equally important or have the same criticality. As with high availability and disaster recovery, SAP systems are divided into different backup classes. Each class receives an individual backup plan, which corresponds to the importance of the data. This classification into backup classes is done similarly to how it is done for high availability, etc.

If the classification of backups is based on the role of the SAP systems, the components can be sorted as shown in Table 2-7.

Table 2-7. *Backup Classes*

Component	Gold	Silver	Bronze
System	Production	Quality	Sandbox, training, development
Virtual machine	Daily	Daily	Daily
Operating system	Every 4 hrs	Every 24 hrs	Every 24 hrs
File system	Every 4 hrs	Daily	Daily
Database	Data Volumes: Daily incremental backup Weekly full backup Log Volumes: Every 15 minutes	Data Volumes: Daily incremental backup Weekly full backup Log Volumes: Every 60 minutes	Data Volumes: Daily full backup Log Volumes: Every 4 hours
SAP-specific directories	Daily incremental backup Weekly full backup	Daily incremental backup Weekly full backup	Weekly full backup

The classification allows the different components to be backed up based on their criticality. Important components are backed up very frequently (such as log volumes) and less critical components are backed up only rarely.

Although storage space in the public cloud is very cheap, efficient retention of backups is important. The backed up data can otherwise lead to a significant cost contribution.

Retention

Today's S/4HANA systems can easily exceed the 10 TB limit and are now reaching a significant size that makes efficient data retention important. A simple calculation of the data to be backed up can illustrate the importance of the topic. For example, an S/4HANA system with a database size of 10 TB becomes a volume of 20 TB to be backed up per month.

How to calculate the needed target size for backup storage?

To calculate the total volume of data to be stored, a system of one size is assumed with the key data shown as an example in Table 2-8.

Table 2-8. *Exemplary System Size*

System Component	Size	Unit
Data Volumes	10,240	TB
Log Volumes	1024	TB
Operating system	256	GB
Change rate	10	%
Full backup	Weekly	
Incremental backup	Daily	

Based on the preceding example, the following volume results for the backup of the data:

- Complete backup: In total, 11.5 TB of backup volume must be calculated for the weekly complete backup.

- Daily backups: The rate of change also determines the volume to be backed up, which is up to 2.05 TB. These daily backups result in a weekly volume of 14.3 TB (7 x 2.05).

- Weekly volume: Based on the full system backup and the sum of the daily backups, the total backup volume is 25.8 TB.

- Monthly volume: The weekly backups of the data result in a total volume of 103.5 TB.

This backup volume must be held in addition to the normal data. In Hyperscaler clouds, the occupied storage must be paid for. Therefore, efficient storage of backup data is very important.

The preceding example shows the relevance of efficient storage of backup data, as the prices of the different storage classes in the Hyperscaler clouds vary greatly. This can be easily illustrated using the Microsoft Azure Cloud:

- Premium SSD storage: A premium disk (P30 with 1024 GiB) costs €125 per month.

- Standard SSD storage: A standard disk (E30 with 1024 GiB) costs €64 per month.

- Standard HDD storage: One standard disk (S30 with 1024 GiB) costs €35 per month.

- Standard BLOB storage: A capacity of 1024 GiB on the hot tier costs €17 per month.

- Standard BLOB storage: A capacity of 1024 GiB on the cold tier costs €8 per month.

- Standard BLOB storage: A capacity of 1024 GiB on the Archive Tier costs €3 per month.

The preceding price examples from mid-2021 show how serious the differences can be and how important it is to store data correctly on the respective storage classes. The Hyperscalers all offer respective storage classes that address different requirements of the SAP S/4HANA systems.

The different storage classes become relevant when it has to be determined for each S/4HANA system where the normal data should be stored and where the backup should be saved:

- Normal storage (SSD, HDD): The normal storage area of the S/4HANA systems should be stored on the normal disks of the Hyperscalers. The disks achieve the necessary performance for HANA-based systems, but are not suitable for storing backups.

- Hot tier: BLOB storage is assumed to be used primarily for backup of large amounts of data, which is not used often anymore. Nevertheless, hot tier classes offer a lot of storage space, and data can be accessed and read again within a short time.

- Cold tier: With BLOB storage of the cold tier classes, it is assumed that the stored data only needs to be read very rarely. Long memories are therefore used here, which keep the data retrievable but no longer offer high speeds.

- Archives: Archive memories are very slow storage media, but they
  are the cheapest option of memory. Here, however, it can take a very
  long time before data can be read again. The Archive class is more for
  long-term archiving.

The correct positioning of the backups depends on the duration for which the
backups need to be stored (retention) and the way in which the data is accessed. Backup
solutions for SAP systems also offer auto-tiering for this purpose, which distributes
the data according to criteria to one of the available storage classes. In addition, these
solutions also have other features that lead to a reduction in backup data. These include
deduplication and compression, which are explained in the following section.

Backup Technologies

There are various procedures for backing up the components. All major Hyperscalers
already offer native backup solutions for this, which also have integration with SAP's
own Backint interface. This means that the backups can also be tracked within the
SAP system.

Regardless of the solution selected, there are basically two different procedures that
are used. These are snapshot-based backups and stream-based backups:

- Snapshot-based solutions: The backups are performed as snapshots
  of the virtual machines and the S/4HANA system within them. A
  snapshot records the current state of the data and the state of the
  S/4HANA system. All data in a VM is thus backed up and initially
  remains on the same storage as the S/4HANA system.

- Stream-based solutions: Backups are backed up from the virtual
  machine via an agent. The agent reads the data and backs up this
  data via pipes to a target environment. The target environment can
  be, for example, a virtual tape library (VTL) or a BLOB storage (BLOB
  = Binary Large Object). In any case, however, it is a second storage
  area that is independent of the storage of the S/4HANA system.

The important difference between both technologies is the whereabouts of the data.
While with a stream-based backup, the data always remains on a different storage area
than the S/4HANA system, with a snapshot-based backup, this backup must first be
transported to a further secondary storage. This also fulfills the usual requirements for
separating the backup areas.

When considering the costs of backups, the enormous price differences between the storage classes were highlighted. Since snapshots always reside on the same storage where the actual data resides, frequent snapshots can lead to an accumulation of data. This accumulation of data on expensive storage is not sensible and should be prevented.

Backup solutions are characterized by intelligent storage of data. Not all data is stored on the fast storage, so that there is no cost explosion. Auto-tiering is used for this purpose, which distributes the data based on access patterns. Data that is not used frequently is stored on a slow storage class. Data that is used very frequently is stored on a fast storage class. Backup solutions can automatically distribute the data and can also redistribute data after it has been written to the storage for the first time.

In addition to auto-tiering, deduplication and compression are among the capabilities of backup solutions that are also important in Hyperscaler clouds. Deduplication of data means the simple storage of redundant data. This is the case with operating systems, for example. Since the operating systems are backed up regularly, but the data does not change significantly and a large part of the data remains the same, the backups also only store the changed data. Redundant data (duplicates) are not stored many times. Deduplication can be expected to reduce backup data by up to 90%.

Compression enables a further reduction of the backup volume. Here, the backups are stored in compressed form. Due to the structure of the data, the backup solutions cannot always achieve the same results and compression rates. In the case of SAP systems, however, a not inconsiderable compression (often up to 50%) can be assumed.

A sound backup solution can help to back up the data properly and cost-effectively. This should always be considered before using the cloud-native solutions, even if a backup solution requires more effort in the initial setup.

Backup Solutions Out of the Cloud

For SAP S/4HANA systems, there are various solutions from the cloud and in the cloud. These include the established providers, such as Veritas or EMC, but also the Hyperscalers, which offer certified solutions.

As of May 2021, there are 42 certified backup solutions for SAP systems. These solutions do not all support the S/4HANA systems, but they have certain limitations. For example, there are providers who have focused strongly on Oracle. For all S/4HANA systems, there are 38 solutions that have achieved certification.

Regardless of which of the available solutions is to be used, certification of the solution by SAP is important. In this regard, a reference should be made to the Backint interface, which is a standardized interface for securing SAP systems.

All solutions that are certified for the Backint interface can also be used to secure S/4HANA systems. If the solution is not certified, an alternative should be considered. Backups are always an important point during audits and checks of SAP systems.

Hyperscalers offer a good starting point for backup in the cloud with native solutions. For example, they offer the following solutions:

- Microsoft: Azure Backup BackInt 1.0

- Google: Google Cloud Storage Backint Agent for SAP HANA

- Amazon: AWS Backint Agent

- Alibaba: Apsara HBR 1.6.0

Hyperscaler solutions are snapshot-based solutions that back up data to primary storage. They can be used to implement simple backup scenarios that meet the most important requirements. However, the solutions have a weakness: they do not allow efficient management of data and do not offer additional features such as deduplication and compression. The retention of the snapshots is not regulated/limited by the solutions, but the snapshots are stored until they are actively deleted again. Thus, the data remains on the primary storage, consuming storage space and causing high costs.

As an alternative to the backup solutions of the Hyperscalers, the established solution providers of backups offer their solutions. Two different classes can be distinguished here:

> Software-as-a-Service: Here, the providers offer the backup solution from the cloud. This means that the customer does not have to worry about configuring backup servers, etc., but can consume the service. The Metallic solution offered by Commvault can serve as an example here.

> Installation on the cloud: Here, the solutions are installed and configured as a separate installation on the cloud. This means that backup servers, agents, etc. have to be installed and configured. The customer has full control here and can make all the settings as required.

Table 2-9. *Some of the Available Backup Solutions*

Vendor	Solution	Backup-as-a-Service/ Installation on the Cloud
Actifio	**Actifio VDP 9.0**	Installation on the Cloud
AISHU Technology Corp.	**AnyBackup CDM 7**	Installation on the Cloud
Alibaba Cloud Computing Limited	**Apsara HBR 1.6.0**	Backup-as-a-Service
Arcserve	**Arcserve Backup 18.0**	Installation on the Cloud
Amazon Web Services, Inc.	**AWS Backint Agent**	Backup-as-a-Service
Microsoft Corporation	**Azure Backup BackInt 1.0**	Backup-as-a-Service
Bacula Systems	**Bacula Enterprise Edition 12.6**	Installation on the Cloud
Libelle AG	**BusinessShadow 6.5**	Installation on the Cloud
Catalogic Software, Inc.	**Catalogic Software DPX 4.6**	Installation on the Cloud
Cohesity, Inc.	**Cohesity DataProtect 6.0 for SAP HANA**	Installation on the Cloud
Cohesity, Inc.	**Cohesity DataProtect 6.5 for SAP HANA**	Installation on the Cloud
Commvault Systems, Inc.	**Commvault V11**	Installation on the Cloud
EMC Corporation	**Data Domain Boost for Enterprise Applications 4.5**	Installation on the Cloud
EMC Corporation	**Data Domain Boost for Enterprise Applications 4.6**	Installation on the Cloud
Dell Marketing LP	**Dell EMC NetWorker 19.3**	Installation on the Cloud
Dell Marketing LP	**Dell EMC PowerProtect Application Agent 19.5**	Installation on the Cloud
Linke	**Emory for SAP HANA 1.0**	Installation on the Cloud
Google Cloud	**Google Cloud Storage Backint agent for SAP HANA**	Backup-as-a-Service
Commvault Systems, Inc.	**Hitachi Data Protection Suite V11**	Installation on the Cloud

(continued)

Table 2-9. (*continued*)

Vendor	Solution	Backup-as-a-Service/ Installation on the Cloud
Hewlett Packard Enterprise	**HPE StoreOnce Catalyst Plug-in 2.2.0 for SAP HANA**	Installation on the Cloud
IBM – International Business Machines Corporation	**IBM InfoSphere Virtual Data Pipeline 8.1**	Installation on the Cloud
IBM – International Business Machines Corporation	**IBM Spectrum Protect for ERP 8.1**	Installation on the Cloud
Commvault Systems, Inc.	**Metallic 1.0**	Backup-as-a-Service
Micro Focus	**Micro Focus Data Protector 10**	Installation on the Cloud
Veritas Technologies LLC	**NetBackup**	Installation on the Cloud
QSFT India Pvt. Ltd.	**NetVault 12.3**	Installation on the Cloud
Rubrik	**Rubrik Cloud Data Management v5.0**	Installation on the Cloud
SEP AG	**SEP sesam 5**	Installation on the Cloud
Veeam Software Group GmbH	**Veeam Backup & Replication v10**	Installation on the Cloud

There are currently still very few providers offering a Backup-as-a-Service solution. It can be assumed that these services will increase in the coming years.

Integration and Network

Cloud computing is characterized by the fact that the services are generally available always and from everywhere. The providers of cloud computing also follow this credo, and thus all public clouds can be accessed via the Internet. However, communication of sensitive company data via the Internet is not acceptable, and so companies implement other ways to access the Hyperscaler clouds.

Access via Internet

All Hyperscaler clouds can be accessed via the Internet. This is done from the company's own network directly to the Hyperscalers. The portals of the public clouds can be accessed as normal via a browser, and so the first steps can be taken without any further costs for a network conversion.

Access via the Internet can be used as an initial option, but is certainly not a long-term solution. SAP S/4HANA systems that are provisioned and only available via the Internet are very vulnerable. In addition, all data exchanged between the SAP S/4HANA system and the company's other IT systems must pass through the Internet. This poses the risk of data manipulation, which is dangerous.

As a first step in using public clouds, access via the Internet is fine, but should be turned off as soon as possible. Access via the Internet can remain as a backup path but should then be supplemented by a virtual private network (VPN).

Azure ExpressRoutes/AWS Direct Connect/Google Cloud Interconnect

The usual way to connect an enterprise network to the public cloud is through direct links out of the network, via a wide area network provider (such as AT&T) to the public cloud.

The direct link creates a connection from the enterprise network to the WAN provider and then on to the public cloud. Here, enterprises often rely on the existing WAN providers, which then have to have the connection terminated in the appropriate regions of the Hyperscalers.

Such connections have significant advantages over a direct Internet connection:

- Higher transmission rates can be achieved, latency can be reduced, and the stability of the connection (fewer dropouts) can be increased.

- There is a higher level of security, as data is transferred point to point, and security can be implemented end to end by the companies.

- For some public cloud providers, direct connections can result in reduced costs for transferring data between/out of the cloud.

When creating the connection, it is important to note that WAN providers are not all present in all Hyperscaler regions. For example, if a customer selects the Amsterdam region and the WAN provider does not have a line there, there are two options:

- The customer can switch to another region, which happens very rarely because regions are chosen wisely and deliberately (e.g., because of regulatory requirements).

- The customer uses another region to terminate the connection and then uses the interregion connection of the public cloud providers. This results in higher hops in the network and thus higher latency, which is very important for SAP S/4HANA systems.

Since all public cloud providers have a connection between their own regions (backbone), customers often switch to the second option and connect the WAN link to another region. Before implementing a new public cloud solution, such points should be considered as they have an impact on the decision.

Creating the connection from the customer network to the public cloud requires a certain setup time. It is not uncommon for this to take more than eight weeks. Since the connection to the public cloud is usually the first step in projects, a lot of time can be lost at the beginning if the connection is ordered too late from the WAN provider.

Some companies pursue a hybrid cloud strategy. Here, the systems can be distributed across two different clouds, for example: SAP S/4HANA systems are run in the Microsoft Azure Cloud, and the non-SAP systems are run in the Google Cloud. In such a case, the company needs to create two connections (Azure and Google) and set up routing between the two connections. Such routing is often done via devices in the on-premise environment of customers. However, this involves a lot of overhead and a loss of performance due to many hops on the network. In addition, these network configurations must still be administered by customers. This can lead to a high level of complexity.

Hybrid Cloud via Cloud Connect Using the Example of Equinix Fabric

To reduce the complexity caused by many different WAN providers, manufacturers offer so-called Cloud Connects. Such Cloud Connects are to be understood as central entry points into the world of Hyperscalers. Here, customers benefit from a central entry point into all clouds and only have to keep a contract with one WAN provider, regardless of the number of connections.

In a Cloud Connect, the connection is established from the customer network via the WAN provider to a Cloud Connect provider. Connections are then made from the central Cloud Connect to the respective public clouds and the respective dial-in nodes of the public clouds. The customer does not need to use another WAN connection for this, but can use the backbone connection of the Cloud Connect providers.

Cloud Connects are a good way to offer multiple clouds via one provider. The offer from Equinix can serve as an example, which can offer a connection to the most important Hyperscalers/public clouds via the so-called Equinix Fabric:

- AWS via Direct Connect

- Azure via ExpressRoute

- Google Cloud via Carrier Peering

- SAP Cloud via SAP Cloud Peering

- IBM Cloud via Direct Link

- Oracle Cloud via Fast Connect

For customers with a maximally heterogeneous infrastructure spread across multiple clouds, a single, simple connection to the Equinix Fabric can be enough to connect all clouds together. This is a major advantage.

Comparison of Connection Types

All customers have the option to choose from the previously mentioned options – shown in Table 2-10 – for connecting to the public clouds. Thus, it is possible to start small at first and begin with the connection to the Internet. However, this cannot be recommended as a long-term connection. Then a direct connection to the public clouds should be created or a Cloud Connect should be used as an alternative.

Table 2-10. *Comparison of Connection Types*

Access	Extend Own Network	Security	Complexity
Internet	No	Very low	Very low
Direct connections	Yes	High	High
Cloud Connect	Yes	High	Medium

Although the Internet can score with very low complexity (customers can start using it immediately), the company's network area cannot extend the public cloud. In addition, the Internet does not offer reliable security for access, data transfer, and the actual protection of the public cloud.

Direct connections to the public clouds are the preferred path for many companies. Here, the network area can be extended, and the security of the SAP S/4HANA systems can be guaranteed in this case. However, the complexity can be very high due to a large number of WAN providers, direct connections with the cloud providers and routing.

Cloud Connects offer the advantages of direct connections and can reduce complexity by simplifying the network layout. The security of the SAP systems is guaranteed here in the same way as with the direct connections.

Example: Cloud Connect to Microsoft Azure in America and to Google in Europe

The company is a global corporation with subsidiaries and branch offices in America and Europe and began to gradually move its IT to the public clouds. A hybrid cloud approach was pursued in order to take advantage of the respective Hyperscalers and because there were already previous business relationships with the respective Hyperscalers. In America, for example, there were various local locations, all of which were connected to the WAN provider. From the WAN provider, there was a connection to Azure in America (ExpressRoute to Atlanta) and a connection to Google Cloud in Europe (Google Cloud Interconnect to Belgium). In addition, the company owned smaller co-location data centers, which were also connected:

- Americas: ExpressRoute to Azure to Atlanta with connection via WAN provider 1

- Americas: 15 smaller locations on WAN provider 1

- Europe: Cloud Interconnect to Google to Belgium via WAN provider 2

- Europe: Co-location data centers in Germany (e.g., Frankfurt and Munich) with connections via WAN provider 2

- Europe: Legacy data center with central switch and with routing infrastructure connecting to WAN provider 2

The company faced the challenge of having two different WAN providers in America and Europe, with which the company had to manage the connection to the clouds, as well as the routing between America and Europe (i.e., the two public clouds). To get out of this bottleneck, the company decided to rely on a central Cloud Connect and reduce the number of WAN providers to one.

The first step was to create the Cloud Connect in Europe. Here, the connection was created out of the existing WAN provider in Europe. The Cloud Connect was created in Belgium, since the Google Cloud also existed there. After that, the connections in America were rebuilt, and the ExpressRoute was dissolved. Instead, the backbone connection through the Cloud Connect provider came into use. All connections to the Microsoft Azure Cloud were handled through the Cloud Connect instead of the ExpressRoute. Further, the WAN provider in the Americas was replaced with the WAN provider from Europe. The smaller co-location data centers in Frankfurt and Munich were separated from the WAN provider in Europe and connected via the Cloud Connect provider's backbone connection. The provider also had a presence in the locations. This allowed the connections from the co-location data centers to the WAN provider to be disconnected. The company's old data center, which contained the central routing infrastructure, was also decommissioned, and routing was implemented via the Cloud Connect provider. All in all, the result was a significantly simplified picture:

- Americas: Different locations on the new WAN provider 2

- Europe: Cloud Connect via existing WAN provider 2

- Europe and America: Use of the Cloud Connect provider's backbone network

By consolidating and using Cloud Connect, the company was able to greatly reduce complexity and ultimately only had to manage one WAN provider.

Automation

The administration of SAP S/4HANA systems can be significantly simplified by automating the daily and recurring manual steps involved in administration. The same automation solutions can be used in the public cloud as in traditional data centers. Hyperscalers, however, also offer solutions for automating work on the public cloud, such as provisioning or start/stop. However, these automations are mostly limited to the services offered by the Hyperscalers. However, this can also automate some important functions and work steps. There are also tools offered by third parties that can be used in the cloud. SAP Landscape Manager (LAMA) is one example of this.

Automation Goals

The complete automation of all tasks of SAP Basis administrators is certainly not possible and is not the goal of automation. Especially when automation is started in the cloud, the following important goals are pursued:

- Process automation: The automation of repetitive work steps in the area of provisioning and operating SAP S/4HANA systems is one of the most important goals.

- Unification of the landscape: The system landscape is to be kept homogeneous. Through automation, systems are provisioned in the same way and thus unified.

- Configuration management: Many companies see the recording of the IT landscape and the maintenance of the configuration items (CIs) as challenging. The databases containing all configuration data (CMDBs) are often not always accurate and maintained. Leveraging Hyperscaler automation can address the issue.

- Keeping landscape up to date: Patching systems on a regular basis is becoming increasingly important due to the growing number of cyberattacks on businesses. For this, Hyperscalers bring the necessary tools to keep the SAP infrastructure up to date.

- Auditing: Audits require accurate data and often a lot of data from the companies. For this purpose, Hyperscalers offer simple options to generate important reports and pass them on to the auditors.

- Tagging: Tags are small pieces of information about SAP S/4HANA workloads that can be assigned to resources in the Hyperscaler portals. This can be used, for example, to identify which resources belong to which projects/departments/teams.

- Schedules: When SAP S/4HANA systems are switched on in the cloud, costs are generated. To minimize costs for systems that do not always need to be 100% available, schedules can be set up that turn resources on and off.

All of the preceding goals can be achieved in the rarest of cases, but rather companies focus on successive implementation. Furthermore, the implementation of complex automation is a very long-term undertaking.

Automation with Hyperscalers

All Hyperscalers offer customers the ability to automate using their own cloud-native tools. These automations can be very lightweight, but can also become increasingly complex.

Simple implementations involve standard operations in a cloud, for example:

- Starting and stopping virtual machines

- Creating, deleting, and modifying resources in the clouds (meaning all resources).

The simpler tasks can be performed using the tools offered by Hyperscalers, such as Azure Automation or even Google Composer.

The somewhat more complex activities, such as creating a new SAP S/4HANA system, are usually not possible via the cloud-native tools. For this, the following steps must be performed, for example:

1. Creating all infrastructure components (storage, virtual machine, network segments)

2. Creating/installing the operating system with the hostname and the desired IP configuration

3. Installing an empty SAP S/4HANA system

4. Filling the SAP S/4HANA system with data

Since the steps must be coordinated with each other, additional tools are required for automation. The automation tools that are already widely used in the public clouds, such as Ansible or Terraform, are ideal for this purpose.

Third-Party Vendors

Automation solutions exist and existed long before Hyperscalers entered the market. Repetitive administration steps were also automated in traditional data centers. At the latest since the introduction of virtualization (e.g., VMware), many tasks have been completely automated by the tools supplied by the virtualization manufacturers. Since Hyperscalers entered the market, there has been a proliferation of automation vendors. At the beginning of public clouds, Hyperscalers did not offer automation solutions, which allowed such vendors, such as Ansible or Terraform, to establish their position in the market.

One of the advantages in using third-party vendors is their strong focus on scripting and reusability. Most third-party solutions use a repository of scripts to get the job done. This repository can be extended with custom scripts, which are specifically customized.

By storing the scripts in a repository and using a third-party solution, Hyperscaler customers can take the existing scripts with them even if they switch platforms (i.e., from Azure to Google Cloud, for example) and use them in the new environment. However, if the customers only use the Hyperscalers' own automation, the work may not be able to be reused.

SAP's Own Automation

It makes sense for all customers to use SAP's own products for automation. Using SAP's solution seems logical, since SAP knows the S/4HANA systems best and can therefore build the appropriate software for them. SAP offers a solution for automating SAP Basis work (SAP LAMA) and a solution for automating repetitive work outside of technical topics (SAP RPA).

SAP Landscape Management is an evolution from SAP Landscape Virtualization Manager (SAP LVM) and SAP Adaptive Computing Controller (SAP ACC). Both products were initially used by SAP in its own data centers. SAP quickly recognized the benefits of the solution for, for example, mass operations in the data centers and quickly extended the solutions with some very interesting functions, such as copying SAP systems. SAP does not necessarily focus on the most common tasks that SAP Basis administrators have to do, but rather on the issues that require a lot of time and energy. These include the copying of SAP systems (copy, clone), as well as the so-called system refreshes (i.e., a copy from PRD to QAS with a renaming of the SID).

Due to its history (first SAP ACC, then SAP LVM), SAP LAMA offers very good support from other technologies, such as hardware manufacturers. For example, SAP LAMA can communicate with NetApp storage via a library. This support was mandatory when SAP ACC and SAP LVM implemented the first functionalities that also required addressing the storage in the data centers. Using the same principle, SAP LAMA also interacts with the public clouds, which all provide an interface for administration.

SAP LAMA exists in two different versions. On the one hand, customers can set up SAP LAMA directly in the data center or the cloud. On the other hand, customers can also use the SaaS version of SAP LAMA. This is provided by SAP, and therefore customers do not have to worry about the administration of the SAP LAMA system. This is also an SAP system that needs to be administered.

SAP Intelligent Robotic Process Automation

In addition to purely technical tasks, companies are also trying to automate other tasks. These are mostly recurring tasks and process steps that can also be performed by nonhuman resources. One way of automating these is SAP Intelligent Robotic Process Automation (SAP iRPA). Robots (bots) are small programs or scripts that perform exactly the same process steps over and over again. The process steps can also be refined via parameterization. Robotic solutions always have to contend with various challenges. Since the robots work on the user interfaces (UI), changes to the UI can result in major changes to the robots, which means that a large number of robots may have to be adapted. This is where SAP comes in and extends the solution. The intelligence in iRPA comes from SAP's use of more intelligent features: machine learning and artificial intelligence. In addition, the robots can now act using interfaces.

SAP has built iRPA as a pure cloud-based solution. Thus, new robots are created in a Cloud Studio via pure UI (without code). Currently, the solution has 200 preconfigured robots, which can be easily customized and deployed. The robots are used in many companies, but less in the technical environment of the administration of SAP S/4HANA systems.

Implementation Effort

Automation of daily work of SAP administrators is quite reasonable and very helpful. Only in this way companies manage to free the administrators' working time from daily tasks, and the administrators can take care of other tasks (such as the introduction of new features).

However, the implementation of automation solutions can become very complex. When using solutions provided by Hyperscalers, customers can get started very quickly and implement initial smaller tasks very quickly. However, as soon as the processes become more complex or several process steps need to be connected, more time needs to be invested for this. The complete implementation of a new solution, such as SAP LAMA, must be carried out as a separate project.

Horizontal and Vertical Scalability

The scaling of SAP S/4HANA systems refers to two directions and is differentiated into horizontal and vertical scaling. Horizontal scaling in SAP S/4HANA systems refers to the expansion of the existing system with more, additional HANA nodes or more application servers. Vertical scaling refers to the growth of the system and the increase in the sizing of the virtual machines and the SAP system due to increased requirements from the business.

Horizontal Scalability

Horizontal scaling describes the expansion of the SAP system through additional application servers or through additional HANA nodes. However, the expansion of the SAP system through additional application servers is not new to the SAP S/4HANA systems, but has existed since the beginnings of the SAP R/3 systems. Back then, too, further dialog instances could be added as additional application servers.

In principle, there are no limits to horizontal scaling, and up to eight or more application servers can be used for very large SAP S/4HANA systems. Often, the additions of application servers are not so much due to the performance limits of the individual servers, but rather certain application servers are only made available to certain groups of users. It is also often the case that application servers are only used for background jobs, since an influence on the end users by long-running jobs is to be avoided.

However, horizontal scaling is not only used for application servers but also for HANA scale-out systems. These HANA systems are used for large business warehouse systems and can thus hold very large amounts of data in the main memory, but distributed across multiple nodes. Especially for BW systems, the requirements for strong data growth exist. The background of the growth is the closings, where a lot of temporary data has to be stored, as well as large data load runs, which also lead to a lot of temporary data. Thus, BW systems show a significantly larger data footprint. This growth is addressed by provisioning through more HANA nodes.

The typical growth of the entire SAP S/4HANA systems is not addressed by horizontal scaling, but usually by vertical scaling.

Example: In many larger implementations of SAP S/4HANA systems, more than one application server is implemented. Very often, individual departments use the respective application servers.

A company from the pharmaceutical sector implemented four application servers for the most important S/4HANA system:

1. Application server: This server was intended for the finance department (FICO). Using the principle of logon groups, the server was integrated into only one group, which was also known only to the finance department.

2. Application server: This server was assigned to the majority of users. Also, here the principle of the logon groups was used, and the group DEFAULT was used for this.

3. Application server: This server was used for all incoming RFC connections. The background was security considerations on the one hand, but also the specific nature of RFC calls and the incoming transactions plus IDOCs.

4. Application server: This server was used for the long-running background jobs. Since there were a lot of background jobs scheduled in the SAP S/4HANA system (often with frequency of ten minutes), the customer decided to have a dedicated application server for this.

By separating the individual areas from each other, the company was able to better separate the load by users, increased security and the overall performance of the SAP S/4HANA system.

Vertical Scalability

Vertical scaling describes the growth of the SAP S/4HANA system through an increase in the size of the servers (HANA servers or application servers) or an increase in the resources of the components. This case occurs when more resources are needed than are available. This can happen when additional users gain access to the system or when new functionalities are to be provided.

Vertical scaling can therefore occur at different levels of the SAP S/4HANA system:

1. Changing the storage class: For some SAP S/4HANA systems, changing the storage from slower SSD storage to fast SSD-based storage may be necessary. This is a vertical scaling, which means more of a change effort, but can provide a huge speed increase.

2. Changing the VM template: For growing systems, other types of virtual machines can be used, which have more CPU and more main memory. These changes usually cannot be made on the fly, but require a reboot of the system. After a new size is used for the VM, the operating system and the SAP components (i.e., either the HANA database or the application servers) still need to be adapted.

3. Changing the HANA database: Changing the HANA database is one of the most common use cases. Here, for example, the allocation of main memory or the number of CPUs is changed to achieve higher performance.

4. Modification of the operating system: After increasing the size of the virtual machine or changing the storage, modifications to the operating system may also be necessary.

5. Modification of SAP application servers: Changing the buffers or even the number of disp+work processes is one of the most common adjustments to scale the SAP S/4HANA system.

Vertical scaling is often done not only for one component but is done for several of the preceding components. An increase in the size of the SAP HANA database can only take place if the virtual machine and the operating system have been adapted beforehand.

Vertical scaling works in both directions: resources can be added and systems can be enlarged. But resources can also be removed and systems downsized again. In the cloud environment, upsizing and downsizing is very important because it can save costs. In the course of effective capacity planning, upsizing and downsizing should be constantly considered. It helps here if the utilization of SAP S/4HANA systems and the respective components is considered over longer periods of time.

Consider Availabilities

Although public cloud providers always talk about unlimited availability of resources, there are limitations. Before planning capacity expansions, customers should ensure that the corresponding target VM templates are also available in the respective regions. It may well be that certain VM templates are not yet available in all regions, and customers will then have to switch to alternatives. Hyperscalers typically always have one/two regions where the latest technology is deployed earliest. Smaller regions for specific markets often cannot offer the full portfolio of services.

At the beginning of the COVID pandemic, there were also resource bottlenecks, sometimes significant, among public cloud providers. This was due to the enormous increase in the use of other Hyperscaler services. This high usage meant that other customers had no or only limited new resources available. The Hyperscalers use the public clouds not only for customers but also for their own services. At the time, it was not possible for customers to simply provision new virtual machines.

Very specifically, customers could no longer order large HANA systems (e.g., M-Class) in the Microsoft Azure Cloud. The underlying machines were used for other services. Microsoft struggled with a surge in Microsoft Teams users at the start of the pandemic. With many employees suddenly having to work from home, resources for MS Teams were steadily expanding. In addition, new requirements for fighting the pandemic emerged, with research institutions creating new and large systems on the cloud to perform complex calculations. All of this ultimately led to a situation where demand could no longer be met by other customers. Microsoft responded by introducing prioritization and requiring customers to register their needs. After such notification, Microsoft decided based on the criticality of the need and allocated (or not) resources to customers.

This example of the pandemic shows that there are limits to scaling in Hyperscalers. Even though such scenarios are very unlikely, bottlenecks can always occur, which nevertheless limit the seemingly unlimited resources.

Summary

This chapter has described the most important aspects of using public clouds for SAP S/4HANA systems. The right sizing of the systems is not only important from the point of view of users and performance but is particularly important because of the costs of such systems. An oversized system did not cause higher costs in the traditional data center world – but in the cloud, this is different and generates high costs. This must be avoided.

In the case of productive SAP S/4HANA systems, it is important to absorb the possible failures of the components of a public cloud (such as the virtual machines) and to continue to ensure the availability of the SAP S/4HANA systems. This was explained in the section on high availability, and an example architecture was also discussed, which is implemented in concrete terms in the sections on the respective Hyperscalers.

In the section on disaster recovery, it was shown how the SAP S/4HANA systems continue to be available through the onboard resources of the Hyperscalers even if a region fails. This can also be done by combining onboard means and the mechanisms of the SAP systems (such as HANA System Replication). The respective sections on Hyperscalers describe the implementation and guide you through the setup step by step.

The two important topics of backing up and restoring data were described, and the options for backing up data using Hyperscaler's own onboard resources, as well as third-party products, were discussed. These differ in how they are used and also in the knowledge required about the products.

The topics of integration and automation were described in this chapter, showing how easy it is to start using public cloud services. Skillful automation can reduce the initial effort required for cloud projects. Automation can save a lot of time and effort, particularly in day-to-day operations.

In order to always meet the requirements of the business departments and to meet the growing demands on the SAP S/4HANA systems, horizontal and vertical scaling were discussed. It is shown how this can be implemented in SAP S/4HANA systems.

The next chapter shows the deployment and migration of SAP S/4HANA systems to the public cloud.

## CHAPTER 3

SAP S/4HANA Deployment and Migration

Before deploying a new public cloud, the target platform must be selected. This is not only done according to technical aspects. Nontechnical aspects such as the contract, regulatory requirements, and other qualitative factors also play a role, which are described here.

Contractual Basis and Support

In this section, we describe some issues surrounding how you choose to use and to pay for your cloud computing and how your use is supported by your vendor.

Important Points to Be Considered

When public clouds emerged in the late 2000s, it was very easy to start using them. All that was needed was a credit card and an account. After that, things were ready to go, and customers could provision their first virtual machines. This still works today, and so the hurdle for entering the world of the public cloud is very low.

In the private customer sector, this approach is absolutely right, as private customers are deterred by too many hurdles when using applications and services. Here, it has to be simple, and a few clicks should take care of all the points so that nothing stands in the way of use. In the corporate environment, however, this is not a viable approach. Here, important questions need to be addressed before the first SAP S/4HANA systems are provisioned in the public cloud:

1. What is the contractual basis for hosting the SAP systems?

2. What service levels (e.g., availability, accessibility, performance) does the Hyperscaler offer and what penalties are offered?

© André Bögelsack, Utpal Chakraborty, Dhiraj Kumar, Johannes Rank, Jessica Tischbierek, Elena Wolz 2022
A. Bögelsack et al., *SAP S/4HANA Systems in Hyperscaler Clouds*, https://doi.org/10.1007/978-1-4842-8158-1_3

3. What liability is offered by the Hyperscaler?

4. What support is required and what levels of support are offered?

5. What is the pricing structure and do credits exist for usage?

These are just some of the most important questions that need to be addressed prior to use, and the answers to which need to be reflected in the contracts.

In the traditional world of service providers, customers could negotiate an individual contract that ideally addressed all points as the customer needed them. In doing so, service providers were very flexible and catered to the individual needs of customers. With the public cloud, however, the situation is different. The Hyperscalers pursue a different strategy here: *all customers receive the same contract.*

From the Hyperscaler's point of view, this makes sense because it means that a large number of customers all have the same contract, and the Hyperscaler does not have to make any distinctions. With so many customers, it is important to use the same contract. From the customers' point of view, this certainly takes some getting used to. The points that were individually regulated in the contracts with the service providers are not negotiable in the contracts with the Hyperscalers. These agreements are inflexible to the maximum, but this also corresponds to the nature of the public cloud.

Amazon Web Services offers the agreement to customers for download on the Internet. The link is as follows (accessed on December 20, 2021): `https://aws.amazon.com/agreement`.

It is important to note that the user agreement is also available in other languages, but the English version of the agreement always takes precedence. In the event of a legal dispute, the English version will always be used as the basis for the contract. Amazon regulates all important points for the use of the AWS services in the user agreement. Here, explicit emphasis is also placed on the obligations of the customers (such as compliance with rights, etc.).

Microsoft is pursuing a different path and would like to offer customers the cloud services in the overarching Enterprise Agreement. The Enterprise Agreement is a comprehensive contract between Microsoft and the customer, which usually starts from 500 users. The agreement is signed, for example, for the use of Office365 when customers use the Microsoft workplace solution. The Enterprise Agreement is considered a framework agreement and can be extended. If a customer is already using Office365 services, the customer can use the new services to the public cloud through the "Server and Cloud Enrollment." The ease of extending the Enterprise Agreement with the SCE also explains why many customers have turned to the Microsoft Azure Cloud. Since there was already an Enterprise Agreement in place, customers could very easily create the contractual basis for the new services. This involved much less effort than signing a new agreement with a new provider.

Google is following a similar path to Microsoft. Here, customers must first sign a Google Cloud Framework Agreement, which regulates the basic points between the customer and Google. Then a separate agreement is signed for the use of each of the various services. These are the service-specific schedules. Thus, specific agreements exist for the use of Google Workplace or also the Google Cloud. The link to the always current documents from Google is as follows (accessed on December 20, 2021): `https://cloud.google.com/terms/service-terms/index.html?hl=de`.

Direct Use or Use via a Partner

There are two ways to use the cloud. On the one hand, customers can use the direct contract with the Hyperscalers. On the other hand, customers can buy the services of the Hyperscalers via a partner (resale). Both options have advantages and disadvantages.

The scenario where the customer contracts directly with Hyperscalers is the common scenario. Here, the customer signs the contracts and thus also has full control over usage, costs, architecture, and all other aspects. However, the disadvantage also lies precisely in this aspect: customers have full control and must also execute this control via appropriate governance. For example, the architecture of the SAP systems must fit the requirements, and the security of the cloud environment must be implemented according to the specifications. The customer is responsible for all aspects of usage and must, for example, also lead the discussions on penalties if a service was only available in the cloud to a limited extent.

The scenario where the customer buys the service from a partner has become less common. Here, the customer's advantages lay in particular in a shift of responsibilities. At the beginning of the public cloud trend, when the first early adopters moved to the public cloud with the SAP systems, there was only limited experience and knowledge on the part of the customers. For this, the customers used the service providers to build the cloud environments, manage, and control them. Thus, the service providers had the duty and responsibility for the environment. In addition, some service providers also offered to combine the service levels for their own services and the services of the cloud. This had the advantage for the customer that only one SLA regime had to be controlled (and not two: with the cloud provider and the service provider). However, the big disadvantage with this scenario is the additional financial effort on the customer's side. The service providers added a surcharge to the cloud providers' services for managing the contracts, as well as standardizing the SLAs. For example, if the virtual machine was offered for €100 per month by the cloud provider, this could quickly become €120 per month from the service provider. For many customers, these additional costs were too much, so this model of reselling services has declined sharply.

Needed Support

All Hyperscalers offer different support contracts/support models, whereby the lowest level of support is already included in the usage fees for all customers. This is usually also free of charge. However, the low support level guarantees that customers can always open tickets and thus have access to the support organization in case of errors/problems.

This basic support is certainly sufficient for private customers, but this is not suitable if productive SAP S/4HANA systems are operated on the public clouds. Then support with the following important features is advisable:

- 24x7 support for resolving technical issues for production systems

- Fast response times for open support tickets when production systems are impacted

- Access to a manager assigned to a customer, through which long-running tickets can be escalated

- Architecture support and regular reviews of the SAP S/4HANA system landscape

- Training/webinars/whitepapers and guidelines

Especially the first points are very important for production environments. If a company initially starts with some sandbox or training systems, minimal support may already be sufficient. However, when the first production systems are migrated to the public cloud, support should be contracted.

DSVGO

A special attention should be directed by all customers to the DSVGO. Here, it is important to take into account the valid current legal requirements according to data storage and data retention plus data processing. These points must be sufficiently well covered and addressed by all customers in the contracts with the Hyperscalers. If the points are not addressed from the perspective of a customer's legal department, this must be discussed and adjusted with the Hyperscaler. As a rule, this should not be the case, but in exceptional cases, there may be discussions about this.

Support for Projects

Some of the large Hyperscalers support customers in using the cloud and in migrating SAP S/4HANA systems to the cloud for the first time. For this purpose, the Hyperscalers set up programs to motivate customers to migrate to the clouds and use them for as long as possible.

The initial step of migrating SAP S/4HANA systems to the cloud can be a very involved step. Customers have to define architectures, the contractual basis has to be created, and a lot of time is needed for coordination and initial walking tests. To reduce these efforts, Hyperscalers support customers in this process and deliver ready-to-use architectures and blueprints. For the execution of the migration of the first SAP systems to the clouds, the Hyperscalers support the customers/partners of the customers monetarily. In this way, the initial pain of migrating to the cloud is kept lower.

Running SAP S/4HANA systems can quickly become expensive due to the very high demands of the systems. In particular, SAP HANA machines are cost drivers in SAP environments. However, Hyperscalers can also counteract the costs here somewhat and provide service credits. These service credits can then be consumed by the customer after the systems have been migrated to the cloud. Customers should ensure that the credits can also be used for the migrated systems and do not apply exclusively to new SAP systems.

With such offers by the Hyperscalers, it must be clear that the goal of the Hyperscalers is to build up the customer relationships and to bind the customers to the Hyperscalers' clouds in the long term. It is obvious that SAP systems which are already running on the cloud will not be migrated out of the cloud again so quickly.

GxP Framework and Important Certificates

For many companies, GxP regulations are important framework conditions under which SAP systems must be operated. This section provides an overview of these regulations.

GxP in General

Companies from the life sciences sector or consumer goods manufacturers are often subject to special requirements with regard to quality management of production, but also IT services. These special requirements for the industries are recorded in the GxP guidelines. The "x" in GxP can stand for different industries, for example, GMP for the manufacturing industry. Besides the manufacturing industry, the GxP principles exist for the following industries:

- GAP: Good Agricultural Practice

- GMP: Good Manufacturing Practice

- GDP: Good Distribution Practice

- GCP: Good Clinical Practice

- GCLP: Good Clinical Laboratory Practice

- GLP: Good Laboratory Practice

- GAMP: Good Automated Manufacturing Practice

- GDocP: Good Documentation Practice

- GEP: Good Engineering Practice

- GSP: Good Scientific Practice

- GVP: Good Pharmacovigilance Practice

When migrating SAP systems to Hyperscaler clouds, companies must ensure that the principles are also met on the public cloud. However, a difference exists from the traditional on-premise world: while in the on-premise world, companies had the data center and server infrastructure under their control, they do not have the Hyperscaler infrastructure under their control. Therefore, it is important whether a Hyperscaler supports GxP and thus commits to the principles or not.

Split of Responsibilities

In general, there is a natural separation of responsibilities for S/4HANA systems on the Hyperscaler cloud. This results from the fact that the Hyperscalers do not have access to the actual customer data and customer systems. So the Hyperscalers can only control a subset of the components and thus ensure GxP compliance. A separation between Hyperscalers and customers can be listed as in Table 3-1.

Table 3-1. *Responsibilities in GxP-Compliant Environments*

Component	Topic	Responsible
Data center	Infrastructure of the data center (including physical access controls)	Hyperscaler
Server	Server infrastructure and security of physical servers	Hyperscaler
Storage	Storage infrastructure including RAID components, connection between server and storage and redundancy	Hyperscaler
Network	Physical components and cabling of all physical network components (including servers and storage)	Hyperscaler
Backbones	Connectivity between the data centers as well as the regions (e.g., Frankfurt to London) using the backbone network of the Hyperscalers	Hyperscaler
Operating system	Setup, configuration, and security of the operating system	Customer
HANA database	Setup, configuration, user and access management, etc.	Customer
SAP application	Operation and management of the technical SAP components (SAP Central Services, application server, etc.)	Customer
SAP data and programs	Data residing in the SAP system and ABAP/JAVA programs	Customer
SAP access	User, passwords, roles, and profiles	Customer
Firewalls and network	All virtual components of the cloud environment	Customer
Encryption	Any encryption of the network traffic, storage, backup, or any other configuration	Customer

The separation of responsibilities in Table 3-1 shows the importance of knowledge of the SAP systems on the Hyperscaler cloud. The Hyperscalers do not have access to the systems operated by the customer on the cloud and therefore cannot ensure the security and compliance of the systems. This must be done by the customers as steps of verification and validation.

Hyperscalers do not individually support the validation and verification of customers and their systems, but contribute to the certifications. It is advisable to contact the chosen Hyperscaler directly and talk through the GxP qualification. Afterward, it can be individually regulated which responsibilities lie with the Hyperscaler and which with the customer and/or service provider.

Additional Certifications

In addition to support for GxP, the major Hyperscalers have other certifications that can be important for customers. For example, some customers must also be able to show during audits that the Hyperscaler clouds have the appropriate certifications (contractor).

SOC 1 and 2

The Service and Organization Control Reports 1 and 2 were created as summaries of various reports, for example, SAS70, which were later replaced by the SOC 1 reports. Similar report names are SSAE18 as the US version, ISAE3402 as the European version, and ASA3402 as the Australian version of the reports. All reports show the effective controls of measures on internal processes. The SOC 2 reports focus on IT security and are derived from the AT101 standard.

If customers run their S/4HANA systems on the Hyperscaler cloud, they must be able to present these reports during audits. It is therefore essential that SOC 1 and SOC 2 are available as standardized reports and are provided by the Hyperscalers.

HIPAA/HITECH/HITRUST

Companies that are subject to the US Health Insurance Portability and Accountability Act (HIPAA) of 1996 must meet certain standards for processing data. This includes not only the processing of data by the same entity but also the processing of data by service providers and the storage of data. HIPAA includes regulations on key healthcare data, such as clinical care, laboratory data, and even test results. HIPAA requirements were later further supplemented by requirements from the Health Information Technology for Economic and Clinical Health (HITECH) Act.

All of the major Hyperscalers support the HIPAA guidelines, but are not themselves certified because the guidelines address operations and setup. For HIPAA purposes, the Hyperscalers are considered the so-called "business associates" – the business partners. Corresponding contracts must be concluded with the Hyperscalers in the sense of HIPAA. These contracts, the customers conclude with the Hyperscalers to ensure HIPAA compliance.

For some time, there was a requirement for HIPAA-compliant customers to use dedicated hosts and instances. It was possible to implement this requirement, but it conflicted with the idea of public cloud and ease of workload customization. The requirement for dedicated hosts and instances has dropped for some time, but customers are advised to familiarize themselves with the terms and requirements to avoid gaps. Some Hyperscalers, such as Microsoft with Azure, also offer blueprints through which customers can familiarize themselves with an example architecture and all the necessary rules for HIPAA/HITECH.

The last important framework in the healthcare industry is HITRUST, which can be seen as an extension of HIPAA and HITECH. It uses both Acts as a foundation and extends them with requirements from other regulatory frameworks, such as ISO 27001 or even MARS-E. There is currently no broad certification by Hyperscalers for HITRUST, as it has not been in existence for very long. Currently (as of 2021), only Microsoft Azure offers certification for HITRUST.

ISO Certificates

In addition to industry-specific certifications and support for such certifications, ISO certifications are very important for customers. The International Organization for Standardization (ISO) is a nongovernmental organization that has gained a very wide reach through its norms and standards. It has over 163 committees for the standardization of a wide variety of topics.

The ISO 27001 standard defines the most important standards for the handling and use of an information security management system (ISMS). This includes best practices that companies should ideally follow. The standard does not define measures, but the framework of them, and thus it is up to the companies to implement the measures.

The three major Hyperscalers Amazon Web Services, Google Cloud, and Microsoft Azure are all certified for ISO 27001. This is the basis of customers to get certified in ISO 27001 as well.

In addition to ISO 27001 certification, there are other certifications offered by the Hyperscalers. The abundance of certifications is to be listed here as an example for Amazon Web Services:

- CSA: Cloud Security Alliance

- ISO 9001 (quality management)

- ISO 27001 (security management)

- ISO 27017 (cloud-specific controls)

- ISO 27018 (personal data protection)

- PCI DSS Level 1 (Payment Card Standard)

- SOC 1 (audit control report)

- SOC 2 (security, availability, and confidentiality report)

- SOC 3 (general control report)

The other Hyperscalers offer similar certifications. This should be verified by the customers accordingly beforehand. Since the situation of certifications changes very quickly, a listing for Microsoft Azure and Google Cloud is omitted.

Management of an SAP S/4HANA Landscape

SAP Solution Manager exists in all SAP environments to administer SAP landscapes and successfully deploy important processes, such as release management via ChaRM. SAP Solution Manager is so deeply integrated into the processes and workflows that it can be found in every current system environment and thus represents the backbone of Application Lifecycle Management in SAP environments.

Important Features of SAP Solution Manager

Solution Manager can support a wide variety of areas in the operation and maintenance of SAP system landscapes. This includes the following most important functions:

- Maintenance management with the maintenance optimizer and system recommendations

- Template management with notifications for changes

- Operation of business processes with a BPO dashboard and job control and schedule management

- Operation of the technical processes with technical monitoring, end-user experience monitoring, and also data volume management

- Documentation of the solution with business blueprints and reverse documentation of the business processes

- Solution implementation with business blueprint models and end-to-end implementation processes for the business processes

- Upgrade management with the possibility to analyze the dependencies during an upgrade

- Incident management for the applications with a framework for automated testing using third-party tools

- Test management with the Business Process Change Analyzer

- Change control management with CTS+

Since Solution Manager was developed in the traditional world of data centers, SAP introduced some important new features with version 7.2 that prepare Solution Manager for new cloud scenarios:

- Solution Manager has been ported to SAP HANA, and it no longer requires a TREX server; instead, the search functionality is fulfilled by the HANA database.

- Solution Manager now fully supports SAP HANA and SAP S/4HANA systems.

- Solution Manager supports the hybrid cloud scenarios and can integrate with and monitor cloud resources.

Application Operation Using SAP Solution Manager

When managing larger SAP S/4HANA landscapes, SAP Solution Manager is essential for controlling operations and monitoring the health of the system landscape. SAP Solution Manager offers important functions that can simplify the daily routine of SAP Basis administrators. SAP Basis administrators can use technical system monitoring to monitor the exact status of the SAP S/4HANA system. The monitoring setup is not significantly different from the previous Solution Manager versions. Some time is required to define the appropriate thresholds and configure the alarms. But once this initial effort is done, the S/4HANA systems, the HANA databases, as well as the underlying virtual machines and operating systems can be monitored via the system monitoring. SAP also introduced job monitoring as a further component. This is limited compared to the functionality of job scheduling systems (such as Atomic's UC4), but can help administrators identify incorrect runs of background jobs. Nevertheless, companies tend to use the functionalities of job scheduling systems.

In addition to monitoring technical components and jobs, SAP has greatly expanded the area of monitoring for business intelligence/business warehouse. Here, customers can centrally monitor SAP Business Warehouse and SAP Business Intelligence solutions. This includes all important services such as System Landscape Transformation (SLT), Data Service Systems, as well as the Business Warehouse Accelerators (BWA). In this way, SAP is expanding the options for monitoring important content issues via the Solution Manager in addition to the technical points.

In addition to the purely technical points for monitoring, SAP has also implemented Process Integration (PI) monitoring. This allows central monitoring of the channels, messages, and system components of the PI systems. Since the PI systems have become neuralgic points in the system landscapes alongside the S/4HANA systems, close monitoring is required here and so administrators must be informed quickly of unsent messages. SAP Solution Manager's PI monitoring can address this.

Another important component for successful system monitoring is the root cause analysis component. This is a function in Solution Manager that has existed for several years and has been successively expanded. It can be used to investigate performance problems in the S/4HANA systems as well as non-availabilities (downtimes) and identify the triggering component. For successful analyses, it is important that all components are set up and configured correctly. SAP Solution Manager can also integrate third-party products.

For professional IT operations of the S/4HANA system landscape, SAP Solution Manager also offers integration with established ITSM (IT Service Management) systems, such as ServiceNow. This allows incidents to be created in the ITSM solutions for the problems detected in the SAP system landscape. This means that there is no need for manual transfer of problems to incidents. This is an alternative to using the company's own ITSM functions from Solution Manager. Many customers have an overarching ITSM tool and use it for centralized control of all ITSM processes. In such a case, the alerts from Solution Manager are passed on to the central ITSM tool.

All in all, the Solution Manager's application monitoring is very important for holistically monitoring the state of the system environment. Thanks to the integrated view of all important components (both technical and application related), Solution Manager makes an important contribution to the stable operation of SAP systems.

Using SAP Cloud ALM

Due to the widespread use of cloud services, SAP faced the challenge that some customers only use cloud-based services from SAP (such as Ariba). These customers do not want to build their own solution, such as Solution Manager, for efficient monitoring, but need a lean solution.

SAP launched SAP Cloud ALM, a new product that acts as part of the SAP Business Technology Platform and offers customers the ability to perform Application Lifecycle Management (ALM) via a cloud-based solution. In order not to limit the possibilities for SAP Cloud ALM too much, SAP is preparing the product to be used in hybrid scenarios as well. Thus, on-premise systems should be able to be monitored in the same way as SAP cloud solutions. However, there is a clear focus on SAP systems in general and SAP's cloud solutions and less on the integration of third-party software.

Many customers are now asking themselves which of the solutions (Solution Manager or Cloud ALM) is the right approach. For this purpose, the functions of the two solutions are compared in Table 3-2.

Table 3-2. *Comparison of Solution Manager and Cloud ALM*

Functionality	Solution Manager	Cloud ALM	Notes
Cloud application management	Low	Complete	
Change management	Complete	Partly	
Project management	Complete	Complete	
Process analysis and governance	Complete	High	
Key performance indicators	Complete	High	
Costs (infrastructure and maintenance)	Partly	Complete	Very low costs for Cloud ALM as provided by SAP
Ready-to-use	Very low	Complete	
Process monitoring	Low	Low	
Support for Intelligent Enterprise	Low	Complete	
Maintenance including upgrades	Low	Complete	Maintenance of Cloud ALM by SAP
Customer experience	Complete	Partly	
Reporting and analytics	Very high	Low	
Support for on-premise environment	Complete	Low	
Test suite	Complete	Very high	
Focused build	Complete	Not supported	
Service desk – ITSM	Complete	Not supported	

SAP Cloud ALM presents itself as a good alternative for controlling primarily cloud-based system environments, which are based on Ariba, Fieldglass, SAP Marketing Cloud, or even the SAP S/4HANA Cloud.

There are several ways to use Cloud ALM:

- If SAP customers are already using cloud products (e.g., Ariba), they can use these directly as part of SAP Enterprise Support.

- If customers do not yet use cloud products, they must sign the SAP Cloud Terms and Conditions and obtain a cloud product from SAP. Then these customers will also get access to Cloud ALM.

Currently, there is no version of Cloud ALM available for evaluation or testing.

Choosing a Hyperscaler

When selecting a future Hyperscaler/public cloud, there are several points for companies to consider. Customers often already have preferences for one or two Hyperscalers. This is based on previous experience or projects which, independent of an overall strategy, had already agreed on a Hyperscaler. In such cases, the already existing environments can later be transferred to the newly selected Hyperscaler or a two-Hyperscaler strategy can be pursued. If a Hyperscaler is selected from scratch, the decision should be based on qualitative and quantitative factors.

Quantitative Factors

In the general selection of a Hyperscaler, there is always one most important criterion that comes into play in all projects: the costs for future operation. Here, the initial setup costs, but especially the later, running costs, play a very important role.

Often, there are only very small differences in prices between the Hyperscalers, and the technologies of the Hyperscalers are comparable, at least for SAP S/4HANA systems. Nevertheless, the expected total price of an SAP S/4 environment plays the biggest role in a decision for/against a Hyperscaler in 99% of cases. However, there are several factors that influence the total price:

- Price per price list: Often, cost estimates are made based only on the Hyperscalers' standard prices. Cost estimates are made on the basis of calculators available on the Internet. As an indicative picture of the expected costs, this is suitable. However, it results in a total price that gives a wrong picture. If the SAP systems/non-SAP systems were moved 1:1 from the old landscape to the new Hyperscaler environment, there would be no cost advantage. A total price determined in this way must therefore be refined.

- Discounts/rebates: All Hyperscalers understand the current market momentum, which will continue for a few more years. They are aware of the current aspirations of customers to move to Hyperscaler clouds. Therefore, the Hyperscalers need to attract the customers and make the switch to the respective clouds attractive. For this purpose, discounts are provided which reduce the overall price. When considering the total cost of ownership, this component is very important. It is important that the larger the landscapes of the customers can become, the greater the discounts that the Hyperscalers can enable.

- Fundings: In addition to the actual discounts, there are other programs within the Hyperscalers which increase the price attractiveness. For example, there are programs that aim to increase the number of SAP systems in the respective Hyperscalers. These programs support customers in migrating SAP systems to the clouds or even provide support for new installations. Similar programs exist for other system types and application areas (such as for Workplace). It should be noted that the more workloads a Hyperscaler is promised, the larger such fundings will be. It therefore makes little sense to request funding for just one new SAP S/4HANA system. Rather, it should be transparently presented how many new systems are expected.

- Reservations: All Hyperscalers offer customers the option to use a virtual machine for a longer period of time and thus achieve a significant price reduction. These reservations/commitments can be obtained from all Hyperscalers. However, they differ in how they can be allocated to individual VMs. For example, at Microsoft, a commitment can be created for a class of virtual machines.

Only by taking the preceding factors into account can a real total price be calculated, which is considered the most important decision factor.

Price cuts   Hyperscalers are cutting prices on a regular basis. Thus, prices do not fall significantly, but in the marginal range on an annual basis. Sharp price reductions occur when serious events occur. For example, AWS and MS Azure prices were significantly reduced when Google entered the market a few years ago. Both competitors faced the situation where a new entrant with significant potential to impact Amazon and Microsoft's business entered the market. In response, prices were lowered to the level of Google in order to remain competitive.

Other events exist which usually lead to price adjustments time and again. These include the introduction of new technologies or new calculation bases (such as reservations/commitments). These events lead to an alignment of the prices for the services between the Hyperscalers, even if they always try to create differentiation through small differences.

Qualitative Factors

The list of quantitative factors in the decision for/against a Hyperscaler is very clear. The qualitative factors, on the other hand, can be very diverse, and the most important and common factors are described as follows:

- Strategy: An important qualitative factor is the strategy of a company in dealing with the public cloud. In the first years of the public cloud, a Hyperscaler was often relied on, and this was defined as the strategic partner. This was accompanied by all the major advantages and disadvantages of limiting oneself to just one Hyperscaler. This is now changing and the majority of companies are relying on a dual cloud strategy. This helps to counter lock-in and continue to interact with both Hyperscalers.

- Market positioning: The positioning of Hyperscalers in the market is certainly important for customers and can contribute to a decision.

However, it should be noted that the top three Hyperscalers are always closely ranked by all major market analysts (Gartner, IDC, Forrester, PAC). Microsoft Azure and Amazon Web Services are very well established due to their long history and have already been able to build up a broad and stable customer base. This also enables the very good positioning in the reports of the market analysts. Google, on the other hand, is often in the position of challenger and thus contributes to market dynamics. When selecting a Hyperscaler, the common market analysts should be consulted.

- Technical features and unique selling points: All Hyperscalers offer a great many services (IaaS, PaaS, and SaaS), which are generally of interest to customers. However, for the operation of SAP S/4HANA systems, there are not too many technical features that are considered unique selling points. The support of very large SAP systems with HANA was indeed a feature in the past, but this was often only used for marketing purposes. In addition, there are features for disaster recovery, which could be interesting for customers of SAP S/4HANA systems. However, since this is changing very quickly and Microsoft, for example, is gradually following suit here, these factors must be examined very thoroughly in order to make a real difference.

- Existing contracts/Enterprise Agreement: A very big factor in the selection of a Hyperscaler may be existing contracts. For a large number of enterprises, contracts with the large Hyperscalers usually already exist for a few smaller services. The effort required to move from these existing contracts to an extended contract that also covers the operation of SAP systems is manageable. If you compare the effort required to extend a contract with the effort required for a completely new contract, many companies tend to opt for an extension. Thus, no long-term, legal reviews become necessary.

- Specifics of the industries: The previous sections have already described the different regulatory regimes for different industries (such as GxP). The support of such regulations, certificates, as well as the implementation are of course very important and crucial for customers of these industries. Although all Hyperscalers support the most important issues here, industry-specific requirements need to be closely examined.

- Appreciation: Every customer appreciates it when they receive preferential treatment. Customers then feel special and valued. This is similar for Hyperscaler companies and customers. Thus, it is important for Hyperscalers to also make prospective customers feel good not only through the account teams but also through an attention from the higher leadership (senior management) of the Hyperscalers. There have been customers who have made this a deciding factor in their choice of Hyperscalers.

- Innovation: All Hyperscalers position innovativeness and outlook in innovation as an important component in decisions for/against a Hyperscaler. These are often important factors for many companies, but it has been shown that these are not critical factors that actually come into play when making a "SAP S/4HANA systems on Hyperscaler A/B/C" decision.

Table 3-3 summarizes these factors. Not all of them are equally weighted in decisions. There are important differences.

Table 3-3. *Weighting for Decision Factors*

Factor	Weighting	Notes
Quantitative Factors		
Total cost of ownership	Very high	
Discounts	High	Part of the TCO
Fundings	High	Part of the TCO
Reservations	Medium	Part of the TCO
Qualitative Factors		
Strategy	Very high	
Market position	Medium	
Features	Medium	
Existing contract	High	
Support for industry	Very high	Can be KO criterion
Appreciation	Medium	
Innovation	Low	

In general, decisions on Hyperscalers are made after careful consideration and are underpinned by scoring models for many companies. The decision for/against MS Azure, Amazon Web Services, or Google Cloud can only be made individually, as all companies are in specific situations. However, the preceding factors can be used as a guide to make a decision.

Deployment and Migration

The public cloud makes it very easy to provision new SAP systems or even consume them directly from the cloud. This section shows how SAP S/4HANA systems can be provisioned and migrated in the cloud.

Transformation Is a Must

In recent years, SAP has pushed its customers to transform their SAP systems through various enhancements and renewals. It started with the enhancement packages, continued with the adaptation of SAP HANA, and is currently culminating in the introduction of new S/4HANA systems.

Before the introduction of the enhancement packages, new functionalities were primarily provided via upgrades of systems. However, such upgrade projects involved massive investments in projects and had a major impact on the business. Due to the high cost of introducing new functions, an alternative to upgrades was sought. SAP found this alternative in enhancement packages, which were easier to implement, but still required greater project effort. For the enhancement packages, the SAP systems had to be updated, but the customers benefited from new functionalities and technical innovations. Many customers took this step to keep their systems up to date and to benefit from the innovations.

After that, there was a very big movement in the SAP system landscapes about the change to SAP HANA. Here, SAP motivated customers to switch to HANA through a number of technical innovations; however, the start was very difficult for SAP. A very complex licensing model for the features of SAP HANA and the SAP systems prevented a broad acceptance and high adaptation rate of SAP HANA at the beginning. In direct comparison to similar technologies, SAP was not yet able to convince with HANA and put a lot of energy into the further development of HANA and making the entire HANA platform robust and mature. Meanwhile, highly critical SAP systems are based on HANA platforms. However, the switch to HANA was a considerably difficult step for all customers and involved a great deal of effort. The adaptations to the ABAP code and the project efforts were significant for many companies, but a majority of SAP customers have adopted the new HANA platform and are running SAP systems on it.

The next big – and currently ongoing – step is the move to S/4HANA. Many companies are currently facing the challenge of converting SAP systems to S/4HANA systems. SAP is linking this technical step not only to a transformation of the technology but also of the business processes in particular. Here, however, companies can take two basic positions and decide how to proceed with the SAP systems:

- Either the company decides to transform the existing system to S/4HANA.

- Or the company decides to make a fresh start and has two system landscapes: an old one and a new one based on S/4HANA.

This fundamental discussion and the basic decision depend on the company's strategy. There is no recipe or general advice that can apply equally to all companies. Each company must analyze its situation and then make the fundamental decision. The majority of customers are currently operating in a hybrid scenario with an old and a new system landscape.

New Approaches Using the Cloud

The provision of services in the public cloud basically follows two different approaches: greenfield or brownfield. The selection of the approach for deployment and migration depends on the prerequisites that the existing IT architecture, if any, entails. Related to this are the requirements for the defined target architecture in the public cloud. When selecting a deployment approach, the current state is consequently compared with the target state of the services to be migrated. First, the scope and nature of the services in the existing environment are considered. Then it is examined whether these services will be migrated completely, partially, or not at all to the public cloud architecture. In the latter case, the services are rebuilt as part of the cloud deployment.

The two approaches, as well as the procedure described, can also be transferred to the deployment of SAP environments in the public cloud. How the approaches differ from each other in relation to SAP and what special features there are in a brownfield migration are explained in the following sections.

Greenfield Deployment

Deployment of services in the IT architecture according to the greenfield approach is understood to mean the complete rebuilding of the service instances as part of the migration. If potential services already exist in the existing IT environment, they are not migrated to the environment in the Hyperscaler public cloud. Greenfield deployment provides for all identified services to be rebuilt in the target environment.

In practice, the greenfield approach with regard to SAP applications is particularly suitable for the deployment of new SAP systems that are not available in the existing architecture. A concrete use case here can be the deployment of an SAP S/4HANA sandbox in the public cloud. Assuming that the sandbox was not previously in use, the deployment is carried out according to greenfield. The greenfield approach is comparatively rare in the practical environment, as an enterprise architecture is often already composed of a large number of existing systems that should continue to be available after migration to the public cloud in order to maintain business capability.

Brownfield Deployment

In contrast to the greenfield approach, brownfield migration involves transferring existing components from the on-premise environment to the target architecture in the public cloud. Migration to the Hyperscaler cloud environment always takes into account at least a subset of the as-is state of the components in the IT architecture. While in a greenfield deployment all services are provided from scratch in the target architecture, the brownfield approach builds on the existing on-premise architecture and its components. In general terms, a distinction is made between two variants in a brownfield deployment: **homogeneous** and **heterogeneous**.

Homogeneous Migrations

On the one hand, migration can involve a complete one-to-one transfer from the on-premise landscape to the public cloud. This strategy is called a homogeneous system copy. When migrating according to this approach, no changes are made, neither at the operating system level nor at the database level. Only a replication of the data is carried out according to the "backup-and-restore" principle. This is understood to mean that the backup is created from the on-premise environment and then restored in the public cloud infrastructure. Therefore, the homogeneous migration is easy to implement with a low downtime.

For SAP systems, the homogeneous strategy can only be applied on condition that the operating system already in use is compatible with the supported operating systems in the public cloud environment. In the Microsoft Azure Cloud, for example, the following systems are supported for running SAP workloads:

- Microsoft Windows Server

- Red Hat Enterprise Linux (RHEL)

- SUSE Enterprise Linux (SLES)

- Oracle Linux for Oracle database management systems

In addition, SAP provides corresponding notes (SAP Note 1928533, SAP Note 2015553) that define the Infrastructure-as-a-Service elements, such as virtual machine types and sizes, that support the operation of SAP systems in the Microsoft Azure Cloud. For a homogeneous system copy to the public cloud, these infrastructure characteristics must already exist in the on-premise environment.

Heterogeneous Migrations

The alternative variant to a homogeneous migration involves deploying the identified components from the as-is architecture to the public cloud by changing the state. This strategy is referred to as heterogeneous system copy. In this approach, at least either the operating system or the database management system is changed. As part of the homogeneous migration, this provides the opportunity to perform release upgrades of the SAP application. Although the analysis of a potential source of errors is more complex in this case, testing is more efficient because the upgrade was performed as part of the migration, which is consequently also tested.

To perform a heterogeneous system copy, SAP recommends using the standardized R3load tool. With the help of this tool, the content from the source database is exported to files, which are then imported into the target database. In addition, the following SAP Software Update Manager (SUM) tools can also be used:

- Software Provisioning Manager (SWPM)

- Database Migration Option (DMO)

Due to the change in the state of the components of the SAP system as a result of upgrades, for example, heterogeneous migration is more complex and entails a higher downtime. However, a key advantage is the increased efficiency for changes in the respective SAP systems.

Sequence of Migration

When deploying SAP systems using the brownfield approach, two procedures are defined for determining the order in which the complete SAP landscape is migrated to the public cloud. As a rule, an SAP landscape is made up of various SAP applications. These can be, for example, SAP ERP (Enterprise Resource Planning), SAP GTS (Global Trade Services), SAP SCM (Supply Chain Management), and SAP BI (Business Intelligence). For each of these applications, there are also several environments in the architecture that serve to maintain consistency in the context of developments and system changes. According to SAP's best practice recommendation, the following environments are established for each application: sandbox, development, quality assurance, and productive. An SAP landscape of a company can be exemplified by Figure 3-1.

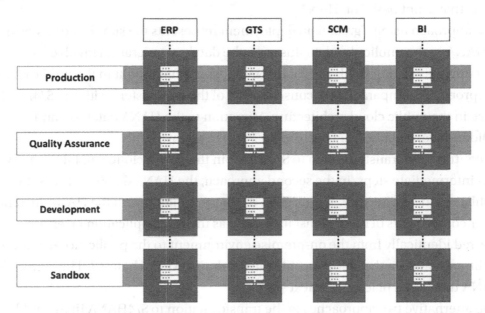

Figure 3-1. *Overall landscape*

Two approaches are available for defining a migration sequence. According to the horizontal migration approach, the sequence for transferring the landscape to the public cloud is defined per environment. In the horizontal approach, the individual environments of the SAP systems are migrated to the cloud architecture in bundles step by step. In relation to the exemplary figure, the sandbox environment and all the SAP instances it contains would therefore be transferred first. However, the horizontal approach is only suitable for the homogeneous migration strategy in order to avoid incompatibilities with the on-premise architecture.

In contrast to the horizontal approach, the order of migration in the vertical approach is based on the SAP applications. In this case, migration takes place step by step per SAP application. For example, from Figure 3-1, all instances of the SAP ERP application would be migrated first in the case of a transfer to the public cloud. This procedure is particularly suitable for heterogeneous migrations in order to maintain compatibility between the instances of an SAP application.

Migration Scenarios for SAP S/4HANA Transformations

The migration of an SAP landscape from on-premise to the public cloud environment can be combined with a conversion to SAP S/4HANA via four approaches. All approaches assume that the on-premise environment hosts an SAP ERP system with any database that is not based on HANA.

The approach using a greenfield deployment represents the simplest transformation to S/4HANA in the public cloud. In this case, the database migration involves transferring the existing database to a HANA database that is built in the public cloud. This approach is comparable to a consolidation of the ECC system with the S/4HANA instance in the public cloud architecture. Migration to the HANA database and consolidation take place in one step, reducing system downtime.

In contrast, the transformation to S/4HANA in the public cloud can take place via various intermediate steps. In the second approach, the HANA database is first built in the public cloud architecture. The original database is migrated to the HANA instance. All other components of the SAP instance, such as the ERP application layer, are transferred identically from the on-premise environment to the public cloud architecture using lift-and-shift. In the first step, only the database level is changed. The conversion to S/4HANA then takes place in the next step.

The alternative two approaches to the transformation to S/4HANA in the public cloud initially involve transferring the existing on-premise environment to the Hyperscaler cloud environment. The migration is done using either lift-and-shift or lift-and-migrate. The lift-and-shift approach assumes that the state of the on-premise SAP instance is compatible with the state of the resources in the public cloud architecture. If, for example, the operating system differs, a corresponding adjustment must be made by applying lift-and-migrate. After the components of the SAP ECC instance have been transferred from the on-premise environment to the public cloud, the next step is either the complete transformation to S/4HANA or, alternatively, first via a migration of the database technology to HANA. In the latter case, the conversion to S/4HANA is implemented in a separate step.

SAP S/4HANA As SaaS Services

It is not always expedient for companies to provision their own SAP systems. The trend toward the use of Software-as-a-Service offerings is becoming increasingly prevalent, and so SAP also offers the option of using SAP S/4HANA systems from the cloud.

Overview

SAP's portfolio comprises a diverse range of SAP solutions for operation in an on-premise environment and operation in the cloud. For SAP S/4HANA, in addition to the conventional edition for in-house operation, SAP also offers a Software-as-a-Service variant in which the SAP S/4HANA system is operated in SAP's own cloud. In general, a distinction is made between on-premise deployment and cloud deployment for S/4HANA. The on-premise variant is operated in a company's own data center or in a Hyperscaler public cloud by the using company itself. The cloud option of S/4HANA is hosted in SAP's own cloud, and two different editions are available: SAP S/4HANA Cloud Essentials Edition and SAP S/4HANA Cloud Extended Edition. The key difference between these editions and a traditional on-premise deployment is the responsibilities in SAP Basis operations. While in an on-premise environment the company itself is fully responsible for operations, in the Essentials Edition and Extended Edition SAP takes over individual areas of Basis operations.

The Essentials Edition and the Extended Edition are hosted entirely in SAP's own cloud. If a company opts for one of these editions, it should therefore be borne in mind that this variant does not allow access to infrastructure components or individual areas of SAP Basis Operation, as SAP takes over operation. From the operational perspective of a user, the business processes in the S/4HANA SaaS variant are basically comparable to an on-premise deployment. Due to the different development and innovation progress, there may be isolated deviations, for example, in the availability of Fiori apps, as new releases are imported at shorter intervals in the S/4HANA cloud deployments. This is due to the lower complexity resulting from standardization and centralized operation by SAP compared to individualized on-premise deployments.

The Essentials Edition and the Extended Edition of the cloud deployment variant differ primarily in the use of resources. The Essentials Edition was originally called "Multi Tenant" because the deployment of the S/4HANA instance in this model takes place in a shared infrastructure in the SAP Cloud. In the Extended Edition, on the other hand, the S/4HANA instance is operated in a dedicated, private infrastructure environment for the customer.

Differences Between the Editions

The following tables show a comparison of the differences between an on-premise deployment, S/4HANA Cloud Essentials Edition, and S/4HANA Cloud Extended Edition. For the comparison, different levels are used: infrastructure, implementation, process, configuration and enhancement, as well as security.

Infrastructure Level

The infrastructure level comprises the areas required for the provision of the respective deployment variant. These areas are summarized in Table 3-4.

Table 3-4. *Infrastructure Level*

Topic	S/4HANA Cloud Essentials Edition	S/4HANA Cloud Extended Edition	SAP S/4HANA On-Premise
Licenses	Subscription based		Bring-your-own-license (BYOL)
Updates	Provided by SAP in automatic fashion	Manual or automatic	Manual
Releases	Once per quarter	Once per half year	Yearly
Data center provider	Predefined by SAP	Chosen by SAP customer	Chosen by SAP customer
Performance	Impacted by all customers	Private instance can be tuned by SAP	Private instance can be tuned by customer

Implementation Level

The implementation level deals with the approach and procedure up to the deployment of an S/4HANA instance in the respective environment. Table 3-5 provides an example of possible timings and approaches.

Table 3-5. *Implementation Level*

Topic	S/4HANA Cloud Essentials Edition	S/4HANA Cloud Extended Edition	SAP S/4HANA On-Premise
Duration	8–16 weeks	Ca. 16 weeks	Depending on customer
Implementation strategy	Greenfield		Greenfield or brownfield

Process Level

In the process level, the functionalities and possibilities related to the operational use of an S/4HANA system are considered from the perspective of end users. Table 3-6 summarizes some aspects of this level.

Table 3-6. *Process Level*

Topic	S/4HANA Cloud Essentials Edition	S/4HANA Cloud Extended Edition	SAP S/4HANA On-Premise
Preconfigured business processes	Obligatory		Optional
Coverage of industries	Finance ERP, professional services, manufacturing, oil and gas	General availability of all 25 industry solutions	
Localization	43 countries 25 languages	64 countries 38 languages	
Graphical User Interface	100% web based Based on Fiori	Based on web and traditional SAP GUI Partly based on Fiori	

Configuration and Enhancement Level

The configuration level – summarized in Table 3-7 – refers in particular to the customizing of an SAP system. Such customization is also often accompanied by various enhancements.

Table 3-7. *Configuration and Enhancement Level*

Topic	S/4HANA Cloud Essentials Edition	S/4HANA Cloud Extended Edition	SAP S/4HANA On-Premise
Customizing (IMG, SPRO)	Simplified (configuration using guides)	Fully available	
In-app enhancements	Yes		
Classical enhancements	No	Yes	
Changes	No		Yes

Security Level

The level of security describes the scope of available security concepts and how they are applicable in the respective S/4HANA instance. Table 3-8 summarizes this level.

Table 3-8. *Security Level*

Topic	S/4HANA Cloud Essentials Edition	S/4HANA Cloud Extended Edition	SAP S/4HANA On-Premise
Infrastructure security	Provided by SAP		Customer specific as client is fully responsible
Risk data theft	Higher risk due to shared environment	Lower risk due to dedicated environment	
Disaster recovery	Shared resources	Dedicated resources	

Overall Comparison

Finally, Table 3-9 provides an overall comparison.

Table 3-9. Overall Comparison

Topic	S/4HANA Cloud Essentials Edition	S/4HANA Cloud Extended Edition	SAP S/4HANA On-Premise
Total cost of ownership	Low	Medium	High
Overall effort for the change management	Very high	High	Depending on customer
Innovation	Entirely depending on SAP	Entirely depending on SAP	Depending on customer and SAP

Advantages and Disadvantages

A central aspect of the cloud deployment approach is the distributed responsibilities. In contrast to an on-premise S/4HANA instance, SAP takes over operations in some areas. By offloading some of the operations, an SAP customer needs fewer human and financial resources to deploy an SAP instance to run business processes. Due to the reduced need for technical knowledge to operate an SAP system, the costs are significantly lower compared to an on-premise deployment.

However, the cost savings from using a cloud deployment comes with the disadvantage that an SAP customer has less influence over the customizability of the S/4HANA instance. For example, if a company has complex business processes and the need for customization of the SAP system is high, the use of SaaS for S/4HANA is conditionally suitable to cover the requirements.

When comparing the advantages and disadvantages of the two deployment approaches, the accessibility and availability to new innovations and functionalities must also be considered. The cloud deployment editions are based on a standardized structure and are operated centrally by SAP. For this reason, the release cycle is shorter than with on-premise deployment, as new functionalities require less adaptation in the standardized S/4HANA instances. Consequently, access to innovations is faster than with an on-premise S/4HANA variant. In addition, when a new functionality is made available, SAP takes over some basic configurations for integration, so that SAP customers usually only have to make a small effort to use new innovations. However, due to the standardization in an S/4HANA cloud deployment, it must be taken into account that the use and integration of an innovation in an on-premise environment may differ.

Overall, the interpretation of the advantages and disadvantages of the respective S/4HANA deployment variants is shaped by the individual strategy of a company. The decision in favor of a model depends on the requirements placed on the SAP S/4HANA system, particularly during operation.

Use Cases

An exemplary use case for the use of a cloud deployment is the low degree of individualization of an S/4HANA instance. This requirement is based on the assumption that a company's business capability is based on standardized processes that are highly aligned with SAP's business processes. Standardization of the operational business reduces the need for customization of a system, which is why an S/4HANA cloud deployment can address this requirement. A prerequisite for this is the ability to outsource isolated areas of basic operations. In particular, internal company compliance must be compliant with the use of SAP's SaaS model. If these assumptions and conditions are met, an S/4HANA cloud edition can also be used as a productive system.

However, a cloud deployment of an S/4HANA instance can also be used as a test environment to gain faster access to new innovations due to the shorter release cycle. The faster availability of new functions in the S/4HANA Cloud edition can give a company an impression of which innovations are suitable for the productive SAP environment, for example, and what added value they bring. The S/4HANA cloud deployment model provides the opportunity to test and evaluate new innovations in a "real" environment before they are made available for the on-premise environment.

Summary

Before using a public cloud for SAP S/4HANA systems, companies should first check the important framework conditions. The contract design is of particular importance here. Since this is based on standard contracts of the Hyperscalers, there is little room for maneuver for the customers with regard to the contracts. More important, however, are the aspects of purchasing the services and the very important support provided by the Hyperscalers. The funding of the Hyperscalers was also described in brief.

Regulatory requirements are a particular focus for many customers. For example, companies from the healthcare sector must be able to implement corresponding specifications – even on the public cloud. The chapter described how this is to be met and how this must be done.

Efficient control of the SAP S/4HANA system landscape is important for every company. The chapter showed how SAP Solution Manager can be used for control and also showed SAP's new cloud-based tool, Cloud ALM. A comparison of both products showed the advantages and disadvantages and facilitated the choice of tool.

The deployment of SAP S/4HANA systems can be carried out using various approaches. These include the reprovisioning of SAP systems with the greenfield approach or the transformation of SAP systems into the cloud with the brownfield approach.

SAP also offers its customers the important SAP S/4HANA systems from the cloud and as cloud editions. The chapter also showed what options are available for purchasing from a cloud operated by SAP.

As the last point in this chapter, the selection of a Hyperscaler was explained in more detail. There are quantitative factors, such as costs, but also qualitative factors, such as market positioning, which contribute to and lead to the selection of a Hyperscaler.

CHAPTER 4

SAP S/4HANA on AWS Elastic Compute Cloud – Concepts and Architecture

This chapter introduces Amazon Web Services Hyperscaler Cloud. Starting with a brief history of AWS, it goes on to introduce the most important services required for hosting, managing, and running the SAP S/4HANA application on AWS. Further, it explains the possible deployment scenarios for SAP S/4HANA on AWS Hyperscaler Cloud and covers the integration aspects.

History of Amazon AWS

Amazon Web Services (AWS) is a subsidiary of Amazon.com, Inc. that provides on-demand cloud computing platforms and APIs to companies (including government owned) and individuals. AWS is the market leader with a global share of around 30% in Cloud World. 13% of Amazon's total revenue ($113.08 billion) comes from the cloud unit. 54% of Amazon's operating income comes from AWS.

AWS that we know today started as an Infrastructure-as-a-Service offering from Amazon.com in 2006. The main benefit that AWS brought with cloud computing was the elimination of upfront capital costs for infrastructure acquisition. Instead, it needed a very low, variable cost based on the specific needs of the company. The companies need not plan for the acquisition of servers or other IT infrastructure months in advance.

© André Bögelsack, Utpal Chakraborty, Dhiraj Kumar, Johannes Rank, Jessica Tischbierek, Elena Wolz 2022
A. Bögelsack et al., *SAP S/4HANA Systems in Hyperscaler Clouds*, https://doi.org/10.1007/978-1-4842-8158-1_4

They could easily ramp up, ramp down, scale up, or scale out the servers based on the requirement. And this revolutionized how infrastructure was hosted and managed and changed the technology world forever.

AWS has been operating SAP workloads since 2008, which is much longer than any other cloud provider. AWS and SAP have been working together on innovations since 2011 to help customers run their SAP landscapes in the cloud. AWS offers the broadest selection of SAP-certified, cloud-native instance types to give SAP customers a choice of processor, storage, networking, operating system, and purchase model to support their unique and changing needs.

More than 85% of customers report cost savings through SAP on AWS, according to an IDC study 2020. With the AWS Migration Acceleration Program (MAP), you receive consulting support, training, and services to migrate eligible SAP workloads. Now more than 5000 customers are using SAP on AWS. AWS is leading the Hyperscaler market share till date, as shown in Figure 4-1.

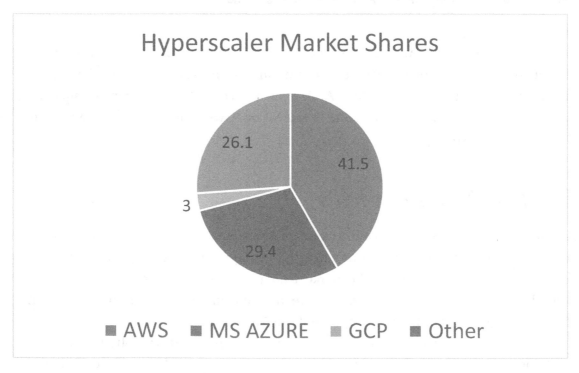

Figure 4-1. *Hyperscaler market share*

New Infrastructure and Innovations

AWS began an infrastructure platform that enabled developers to build and test new apps. AWS has more than one million users, including Netflix and Airbnb. Because of the huge customer base, AWS has extensive experience and better understanding of cloud service usage by customers. It is continuing to create new infrastructures and innovations to meet its customer needs around the world.

AWS has developed platforms for databases, developer apps, tools, analytics, etc. It has set up a full-featured platform of services that has given them the forefront as the cloud service provider.

Fast and Easily Scalable Solutions

AWS offers fast and simple scalable solutions for its customers. AWS has the following strength:

– Huge and diversified customer base

– Wide spectrum of acquiring strategic tools, for example, native cloud applications and ebusiness hosting

– Substantial tech alliance including software vendors that integrate their solutions with AWS

– Large-scale network of partners that provide app development expertise, managed services and professional services such as data center migration

– Extensive choice of IaaS and PaaS capabilities

– Expeditious service offerings and higher-level solution expansion

So, having an enormous capacity offer by AWS helps to find solutions for its business challenges. For example, companies can use AWS autoscaling to match their load demands instead of maintaining top loads in traditional data centers. Companies can adjust the number of servers added or remove them depending on the load, by using AWS autoscaling. Autoscaling also helps aid companies to identify when a server is not stable, then terminate and launch it on another server to replace and run it on a stable environment. So, the advantage of using AWS offers companies vast solutions for their different needs under one umbrella.

Still AWS is dominating the cloud computing market because of its service offerings to the customers. Other competitors like Microsoft, Google, and others could achieve higher growth than AWS sometimes. However, by providing improved infrastructure, reduction in price, ever-evolving innovation, AWS yet successfully maintained the leading position in cloud computing.

Three Reasons Why AWS Is Dominating the Cloud Marketplace

It has been around for the longest.

In 2006, AWS started infrastructure offering. Throughout these years, it not only built a wide customer base providing major cloud computing platforms but also revamped its product. Whereas Microsoft Azure was launched in 2010, Google App Engine (a predecessor to Google Cloud) was released in 2008, and IBM Cloud didn't become public until the 2009 LotusLive collaboration suite.

A year of time for free testing

The free tier offering from AWS allows its users to get a hands-on experience in the AWS cloud platform without any cost, before fully migrating to the AWS cloud. Users have access to AWS Free Tier services like Amazon EC2 (cloud computing capacity), Amazon S3 (cloud storage), and Amazon RDS (Relational Database Service) for 12 months. So, they can utilize a one-year duration before making any official commitment. The subscription movement from AWS Free Tier is very easy. The test tier can shift over to full-service AWS, and business can run as usual.

Much bigger than its competitors

An article written last May in Forbes discussed a Gartner report that estimated "AWS has more than ten times the computing capacity of the next 14 largest infrastructure vendors combined." AWS has multiple data centers across the globe. As it stands, AWS has quite a few numbers of availability zones around the globe. In the upcoming year, the company already planned to add 11 availability zones in five more geographic regions. AWS is able to meet your essentials in case you are trying to improve your IT infrastructure or a multinational company (MNC) looking for scalable cloud processing.

Reasons for AWS

The following sections provide a quick summary of the advantages of choosing AWS.

Easy to Use

With AWS, application providers, independent software vendors, and manufacturers can quickly and securely host your applications, whether it's an existing application or a new SaaS-based application. You can use the AWS Management Console or the well-documented web services APIs to access the AWS platform for hosting applications.

Flexible

In AWS, you get a choice of operating system, database, web application platform, programming language, and other services you need. Figure 4-2 shows some of the many services that are available.

Moreover, with AWS, you get a virtual environment where you can load the software and services your application needs. In this way, the migration of existing applications is made easier and more accessible, and at the same time, it offers a variety of options for implementing new solutions.

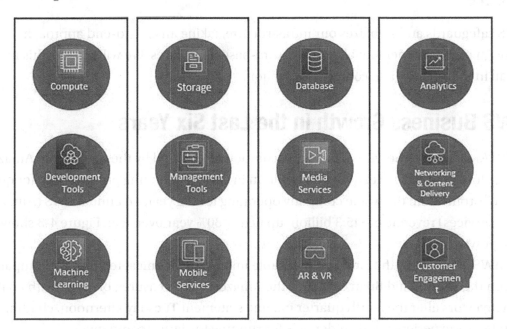

Figure 4-2. *Amazon Web Services list at a glance*

Economical

You only pay for the computing power used, the memory used, and other resources that you use and do not have to enter into long-term contracts or provide upfront services.

Reliable

With AWS, you take the benefit of a scalable, reliable, and secure global computing infrastructure that is the virtual backbone of Amazon.com's multibillion-dollar online retail business and has improved for over a decade.

Scalable and Extremely Powerful

Using AWS tools, autoscaling and elastic load balancing, your application can be scaled as desired automatically.

Secure

AWS safeguards and stabilizes our infrastructure, taking an end-to-end approach through physical, operational, and software-based measures. We will discuss this in detail in the Security and compliance section.

AWS Business Growth in the Last Six Years

AWS (Amazon Web Services), the cloud computing giant led by the now-future Amazon CEO, closed out 2020 with quite $13.5 billion in annual operating profits, liable for quite 63% of profits from the whole company operating for the year, on annual AWS (Amazon Web Services) revenue of $45.3 billion, up nearly 30% year over year. Figure 4-3 shows this growth trend.

AWS is "arguably the foremost profitable important technical technology company within the world," said Brian Olsavsky, the Amazon chief treasurer, on a call with analysts and investors after the fourth quarter income statement Tuesday afternoon, chatting with Jassy's experience and credentials for running the larger company.

The bottom line is that Amazon is constant to maximize its position because the leader publicly cloud computing. Jassy has necessarily built a corporation within an organization since the launch of AWS (Amazon Web Services) quite 15 years ago, one among the factors that made him the choice of the AWS board to succeed founder Jeff Bezos as the Amazon CEO.

Figure 4-3. *AWS business growth from 2014 to 2020[1]*

Offered Cloud Services

AWS is the leading Hyperscaler cloud service provider that offers on-demand cloud-based services under IaaS and PaaS offering with pay-as-you-go pricing for hosting and running SAP applications. The history of AWS hosting SAP applications goes back to 2008, and AWS has been SAP's Global Technology Partner since 2011. Through all these years, the offerings have matured, and AWS now has 5000+ customers running SAP.

---

[1] www.google.com/url?sa=i&url=https%3A%2F%2Fwww.geekwire.com%2F2021%2Famazon-web-services-posts-record-13-5b-profits-2020-andy-jassys-aws-swan-song%2F&psig=AOvVaw067VWQqXzJECTndfaUAUh4&ust=1641300541073000&source=images&cd=vfe&ved=0CAsQjRxqFwoTCIC-7o_PlfUCFQAAAAAdAAAAABAD

The current list of services runs over 200. AWS offers infrastructure services that can be used to deploy and run SAP products. The services that are required for hosting and running SAP applications are described in the following sections.

Compute

Amazon Elastic Compute Cloud (Amazon EC2) provides a secure and scalable compute capacity that supports virtually any workload for SAP. The offering is wide, the smallest being with 2 vCPUs and 3.75 GB RAM (VM supporting 1995 SAPS) to as large as 448 vCPUs and 24,576 GB RAM (Bare Metal supporting 444,330 SAPS).

For the latest list of certified Amazon EC2s that can run SAP workloads, refer to SAP Note: **1656099 – SAP Applications on AWS: Supported DB/OS and AWS EC2 products**.

For running HANA databases, SAP also provides a list of certified and supported SAP HANA Hardware. This can be referenced at

`www.sap.com/dmc/exp/2014-09-02-hana-hardware/enEN/#/solutions?filters=v`
`:deCertified`

An EC2 instance is normally launched using an Amazon Machine Image (AMI). AMIs are like preconfigured templates which contain the desired configurations like operating systems and settings, applications, and software configurations that you aim to have when an EC2 instance is launched.

SAP and AWS suggest that while launching EC2 instances for SAP workloads, use Amazon Machine Images (AMIs) with Hardware Virtual Machine (HVM) virtualization instead of PV (*paravirtualized AMIs*). With this, the migration to future instance types – once supported – will become simpler.

For more details on HVM and PV AMIs, refer to the Amazon documentation:

`https://docs.aws.amazon.com/AWSEC2/latest/UserGuide/virtualization_`
`types.html`

Storage

AWS offers block storage as well as object-based storage to support operations of SAP workloads. The main AWS storage services that are used in SAP are

- Amazon Elastic Block Store (Amazon EBS)
- Amazon Elastic File System (Amazon EFS)

- Amazon FSx for Windows File Server

- Amazon Simple Storage Service (Amazon S3)

Amazon Elastic Block Store (Amazon EBS)

EBS is a persistent block storage volume that is attached to EC2 instances. It offers similar functions as the Storage Area Network (SAN). EBS volumes are like raw, unformatted block devices that can be mounted on EC2 instances, and then file systems can be carved out on top of these volumes to host SAP or database-related files.

All the file systems that do not require sharing for SAP applications and HANA databases should be hosted on EBS.

Amazon Elastic File System (Amazon EFS)

EFS is a shared file system service in Amazon. In applications where you have the requirement for a common file system, shared across all applications, you use EFS.

EFS is not supported on servers with Windows OS.

For SAP, EFS can be used for shared file systems like sapmnt and trans directories and, in the HANA DB side, for HANA share.

Amazon FSx

FSx is an AWS managed file storage built on Microsoft Windows Server. This again is used for common file systems, shared across all applications hosted on a Windows server.

When you plan to use EFS and FSx, the overhead for file server provisioning, management, and administration is taken care of by AWS.

Amazon Simple Storage Service (Amazon S3)

S3 is an object-based storage service that provides highly scalable, reliable, fast, and inexpensive data storage infrastructure. Objects are redundantly stored on multiple devices across multiple facilities in an Amazon S3 Region.

In the case of SAP, S3 normally can be used for the long-term storage of backups.

Networking

Amazon networking services provide a reliable, secure, and highly available environment to host your SAP workloads. The main services that are used in the context of SAP are

- Amazon Virtual Private Cloud (Amazon VPC)

- AWS Site-to-Site VPN

- AWS Direct Connect

- Amazon Route 53

- Amazon Time Sync

Amazon Virtual Private Cloud (Amazon VPC)

VPC is part of AWS Networking Foundations, and it enables you to define an isolated virtual network area within the AWS Cloud. This can be loosely compared to the dedicated and secured section in your on-premise data center where you host and run SAP applications and databases.

A VPC is completely under your ownership where you define subnets (in your own IP address range) and communication paths (route tables and network gateways) for hosting and accessing applications.

Resources like EC2s, gateways, and load balancers for hosting and running SAP are provisioned in VPC. Communications are tightly secured with features like *Security Groups* (SG) and *Network Access Control Lists* (NACLs).

AWS Site-to-Site VPN

Your VPC is an isolated network zone in AWS. If you want to enable communications from your on-premise network to your VPC, you can use a Site-to-Site VPN as shown in Figure 4-4.

The connection of AWS VPC to an on-premise network can be facilitated with a virtual private gateway or a transit gateway as the gateway for the Amazon side. And in the on-premise side, there is a customer gateway which can be a physical device or software application for the Site-to-Site VPN connection.

The data flows through an encrypted link called the VPN tunnel. Each VPN connection includes two VPN tunnels which you can simultaneously use for high availability.

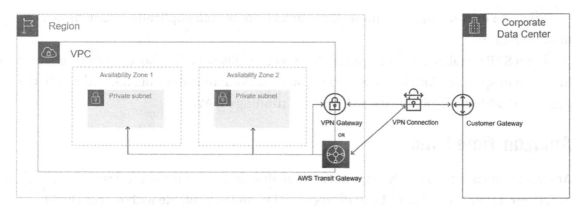

Figure 4-4. *AWS Site-to-Site VPN*

The same VPN gateway/AWS Transit Gateway can be used to connect multiple on-premise locations. With this setup, the users in offices can connect to SAP applications hosted on AWS.

AWS Direct Connect

Direct Connect lets you establish a dedicated private network connectivity between your data center and AWS. The connection can be of two types – dedicated or hosted.

For getting the connection established, you need to work with a partner in the AWS Direct Connect Partner Program. They will help you establish the required network circuits between an AWS Direct Connect location and your data center, office, or co-location environment:

- Dedicated connection: This is a physical Ethernet connection associated with just one single customer.

- Hosted connection: This is a physical Ethernet connection that an AWS Direct Connect Partner provisions on behalf of a customer.

Amazon Route 53

This is the DNS (Domain Name System) service from Amazon. By design, it is auto scalable and is highly available. Route 53 offers three main functions:

- Domain name registration

- DNS routing

- Health checking

Route 53 lets you register a name for your website or web application, known as a domain name.

In an SAP installation, it is required that you use fully specified hostnames (including the domain specification) in URLs. You register the domain with Route 53, and it helps in name and address resolution for SAP systems running on AWS.

Amazon Time Sync

Amazon Time Sync is a highly accurate and reliable time synchronization service. It is delivered over the Network Time Protocol (NTP) and is available with no cost in all public AWS regions to all instances running in a VPC.

For the accessibility of the service, you need to link to the local IP of AWS 169.254.169.123. The traffic does not traverse out of the AWS network and so is fully secured for access from your private network.

When you install multiple SAP applications in your landscape, the fleet of EC2 instances (running Windows or Linux) need to be in time sync. This is especially recommended when you run distributed SAP systems where SAP applications and databases are hosted on separate EC2 instances. Amazon Time Sync can help keep the operating system time for all the EC2s in sync.

Identity Management

AWS Identity and Access Management (IAM) enables you to securely manage access to AWS services and resources. You create users and groups and associate permissions to permit or prohibit access to AWS services.

The IAM service too is available with no usage cost.

IAM provides you with a very fine-grained access control using a least privilege security model to access AWS services and actions. It offers a multifactor authentication feature and can be integrated with your corporate directory such as Microsoft Active Directory.

For SAP landscapes running on AWS, you can leverage IAM roles to permit access control to AWS services, for example, allow SAP Basis resources to launch, stop, and start EC2 instances but not terminating them.

Security and Compliance

AWS offers several security resources that can be leveraged to secure the environment running SAP on AWS:

- IAM service (to centrally manage users, security credentials such as passwords, access keys, and permission policies that control which AWS services and resources users can access).

- OS hardening to lock down the OS configuration. For example, to avoid providing a NetWeaver administrator with root credentials when logging into an instance.

- Encryption can be used to protect data at rest and in transit.

- Security Groups are like virtual firewalls for EC2 that control inbound and outbound traffic.

- The Network Access Control List is another layer of security for your VPC that acts as a firewall for controlling traffic in and out of one or more subnets.

- API call logging: All the API calls to the SAP applications can be recorded with AWS CloudTrail. The information recorded includes the identity of the API caller, the time of the API call, the source IP address of the API caller, the request parameters, and the response elements returned by the AWS service.

- Notifications on access: Amazon Simple Notification Service (Amazon SNS) or third-party applications can be used to send notifications about SSH logins to your email address or mobile phone number.

In addition, there are several standard guidelines and best practices available from AWS as well as the SAP side to secure the SAP landscape running on AWS and keep them compliant.

Management Tools

AWS Management tools help you manage the services and resources in the AWS Cloud. When you install and run an SAP landscape in the AWS Hyperscaler cloud, it involves various AWS services. AWS Management tools help you control and manage them optimally while ensuring compliance and security and importantly keeping control over the operation cost.

There are two ways you can access AWS Management tools:

- AWS Management Console

- AWS Command Line Interface (AWS CLI)

AWS Management Console

It is the web interface service that helps you provision and administer AWS resources. It is one of the first landing places when you start with your journey to run SAP on AWS. It helps you provision and manage AWS resources for SAP AWS.

AWS Command Line Interface (AWS CLI)

CLI is an open source tool that enables you to interact with AWS services using commands in the command-line shell such as bash, tcsh (Linux), or PowerShell, cmd (Windows).

With CLI, you can create scripts that can automate both build and run activities for SAP applications and databases in AWS.

Key Management Tools that are available in AWS are

- AWS CloudFormation

- Amazon CloudWatch

- AWS CloudTrail

- AWS Config

These available management tools can be broadly categorized into three groups based on functionalities they offer:

- Provisioning tools include AWS CloudFormation.

- Monitoring tools include Amazon CloudWatch.

- Operation management and governance tools include AWS CloudTrail and AWS Config.

AWS CloudFormation

This service of AWS offers the option to provision and manage AWS and third-party resources with the Infrastructure as Code option.

Using the CloudFormation template, you can put the desired state of the resources along with their dependencies in the form of code. And thus, you can launch and configure them together as a stack once or multiple times ensuring identical state every time.

This feature becomes very handy in the case of SAP provisioning where you have to install multiple SAP applications as well as disaster recovery systems that should be identical in setup.

Amazon CloudWatch

This is the central monitoring service for AWS. CloudWatch collects monitoring and operational data for the resources and services running in AWS and on-premise. By collecting logs and metrics, you can see the detailed operation status troubleshoot issues and discover insights as well as actionable alarms/event can be set to automate actions. Thus, you can keep your applications running smoothly with the help of Amazon CloudWatch.

When you host and run an SAP landscape in the AWS cloud, it conglomerates various AWS services like EC2, EBS, network services, etc. AWS collects the metrics for every active service in your account, and the CloudWatch home page displays them all at one central location. Thus, you have a consolidated view of resources' health and status with Amazon CloudWatch.

Amazon CloudTrail

When an application is hosted in the AWS Hyperscaler cloud, naturally there would be activities performed by users via the AWS Management Console and AWS Command Line Interface or by roles or other AWS services via AWS SDKs and APIs. It's very important to keep track of every action performed in AWS account the activities to ensure a streamlined operation and most importantly security of the environment. The AWS CloudTrail service tracks all user activities and API usage in the AWS environment.

By default, CloudTrail is enabled for your AWS account when you create it. All the activities in your AWS account are recorded as events in CloudTrail. These events can be analyzed to ensure compliance and reduce operational risks.

When you run an SAP system in the AWS Hyperscaler cloud, CloudTrail becomes a very important tool for governance, compliance, and operational and risk auditing.

AWS Config

The AWS Config service is like a record keeper of all the configurations of AWS resources in your AWS account. When you turn on AWS Config (which is done at the region level), it goes on to discover all the active resources in your AWS account and generates a snapshot record, in the form of configuration items, of the current configuration states of the resources. Additionally, it also captures the detail around how the resources are related to one another. And it further tracks and maintains a historical record of all the changes in configuration done to an AWS resource.

Thus, you get an option to automatically evaluate your resource configurations against desired configurations.

When running an SAP application in AWS, the landscape can be large and can grow with time. To keep track of related AWS resources and their configuration state to standard AWS Config, it is a very important tool to be used.

Regions and Availability Zones/Sets

AWS Region

Regions are geographic locations across the globe where Amazon hosts their cloud computing resources. AWS regions are independent and isolated from one another, helping achieve greater fault tolerance and improved stability and resiliency of hosted SAP applications. At the time of writing this book, there are 25 AWS regions. Region details and AWS Code can be referenced here:

`https://docs.aws.amazon.com/general/latest/gr/rande.html#region-names-codes`

Availability Zones

Within each region, cloud computing resources are hosted in isolated locations that are known as availability zones. These are illustrated in Figure 4-5. Availability zones are basically a cluster of data centers within a region whose setup has been engineered such that they are isolated from any kind of impact in other availability zones in that region. The number of availability zones in a region varies from two to five.

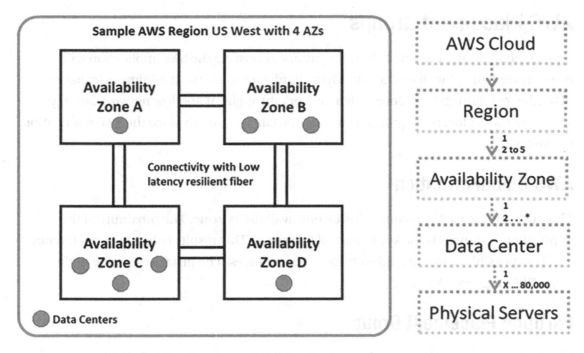

Figure 4-5. *AWS regions and availability zones*

In an AWS region, the availability zones are interconnected with fully redundant and dedicated metro fiber. This ensures a high-bandwidth, low-latency communication throughput between the services of availability zones.

Each availability zone is fed from different segments of the utility provider and has redundant connections to multiple tiers on Internet service providers. This ensures the availability and connectivity of services are least impacted due to faults in related external factors.

All the network traffics between the availability zones are encrypted.

With a dedicated metro fiber, the offered throughput is such that a synchronous replication is easily accomplished without any latency.

Availability zones are physically separated by a meaningful distance, many kilometers, from any other availability zone, although all are within 100 km (60 miles) from each other.

Availability zones offer another feature called the placement group that ensures protection against correlated hardware failure or failure due to natural calamities like flood, fire, tornadoes, etc.

AWS Placement Groups

A placement group determines how the instances hosting the SAP application will be organized and placed on the underlying hardware to ensure a minimum impact of hardware failure and achieve a high network throughput and low network latency. There are three placement group strategies that can be used to place the SAP application instances.

AWS CloudFormation

This strategy places the instances inside one availability zone. The proximity of the application instances is the key feature of this setup. This results in low network latency and best possible communication among the instances. The instances can be in the same VPC or peered VPC.

Partition Placement Group

In this strategy, AWS offers you the option to club your instances in a logical partition. And when provisioning the instances in a logical partition, AWS ensures that they are placed on separate underlying hardware, thus ensuring protection against correlated hardware failure. Groups of instances in one partition do not share the underlying hardware with groups of instances in another partition.

Spread Placement Group

This strategy places the instances across distinct underlying hardware such that each instance runs on a separate physical hardware rack. The spread placement group can spawn one or multiple availability zones.

Spread and partition placement groups are distinct with a feature of instance grouping. While partition placement groups are made up of multiple instances in the partition, spread placement groups have a single instance. They are then spread across different hardware in the availability zones.

Planning S/4HANA Implementation: Selection of Region

When you plan to implement your S/4HANA system, the selection of an appropriate region is crucial. The region selection is determined by the AWS account that you create. The following factors should be considered while selecting the AWS region:

Regulatory compliance: Check for legal requirements of your country/territory for hosting and storing financial and user data. Special attention should be paid when you are choosing the region pair for your disaster recovery setup. Country-specific laws should be considered related to the transfer and storage of financial and user data.

User proximity: The AWS region preferably should be closer to your majority user base. This will help achieve lower latency and higher throughput.

Run cost: While selecting a region, cost is an important factor. The price of EC2 and other services like egress traffic varies in AWS regions. So select an AWS region that has a lower hosting cost for EC2 instances and that offers the best price-performance ratio.

An AWS price calculator can be used to get an approximate cost: `https://calculator.s3.amazonaws.com/index.html`

Planning S/4HANA Implementation: Selection of Availability Zone

When planning the deployment of SAP S/4HANA instances (SAP application instance and database), one of the primary requirements is an always available system. There should be no unplanned downtime, especially because of any issue in the underlying hosting hardware.

High availability becomes a mandatory requirement for almost all production SAP S/4HANA systems. Business-critical production systems can't afford any unplanned outages. So, planning the SAP S/4HANA instances for high availability is crucial. Any high availability setup requires additional hardware with a complex setup. So the associated hardware and maintenance run cost becomes one of the limiting factors.

Deploying instances in availability zones ensures high availability or increased availability applications and database instances based on the strategy selected, keeping cost in view.

Selection of Availability Zone – Non-production SAP S/4HANA System

Normally for non-production systems (development, quality assurance, test, or training systems) of SAP S/4HANA, the requirement is limited to maximum availability. This can be ensured with the following approach:

- SAP systems with more than one application server instance (D<nn>): Place them in partition or spread placement groups.

- All SAP S/4HANA components: ASCS, app servers, and databases run on separate EC2 instances.

This setup is illustrated in Figure 4-6 and is suitable when the RTO/RPO is high, in several hours/days. The downtime for the restoration of operation in case of hardware failure is high.

This setup with application servers in a placement group ensures that another application server is available even when one fails due to any hardware issue.

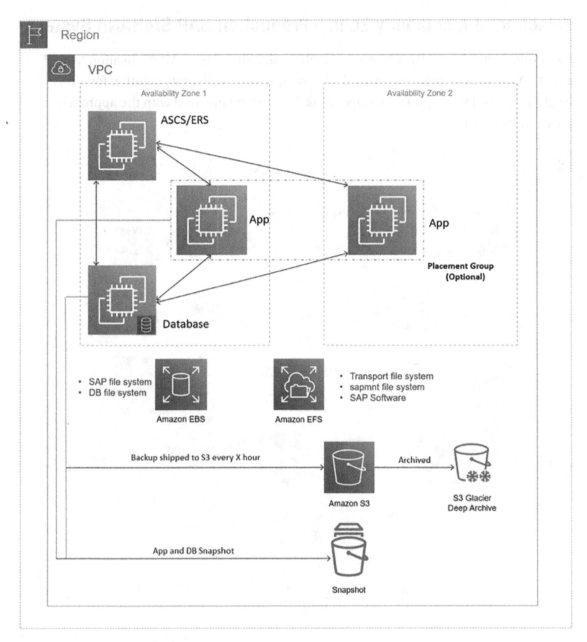

Figure 4-6. *Availability zone selection for non-prod systems*

Selection of Availability Zone – Production SAP S/4HANA System

For production SAP S/4HANA systems, high availability of the SAP application as well as HANA database instance is crucial. This requires an availability solution for all single-point-of-failure (SPOF) components. This can be ensured with the approach shown in Figure 4-7.

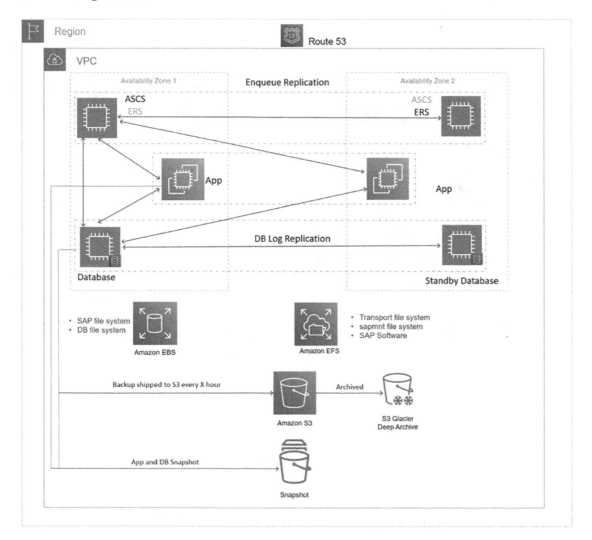

Figure 4-7. *Availability zone selection for production systems*

Placement group configuration is optional.

Additional benefits of deploying SAP S/4 systems in a multi-availability zone setup are as follows:

- Backups can be taken from the standby HANA database instance.

- Reduced system outage while applying patches or performing upgrades.

In AWS, the deployment of EC2 instances is more controllable with regard to the selection of availability zones. During the provisioning of an EC2, you have the option to select the AZ within the region in which the instance will be provisioned.

So, in an SAP S/4HANA system with more than one SAP application server, you can control in which AZ the instance will be provisioned. This makes the placement group redundant as you already have control on the placement of instances.

The AWS Console

The AWS Management Console is a web-based portal that allows users to securely access and manage Amazon Web Services. A user needs an ID and password to log in. Normally, a multifactor authentication can be enabled to enhance login protection, and users are requested to enter the device's authentication code.

Like any modern interface, the AWS Management Console also provides access from mobile devices like phones or tablets. Apps are available for Android and iOS.

Supported Browsers

The AWS Management Console supports the three latest versions of Google Chrome, Mozilla Firefox, Microsoft Edge, Apple Safari, and Microsoft Internet Explorer 11. These are listed in Table 4-1.

Note   The AWS Management Console does not support an Internet Explorer version lower than version 11.

Table 4-1. *Browser Support*

Browser	Version	Services
Apple Safari	Latest three versions	All services
Google Chrome	Latest three versions	All services
Mozilla Firefox	Latest three versions	All services
Microsoft Edge	Latest three versions	All services
Microsoft Internet Explorer	11	All services

User for Management

There are two types of users that can be used to log in to the AWS Management Console:

- Root user
- AWS Identity and Access Management (IAM) user

AWS Root User

When you log in to AWS for the first time, you sign up as a new user. This is basically setting up the AWS account. The sign-in user ID gets complete access to all AWS services and resources in the created new account. This identity becomes the root user of that AWS account.

The root user is the most powerful user of your AWS account, and it is strongly recommended not to use the root user for everyday tasks. Once the account has been set up, proceed as follows:

- Create your first IAM user with administrator permissions.
- Lock away the access keys for the root user securely.
- Use the root account to perform restricted tasks.

Note   The root user cannot be denied access via IAM policies.

The AWS Organizations service control policy (SCP) can be used to limit the permissions of the root user.

Tasks that require root user credentials

- Change root user account settings: If you want to change root user account settings such as the account name, email address, root user password, and root user access keys, you need to log in with the root user.

- Restore IAM user permissions: As a firefighter ID, in case the IAM administrator accidentally revokes their own permissions, you can sign in as the root user to edit policies and restore those permissions.

- Activate IAM access to the Billing and Cost Management console.

- Close your AWS account.

- Change or cancel the AWS Support plan.

- Configure an Amazon S3 bucket to enable MFA (multifactor authentication).

- Edit or delete an invalid VPC ID or VPC endpoint ID from the S3 bucket policy.

- Sign up for GovCloud.

- View certain tax invoices.

- Register as a seller in the Reserved Instance Marketplace.

AWS Identity and Access Management (IAM) User

An IAM user is another way (and recommended way) to sign in to the AWS Management Console and perform interactive tasks. The first IAM user ID with an administrator permission is created by the root user after the first login. Henceforth, all other IAM users are created by the IAM administrator with appropriate permissions by making them a member of a user group that has appropriate permission policies attached (recommended) or by directly attaching policies to the user.

An IAM user is used for the day-to-day administration and management of or interaction with AWS services and resources. The IAM ID can either represent a person or a service that can interact with AWS.

An AWS IAM user is identified by a username and password to sign in to the AWS Management Console and up to two access keys that can be used with the API or CLI.

IAM Role and IAM User Group

An IAM role is used to assign permissions to a user, enabling them to perform a task in the AWS Console.

An IAM user group is an entity for AWS IAM user management. IAM users can be grouped for ease of administration into IAM groups. It is easy to assign and manage permission policies for a group of users who need identical rights in the AWS Management Console.

IAM roles and IAM users are similar entities with respect to permission policies, enabling the bearer to perform allowed tasks. The only difference is that IAM users have a password or access key associated with them. Use IAM roles at places where an activity is to be performed by an application rather than a user.

For example, an AWS application running on an EC2 wants to use a certain AWS service. Rather than creating an IAM user with a password and associating it to the application or embedding the credentials in the application, use an IAM role assigned to the EC2. Thus, the application running on EC2 will be authorized to perform the task allowed by the associated policies to the IAM role.

Getting Started with the AWS Console

1. Open a web browser.

2. Enter the URL **https://console.aws.amazon.com/console/home** to access the AWS Management Console.

3. Enter AWS or IAM account credentials, as shown in Figure 4-8.

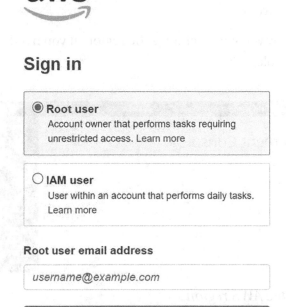

Figure 4-8. *AWS Console Getting Started*

Note   For AWS GovCloud (US) region access, the AWS Console URL is different.
In the browser, open `https://console.amazonaws-us-gov.com`.
Sign in to the Management Console using IAM account credentials.

Changing the Region

Except for a few services, all the resources that you create in your AWS account are tagged to an AWS region. So, after logging in to the AWS Management Console, it is imperative to select your AWS region.

Some AWS services operate across all regions. You don't need to switch regions to navigate to these services:

- AWS Identity and Access Management (AWS IAM)

- AWS Management Console

- Amazon CloudWatch

Figure 4-9 shows how you would change the region, if you need to do so, from the AWS Management Console.

Figure 4-9. *Change the AWS region*

Navigating to Services

Once you are logged in to the AWS Management Console and the right region has been selected, there are different ways available to navigate to or find an AWS service. To display all the available services grouped by category, you can navigate as shown in Figure 4-10.

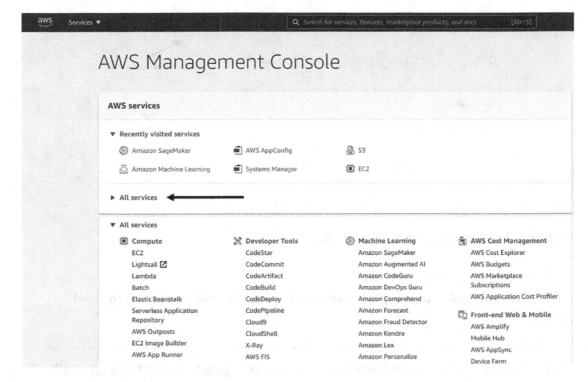

Figure 4-10. *Navigating to services*

Search AWS Service

In order to search for any AWS service, the AWS Management Console is the right starting point. It has a search bar at the top of the screen where you would just need to enter the name of the service you are looking for. Figure 4-11 shows the location of the search bar.

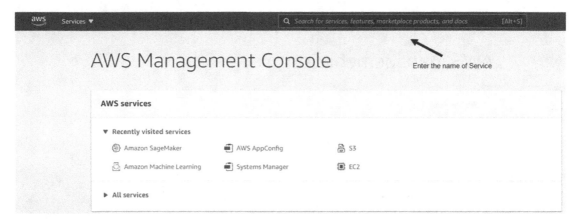

Figure 4-11. *Search for an AWS service*

Enter the name of the service.

The AWS Console landing page displays the common and most recently used services.

Tip   You can also use your keyboard to quickly navigate to the top search result. First, press Alt+S (Windows) or Option+S (macOS) to access the search bar. Then start entering your search term. When the intended result appears at the top of the list, press Enter.

A Favorite menu can be created, and your service of interest can be added to Favorite. To add a service to Favorite, pause on the name of the service that you want to add as a favorite, then click the star on the left to the service name.

Your AWS session remains active for 12 hours after your login in the AWS Management Console. You need to click "login to continue" to log in again and continue your work.

Billing and Cost Management Service

At the time of setting up your AWS account, you are required to provide information about your credit card. The monthly cost incurred by the usage of all the AWS services in your account is charged to this card. So, one of the important tasks of an AWS administrator is to keep track of expenses in AWS. It's critical to monitor the usage and analyze and control the spending for the usage of AWS services in your AWS account.

You need a permission to see the information about the charges. To get your billing information, navigate as follows:

1. Go to the navigation bar and select the account for which you want to see the billing information.

2. Select "My Billing Dashboard" from the menu as shown in Figure 4-12.

3. The AWS Billing and Cost Management dashboard gives the summary and a breakdown of your monthly spending. An exemplary dashboard is shown in Figure 4-13.

Figure 4-12. *Billing information*

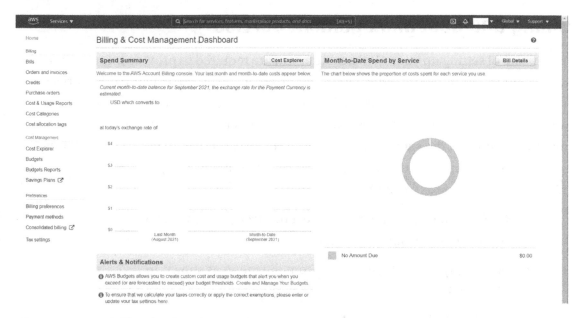

Figure 4-13. *Billing information*

The Billing and Cost Management service helps you perform the following tasks:

- Estimate and plan your AWS costs.

- Set a cost threshold and receive alerts if the limit is breached.

- Assess your biggest investments in AWS resources.

- Manage multiple AWS accounts in one place.

Integration into Core Services

When you plan to implement SAP S/4HANA in AWS, you need to plan for the setup of the SAP landscape. The AWS IaaS feature is used where all the infrastructure to host the SAP application is provided on demand as a service in AWS.

For hosting any application of AWS under IaaS, you need to prepare a VPC (Virtual Private Cloud) in AWS. VPC is a logically isolated private section of the AWS Cloud where you can launch AWS resources that are dedicated to you. This is similar to a section of your on-premise data center which is dedicated for the implementation and usage of an application. An exemplary VPC is shown in Figure 4-14.

Any customer planning to implement SAP S/4HANA has its own existing corporate network footprint. It is advisable and most of the time required to integrate AWS VPC to existing corporate networks so that some of the critical features of on-premises can be extended and used in AWS, for example, Active Directory Federation Services (ADFS) for single sign-on (SSO) based on Security Assertion Markup Language (SAML). SAP BW can access the legacy application file server via SFTP.

Most of the companies manage users and identities via Active Directory that has been set up on-premise. While setting up an identity in AWS, customers prefer to manage the identity via the on-premise AD so that critical user data like ID and password do not leave the corporate network. In such scenarios, the AWS VPC needs to be integrated with on-premise services.

Keeping security in view in any SAP deployment in AWS, the components are placed with the minimum allowed access model. For this, the components are grouped, and segregation is achieved by placing them in different subnets. Access is controlled through *Security Groups* (SGs), *route tables* (RTs), and *Network Access Control Lists* (NACLs).

RTs are sets of network rules that determine the direction of network traffic.

SGs are stateful firewalls that operate at the EC2 or NIC level controlling both inbound and outbound traffic.

NACLs are stateless firewalls equivalent of firewalls of the on-premise network setup that operate on the subnet level controlling the inbound and outbound traffic.

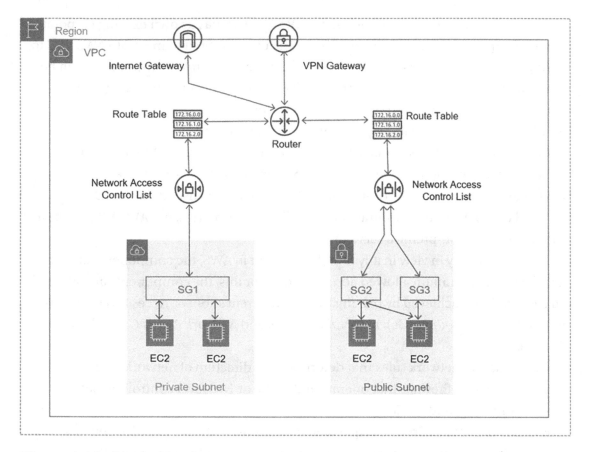

Figure 4-14. *Integration into core services*

In an SAP ecosystem with SAP S/4HANA, the placement of systems and components and their related access mechanisms can be understood as follows:

- Databases of SAP systems like S/4HANA, BW/4HANA, GTS, GRC, etc. are the holy grail of any organization and are strongly safeguarded. They can be placed in one subnet – the database subnet.

- Application servers of SAP systems are the main components that are accessed by business users. The request for access can be from users in a corporate network (Intranet) or from external users (Internet). They are thus placed in a separate subnet, and access is controlled with different SGs and NACLs, allowing the application server to communicate with the DB and users to communicate with application servers.

- Middleware components of SAP like PO.

- SAP systems like SAP Router, SAP Web Dispatcher (or other reverse proxies), and SAP Cloud Connector require access from the Internet. They need to be placed in a separate public subnet.

- SaaS applications like SAP Fieldglass, Concur, and Workday can also connect to the SAP ecosystem. The connectivity is managed via the public subnet discussed earlier.

- In addition, there are management components like Active Directory and DNS server and monitoring solutions like SAP Solution Manager that require connectivity to all the components in the landscape.

To ensure connectivity, there are some AWS services that come to aid. These services are the following:

VPN Gateway

When it is required to connect an on-premise network to AWS over a VPN, it is required to have a virtual private gateway (also called VPN Gateway) in the AWS side and a customer gateway in the customer side.

A VPN Gateway is always associated with a VPC.

NAT Gateway and NAT Instance

They facilitate the connection of instances in private subnets to the Internet, other VPCs, or on-premise networks. The communication through NAT devices is established such that only outbound traffic is allowed. They do not allow any incoming request.

A NAT instance is an AWS managed NAT device, while a NAT Gateway is a self-managed NAT service created on EC2 instances.

Internet Gateway (IGW)

This VPC component facilitates communication between the VPC and the Internet. It offers two functions:

- It provides a target in VPC route tables for Internet-routable traffic.

- It provides a Network Address Translation (NAT) for instances that have been assigned public IPv4 addresses.

Normally, an Internet Gateway gets created with the creation of a VPC.

Route 53

Route 53 is a highly available and scalable cloud Domain Name System (DNS). It facilitates the translation of human-readable names like `www.example.com` into numeric IP addresses like 192.0.2.1.

AWS S3

Amazon Simple Storage Service (S3) is an object-based storage service primarily used to store backups of SAP databases.

Amazon CloudWatch

Amazon CloudWatch is a central monitoring and alerting tool that collects metrics and logs from connected resources in AWS or on-premise.

AWS Config

An AWS Config service keeps a record of the configuration of AWS services. It continuously monitors the resource's status and records any change. It helps automate the evaluation of recorded configurations against desired configurations.

Transit gateway

It can be used to connect VPCs and on-premises networks. You use a transit gateway or virtual private gateway as the gateway for the Amazon side of the Site-to-Site VPN connection.

There are several possible architectures to place the systems and components keeping business connectivity in the center wrapped with strict security at each layer.

Internal Access Architecture

In this setup, the SAP application in AWS is accessed only via a corporate network.

This setup with the hub-and-spoke model contains four subnets:

- Public subnet: This subnet contains a SAP router and a NAT gateway or NAT instance. Only the specified public IPs from SAP are allowed to connect to the SAP router. See SAP Note 28976, Remote connection data sheet, for details.

- Application subnet: The SAP application servers are placed in this subnet and access is made possible via SAP GUI or HTML via a browser from within the corporate network. Also, for the SAP support, the subnet connects to a public subnet where the NAT Gateway or NAT instance enables connectivity to the SAP support.

- Database subnet: This is the core of enterprises, where databases are placed in this separate subnet, with allowed connectivity only from the application subnet.

- Management subnet: This is a private subnet that hosts administration, monitoring, and management tools like bastion host (RDP server), Microsoft System Center Configuration Manager (SCCM), and BODS Database Designer tools.

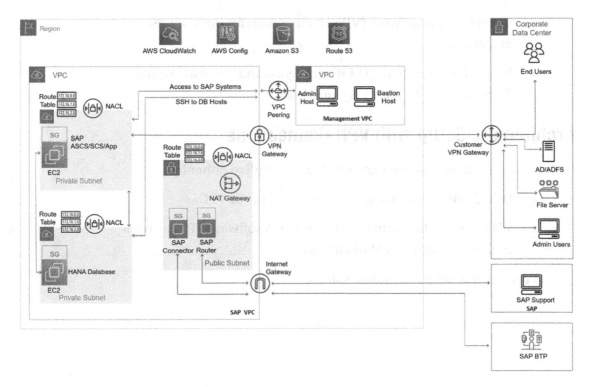

Figure 4-15. *Intranet-only access architecture*

Applications in the intranet-only access subnet are required for supporting as well as some tasks that require installation of FAT clients, for example, SAP HANA Studio, SAP BODS Designer Tool.

For the management layer, the hosts can be put in a separate VPC as depicted earlier, or they can be hosted in the SAP VPC in a separate subnet.

The preceding scenario shows the setup in a single region. For high availability, the setup will extend in multiple AWS availability zones, and for disaster recovery, the setup will extend in multiple AWS regions.

Internal and Limited External Access

In addition to access of SAP applications from a corporate network (intranet access), it is crucial to connect the system to some trusted external applications, normally referred to as trusted third-party applications in the SAP world. SAP's Process Orchestration (PO)/Process Integration (PI) or non-SAP products like MuleSoft are the middleware components that act as a bridge in this scenario. For connectivity, there are typical options:

- Virtual private network (VPN) connections for both ingress and egress

- Elastic Load Balancing (ELB) for ingress and Network Address Translation (NAT) Gateway for egress

Architecture Setup with VPN Connections

In this setup, both ingress and egress traffic are handled either by

- Using a virtual private gateway (VGW) in your VPC.

- With a dedicated software VPN server. A software VPN server is available in the AWS Marketplace.

A VPN entity is put in the public subnet.

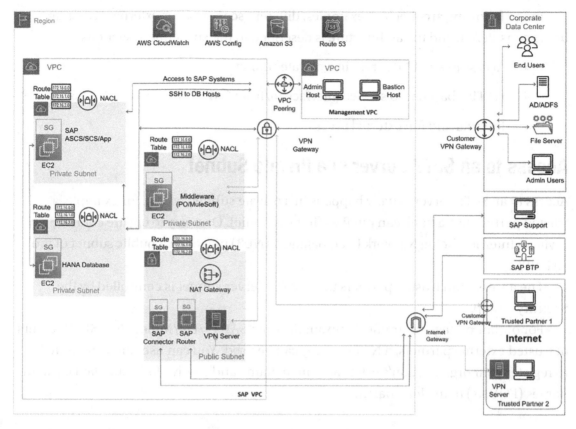

Figure 4-16. *Internal and limited external access*

Architecture Setup with Elastic Load Balancing (Ingress)/NAT Gateway (Egress)

There are two types of Load Balancers (LBs):

- Network Load Balancer

- Application Load Balancer

A Network Load Balancer operates at the network layer and deals with TCP traffic load balancing, while an Application Load Balancer operates at the application layer and is the ideal choice for HTTP or HTTPS traffic load balancing.

In the following architecture examples, different scenarios for external access are being considered, and the architecture is described in the subsequent sections:

- Access to an SFTP server in a private subnet

- HTTPS-based web service interface to/from SAP PI/PO

- Internal and full external access

Access to an SFTP Server in a Private Subnet

Access to an SFTP server usually happens in a private subnet, where, for example, a trusted partner like a bank can put files (ingress traffic). One way to ensure connectivity is via an Internet-facing Network Load Balancer (NLB) placed in a public subnet of the SAP VPC.

The access from trusted partners to the SFTP server subnet is controlled by the Security Group.

For outbound (egress) traffic, for example, from SAP PI/PO/MuleSoft to SFTP servers of trusted external partners, a NAT gateway can be used. You can use Amazon Route 53 to register your organization's external domain name and resolve fully qualified domain names (FQDNs) to the load balancer.

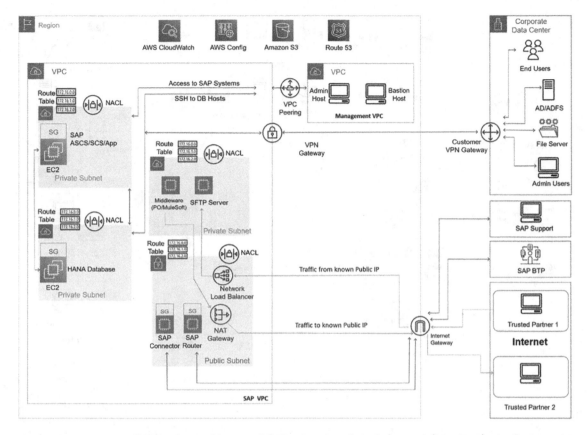

Figure 4-17. *Architecture setup with Elastic Load Balancing (ingress) and NAT Gateway (egress)*

HTTPS-Based Web Service Interfaces to/from SAP PI/PO

In this scenario, the web services in PI/PO are accessed from external partners over the Internet with the HTTPS protocol. And PI/PO can connect to external trusted partners over the Internet.

Ingress traffic (from third party to PI/PO) can be handled with an Application Load Balancer.

Access from known IPs will be controlled through the security group attached to the load balancer.

Egress traffic (from PI/PO to third party) can be enabled and controlled by NAT gateway.

Amazon Route 53 can be used for domain name registration and FQDN resolution.

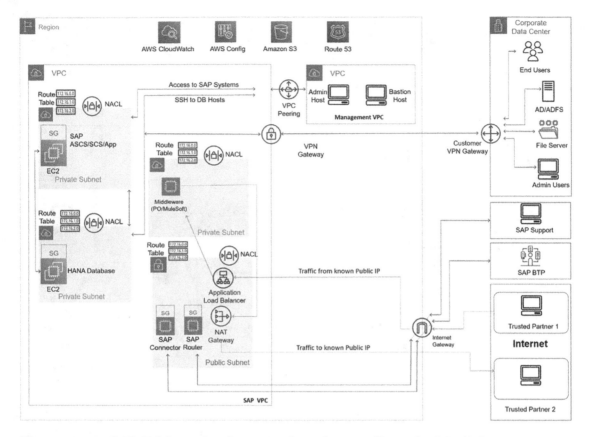

Figure 4-18. *HTTPS-based web service interfaces to/from SAP PI/PO*

Internal and Full External Access

In this scenario, along with internal access, access from the Internet is also required. A typical use case scenario for that is access to systems with SAP Fiori, or if there is Internet-facing SAP Enterprise Portal.

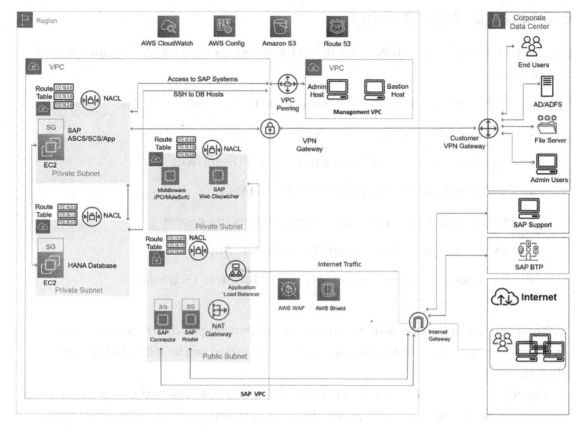

Figure 4-19. *Internal and full external access*

All the Internet traffic into the SAP can be facilitated through an Application Load Balancer (ALB) placed in a public subnet. Traffic from ALB goes to the SAP Web Dispatcher, which is a reverse proxy for SAP S/4HANA system Fiori applications.

The protection of ALB can be ensured with the following AWS services:

The AWS Web Application Firewall (WAF) for Application Load Balancers prevents common application layer exploits like SQL injection attacks.

The WAF for ALB provides additional protection by constructing Access Control Lists (ACLs), rules, and conditions that control traffic from predefined IP addresses.

Refer to the following blog:

```
https://aws.amazon.com/blogs/aws/aws-web-application-firewall-waf-for-
application-load-balancers/
```

AWS Shield is a managed distributed denial of service (DDoS) protection service that safeguards web applications running on AWS. There are two tiers of AWS Shield: Standard and Advanced. There is no additional charge for AWS Shield Standard.

Example Landscape Setup

Consider a typical SAP S/4HANA Greenfield implementation. The SAP components to be installed include

- SAP S/4HANA 2021 with embedded Fiori

- SAP Web Dispatcher as a reverse proxy

- SAP Adobe Document Service to support PDF services

- SAP BODS for data migration to SAP S/4HANA

- SAP Solution Manager as the central monitoring system

- SAP Router to facilitate connection with SAP Support

- SAP Cloud Connector to connect to SAP Business Technology Platform

You can have additional SAP systems as well depending on the requirements in your implementation. The approach followed for a system can be extended to any additional system.

The SAP systems will be implemented in AWS VPC. In addition, the implementation will connect to the following on-premise components that are already existing in the customer landscape:

- AD/ADFS as the central user store.

- Legacy file server.

- Also, the admin users in the on-premise network will connect to AWS for administration, management, and monitoring.

Proposed architecture setup
The setup can be prepared as follows:

- VPC 1 for hosting SAP systems

- VPC 2 for hosting management systems

Create the following subnets in VPC 1:

- Private subnet 1 for hosting databases

- Private subnet 2 for hosting SAP applications

- Public subnet 1 to host external-facing applications like SAP Router
  and Cloud Connector to connect to SAP Support Hub and SAP
  Business Technology Platform (BTP)

Create the following subnet in VPC 2:

- Private subnet 3 for management instances

The security of each subnet is ensured via a route table and Network Access Control List. As discussed, a route table contains a set of rules called routes that determine the flow of traffic.

NACLs control the inbound and outbound traffic with appropriate allow and deny rules.

In addition, a Security Group can be created for each SAP application and database to ensure only the explicitly allowed systems/IPs can interact with the EC2 hosting the application/database.

Some other AWS services that are required for the setup of the SAP landscape are

- NAT Gateway: A Network Address Translation (NAT) service
  that facilitates the connection of systems in private subnets to
  external systems

- Amazon CloudWatch: To collect and analyze monitoring data

- Amazon S3: As a long-term storage solution for backups

- Amazon Route 53: Amazon DNS service

- AWS Config: A service that helps you assess, audit, and evaluate the
  configurations of deployed AWS resources

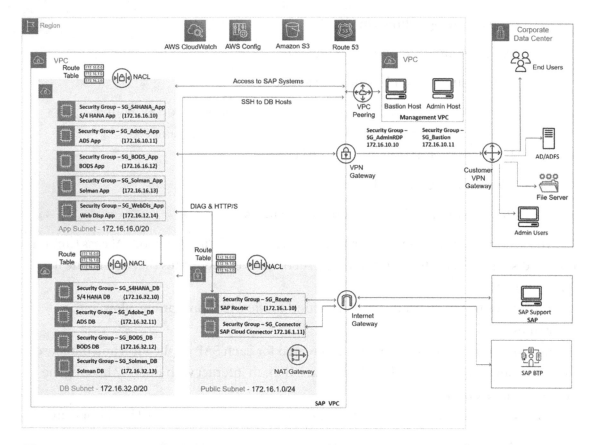

Figure 4-20. *Example scenario*

This is an indicative setup. The following additional configuration setup points should be considered:

- In the Management VPC, two hosts have been considered: one for the administration team and another for the project team. You can decide to have one host as well with proper access control.

- The Security Group configuration is separate for each application. You can club the EC2s with similar usage type for identical access mechanism and assign one Security Group.

- Refer to the AWS documentation "Security group rules for different use cases" for further information on Security Groups:

  `http://docs.aws.amazon.com/AWSEC2/latest/WindowsGuide/`
  `security-group-rules-reference.html`

An indicative subnet setup can be as shown in Table 4-2.

Table 4-2. *Indicative Subnet Setup*

	CIDR	Route Table	NACL	System	IP	Security Group
SAP VPC	172.16.0.0/16	–	–	–	–	–
Management VPC	172.16.10.0/24	–	–	–	–	–
Customer DC	172.16.128.0/18	–	–	–	–	–
Public subnet	172.16.1.0/24	RT_Sub_Public	NACL_Public	SAP Router	172.16.1.10	SG_Router
				SAP Cloud Connector	172.16.1.11	SG_Connector
SAP VPC – application subnet	172.16.16.0/20	RT_Sub_App_Private	NACL_App_Private	SAP S/4HANA	172.16.16.10	SG_S4HANA_App
				SAP Adobe Service	172.16.16.11	SG_Adobe_App
				SAP BODS	172.16.16.12	SG_BODS_App
				SAP Solution Manager	172.16.16.13	SG_Solman_App
				SAP Web Dispatcher	172.16.16.14	SG_WebDisp_App
SAP VPC – database subnet				SAP S/4HANA DB	172.16.32.10	SG_S4HANA_DB
				SAP Adobe Service DB	172.16.32.11	SG_Adobe_DB
				SAP BODS DB	172.16.32.12	SG_BODS_DB
				SAP Solution Manager DB	172.16.32.13	SG_Solman_DB
Management VPC – admin host		RT_Sub_Adm_Private	NACL_Adm_Private	Admin RDP host	172.16.10.10	SG_AdminRDP
Management VPC – bastion host		RT_Sub_Bast_Private	NACL_Bast_Private	Bastion host	172.16.10.11	SG_Bastion

The rules for SG, NACL, and route tables depend on the instance number that you select for the SAP application and HANA DB. A detailed port for SAP can be referenced at "TCP/IP Ports of All SAP Products": `https://help.sap.com/viewer/ports`.

Active Directory

Microsoft Active Directory is a directory service developed by Microsoft. It's one of the most common products that is used by most companies to manage directory-based services such as

- Domain Service

- Lightweight Directory Service

- Certificate Service

- Right Management Service

- Federation Service

Active Directory was made General Available (GA) in the year 1999. Over the years, several features and functionalities were added. The part of Active Directory in charge of the management of domains was rechristened Active Directory Domain Service (ADDS). And Active Directory became an umbrella product for a broader range of directory-based services.

ADDS is used to manage the domain of a company. It stores information about users, computers, file systems, printers, and other resources and offers authentication and authorization services. It is also used to manage group policies, encryption of systems in the landscape, Domain Name Services, Remote Desktop Services, Exchange Services, and SharePoint Servers.

Figure 4-21. *ADDS features*

In the AWS cloud, there are three options to use Active Directory Domain Services (ADDS):

1. AWS Managed Microsoft Active Directory Service

2. Self-managed ADDS deployment in the AWS cloud

3. Extend the existing on-premises ADDS to AWS

AWS recommends creating a separate account for identity services like AD and limiting the access to a small administrator group. While you plan to implement any of the three solutions, ensure that the AWS AD is deployed in a VPC that is reachable from all the VPCs that have workloads depending on Active Directory. Again, the hub-and-spoke model for VPC deployment can be used, with AD VPC acting as the hub and all Directory Consumer VPCs connected to this AD VPC using VPC peering.

AWS Managed Microsoft Active Directory Service

In this solution, the Active Directory instance is maintained by AWS. The setup includes the following components:

- A VPC

- Public and private subnets in two availability zones to ensure high availability

- Public subnets in the AZs that have a NAT Gateway and an RD Gateway

- NAT gateways to allow outbound Internet access for resources in private subnets

- RD Gateway instances in an autoscaling group to help secure remote access to instances in private subnets

- AWS Systems Manager Automation to set up and configure ADDS and AD-integrated DNS

- AWS Secrets Manager to store passwords

- AWS Directory Service to provision and manage ADDS in private subnets

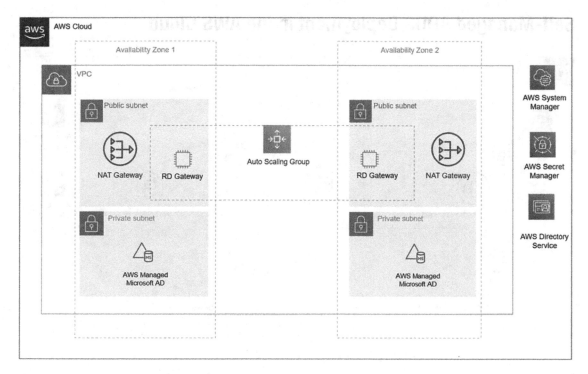

Figure 4-22. *AWS Managed Microsoft Active Directory Service*

Self-Managed ADDS Deployment in the AWS Cloud

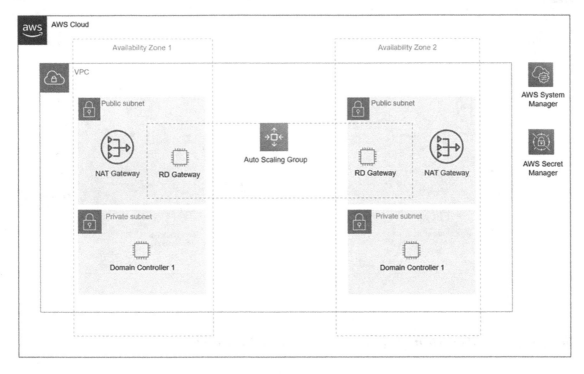

Figure 4-23. *Self Managed ADDS Deployment in AWS cloud*

In this solution, the Active Directory instance is installed and managed by the customer IT team. The setup includes the following components:

- A VPC configured with public and private subnets in two availability zones for high availability

- Public subnets in the AZs that include an instance of a NAT Gateway and an RD Gateway

- NAT gateways to allow outbound Internet access for resources in private subnets

- RD Gateway instances in an autoscaling group to help secure remote access to instances in private subnets

- Private subnets in the AZs that include the following

- A Windows Server forest and domain functional level, including security groups and rules for traffic between instances

- AWS Systems Manager Automation documents to set up and configure ADDS and AD-integrated DNS

- AWS Secrets Manager to store passwords

Extend the Existing On-Premises ADDS to AWS

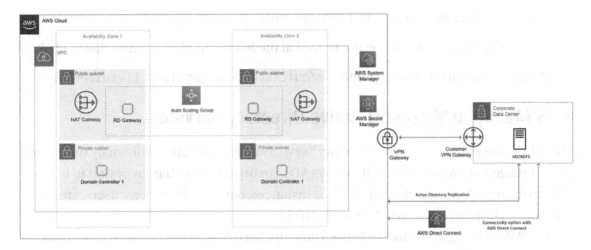

Figure 4-24. *Extend Existing On-Premises AD DS to AWS*

In this solution, the Active Directory instance in the corporate data center acts as the primary domain controller. The Windows instances set up in the private subnet are connected to on-premise AD and promoted as domain controllers.

The secure connectivity from AWS to the corporate data center is ensured with the VPN gateway that connects to the Customer VPN gateway. AWS Direct Connect can be used as well for connectivity.

The setup includes the following components:

- A VPC configured with public and private subnets in two availability zones for high availability

- Public subnets in the AZs that include an instance of a NAT Gateway and an RD Gateway

- NAT gateways to allow outbound Internet access for resources in private subnets

- RD Gateway instances in an autoscaling group to help secure remote access to instances in private subnets

- Private subnets in the AZs that include the following

- A Windows Server forest and domain functional level, including security groups and rules for traffic between instances

- AWS Systems Manager Automation documents to set up and configure ADDS and AD-integrated DNS

- AWS Secrets Manager to store passwords

The deployment detail can be referenced at the following AWS documentation link:

`https://aws-quickstart.github.io/quickstart-microsoft-activedirectory/`

AWS Managed Microsoft Active Directory Service

AWS offers the Microsoft Active Directory Service as a SaaS solution known by the name AWS Managed Microsoft Active Directory (AD). An organization has an option to use this AD service on AWS connecting all the EC2 instances, database instances, users, groups, and devices like conventional Microsoft ADDS.

The AWS Managed Microsoft Active Directory Service also offers the other domain controller services of ADDS described earlier such as the management of group policies, password policies, Kerberos-based single sign-on, etc. To manage AWS Managed AD, no special tool is required. It works identical to on-premise Microsoft ADDS.

AWS Managed Microsoft Active Directory being a SaaS solution has built-in high availability on AWS infrastructure. The domain controller is internally monitored by AWS that detects any fault and replaces it in case of failure in the same AZ with the same IP access, thus ensuring no disruption. AWS handles all patching and keeps the software updated. Also, it is configured with data replication and automated daily snapshot. This saves any organization from the complexity of hosting, managing, monitoring, and keeping the ADDS up to date.

Implementation Considerations for AWS Managed Microsoft Active Directory As Central ADDS

If an organization plans to implement AWS Managed Microsoft Active Directory, the on-premise users and resources can be connected to this central directory service and maintained seamlessly. It can be integrated with Active Directory Federation Service (AD FS) and AWS Single Sign-On to provide seamless single sign-on experience to users such as SAP Fiori business users.

You can also connect your Microsoft Network Policy Server (NPS) with Amazon Managed AD. When you set up AWS Managed AD, an administrative account gets created. It has delegated management rights over the Remote Access Service (RAS) and Internet Authentication Service (IAS) security groups. This enables you to register NPS with AWS Managed Microsoft AD and manage network access policies for accounts in your domain. AWS Managed Microsoft AD has two available product editions – Standard and Enterprise:

- Standard Edition: Suitable for small and midsize businesses with up to 5000 employees. It provides storage capacity to support up to approximately 30,000 directory objects, such as users, groups, and computers.

- Enterprise Edition: Suitable for large enterprises with up to approximately 500,000 directory objects.

The upper limit is an approximation. The directory may support more or less directory objects depending on the size of the objects and the behavior and performance needs of the applications.

Implementation Considerations for AWS Managed AD with SAP S/4HANA DR Consideration

With AWS Managed Microsoft AD, it is possible to set up multiregion replication. With this setup, you can be prepared when there is a region failure, and you must invoke disaster recovery for your SAP application including S/4HANA. The directory identifier (directory_id) remains the same in the DR region and is deployed in the same AWS account as your primary region.

With the replication setup of AD, AWS deploys domain controllers in the DR region and replicates all the primary region AD's directory data, including users, groups, Group Policy Objects (GPOs), and schema. Thus, the directory will be ready in your DR region offering the desired services in case of a disaster.

How to Create an AWS Managed Microsoft Active Directory

An AWS Managed Microsoft Active Directory setup creates a highly available pair of domain controllers (DC) connected to the Virtual Private Cloud (VPC). The domain controller EC2s run in separate availability zones in your region.

The two EC2 instances on which the DC runs are managed by AWS, and you don't have access on their operating systems. Each EC2 has two elastic network interfaces (ENIs), ETH0 and ETH1. ETH0 is the management adapter for AWS and is not accessible from your account. ETH1 is created within your account.

The management IP range of the directory's ETH0 network is 198.18.0.0/15.

You cannot associate Elastic IP to those ENIs.

Prerequisite information includes the following:

- AWS Managed Active Directory Edition. Standard Edition or Enterprise Edition of AWS Managed Microsoft AD. Refer to AWS Managed Microsoft AD available product editions for selection.

- The VPC which will be managed by the AD.

- Two subnets in different availability zones where Active Directory Windows servers will be deployed.

The AWS Directory Service does not support using a Network Address Translation (NAT) with Active Directory. Using NAT can result in replication errors. The creation of Active Directory takes approximately 20–40 minutes:

1. Log in to the AWS Management Console.

2. In the Navigation pane, choose Directories and select Set up directory.

3. In the next screen, choose AWS Managed Microsoft AD, and click Next.

4. On the Enter directory information page

    - Edition: Standard or Enterprise

    - Directory DNS name: The fully qualified name for the directory

- Directory NetBIOS name: The short name for the directory, such as CORP

- Directory description: An optional description for the directory

- Admin password: The password for the directory administrator "Admin" that gets created automatically

5. Click Next.

6. On the Choose VPC and subnets page, provide the information about the VPC which will be managed with AD:

   - VPC: The VPC for the directory.

   - Subnets: Choose the subnets for the domain controllers in which it will be deployed. The two subnets must be in different availability zones.

7. Click Next.

8. On the Review & create page, review the directory information for correctness. Choose Create directory.

Provisioning can take up to 40 minutes. Once created, the status value changes to active. The result is a pair of highly available AWS Managed AD that gets created with its own security group. The SG has predefined inbound and outbound security rules that ensure secure traffic within the VPC, from other peered VPCs, or from networks that you have connected using AWS Direct Connect, AWS Transit Gateway, or virtual private network.

It is highly recommended not to change the default rules, or you may end up losing connectivity to AD.

DNS Name Resolution with Route 53 Resolver

Organizations adapting a hyperscaler cloud can have resources distributed over multiple accounts and VPCs. And more commonly, they have an on-premise footprint as well for servers/systems. When servers come up on the cloud, a hybrid network setup comes up, and, in such setup, there are multiple domains and private hosted zones, and it is required to have a unified DNS setup. Also, it is important to keep the latency low. So, an ideal setup is to provide name resolution services in the same local network where the resource is located. Normally for on-premise, there is a DNS server, and in AWS, a DNS service is provided by Route 53.

In a hybrid setup, it is required to have a bidirectional query forwarding such that the query from on-premises for AWS resources can be resolved in Route 53, and the query from AWS VPCs for on-premise resources can reach on-premises DNS. A setup further gets complex when there are multiple accounts with multiple VPCs with multiple domains, and it is required to have a unified DNS service.

To achieve this integrated DNS requirement, Route 53 Resolver for Hybrid Clouds can be used. It enables a bidirectional querying between on-premises and AWS over private connections for DNS name resolution.

To support DNS queries across hybrid environments, Route 53 Resolver provides two capabilities:

1.   Route 53 Resolver endpoints for inbound queries

2.   Conditional forwarding rules for outbound queries

Set up an Integrated DNS View for Amazon VPCs and On-Premise Networks

This is a typical setup that consists of the following network elements:

- An on-premise DNS

- VPCs from multiple AWS accounts, each with its own Route 53 Resolvers

Suggested architecture setup

1.   Connect all spoke VPCs to hub VPCs using AWS Transit Gateway.

2.   Connect on-premise to hub VPCs using a VPN or AWS Direct Connect.

3.   Configure Route 53 Resolver inbound and outbound endpoints:

- An inbound endpoint specifies the IP that you want DNS resolvers on your network to forward DNS queries to.

- To forward DNS queries from your VPCs to your network, you create an outbound endpoint. An outbound endpoint specifies the IP addresses that queries originate from.

While creating endpoints, it is recommended to specify IP addresses in at least two subnets across two availability zones to ensure high availability of the endpoints.

Configure the Route 53 Resolver with private hosted zones in hub VPCs and associate them.

All VPCs will need to associate their private hosted zones to all other VPCs, so complete the cross-account private hosted zone–VPC association between the spoke VPCs.

Create forwarding rules with the following in mind:

- Create conditional forwarding rules that specify the on-premises domain names of the DNS queries that you want to forward to on-premises DNS resolvers.

- You need to create one forwarding rule for each domain name and specify the name of the domain for which you want to forward queries.

- After you create a forwarding rule, you must associate the rule with one or more VPCs. When you associate a rule with a VPC, the resolver starts to forward DNS queries for the domain name that's specified in the rule to the DNS resolvers that you specified in the rule. The queries pass through the outbound endpoint that you specified when you created the rule.

Working Solution for Scenario: Query from On-Premise to AWS Route 53

In this scenario, a request for DNS name resolution originates from on-premise for a resource in the AWS cloud.

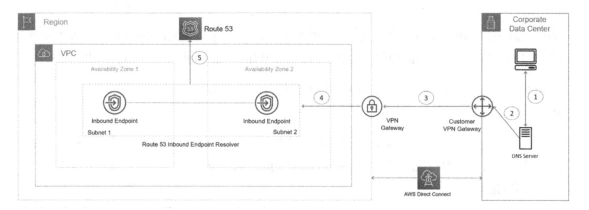

Figure 4-25.   *Query from on-premise to AWS Route 53*

Connectivity between on-premise and the AWS cloud can be via a VPN or AWS Direct Connect or both:

1. A client in an on-premise network initiates a DNS request, and it goes to the on-premise DNS server. With the configuration in place in the on-premise DNS server, it identifies that the request is for an AWS domain.

    The on-premise DNS server forwards the request to Route 53 Inbound Endpoint Resolver.

2. The request is forwarded to the customer VPN gateway.

3. This then goes to AWS VPN gateway to Route 53 Inbound Endpoint Resolver.

4. For name resolution, the request from Inbound Endpoint Resolver goes to Route 53 in AWS.

Route 53 resolves the name, and the response is sent back to the client on-premise.

Working Solution for Scenario: Query from AWS Resource for On-Premise DNS

In this scenario, a request originates from an EC2 in one of the spoke VPCs. The domain queried is one from an on-premise DNS. The flow of network traffic is depicted in Figure 4-26.

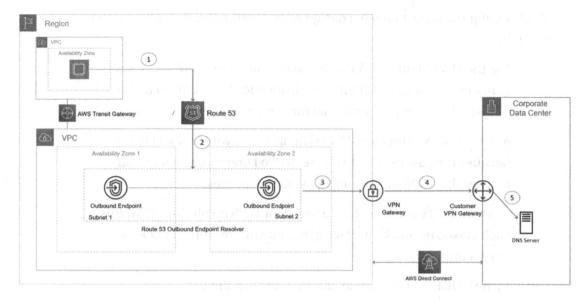

Figure 4-26. *Query from an AWS resource for an on-premise DNS*

1. An EC2 instance in a spoke VPC initiates a DNS lookup. This spoke VPC is connected to a hub VPC that has endpoints via Transit Gateway. Route 53 receives the request, and with the resolver rules in place, it determines the request is for the on-premise domain.

   If the resolver rule matches, the request is forwarded to the on-premise DNS.

2. The request is forwarded to the outbound endpoint.

3. The outbound endpoint sends the request to the AWS VPN Gateway.

4. The AWS VPN Gateway forwards the request to the Customer VPN Gateway.

5. The Customer VPN Gateway sends the request to the on-premise DNS server.

The on-premise DNS resolves the name and sends back the reply to the requester EC2.

While configuring, the following design considerations can result in better connectivity:

- Put the DNS in the hub VPC so that all connected spoke VPCs can connect seamlessly with this central location. The traffic can be managed by using a conditional forwarder.

- Make all Active Directory DNS domains resolvable for all clients, because they are using it to locate Active Directory services and register their DNS names using dynamic updates.

- Amazon EC2 instances should use .2 for DNS resolution. With this, each elastic network interface gets a maximum of 1024 packets per second.

- In the DHCP, set the domain name servers to point to AmazonProvidedDNS and not to the resolver endpoints. Use forwarding rules to ensure AmazonProvidedDNS has the view of the DNS you need.

- Keep the DNS name resolution local to the AWS region to reduce latency.

- Use the Amazon DNS server as a forwarder for all other DNS domains that are not authoritative on your DNS servers on Active Directory domain controllers. This setup allows your DCs to recursively resolve records in the Amazon Route 53 private zone and use Route 53 Resolver conditional forwarders.

AWS reference document: `https://docs.aws.amazon.com/Route53/latest/ DeveloperGuide/resolver.html`

Monitoring AWS Managed ADDS

ADDS is one of the critical services for organizations, and it is crucial to monitor resources. There are several options available in Amazon to monitor AWS Managed AD:

- Active monitoring of directory security logs with Amazon CloudWatch Logs.

- Integrate with the Simple Notification Service (SNS) to get notifications about any directory change.

- Connect to AWS CloudTrail to store logs for audit.

AWS does not allow the installation of monitoring agents on AWS Managed Microsoft AD domain controllers.

Dynamic Host Configuration Protocol (DHCP)

When you set up an infrastructure in the AWS cloud to host an application, it includes several components. As these components get included in the network, they get their unique individual identity through an IP address. Along with IPs, other TCP/IP communication configuration parameters also need to be assigned to the components, and these include a subnet mask, default gateway, DNS address, name server, and time server.

As the network and the list of network components in the landscape grow, manual assignment (or reclaim), management, and tracking become a cumbersome process. And here comes the Dynamic Host Configuration Protocol (DHCP), a network management protocol, to aid the automatic assignment of IPs and other network parameters centrally.

DHCP works on a server/client model. There is one central DHCP server in the landscape and DHCP-enabled client that can receive the parameters from DHCP servers. Normally, Windows-based client operating systems have the DHCP client included. On Linux operating systems, you can either run dhclient to set up a DHCP client or configure the /etc/network/interfaces file to use DHCP.

When a device such as a VM connects to a network, generally while booting only, the included DHCP client software sends a DHCP broadcast query asking for the mandatory network information. The DHCP server of the network responds back with the information. What information needs to be supplied can be configured by an administrator.

A DHCP server manages a record of all IP addresses allocated to the network nodes. These individual network components are identified using the unique MAC (Media Access Control). Any duplication of IP assignment is prevented.

When you create the VPC, AWS automatically creates a default set of DHCP TCP/IP communication parameters and associate them to the VPC. So, any AWS service that gets created in the VPC inherits these parameters. The default DHCP options also include two options – domain name and domain name server:

```
domain.name = <domain_name_of_your_region> e.g. sa-east-1.compute.internal
domain-name-server = AmazonProvidedDNS
```

The default `AmazonProvidedDNS` associated to the VPC is also known as Route 53 Resolver and runs on one of the reserved IPs of the VPC. In IPv4, this IP will be assigned out of a network range of VPC +2. For example, if you have assigned the CIDR range 172.16.0.0/16 to your VPC, then 172.16.0.2 will be the IP of the DNS server of the VPC. For VPCs with multiple IPv4 CIDR blocks, the DNS server IP address is in the primary CIDR block. The DNS server does not reside within a specific subnet or availability zone in a VPC.

By default, any service that is created in the VPC gets an unresolvable host like you see in Table 4-3.

Table 4-3. *Region Resolution*

Region	Private Hostname	Public Hostname
US East (N. Virginia) us-east-1	IP-<Private_IP>.ec2.internal	ec2-<Private_IP>.compute-1.amazonaw. com
Other regions	IP-<Private_IP>.compute.internal	ec2-<Private_IP>.compute.amazonaw.com

You must configure your own DHCP options set for your VPC. While setting up the custom DHCP options sets, keep the following considerations in mind:

- Once set, the DHCP options can't be modified.

- A VPC can be associated to only one set of DHCP options set at a time. Though you can have multiple sets configured.

- Create new options and associate them to a VPC in case you need different DHCP options for a VPC.

- For a running VPC, if you associate a new DHCP options set, all the existing instances and future components use the new options automatically. No restart is needed, though it may take some time to renew or is force renewed manually.

The DHCP options sets that can be adapted to your custom values are listed as follows:

- `domain-name-servers`: The name of your DNS server that will be used for name resolution.

- `domain-name`: The custom domain name for your instances.

- `ntp-servers`: The name of Network Time Protocol (NTP) servers to keep time in sync across all instances.

- `netbios-name-servers`: The name of the NetBIOS name servers.

- `netbios-node-type`: The NetBIOS node type (1, 2, 4, or 8). It is recommended to specify 2 (point-to-point, or P-node). In AWS, broadcast and multicast are not currently supported.

Working with DHCP Options Sets

This is one of the first tasks that you perform after you have set up your first VPC. As stated, with the provisioning of the VPC, AWS assigns a default DHCP with its own options sets. You need to adapt them to suit the requirement of your organization. During sustained operations, also it may be required to change to a new options set. Broadly, the activities with the options set can be categorized as follows:

1. Create DHCP options set

2. Delete DHCP options set

3. Change DHCP options set associated to VPC

4. Remove DHCP options set associated to VPC

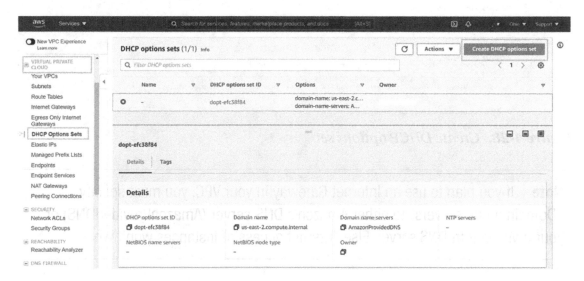

Figure 4-27. *DHCP options set*

Create DHCP Options Set

In order to create a DHCP options set, you would need to populate all needed values for every option as shown in Figure 4-28.

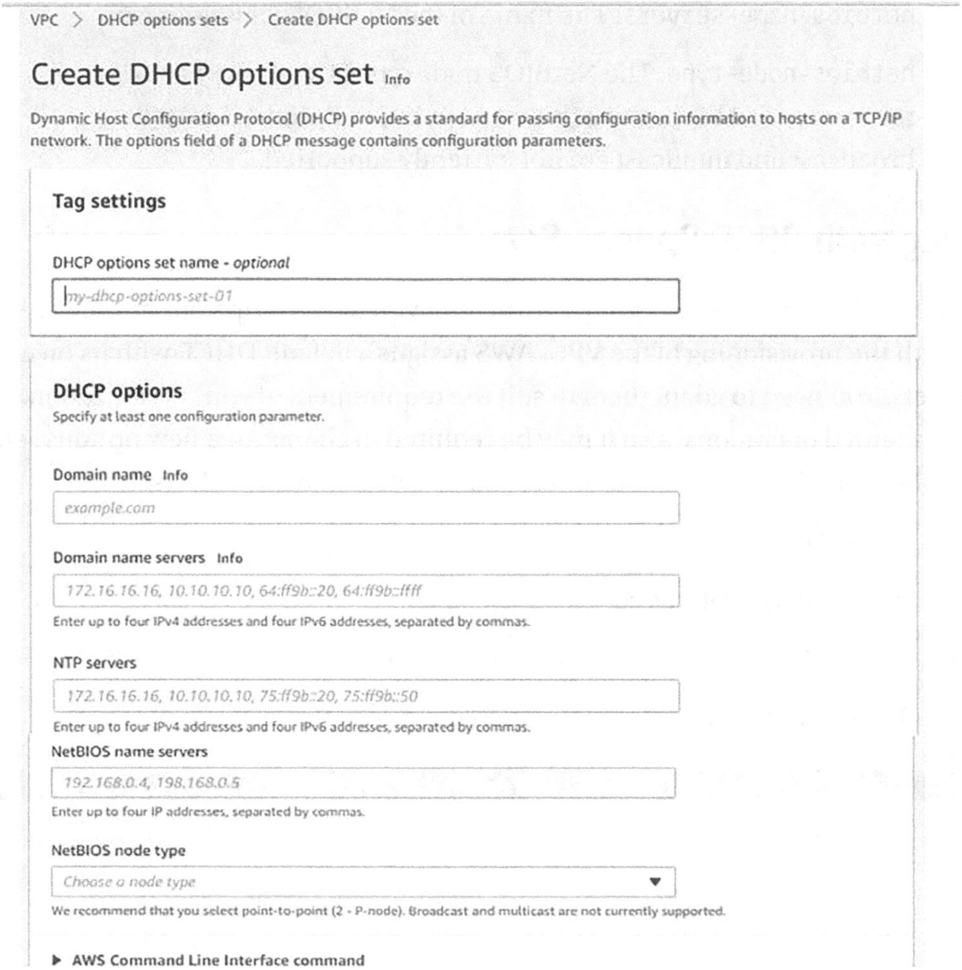

VPC > DHCP options sets > Create DHCP options set

Create DHCP options set Info

Dynamic Host Configuration Protocol (DHCP) provides a standard for passing configuration information to hosts on a TCP/IP network. The options field of a DHCP message contains configuration parameters.

Tag settings

DHCP options set name - *optional*

| my-dhcp-options-set-01 |

DHCP options
Specify at least one configuration parameter.

Domain name Info

| example.com |

Domain name servers Info

| 172.16.16.16, 10.10.10.10, 64:ff9b::20, 64:ff9b::ffff |

Enter up to four IPv4 addresses and four IPv6 addresses, separated by commas.

NTP servers

| 172.16.16.16, 10.10.10.10, 75:ff9b::20, 75:ff9b::50 |

Enter up to four IPv4 addresses and four IPv6 addresses, separated by commas.

NetBIOS name servers

| 192.168.0.4, 198.168.0.5 |

Enter up to four IP addresses, separated by commas.

NetBIOS node type

| Choose a node type ▼ |

We recommend that you select point-to-point (2 - P-node). Broadcast and multicast are not currently supported.

▶ AWS Command Line Interface command

Figure 4-28. *Create DHCP options set*

Note   If you plan to use an Internet Gateway in your VPC, you must specify "Domain name servers" to either Amazon's DNS server (AmazonProvidedDNS) or your own custom DNS server. Else, Internet access of instances won't work.

Edit DHCP Options Set

Editing a DHCP options set is done by accessing the actions on the main menu of the VPC. In the drop-down menu, you see the option to edit the DHCP options set as shown in Figure 4-29.

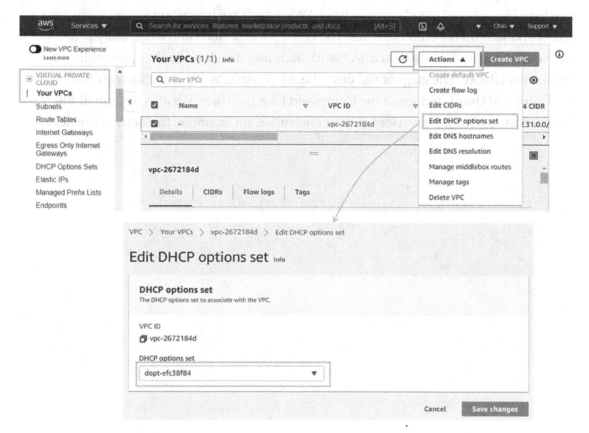

Figure 4-29. *Edit DHCP options set*

Summary

This chapter provided an overview about the core concepts for running SAP workloads on AWS. You did learn about the history of AWS and the main reasons for using AWS for running your core SAP workloads in that public cloud. The chapter also described and listed the offered cloud services from AWS, which are important for deploying the SAP workloads on the cloud later on. The concepts of regions and availability zones were explained and how to place SAP workloads into the cloud so that you achieve a higher availability. The chapter did describe the console, which you can use either via the Graphical User Interface or the Command Line Interface. We also described the integration into the core services of your enterprise, for example, the Active Directory.

CHAPTER 5

SAP S/4HANA on AWS Elastic Compute Cloud – Deployment

SAP S/4HANA is SAP's modern ERP solution that is powered by in-memory database HANA and is in the core of mission-critical digital business of most big enterprises across the globe. The HANA database which is in the heart of this digital business runs in its full potential when hosted on purpose-built hardware for harnessing its power. And this is one of the reasons SAP has the SAP Integration and Certification Center (SAP ICC) that tests and certifies Infrastructure-as-a-Service (IaaS) platforms, along with other certifications like the storage solution that supports SAP HANA. The list of certified and supported SAP HANA Hardware can be referenced at

`www.sap.com/dmc/exp/2014-09-02-hana-hardware/enEN/#/solutions?filters=v`
`:deCertified`

AWS offers a wide range of Elastic Compute Cloud (EC2) instances to host and run SAP HANA and S/4HANA application servers, the smallest being with 2 vCPUs and 3.75 GB RAM (VM supporting 1995 SAPS) to as large as 448 vCPUs and 24,576 GB RAM (bare metal supporting 444,330 SAPS). In the scale-out scenario, you can now run SAP S/4HANA workloads of up to 48 TB of memory.

The following section will detail some exemplary scenario to host and run SAP S/4HANA workload in the AWS Hyperscaler Cloud.

© André Bögelsack, Utpal Chakraborty, Dhiraj Kumar, Johannes Rank, Jessica Tischbierek, Elena Wolz 2022
A. Bögelsack et al., *SAP S/4HANA Systems in Hyperscaler Clouds*, https://doi.org/10.1007/978-1-4842-8158-1_5

Exemplary Architecture

The SAP S/4HANA system can be deployed on highly available, fault-tolerant, and affordable way with AWS Infrastructure-as-a-Service model. In this chapter, you will have a clear understanding of how to provision an SAP S/4HANA system with different types of architecture on AWS with a specific availability SLA.

The common architecture discussed are

- Single-AZ and single-node architecture

- Single-AZ and multinode architecture

- Multi-AZ, single-node SAP S/4 high availability architecture

Deployment Scenarios

Single-AZ and Single-Node Architecture

This is the default cost-minimized architecture to deploy an SAP system on AWS. Figure 5-1 shows a diagram illustrating this architecture.

The main features of this deployment are

- The SAP system is deployed in a single availability zone.

- You get 99.99% (four nines) VM availability SLA that means the maximum EC2 instance can be unavailable for 4.32 minutes per month.

- This is a self-healing architecture. In case the underlying EC2 fails because of any hardware issue, AWS reboots that EC2 and automatically brings it up on another healthy hardware with the same configuration. You only need to take care of the application part.

The VM availability SLA should not be mixed with the SAP S/4HANA application availability SLA. During the reboot, it is to be noted that AWS does not guarantee on your application data; if data gets corrupted, then the only option is to restore the data to bring the services back to normal. This is the default cost-minimized architecture which is the best for non-production workload and also can be used for noncritical production workload.

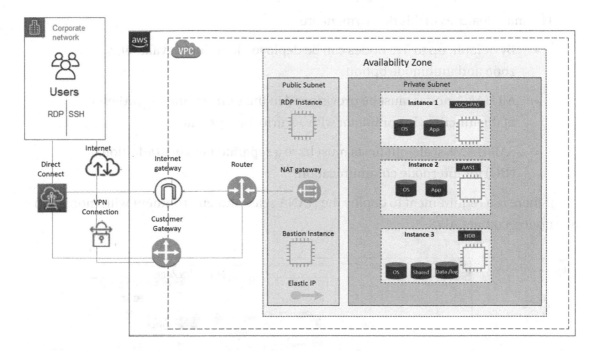

Figure 5-1. *S/4HANA single-AZ, single-node architecture*

In this setup, the SAP application and the HANA DB are deployed in the same VPC, the same availability zone, and normally the same subnet. Network segmentation totally depends on customer requirements like

- Microsegmentation: Different subnets for each SAP SID.

- Prod/non-prod segmentation: Production applications and databases are provisioned in one subnet, and non-prod applications and databases are provisioned in a different subnet.

The best practice is to put the SAP and DB in different subnets to restrict the direct access to the database. SAP applications (PAS and AAS) and HANA databases are installed as per the SAP standard installation guide. VM and OS requirements for SAP deployment are explained in detail in the next section.

Single-AZ and Multinode Architecture

This SAP S/4 deployment is illustrated in Figure 5-2. It is normally used for HANA scale-out environments.

The main features of this deployment are

- By default, up to five nodes can be deployed in a single availability zone and multinode option.

- All HANA nodes must be provisioned in the same subnet regardless of the function, in compliant with security best practice.

- SAP HANA scale-out hosts must have a separate network (additional NIC) for internode communication.

If there is a requirement to deploy the HANA scale-out environment with more than five nodes, contact AWS.

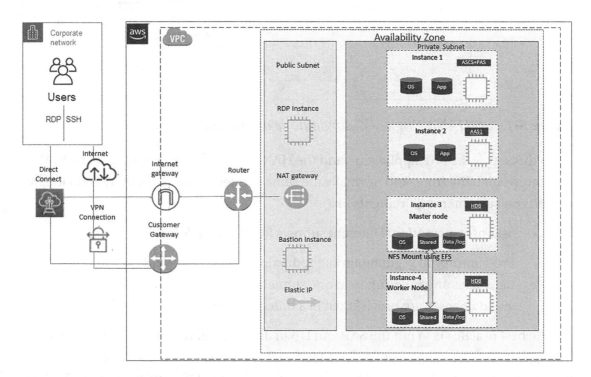

Figure 5-2. *S/4HANA single-AZ, multinode architecture*

SAP S/4 and HANA databases must be installed as per the SAP standard guide. VM and OS requirements for SAP deployment are explained in detail in the next section. The parameter "`listeninterface`" in section [communication] must be set to ".internal" or contain a CIDR netmask. Please follow the SAP KBA – 2183363.

Multi-AZ, Single-Node SAP S/4 High Availability Architecture

AWS multi-AZ deployment offers you to run business-critical SAP workloads with a high resiliency, fault-tolerant, and highly available environment. There is very less probability of business impact in case of any application breakdown, unexpected hardware failure, or unavailability of the entire single availability zone.

The infrastructure setup involves the following steps:

- Select the availability zones for the deployment of the SAP S/4HANA system.

- Create separate subnets for hosting the application and the database, separately in both AZs.

One important infrastructure limitation of hosting the infrastructure in AWS AZs is that you can have a shared subnet between AZs. This means you cannot assign a common IP to ASCS/ERS or HANA DB to address them when they are in two separate AZs. This limitation can be overcome with the use of Overlay IP (OIP).

Option A: Overlay IP Using AWS Transit Gateway

You can set up an SAP HA environment on AWS using Overlay IP in two ways. The first option we will discuss is shown in Figure 5-3. This option overlays the IP using the AWS Transit Gateway.

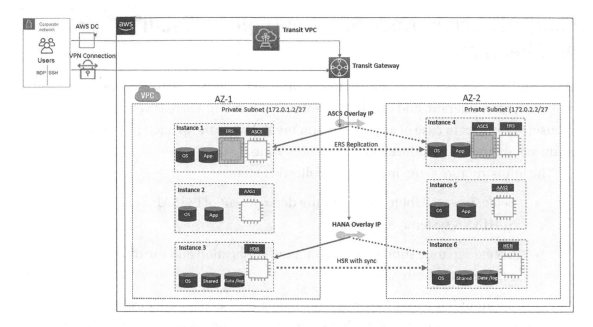

Figure 5-3. *S/4HANA multi-AZ, single-node with Transit Gateway architecture*

With Transit Gateway, you can use AWS route table rules which allow an Overlay IP address to communicate with an SAP instance without having any additional component like Network Load Balancer. You can easily connect to Overlay IP from another VPC, another subnet, or through Direct Connect from your corporate network.

AWS Transit Gateway works as a hub that controls the traffic, which is routed among all the connected networks, which act like spokes. Transit Gateway routes packets between the source and the destination as per the Transit Gateway route tables. You can configure these route tables to fetch routes from the route tables for the attached VPCs and VPN connections. You can also add static routes to the Transit Gateway route tables. You can add the Overlay IP address or address CIDR range as a static route in the Transit Gateway route table with a target as the VPC where the EC2 instances of the SAP cluster are running. This way, all the traffic is routed toward the Overlay IP addresses.

In above illustration, you have one VPC to isolate the network from other AWS virtual networks; within the VPC, you have two availability zones AZ1 and AZ2. Now you have to create a private subnet with a specific CIDR range in AZ1 (172.0.1.2/16) and AZ2 (172.0.2.2/16). Your private subnet cannot be spanned across availability zones. Now install S/4 ASCS in AZ1 (instance 1 in the diagram) and Standalone Enqueue Server 2 (ENSA2) in AZ2 (instance 4 in the diagram). SAP defined the new enqueue server ENSA2 as the default installation from S/4 1809 and concept to bring this feature to manage the lock table smoothly and efficient way which ensures the consistency of data in an ABAP system.

The ASCS and ERS or ENSA2 service needs to be installed with a virtual host associated with a virtual IP which is known as Overlay IP. An S/4 application instance needs to be installed in both AZs (instance 2, instance 3) to avoid the outage in case of zone failure. Now the HANA DB needs to be installed in both AZs (instance 3, instance 4) with a virtual host associated with Overlay IP, and the HANA System Replication with synchronous replication mode needs to be configured between the two HANA DB.

The overlay IP always points to the active ASCS or HANA DB node, in case node failure or any disruption of services, ASCS or HANA DB failover to availability zone 2 and Overlay IP switch to AZ 2 active nodes. End users will not get impacted with the node failure as they always connect to Overlay IP, and Overlay IP always points to active nodes.

Follow the AWS standard guide to configure the AWS Transit Gateway. The SAP HA cluster setup on different flavors of OS will be described later in this chapter.

`https://docs.aws.amazon.com/vpc/latest/tgw/tgw-getting-started.html`

Option B: Overlay IP Routing with Network Load Balancer

The other option is to overlay your IP routing. This option is illustrated in Figure 5-4.

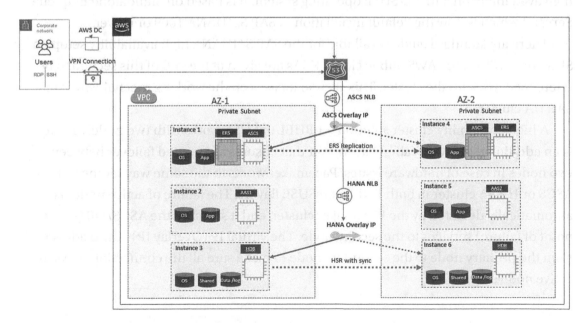

Figure 5-4. S/4HANA multi-AZ, single-node with NLB architecture

If you do not have scope to use AWS Transit Gateway, you can use Network Load Balancer to access the Overlay IP addresses from an external network. NLB works at the network layer, the fourth layer in the OSI model which can accept millions of requests per second. It receives a request from an external network and selects a target as per the Network Load Balancer target group and routes the request to the specific Overlay IP address.

The installation of the SAP S/4 application and HANA DB is the same as explained in the previous section. In order to configure the Network Load Balancer in a proper way, you can follow the AWS standard guide, which is accessible in the following link:

```
https://docs.aws.amazon.com/elasticloadbalancing/latest/network/create-
network-load-balancer.html
```

SAP HA Cluster Setup

SAP NetWeaver/HANA High Availability Setup on RHEL and SUSE

This section will explain the idea on how to set up a cluster solution to configure SAP on high availability on a RHEL/SUSE operating system. It is based on Standalone Enqueue Server 2 which is now the default installation in SAP S/4HANA 1809 or newer.

There are standard guides available for the SAP S/4HANA high availability setup on SUSE or RHEL on the AWS public cloud. KBAs are given at the end of this section to be referenced to set up the cluster. This section focuses on the working mechanism of the SAP HA cluster.

A high availability cluster solution for RHEL or SUSE works with two nodes. There is an additional software called Pacemaker that ensures automated failover between two nodes in case of hardware issues. Pacemaker works in the same way for the S/4 ASCS or HANA cluster in both RHEL and SUSE flavors. The failure of active nodes is automatically detected by the Pacemaker cluster, and it switches the ASCS/DB (single point of failure) services to the second node. The virtual IP (Overlay IP) is also adjusted from the primary node to the secondary node to make sure all the connection flows to active node only.

Importance of fencing: During a normal operation, there is no work of fencing agents in the cluster solution. A cluster communicates through Corosync, and a cluster of both nodes continuously updates each other of the health status of the nodes. A problem starts when one of the nodes stops responding. There are two possible scenarios:

- The primary node is not available due to a crash or panic reboot.

- The primary server is available, but due to a network issue, it is not reachable.

In the first case, the cluster will perform the failover to the secondary (healthy) node. In the second case, the failover must not happen as both nodes are active or available. This situation is called split brain or dual primary, and this is super dangerous in the HANA cluster as on both nodes the HANA database is running independently. So, imagine some transaction getting recorded in node 1 and some in node 2. This can result in serious data inconsistency for business, even loss of data. To prevent this situation, the Pacemaker cluster introduces a fencing mechanism called STONITH (shoot-the-other-node-in-the-head). Just in case there is any communication issues between the nodes, then the healthy node will kill the faulty/noncommunicating node to ensure both nodes are not active at the same time.

The following are the high-level steps to install the SAP S/4 application server or SAP HANA database on the HA environment on a RHEL or SUSE platform:

1. Build the AWS cloud foundation: The AWS cloud foundation design and implementation is the first step to start any project on the AWS cloud. It starts with region selection, network design (VPC, subnet, firewall, Transit Gateway or Network Load Balancer, Route 53), security and resource policies, on-premise to AWS connectivity, AD authentication, and so on. Some of these services are already explained in previous sections, and a few like security will be explained in the security section later in this chapter.

2. EC2 instance provisioning: You need to provision the SAP NetWeaver certified and SAP HANA certified EC2 instances. You can deploy this manually or in an automated way with SAP recommended OS settings for a specific OS release (RHEL for SAP solution or SLES for SAP solution). VM provisioning is explained in detail in the "Compute" section later in this chapter.

3. File system layout: You need to have the following directories to configure the SAP and HANA high availability:

- ASCS server local FS: /usr/sap/<SID>/ASCS<nn>

- ERS server local FS: /usr/sap/<SID>/ERS<nn>

- Shared FS: /sapmnt, /usr/sap/trans, /usr/SAP/<SID>/SYS

- Application server local FS: /usr/sap/<SID>/D<nn>

On Linux OS, Amazon Elastic File System (EFS) can be used for shared directories to be mounted as NFS in different servers. For Windows, FSx is the file share option mounted as SMB drive. For both the HANA nodes, you should have the following file systems with the same size:

- /usr/sap

- /hana/shared

- /hana/data/<SID>

- /hana/log/<SID>

- /hana/backup

- /hana/* file system type should be XFS, and the rest are EXT4 type.

Please follow this sequence to create the environment:

1. Create the Overlay IP addresses: Create the virtual IP or overlay IP in AWS and associate the same with all the HA nodes.

2. Install S/4 ASCS and ERS: Install ASCS in one node and ERS in another node with a virtual host and Overlay IP as per the SAP HA standard guide.

3. Configure the cluster setup: Set up the Pacemaker configuration in both ASCS and ERS nodes.

4. Install HANA DB: Install the stand-alone HANA DB in both the DB nodes with a virtual hostname and Overlay IP as per the standard SAP guide.

5. Configure HANA System Replication: Configure HSR with synchronous operation mode and log-replay replication mode.

6. Set up the Pacemaker cluster: Set up the Pacemaker cluster on both ASCS/ERS and HANA nodes separately.

7. Install S/4 application servers: Install additional S/4 application servers in both the availability zones. Application servers are not part of the cluster.

8. Test the cluster: Perform a cluster failover test.

It is very critical for any production system setup with HA to have a robust cluster setup to avoid any unplanned outage because of hardware issues. So, after the cluster setup, perform a rigorous cluster testing. Table 5-1 summarizes a sample cluster test plan.

Table 5-1. *Test Cases for HA Clusters*

Test Scenario	Expected Outcome
Application – SAP Cluster	
Switch ASCS from primary to secondary	ASCS should move to the secondary node, and the user session should remain intact
Switch ASCS from the secondary to the primary node	ASCS should move to the primary node, and the user session should remain intact
Kill Message Server in the primary node	ASCS should start on the secondary node, and the user session should be intact
Kill Message Server in the secondary node	ASCS should start on the primary node, and the user session should be intact
Kill ASCS sapstartsrv in the primary node	ASCS should move to the secondary node, and the user session should remain intact
Kill ASCS sapstartsrv in the secondary node	ASCS should move to the primary node, and the user session should remain intact
Reboot the primary ASCS node	ASCS should move to the secondary node, and the user session should remain intact
Reboot the secondary ASCS node	ASCS should move to the primary node, and the user session should remain intact

(continued)

Table 5-1. (*continued*)

Test Scenario	Expected Outcome
Isolation of the storage for one node (A/B)	ASCS service should start automatically on the other node
Application – DB Cluster	
Perform manual failover from primary to secondary	HDB should run on the secondary node; the user session should remain intact
Perform failback from secondary to primary	HDB should run on the primary node; the user session should remain intact
Stop DB on the primary node	HDB should run on the secondary node; the user session should remain intact
Stop DB on the secondary node	HDB should run on the primary node; the user session should remain intact
Kill hdbindexserver in the primary node	HDB should run on the secondary node; the user session should remain intact
Kill hdbindexserver in the secondary node	HDB should run on the primary node; the user session should remain intact
Kill other DB services in the primary node	HDB should run on the secondary node; the user session should remain intact
Kill other DB services in the secondary node	HDB should run on the primary node; the user session should remain intact
Reboot the primary DB node	HDB should run on the secondary node; the user session should remain intact
Reboot the secondary DB node	HDB should run on the primary node; the user session should remain intact

Follow the standard S/4 on AWS KBAs to set up the high availability solution on a RHEL or SUSE platform:

- S/4 high availability for SUSE: https://documentation.suse.com/ sbp/all/html/SAP_HA740_SetupGuide_AWS/index.html

- SAP HANA high availability for SUSE: `https://documentation.suse.com/sbp/all/html/SLES4SAP-hana-sr-guide-PerfOpt-15_AWS/index.html`

- S/4 high availability for RHEL: `https://access.redhat.com/articles/3916511`

- SAP HANA high availability for RHEL: `https://access.redhat.com/articles/3569621`

SAP NetWeaver Availability Setup on Windows Platform

When setting up an S/4HANA system or a NetWeaver system, you can host an application server on a Windows Server operating system. The Windows-native high availability solution – Windows Server failover cluster – is used for the HA configuration. You can configure an SAP high availability setup for ASCS and ERS services in two ways on the Windows platform:

- Windows Server Failover Clustering (WSFC) using the Amazon FSx file share solution

- Windows Server Failover Clustering (WSFC) using the SIOS Protection Suite on AWS

Windows Server Failover Clustering (WSFC) Using Amazon FSx File Share Solution

This solution uses Amazon FSx file systems to host shared directories needed for ASCS and ERS. Amazon FSx is an AWS fully managed file system (same as EFS for Linux OS) which can be shared across availability zones. Use a multi-AZ Amazon FSx file for a Windows file share. Refer to the following AWS guide to set up SAP S/4 high availability on Windows using the Amazon FSx file share:

`https://aws.amazon.com/blogs/awsforsap/how-to-setup-sap-netweaver-on-windows-mscs-for-sap-ascs-ers-on-aws-using-amazon-fsx/`

Windows Server Failover Clustering (WSFC) Using SIOS Protection Suite on AWS

SIOS Protection Suite is a third-party software provided by SIOS Technology. It is tightly integrated with the WSFC cluster to perform smooth failover in case of a zone failure or disruption of services. The SIOS DataKeeper part of SIOS Protection Suite is a server-based replication solution (same as the NFS or GFS file share solution) that performs block-level data replication across the availability zones to manage the Windows HA solutions. Here, the recommendation is to provision separate VMs in both zones for shared file systems which are to be replicated synchronously and mounted to ASCS/ERS servers, so there will not be any disruption of services in case of zone failure.

Refer to the following AWS guide to set up SAP S/4 HA on Windows using SIOS Protection Suite: `https://aws.amazon.com/blogs/awsforsap/deploying-highly-available-sap-systems-using-sios-protection-suite-on-aws/`.

Compute

Computes are the core services for hosting SAP applications and HANA databases. In this section, you will learn the available templates released by AWS that have been certified to host the SAP workload.

This will help to choose the appropriate EC2 template. This section further describes how to provision the template, which build-related information are available, how to provision the EC2 template and which build-related information are required to enable the EC2 to finally host the SAP workload.

Compute refers to the amount of computational power required to fulfill your workload. Being an architect, your responsibility is to properly size the compute to host the SAP workload (large, medium, small). It should not be oversized resulting in customer spending more than required or undersized which may lead to impaired performance of the production instance, hampering business, and unpleasant user experience.

AWS has a wide range of SAP certified compute on offer to host the SAP workload. The elasticity feature of the AWS cloud can be used to adapt the compute power to the usage load requirement. This means you don't necessarily need to plan for a large instance upfront.

The available EC2 instances in AWS are segregated based on CPU, memory, storage, and network performance. Depending on the usage type, you can provision a suitable EC2, for example, for an application server expecting heavy compute load, you can provision a CPU-optimized EC2, while for HANA DB, you can opt for a memory-optimized EC2 instance.

Available EC2 Instance Family

Amazon provides a wide range of EC2 instance types to support all types of workload.

Compute-optimized instance types are best for workloads where you need high-performance processors: C* (C4, C5, C5a, C6g, etc.).

Storage-optimized instance types are used where you need high, sequential read/write operations to a large dataset locally. They provide low latency and very high IOPS: D*, H1, I3, I3en

General-purpose instance types are CPU- and memory-balanced instance types and ideal for small- and medium-sized databases or workloads: M*, T* (M4, M5, M5a, T2, T3, T3a, etc.)

Memory-optimized instance types are ideal for workloads that process a large dataset in memory and are best used in in-memory databases like HANA: R* (r4, r5, r5a, r5ad, etc.).

Amazon also provides bare-metal solutions to support very high memory workload like u6tb1.metal, u-9tb1.metal, u-12tb1.metal, u-18tb1.metal, and u-24tb1.metal.

EC2 Instance Licenses

For running SAP workload on EC2, you have the following options to procure the usage license:

- On-Demand Instance: With On-Demand Instances, you pay by hour or by minute, depending on the instances you're running and based on your uses. No long-term contracts or upfront payments are required. You can flexibly increase or decrease the computing capacity depending on the application requirements and only pay the hourly rate for the instances used. This is very useful if you run your workload during specific times only.

- Reserved Instance: Amazon EC2 Reserved Instances (RI) provide a significant discount (up to 72%) compared to On-Demand pricing and provide a capacity reservation when used in a specific availability zone. You should use a reserved instance for all the production workload.

- Dedicated host: This is the bare-metal solution offering explained earlier. A dedicated host is a physical EC2 server that is reserved exclusively for your use. With dedicated hosts, you can save costs by using your existing server-based software licenses, like Windows Server, SQL Server, and SUSE Linux Enterprise Server (according to your license terms and conditions). This can be booked on-demand or as a reserved instance (with 70% discount) as per your usages.

SAP S/4 Certified EC2 Instance Types

AWS has worked closely with SAP to certify a set of EC2 instances for SAP and HANA workload. Follow the link to get the updated latest generation SAP certified EC2 instance types:

`https://aws.amazon.com/sap/instance-types/`

Also, refer to the SAP Note 1656099 "SAP Applications on AWS: Supported DB/OS and AWS EC2 products" that gives you the latest information about AWS EC2 instance types that are currently supported on Amazon Web Services (AWS) infrastructure.

EC2 Provisioning

This section will walk you through the components, services are required to provision the virtual machines on AWS and high-level steps to provision the VM. First, you need to assess and gather customer requirements to build the cloud foundation or landing zone which include the following components:

- Region: Select the primary and DR region.

- Availability zones: Select the availability zones and single-AZ or multi-AZ deployment.

- Networking: Design network segmentation with the following items.

- Virtual Private Cloud (VPC): The number of VPCs required like Management VPC and SAP VPC to isolate from other virtual networks.

- Private subnet: Design a private subnet for SAP workload like one subnet for each SAP SID or one subnet for non-production workload and one for production workload or different subnets for the SAP S/4 application and HANA DB layer.

- Public subnet: Bastion host on a public subnet with an Elastic IP address to access the EC2 instances.

- Internet Gateway to access the Internet.

- NAT Gateway: A NAT gateway allows the outbound Internet access for private subnet resources.

- AWS connectivity: You can connect to AWS VPC with your corporate network in two ways.

- VPN connection: Encrypted IPSec connection between on-premise and AWS VPC. You can create multiple VPN connections with one VPC; it's fast and simple to set up.

- Direct Connect: Using Direct Connect, you can connect to AWS VPC with your data center. Direct Connect provides high bandwidth and throughput.

- Security: Define a security policy to restrict the inbound/outbound traffic.

You have to create an AWS account to provision any resources on AWS. Once your AWS landing zone is ready, then you are good to start with deploying S/4 and HANA VMs. You need to have the following information to provision an S/4 application or HANA DB server on AWS:

1. Account ID.

2. IAM roles/policies.

3. VPC/subnet/region.

4. Security group.

5. S3 bucket (if required to attach).

6. Storage volumes and file system layout: Mount point, volume (physical and logical), size, type of storage (EBS/EFS), file system type.

7. Instance size.

8. Platform (Windows/RHEL/OEL).

9. Physical and logical hostname.

10. UID/GID information.

11. OS packages should be installed as per the SAP recommendation.

12. Server tagging information.

Now you can deploy the cloud foundation and EC2 instances in a manual way or fully automated way with a script.

Manual Deployment with AWS Console

This example walks you through the look and feel of the AWS console and how to create resources on AWS. The process is shown in Figure 5-5.

Create a Direct Connect connection: Search the service from the AWS console or go to All Services ➤ Networking & Content Delivery ➤ Direct Connect.

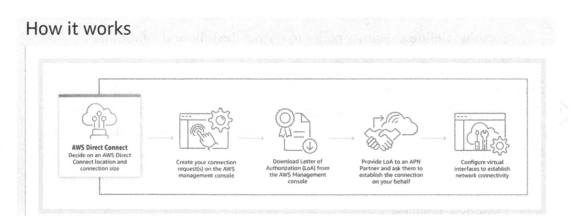

Figure 5-5. *Manual deployment – step 1*

Click create connection. After giving all the details like name, your location from where you want to connect to AWS, required bandwidth, your on-premise network provider, and BillTo tag, create a connection as shown in Figure 5-6.

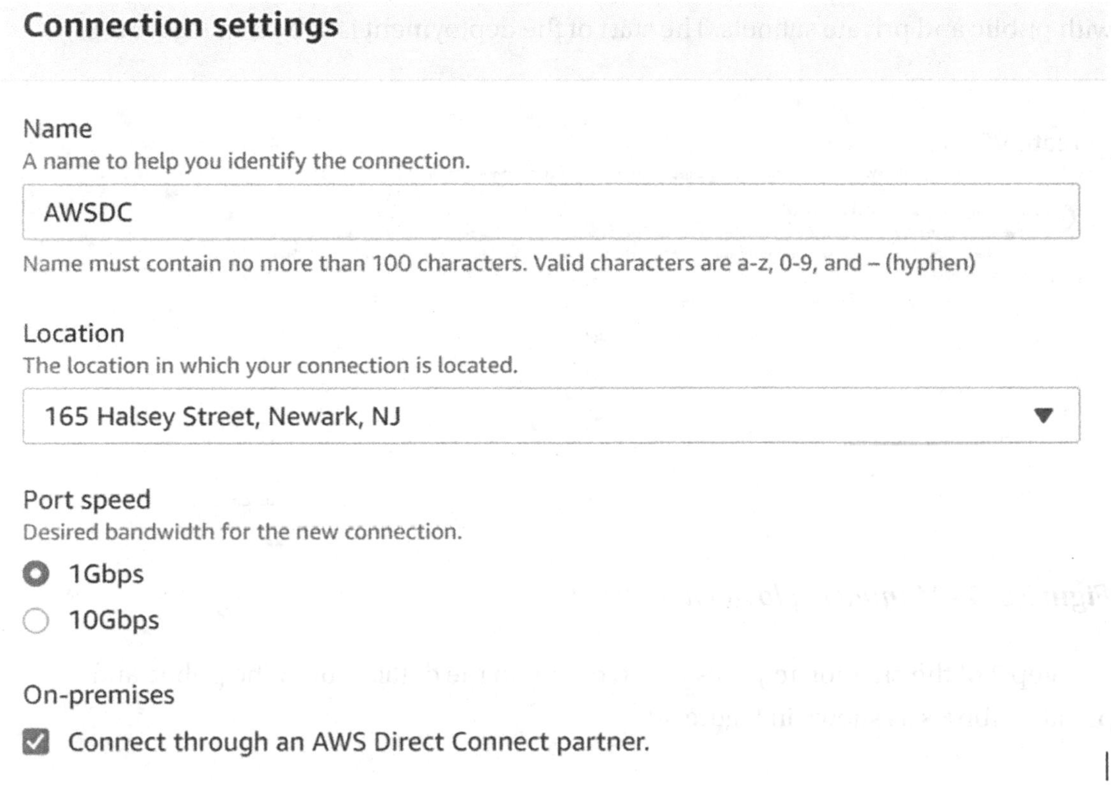

Connection settings

Name
A name to help you identify the connection.

AWSDC

Name must contain no more than 100 characters. Valid characters are a-z, 0-9, and – (hyphen)

Location
The location in which your connection is located.

165 Halsey Street, Newark, NJ ▼

Port speed
Desired bandwidth for the new connection.

◉ 1Gbps

◯ 10Gbps

On-premises
☑ Connect through an AWS Direct Connect partner.

Figure 5-6. *Manual deployment – step 2*

You can choose the service provider for the connection from a list of providers as shown in Figure 5-7. After that step, the connection would be created and established.

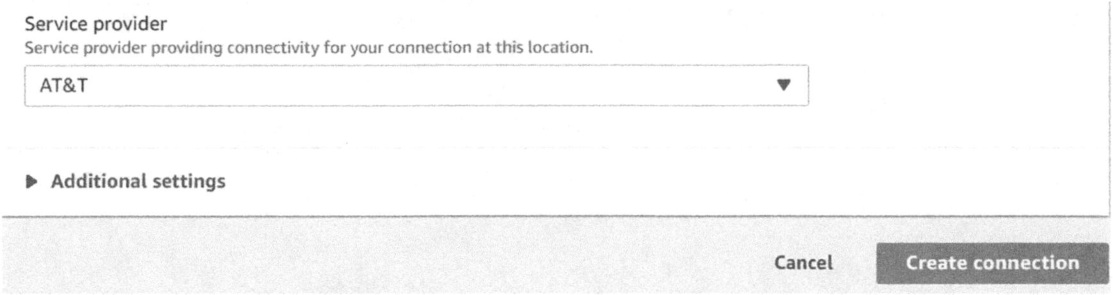

Service provider
Service provider providing connectivity for your connection at this location.

AT&T ▼

▶ Additional settings

Cancel   **Create connection**

Figure 5-7. *Manual deployment – step 3*

Create VPC, Subnet, NAT Gateway (Create Elastic IP Address Before You Create VPC)

After the connection was created successfully, the next step will be to create the VPC with public and private subnets. The start of the deployment is shown in Figure 5-8.

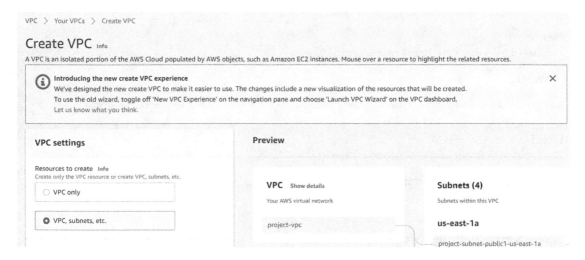

Figure 5-8. *Manual deployment – step 4*

Step 2 of the creation requires you to maintain the details about the public and private subnets as shown in Figure 5-9.

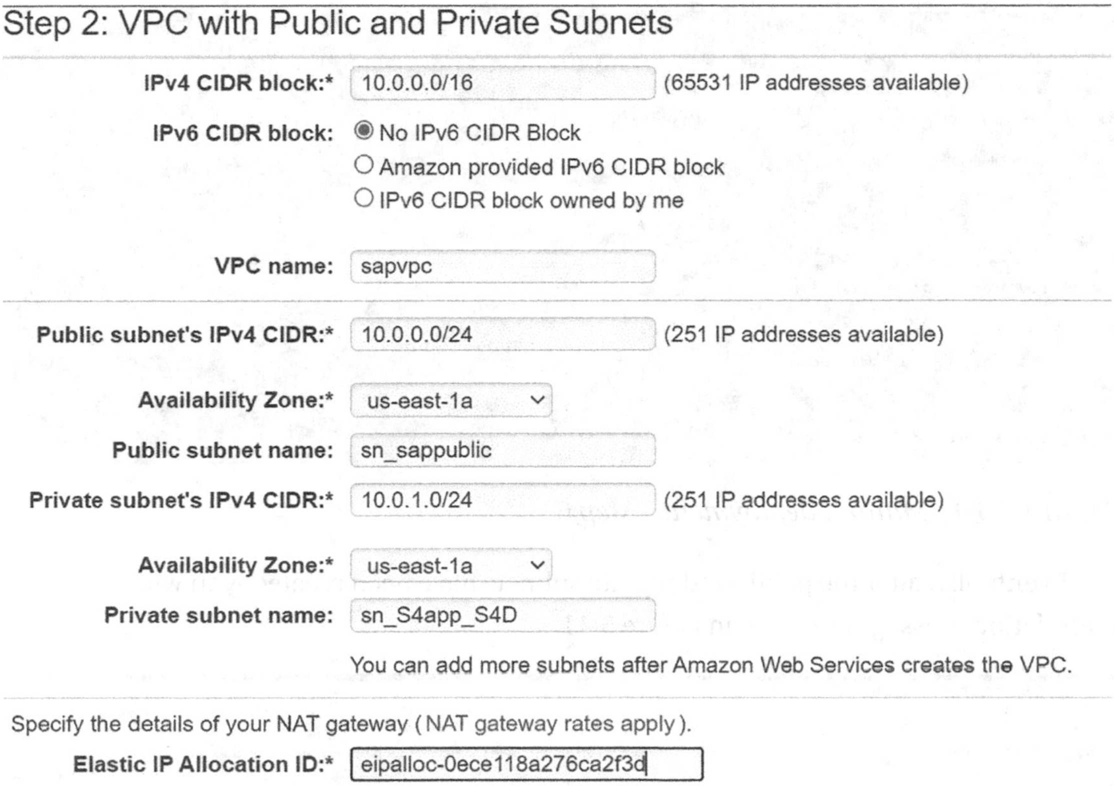

Step 2: VPC with Public and Private Subnets

IPv4 CIDR block:*	10.0.0.0/16 (65531 IP addresses available)
IPv6 CIDR block:	◉ No IPv6 CIDR Block ○ Amazon provided IPv6 CIDR block ○ IPv6 CIDR block owned by me
VPC name:	sapvpc

Public subnet's IPv4 CIDR:*	10.0.0.0/24 (251 IP addresses available)
Availability Zone:*	us-east-1a ⌄
Public subnet name:	sn_sappublic
Private subnet's IPv4 CIDR:*	10.0.1.0/24 (251 IP addresses available)
Availability Zone:*	us-east-1a ⌄
Private subnet name:	sn_S4app_S4D

You can add more subnets after Amazon Web Services creates the VPC.

Specify the details of your NAT gateway (NAT gateway rates apply).

Elastic IP Allocation ID:*	eipalloc-0ece118a276ca2f3d

Figure 5-9. *Manual deployment – step 5*

After you maintained the details about the public and private subnets and click next, it will take some time to create the subnets. During that time of waiting, you will see the status message as shown in Figure 5-10.

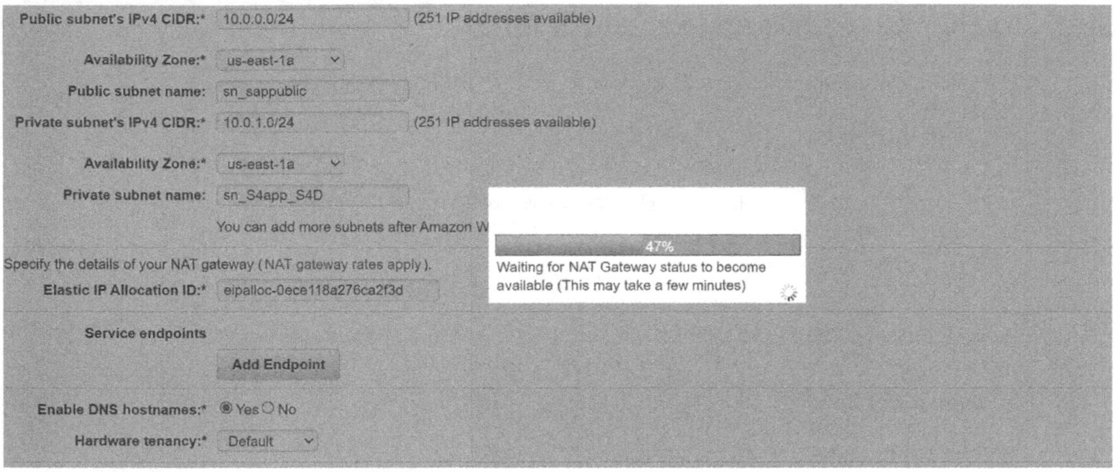

Figure 5-10. *Manual deployment – step 6*

Eventually, after the public and private subnets have been created, you will see a completion message as shown in Figure 5-11.

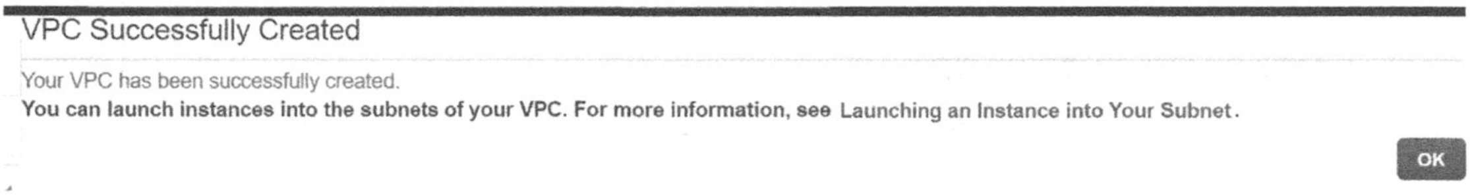

Figure 5-11. *Manual deployment – step 7*

Now your basic cloud foundation is ready, and you can deploy SAP S/4 and HANA VMs as follows. Here in the example, we choose SLES for SAP 15 SP1 AWS Machine Image with pay-as-you-go (PAYG) subscription. You can use bring-your-own-subscription as well. The first step to deploy the machine is to choose the Amazon Machine Image, which is tailored for the needs of SAP. In Figure 5-12, you can see an example of such an SAP-tailored AMI.

Figure 5-12. *Deployment of SLES AMI*

After choosing the AMI, the associated and certified instance types are listed. This allows you to choose the right sized VM for your new SAP system. Each VM template differs in the number of CPUs and memory and, hence, incurs higher/lower costs. Those are also shown for each instance type. Figure 5-13 shows the list of instance types and costs for the SLES operating system.

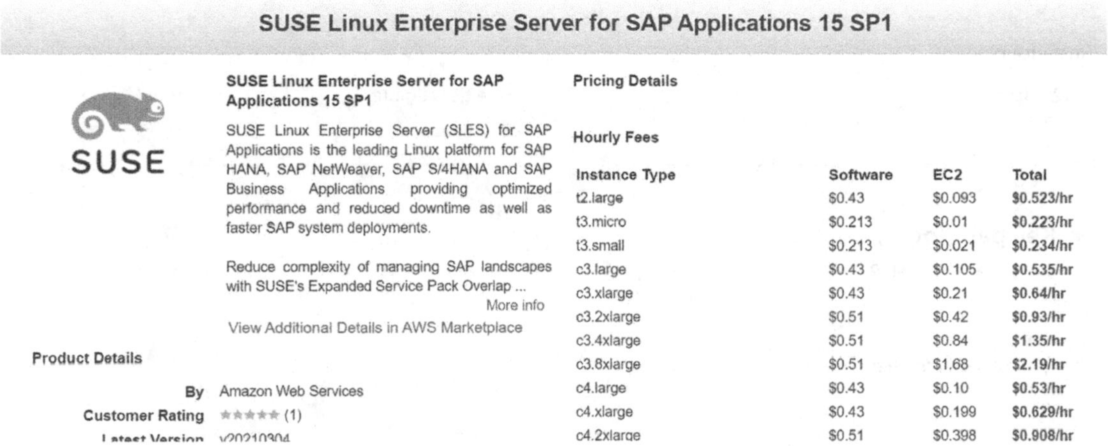

SUSE Linux Enterprise Server for SAP Applications 15 SP1

SUSE Linux Enterprise Server for SAP Applications 15 SP1

SUSE Linux Enterprise Server (SLES) for SAP Applications is the leading Linux platform for SAP HANA, SAP NetWeaver, SAP S/4HANA and SAP Business Applications providing optimized performance and reduced downtime as well as faster SAP system deployments.

Reduce complexity of managing SAP landscapes with SUSE's Expanded Service Pack Overlap ...
More info
View Additional Details in AWS Marketplace

Product Details

By	Amazon Web Services
Customer Rating	★★★★★ (1)
Latest Version	v20210304

Pricing Details

Hourly Fees

Instance Type	Software	EC2	Total
t2.large	$0.43	$0.093	$0.523/hr
t3.micro	$0.213	$0.01	$0.223/hr
t3.small	$0.213	$0.021	$0.234/hr
c3.large	$0.43	$0.105	$0.535/hr
c3.xlarge	$0.43	$0.21	$0.64/hr
c3.2xlarge	$0.51	$0.42	$0.93/hr
c3.4xlarge	$0.51	$0.84	$1.35/hr
c3.8xlarge	$0.51	$1.68	$2.19/hr
c4.large	$0.43	$0.10	$0.53/hr
c4.xlarge	$0.43	$0.199	$0.629/hr
c4.2xlarge	$0.51	$0.398	$0.908/hr

Figure 5-13. *Overview of instance types and costs*

In the next step for the deployment, you will have to choose the right instance type. You also see the sizing of each instance type, like CPUs and memory, but also the limitations toward the storage (Elastic Block Storage – EBS only) and the connectivity to the network. This is shown in Figure 5-14, where we choose the instance type r5.

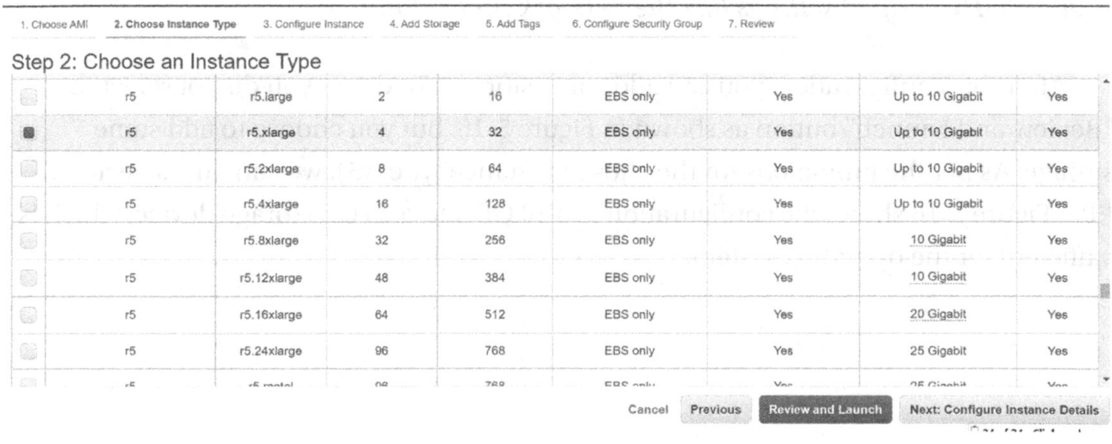

1. Choose AMI	2. Choose Instance Type	3. Configure Instance	4. Add Storage	5. Add Tags	6. Configure Security Group	7. Review

Step 2: Choose an Instance Type

☐	r5	r5.large	2	16	EBS only	Yes	Up to 10 Gigabit	Yes
■	r5	r5.xlarge	4	32	EBS only	Yes	Up to 10 Gigabit	Yes
☐	r5	r5.2xlarge	8	64	EBS only	Yes	Up to 10 Gigabit	Yes
☐	r5	r5.4xlarge	16	128	EBS only	Yes	Up to 10 Gigabit	Yes
☐	r5	r5.8xlarge	32	256	EBS only	Yes	10 Gigabit	Yes
☐	r5	r5.12xlarge	48	384	EBS only	Yes	10 Gigabit	Yes
☐	r5	r5.16xlarge	64	512	EBS only	Yes	20 Gigabit	Yes
☐	r5	r5.24xlarge	96	768	EBS only	Yes	25 Gigabit	Yes
☐	r5	r5.metal	96	768	EBS only	Yes	25 Gigabit	Yes

Cancel | Previous | Review and Launch | Next: Configure Instance Details

Figure 5-14. *Choosing the instance type*

Once the instance type is chosen, you will need to select a couple of options and specify some important details. For example, you need to assign the network and subnet but also settings for the domains and some additional behavior settings. In Figure 5-15, we have chosen the network "sapvpc," to which the new VM will be assigned.

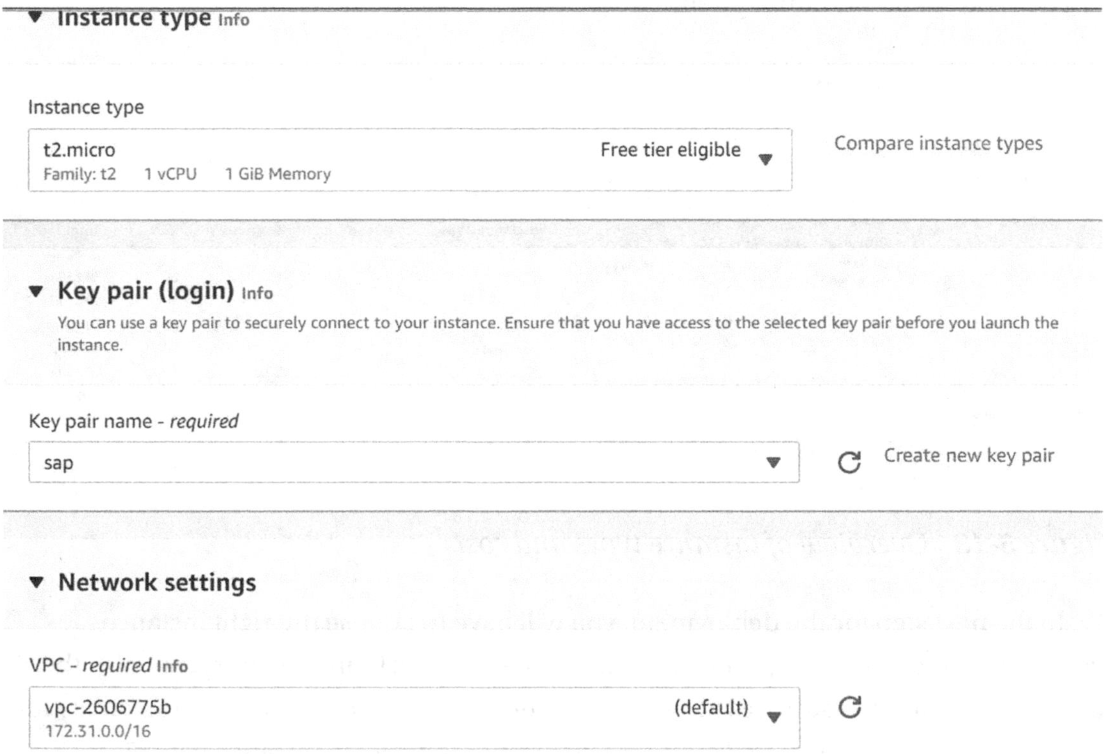

Figure 5-15. *Adjust settings like the network and subnet*

After this configuration, you can add some storage. To do so, you do not select the "Review and Launch" button as shown in Figure 5-16, but you choose to add some storage. As per the limitations for the chosen instance type (r5), we can only select EBS. Figure 5-16 shows the configuration of a 10 GB and a 25 GB storage device, which is sufficient for the operating system.

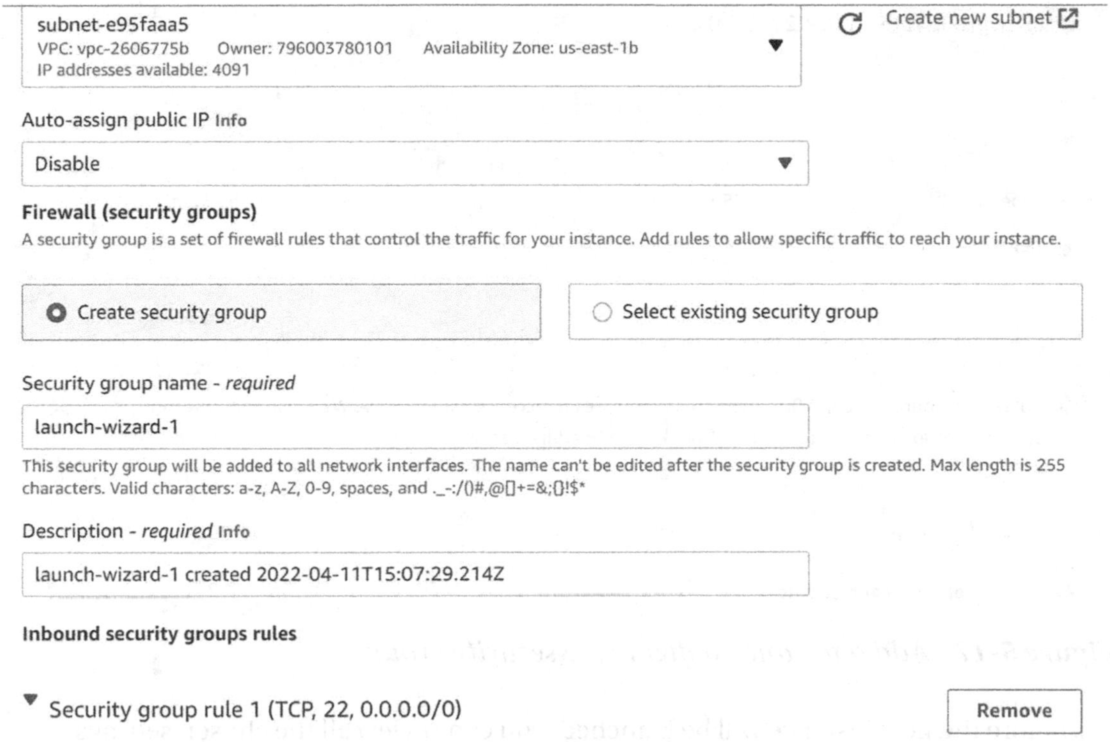

subnet-e95faaa5
VPC: vpc-2606775b   Owner: 796003780101   Availability Zone: us-east-1b
IP addresses available: 4091

▼   ⟳   Create new subnet ↗

Auto-assign public IP Info

Disable   ▼

Firewall (security groups)
A security group is a set of firewall rules that control the traffic for your instance. Add rules to allow specific traffic to reach your instance.

○ **Create security group**   ○ Select existing security group

Security group name - *required*

launch-wizard-1

This security group will be added to all network interfaces. The name can't be edited after the security group is created. Max length is 255
characters. Valid characters: a-z, A-Z, 0-9, spaces, and ._-:/()#,@[]+=&;{}!$*

Description - *required* Info

launch-wizard-1 created 2022-04-11T15:07:29.214Z

Inbound security groups rules

▼ Security group rule 1 (TCP, 22, 0.0.0.0/0)   Remove

Figure 5-16. *Do not launch the VM, but configure the storage*

As a next step after configuring the storage, you can configure tags. Those are used
to manage cost allocations or specify the owner of a specific machine. In Figure 5-17, we
specify a tag called "SAP S/4 S4D" and set the value to "600099." Afterward, we define
the security group for the new VM. This is based on the recommendations from the AWS
Marketplace and contains, for example, some frequently used ports (22 and 80), which
will be added to the security group for this machine.

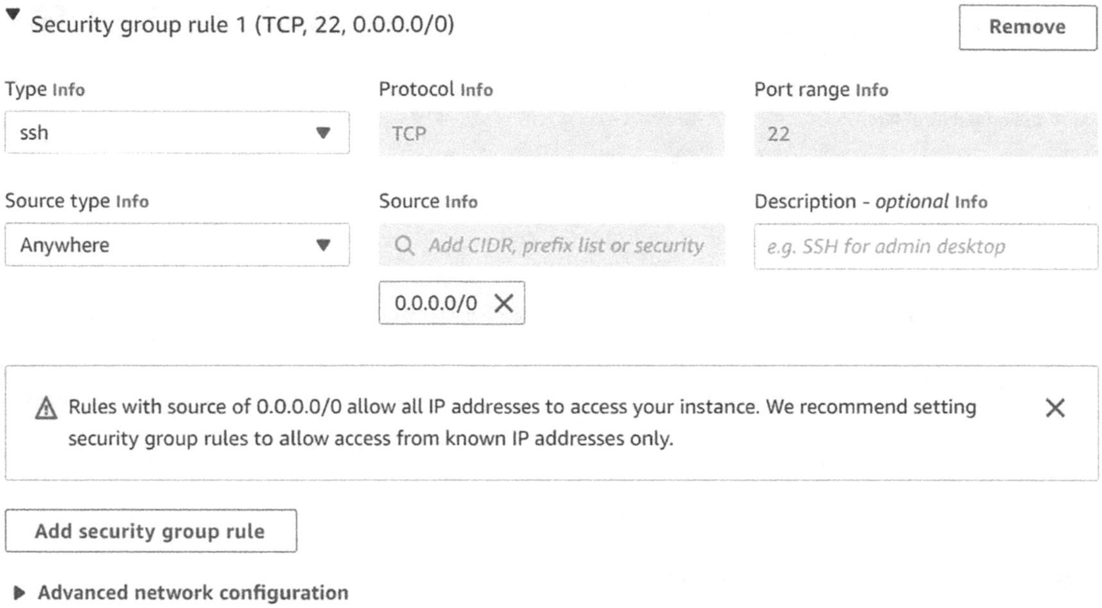

▼ Security group rule 1 (TCP, 22, 0.0.0.0/0)

Remove

Type Info

ssh ▼

Protocol Info

TCP

Port range Info

22

Source type Info

Anywhere ▼

Source Info

Q Add CIDR, prefix list or security

0.0.0.0/0 ✕

Description - optional Info

e.g. SSH for admin desktop

⚠ Rules with source of 0.0.0.0/0 allow all IP addresses to access your instance. We recommend setting   ✕
security group rules to allow access from known IP addresses only.

Add security group rule

▶ Advanced network configuration

Figure 5-17. *Add a tag and configure the security group*

Before the new instance will be launched, you can review all the chosen settings
and options and, if required, return back to the specific step to change anything. The
summary as shown in Figure 5-18 contains all the settings, which we have chosen for the
deployment.

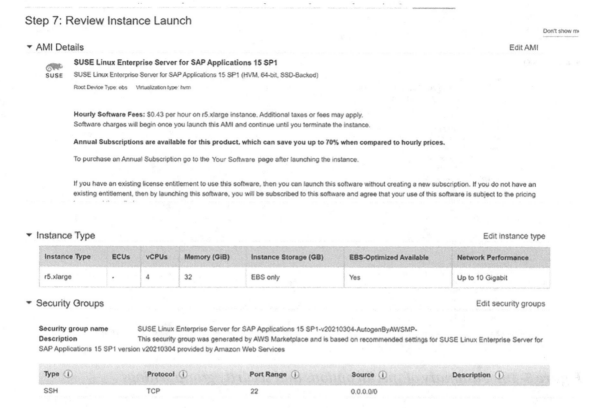

Figure 5-18. *Review all settings before deploying the machine*

The summary contains a lot of details and also lists the details about the security group as well as the chosen storage. This is shown in Figure 5-19.

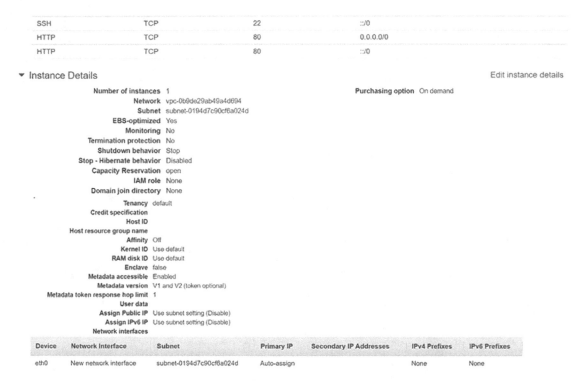

SSH	TCP	22	::/0
HTTP	TCP	80	0.0.0.0/0
HTTP	TCP	80	::/0

▼ Instance Details   Edit instance details

Number of instances	1
Network	vpc-0b9de29ab49a4d694
Subnet	subnet-0194d7c90cf6a024d
EBS-optimized	Yes
Monitoring	No
Termination protection	No
Shutdown behavior	Stop
Stop - Hibernate behavior	Disabled
Capacity Reservation	open
IAM role	None
Domain join directory	None
Tenancy	default
Credit specification	
Host ID	
Host resource group name	
Affinity	Off
Kernel ID	Use default
RAM disk ID	Use default
Enclave	false
Metadata accessible	Enabled
Metadata version	V1 and V2 (token optional)
Metadata token response hop limit	1
User data	
Assign Public IP	Use subnet setting (Disable)
Assign IPv6 IP	Use subnet setting (Disable)
Network interfaces	

Purchasing option On demand

Device	Network Interface	Subnet	Primary IP	Secondary IP Addresses	IPv4 Prefixes	IPv6 Prefixes
eth0	New network interface	subnet-0194d7c90cf6a024d	Auto-assign		None	None

Figure 5-19. *Summary of special options and security group settings*

Before finally launching the instance, you can review the storage and the sizing of the storage. If you are ok with that, you can go ahead and get the new VM created and launched by hitting the button "Launch" as shown in Figure 5-20.

▼ Storage   Edit storage

Volume Type ⓘ	Device ⓘ	Snapshot ⓘ	Size (GiB) ⓘ	Volume Type ⓘ	IOPS ⓘ	Throughput (MB/s) ⓘ	Del on Ter ⓘ	E
Root	/dev/sda1	snap-0b1abedb626e899ec	10	gp2	100 / 3000	N/A	Yes	E...
ebs	/dev/sdb		25	gp2	100 / 3000	N/A	No	Enc

▼ Tags   Edit tags

Key	Value
SAP S/4 S4D	600099

Cancel   Previous   **Launch**

Figure 5-20. *Summary of storage and launch options*

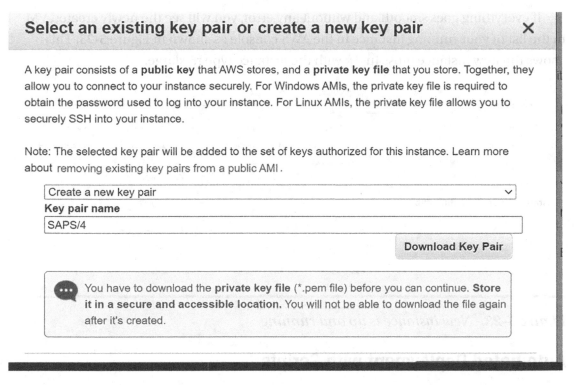

Select an existing key pair or create a new key pair ✕

A key pair consists of a **public key** that AWS stores, and a **private key file** that you store. Together, they allow you to connect to your instance securely. For Windows AMIs, the private key file is required to obtain the password used to log into your instance. For Linux AMIs, the private key file allows you to securely SSH into your instance.

Note: The selected key pair will be added to the set of keys authorized for this instance. Learn more about removing existing key pairs from a public AMI.

Create a new key pair   ⌄
Key pair name
SAPS/4

Download Key Pair

... You have to download the **private key file** (*.pem file) before you can continue. **Store it in a secure and accessible location.** You will not be able to download the file again after it's created.

Figure 5-21. *Select or create a key pair*

For the access to the newly created machine, a key pair can be chosen, if you already have one stored in AWS, or you can go ahead and create a new one as shown in Figure 5-21. This is needed in order to gain the access to the machine after the successful deployment. The deployment can take quite a while, depending on the size of the machine and the number of settings to be applied. But overall, the deployment is rather quick, and you will see a screen like in Figure 5-22, which also shows you the current step in the deployment.

Launch Status

Initiating Instance Launches
Please do not close your browser while this is loading
Creating security groups... Successful
Authorizing inbound rules... Successful
Verifying entitlement to product...

Figure 5-22. *Deployment is in progress*

If everything goes smooth and without any error, you will see the newly created VM in the list of your running instance in the AWS console as shown in Figure 5-23. This shows the new instance mpss4us1p with the instance type r5.xlarge.

Figure 5-23. *New instance is up and running*

Automated Deployment with Scripts

When you deploy SAP systems in AWS, you need to deploy identical instances, for example, deployment of Additional Application Servers or setup of landscape in a disaster recovery region which needs identical setup as production. There is an option of automated deployment of infrastructure as well as SAP applications through scripts. Terraform and Ansible are two available tools that can aid this.

Terraform

Terraform is an infrastructure automation tool. It uses easy-to-write templates in HCL (HashiCorp Configuration Language). It offers built-in functions and conditions and has a vast array of modules and providers for working with cloud and on-premise systems. One of the unique selling points of Terraform is that it is cloud agnostic, that is, the code works on all popular clouds. If you plan to use Terraform, you don't need to deploy any agent, only the binary code on the server is sufficient to perform the provisioning tasks.

In AWS, Terraform can be used to create the SAP and DB infrastructure automatically as per the Terraform configuration files. Terraform workflows depend on their commands – plan, apply, and destroy. And to invoke this, you need to have an initialized working directory.

Visit the GitHub repository and go through the sample Terraform scripts and modules and execute them to create your first infrastructure on AWS for SAP automatically:

```
https://github.com/aws-samples/terraform-aws-sap-netweaver-on-hana
```

Ansible

Ansible, which is owned by Red Hat, is an open source tool that enables the automation, configuration, and orchestration of infrastructure. Ansible is very reliable for repeated deployment, infrastructure update, and configuration management. And all these can happen from one central location called control machine via SSH. Ansible also offers a vast array of modules for most OS-level utilities.

Ansible uses YAML syntax to create the configuration file. Ansible too is an agentless tool, and only binary code is required on the server to perform the tasks.

Ansible can be used to automate the OS configuration and SAP and DB application deployment. Like Terraform, you also need to execute the Ansible script from a tool server to deploy the application on managed servers. The yml (*.yml) file is the main configuration file in Ansible which contains all the tasks to configure the infrastructure and deploy S/4 and HANA applications.

```
https://software.opensuse.org/download.html?project=systemsmanagement&package=ansible
```

Terraform uses API calls to provision cloud resources like deploying EC2 instances, disk provisioning and load balancer setup, and so on, whereas the Ansible script is used to configure OS settings like mounting the disk, FS layout, user group creation, OS parameter settings, and installation of an SAP application and database. Figure 5-24 depicts how it works.

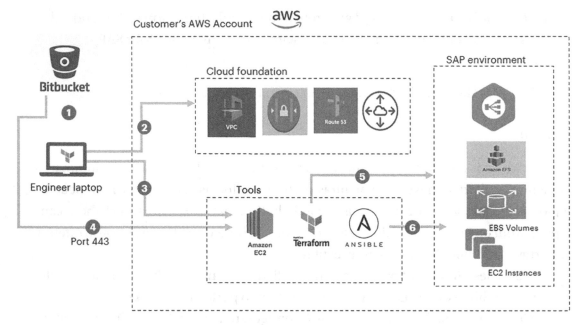

Figure 5-24. *VM and SAP automated deployment*

For a fully automated deployment, you would follow the six steps as shown in Figure 5-24:

1. Clone the Terraform Git repository to the laptop.

2. Launch Terraform from the laptop to provision the cloud foundation like the VPC, subnet, Route 53, NLB, Transit Gateway, etc.

3. You need to provision one tool server on AWS from where you can launch Terraform and Ansible to provision VM and SAP.

4. Clone the Terraform and Ansible Git repository to the tool server.

5. Launch Terraform from the tool server to deploy SAP infrastructure.

6. Launch Ansible from the tool server for OS configuration and to deploy S/4HANA application.

Storage

This section gives an introduction of the main storage types of AWS that are used when hosting the SAP landscape on the AWS cloud. As a recap, the main AWS storage services that are used in SAP are shown in Figure 5-25:

- Amazon Elastic Block Store (Amazon EBS)

- Amazon Elastic File System (Amazon EFS)

- Amazon FSx for Windows File Server

- Amazon Simple Storage Service (Amazon S3)

The section elaborates the available storage types in Amazon, based on the requirements of the S/4 system, and it provides guidance to the general storage layout (stripping) as well as possible sizing for S/4 systems (database and application servers). We will also discuss cost-optimized solutions for running noncritical SAP systems, for example, read-only archive systems. Based on the DR requirements, you may need to choose specific settings (geo-replication) for some of the storages. The relationship between the different storage types is shown in Figure 5-25.

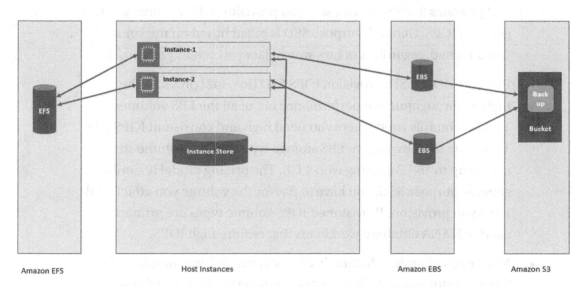

Figure 5-25. *Relationship between the different types of storage options*

Amazon EBS

EBS (Elastic Block Store) provides durable, block-level storage volumes to be attached to specific EC2 instances. They function similar to Storage Area Network (SAN) devices, much like raw unformatted block device from where you can carve out the file systems. Normally, all the file systems of an SAP application server and database that does not require sharing are created out of EBS volumes. EBS by its configuration offering from AWS is on a high availability setup. They are replicated across multiple servers in an availability zone that ensures HA.

You can attach multiple EBS volumes to a single EC2 instance, but you cannot attach the same EBS volume to multiple EC2 instances. EBS volumes are independent on the EC2 instance lifetime. You can keep the EBS volume after terminating the EC2 instance. EBS is not expandable across the availability zones. If you need to replicate the content across availability zones, you can take a snapshot of existing EBS, transfer the snapshot to another zone, and restore. AWS offers different EBS volume types:

- General-purpose SSD: General-purpose SSD (gp2 and gp3) provides cost-effective storage with strong performance. This is best suited for small- to medium-sized workload. It's available from 1 GB till 16 TB and provides 3 IOPS per GB, so if you provision 1 TB volume, you will get 3000 IOPS. General-purpose SSD is billed based on the volume you attached, regardless of how much data you actually stored.

- Provision IOPS SSD: Provision IOPS SSD (io1, io2) provides the highest throughput and performance out of all the EBS volumes. This is primarily used where you need high and consistent IOPS rate. This is the most expensive EBS storage type, and the volume size can go up to 16 TB starting with 4 GB. The pricing model is similar to general-purpose SSD; you have to pay for the volume you attach and IOPS you provision. Provisioned IOPS volume types are primarily used in HANA database workloads that require high IOPS.

- Magnetic Volumes: A Magnetic EBS (st1, sc1) volume provides the lowest performance with lowest cost among all the EBS volumes. It's useful where data needs to be accessed infrequently and for sequential reads. It is not recommended to use Magnetic Volumes for SAP workloads.

Amazon EC2 Instance Store

EC2 instance stores also provide block-level storage like EBS, but they are ephemeral data stores. Instance stores are physically attached with an EC2 host; hence, if you terminate the EC2 instance, your instance storage data is lost. It is ideal for temporary storage like buffer, cache, or data that replicates across instances. Instance stores should not be used to SAP workload file systems, but you can use them in swap space.

Amazon EFS

As explained in Section 4.2, EFS and FSx are Amazon-managed highly available shared file systems used to store SAP file systems that need to be shared across application servers. And in the case of high availability configuration, they are also used to host file systems for ASCS/SCS and ERS HANA share and HANA backups.

EFS is exclusively used with Linux operating systems, while FSx is used with the Windows Server operating system. Refer to the following standard AWS guide to know how to create an EFS file system step by step:

```
https://docs.aws.amazon.com/AWSEC2/latest/UserGuide/EBSEncryption.html
```

Amazon S3 (Simple Storage Service)

Amazon S3 is an object storage which you can use to store and retrieve any type and any amount of data from anywhere over the Web. S3 offers you to pay only for the storage you actually use. For the SAP landscape, S3 is commonly used in the following cases:

- *Store backup (DB, VM snapshot, etc.) and archive data.*

- *Disaster recovery.*

- *Content, media, and software storage.*

S3 also offers different types of storage classes like general purpose, infrequent access, and archive to support different types of use cases. S3 components are explained briefly in the following.

Buckets: An S3 bucket is a container for objects to store in S3. A bucket is a global entity and is not limited to your AWS account. This means bucket names should be unique across all AWS accounts. Although bucket namespace is global but you can create an S3 bucket in your specific region and close to set-off end users in order to minimize the latency and to ensure fast transfer of the files or even you can create in different region than primary to support in disaster scenario.

Objects: Objects are files which are stored in S3 buckets. Objects can store any type of data in any format, but you can store data up to 5 TB in a single bucket with unlimited number of objects. Each object consists of data (actual data) and metadata (information about data).

Keys: A key is a unique identifier of every object which is stored in an S3 bucket. A key can be a file name which should be unique in a single bucket, but the same key (or file name) can be used in different buckets.

Object URL: An Amazon S3 object can be accessed with a specific URL formed using a service endpoint, a bucket name, and an object key like

```
http://testbucket.s3.amazonaws.com/test.doc
```

Here, testbucket is the bucket name, and test.doc is your key or file name.

Durability and availability: Amazon S3 provides very high durability and very high availability; the Amazon S3 standard storage is designed for 99.999999999% durability and 99.99% availability. S3 achieves durability by automatically replicating the data in all locations in a specific region. If you don't need high durability for noncritical data, you can use Reduce Redundant Storage (RRS) at a lower cost with 99.99% durability.

Data consistency: Amazon S3 guarantees on data consistency as by default it replicates your data in different servers or locations within a region. Changes may take a moment, so in some cases you can get stale data, specifically if you PUT new data on an S3 object and subsequent GET will return old data; so for an eventually consistent read, you will get either old data or new data, but there will not be any data inconsistency.

Access control: Amazon S3 uses the Amazon Access Control List (ACL) and IAM to grant the access on the S3 bucket or object level. You can grant WRITE, READ, and FULL CONTROL at the bucket or object level.

Storage class: You need to understand the different types of storage class available in S3 to define the backup and archive storage strategy in a cost-effective way. There are mainly three storage classes available:

- Amazon S3 Standard: The Amazon S3 Standard provides the highest durability, availability, low latency, and high performance on your data transfer between EC2 and S3. The Amazon S3 Standard is very useful for frequently accessed short-term or long-term storage data.

- Amazon S3 Standard IA: Standard Infrequent Access also offers the same durability, availability, and low latency like the standard storage class, but this is used for less frequently accessed data. If you have to store data for a minimum of 30 days, you can use this for long-term stored data which are accessed less frequently, and cost-wise it's much cheaper than the standard storage class.

- Amazon Glacier: The Amazon Glacier storage class allows you to store the archive data or long-term backup with the lowest price. It also provides durability and security to your data. Data retrieval from Glacier can take several hours. Also, retrieval can be expedited incurring additional costs. Now you can plan your cloud storage based on the preceding three classes; mainly, you need to focus on "how frequently data access is required," "retention period," and obviously "cost."

For further details, we recommend reading through the user guide from Amazon, using the following link:

```
https://docs.aws.amazon.com/AWSEC2/latest/UserGuide/AmazonS3.html
```

Storage Layout for S/4HANA System

An SAP system can be set up with one of the three possible deployment options. This section will detail the storage layout setup required for each.

Standard System Deployment

In this deployment option, all the components of the SAP application – ASCS/SCS, ERS, and PAS – and HANA database run on one single EC2 host. This deployment is only suitable for small non-production instances.

If you plan to run an SAP S/4HANA application server on a Windows Server host, you need separate EC2 instances for the application and the HANA database.

Distributed System Deployment

In this deployment option, each component can run on separate hosts:

- An EC2 for ABAP Central Services instance (ASCS instance)

- An EC2 for SAP HANA database

- An EC2 for PAS

- Additional EC2s, optionally Additional Application Servers (AAS)

High Availability System Deployment

In this deployment option, each component must run on a separate host, and the high availability setup will be done to secure the single-point-of-failure (SPOF) components for the S/4 application (ASCS/ERS) and HANA DB.

Indicative File System Setup for Non-high Availability Setup

There are clear recommendations for which storage type can be used for which file system/mount point of the SAP system. For SAP systems running without any high availability solution, Table 5-2 provides an overview.

Table 5-2. *Indicative FS Layout for Non-HA*

Mount Point Detail	Mount Point Name in SAP	Suggested Storage Type
SAP Application Server		
Local directories	/usr/sap/<SID>/usr/sap/hostctrl /swap	EBS gp3
Physically shared directories	/sapmnt/<SID>/usr/sap/trans	EFS
Logically shared directories	Hyperlinks for global, profile, run, and dbg subdirectories	–
HANA Database		
Local directories Root HANA share System instance	/ /hana/shared/ /usr/sap	EBS gp3
Local directories Data Volume Log Volume	/hana/data /hana/log	EBS io1 or EBS io2

Indicative File System Setup for High Availability Setup

For the HA setup, the SPOF file systems need to be on HA, and EFS is one the suitable options to host such file systems. Compared to non-HA SAP systems, those systems using a high availability solution have special mount points for special file systems. Table 5-3 shows the mount points and the suggested storage type.

Table 5-3. *Indicative FS Layout for HA*

Mount Point Detail	Mount Point Name in SAP	Suggested Storage Type
SAP Application Server		
Local directories	/usr/sap/ /usr/sap/hostctrl /swap	EBS gp3
Physically shared directories (SPOF file systems)	/sapmnt/<SID> /usr/sap/trans /usr/sap/<SID>/SYS /usr/sap/<SID>/ASCS<nn> /usr/sap/<SID>/ERS<nn> /<sapmedia>*	EFS
Logically shared directories	Hyperlinks for global, profile, run, and dbg subdirectories	–
HANA Database		
Local directories Root System instance	/ /usr/sap	EBS gp3
Local directories Data Volume Log Volume	/hana/data /hana/log	EBS io1 or EBS io2
Physically shared directories	/hana/shared/	EFS

* It is preferable to keep /<sapmedia> (a directory that holds all SAP installation media downloaded from the SAP Support Portal) in a shared location so that it is accessible from all the servers. So EFS has been recommended. It is not a SPOF.

The following aspects related to file system hosting should be taken into account while planning to configure the SAP application and HANA DB file systems:

- HANA data and log volumes must be configured on SAP-certified storage options for HANA workloads. To achieve the optimal throughput or performance, SAP certifies EBS volumes (gp2, gp3) and provisions IOPS SSD (io1, io2) for SAP HANA workloads.

- For non-production HANA databases, you can opt for general-purpose SSDs (gp2/gp3), unless you have a pressing requirement for high IOPS.

- For production instances that are mission critical, you should provision IOPS SSD (io1, io2).

- Keep in mind the cost while deciding the storage tiers. IOPS SSDs can be 1.5 times (or more) costlier than general-purpose SSDs.

- AWS has recently launched the gp3 type EBS volume. It is now recommended to use the gp3 type SSD as this offers better throughput or performance and is cost-effective compared to gp2 type EBS volume.

- EFS volumes are up to three times costlier than EBS volumes. So, for a standard installation, prefer putting the file system in EBS as they are accessed from the same host.

- It is possible to stripe multiple EBS volumes together to achieve more IOPS and larger capacity. This is especially applicable for hosting HANA DB's data files.

- With SAP HANA 2.0 SPS03, the HANA indexserver is able to distribute its I/O activity across multiple HANA data files. These files can be located on different disks. If you opt for this setup, you can save yourself from the additional overhead of EBS striping.

- Ref: Partitioning Data Volumes - SAP Help Portal

- `https://help.sap.com/viewer/6b94445c94ae495c83a19646e`
  `7c3fd56/2.0.05/en-US/40b2b2a880ec4df7bac16eae3daef756.`
  `html?q=hana%20data%20volume%20partitioning`

- 2400005 – FAQ: SAP HANA Persistence

- For a view of the HANA storage configuration for /hana/data and /hana/log, you can refer to the AWS documentation – **Storage Configuration for SAP HANA**: https://docs.aws.amazon.com/sap/latest/sap-hana/hana-ops-storage-config.html.

- Enable EBS optimization while launching the EC2 instance for hosting the SAP application/DB. With this setup, the burst performance of the EBS volumes is almost guaranteed. When attached to an EBS-optimized instance

    - General-purpose SSD (gp2 and gp3) volumes are designed to deliver their baseline and burst performance 99% of the time.

    - Provisioned IOPS SSD (io1 and io2) volumes are designed to deliver their provisioned performance 99.9% of the time.

Refer to the AWS documentation for instructions on how to enable EBS optimization for an instance:

https://docs.aws.amazon.com/AWSEC2/latest/UserGuide/ebs-optimized.html

PAYG vs. Commitment – Calculator

Although the public cloud can offer great potentials for savings, the tricky question remains for a lot of customers, if they should commit to a workload for some time or if they want to benefit from the flexibility. This has a big monetary impact and will be discussed in this section. We will also show the calculator for having a better idea about the break-even for the decision.

In AWS, you can purchase an EC2 instance in the "On-Demand" or "Reserved Instance" category based on your usage.

On-Demand Instances

On-Demand Instances enable you to pay for what you use; you have to pay only for the time of EC2 instances running, and if you stop it, you don't need to pay for compute, only you have to pay for the storage attached to the instances. This is very useful and cost-effective in cases where you have limited usage of instances like sandbox, training, non-prod instances, etc. You can schedule the start and stop automatically if you know the usage duration. For example, you can automatically start it before starting the business hours and stop the instance after business hours. On-Demand Instances are very useful and cost-effective in those cases where you don't have any long-term commitment.

There is a default limit of running a total number of On-Demand Instances per AWS account per region. The limit depends on the number of vCPUs. You can have a certain number of vCPUs per AWS region and per account, but you can increase this limit by raising a request through the AWS Support Portal.

Reserved Instance

In a Reserved Instance model, you will get a significant discount compared to the On-Demand Instance cost. You need to provide one-year or three-year long-term commitment. You will get more discount for longer commitment.

A Reserved Instance will not get renewed automatically if it expires; you must purchase the reserved instance again, else it would be converted to an On-Demand Instance once it expires.

It is a very useful and cost-effective option for your production workload where your EC2 instance must be running 24 hours throughout the year.

The Reserved Instance price depends on four attributes:

- Instance type (small or large)

- Region (purchased on which region)

- Tenancy (default or dedicated)

- Platform (Unix or Windows)

A Reserved Instance offers two classes: *Standard* and *Convertible*. In a Standard class, you will get a significant discount, but you cannot exchange the instance type, only you can modify it. Convertible comes with a lower discount compared with the standard class, but you can exchange the instance type with another convertible instance, and it can also be modified.

A Modified Reserved Instance means you can change the instance type within the same family. You can modify the instance type from m4* to m5* provided your instance footprint size is the same, but you cannot modify an m4* to c* instance type. Only the Linux/Unix platform can be modified.

An Exchange Convertible Reserved Instance means you can exchange the instance type from one family to any other family with the same or higher footprint size than the original instance type.

Payment Option

You have to pay for Reserved Instances regardless of whether you are using it or not. There are three payment options available in the Reserved Instance category:

- All Upfront: Full payment must be made before starting the instance, no other charges to be paid throughout the term. You get a maximum discount with this payment option.

- Partial Upfront: A portion of the total cost must be paid before starting the term, and the remaining will be billed with a discounted hourly rate.

- No Upfront: You don't need to pay anything upfront; you will be billed a discounted hourly rate.

AWS Calculator

You can calculate the BOM (Bill of Materials) of your project through the AWS calculator. This section will show you how the AWS calculator is used in your regular business. Go to `https://calculator.s3.amazonaws.com/index.html`, and you will see a similar screen like the one in Figure 5-26.

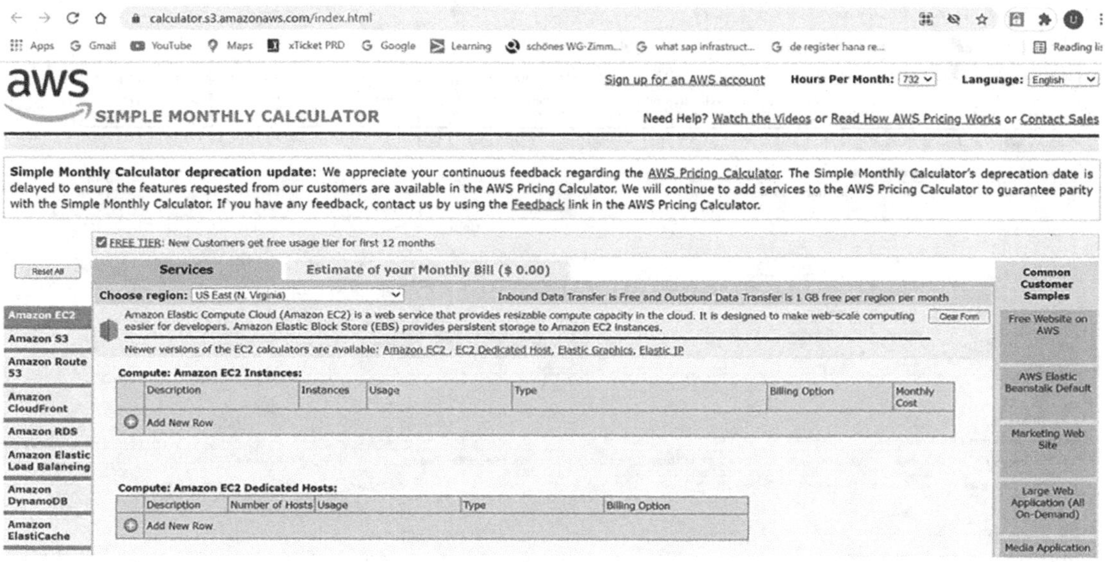

Figure 5-26. *AWS calculator – initial screen*

Here, you can see all the AWS services in the left pane, which you need to calculate the cost, and "Services" and "Estimate of your Monthly Bill" at the top pane. In this example, we will estimate the cost of the EC2 instance and EBS volume with the "On-Demand" and "Three years Reserved Instance" category.

We will take two r* family instance types and 2048 GB "Provisioned IOPS SSD (io2)" EBS volume into our consideration.

On-Demand Instance Cost

Click "Add New Row" in the "Compute: Amazon EC2 Instances" section and enter the details as per your requirement. In the same way, enter the details in the "Storage: Amazon EBS Volumes" section as you can see in Figure 5-27.

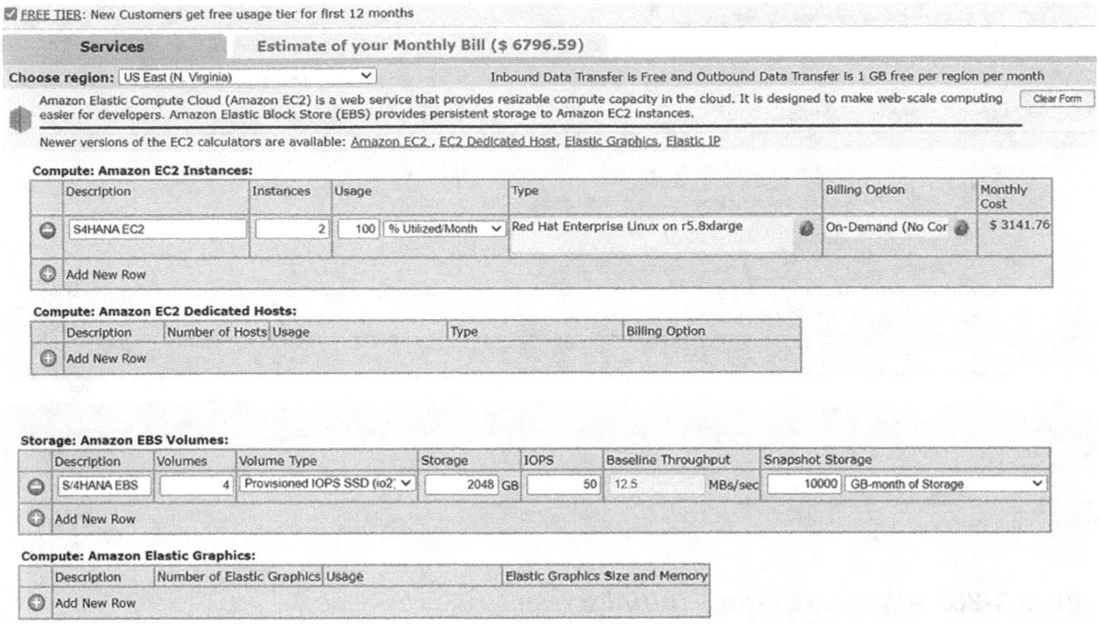

Figure 5-27. *Add the instance and storage*

In Figure 5-28, you can see the estimated monthly bill of $6796.59 for two r5.8xlarge instances and 4 IOPS SSD (io2) volume with 2048 GB. If you click the Estimate tab, you can see the breakdown as well.

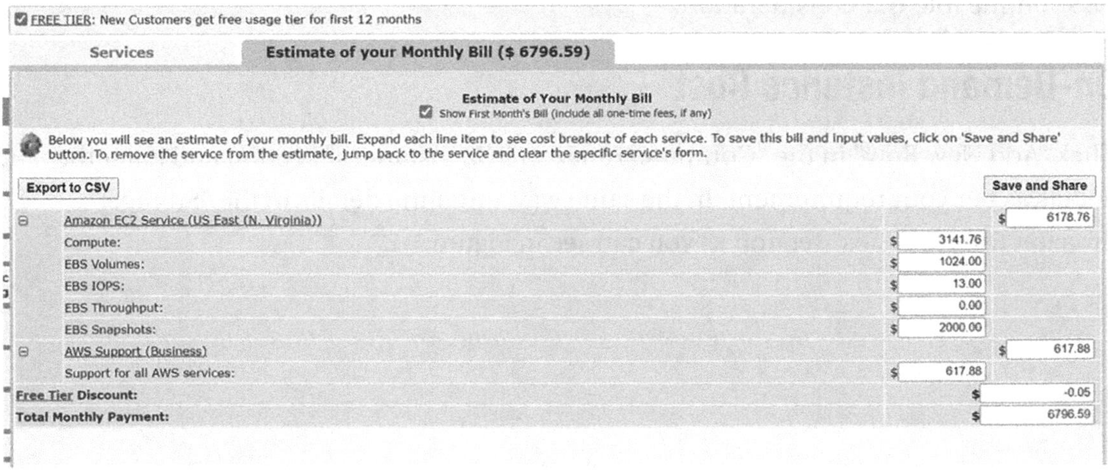

Figure 5-28. *Breakdown of monthly costs*

If you change the billing option for the instance from on-demand to a three-year upfront payment, the overall costs will significantly reduce. This billing option is shown in Figure 5-29, and you can see the monthly cost of $0.00.

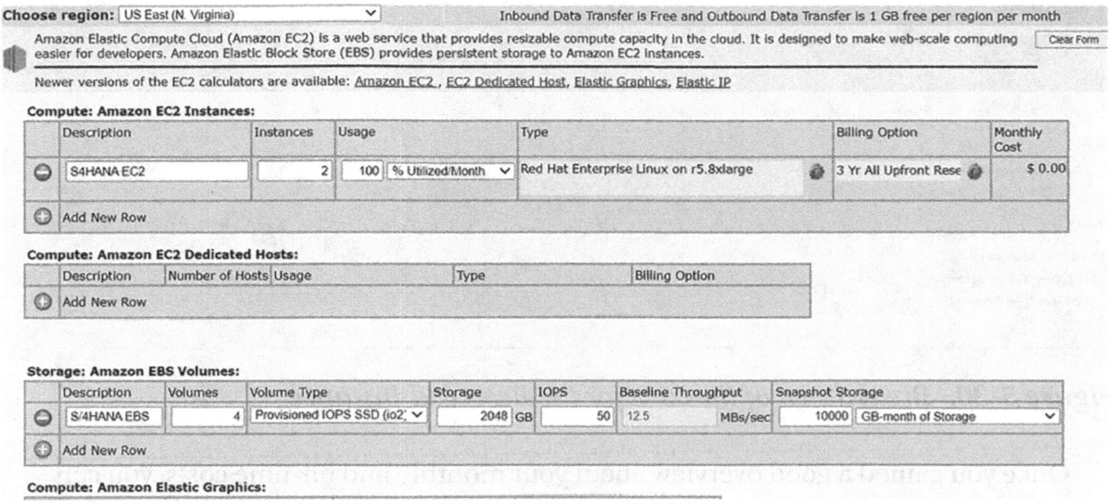

Figure 5-29. *AWS calculator - step 4*

Reserved Instance Cost

In order to understand the costs for a Reserved Instance, you will need to switch to the tab "Estimate of your Monthly Bill" to see the breakdown of the costs. This is shown in Figure 5-30, where the total on-time cost of $50,150 is shown plus the monthly cost of $3340.

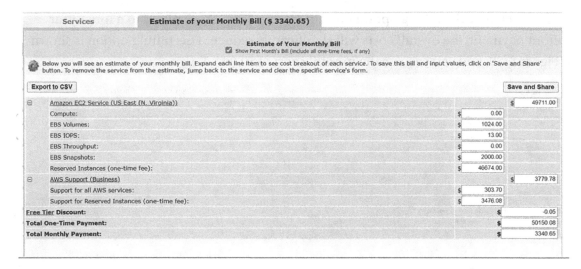

Figure 5-30. *Breakdown of the costs for the Reserved Instance*

Once you gained a good overview about your monthly and on-time costs, you can switch back to the main tab Services to review your input as shown in Figure 5-31.

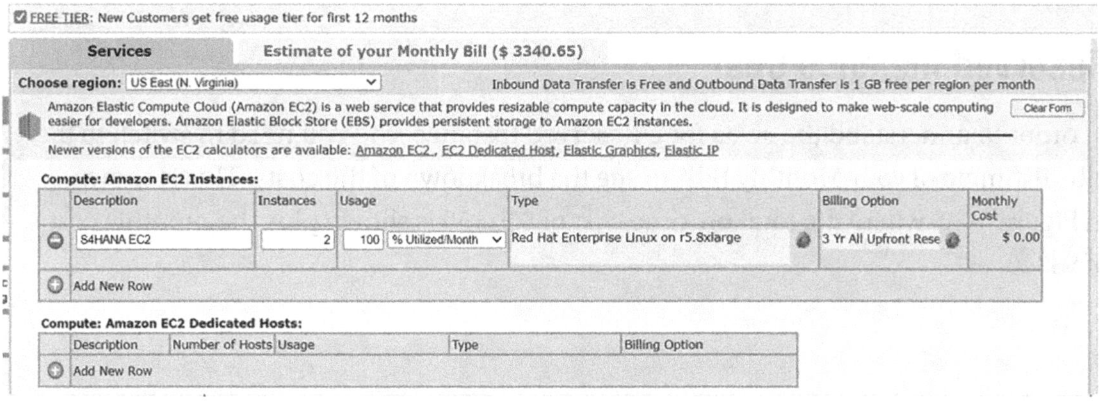

Figure 5-31. *Back to the Services tab*

Security on AWS

Security is of paramount importance when you plan to host your SAP landscape in the AWS cloud. AWS promises to be one of the most secure environments and ensures protection at every layer engaged in hosting and running an SAP landscape. The security in AWS works with the Shared Security Responsibility Model:

- AWS owns the security of the cloud infrastructure.

- The customer is responsible for the security of SAP workloads deployed on AWS – for example, for application, data, identities, and connectivity.

Figure 5-32 shows the AWS Shared Security Responsibility Model for SAP systems deployed in AWS.

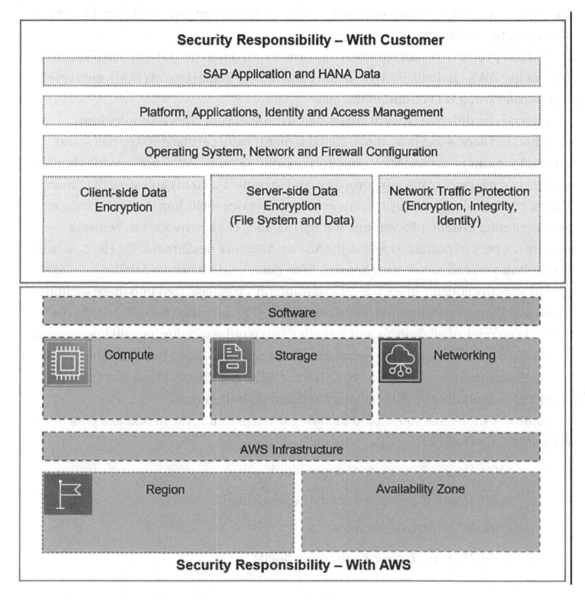

Figure 5-32. AWS Shared Security Responsibility Model

In this model, the security **of** the cloud is the responsibility of AWS, while the security **in** the cloud is the responsibility of customers. AWS takes care of the security part of the underlying infrastructure like compute, storage, global network, etc., and you are responsible for everything you deploy on the cloud like the operating system, SAP application, network, firewall setup, etc.

AWS offers a wide range of security tools for the protection of the network, configuration management, access control, and data security. And to keep track of changes, AWS provides monitoring and logging tools that can provide full visibility into what is happening in your environment.

You can protect AWS accounts and resources with different AWS-provided security features like AWS credentials, AWS Identity and Access Management (IAM), encrypted data transfer using HTTPS endpoints, etc.

You can use different types of credentials to protect your AWS resources from unauthorized access like passwords, digital signature and certificates, key pairs, and multifactor authentication (MFA). Not only account security, AWS also provides built-in security in each layer of the infrastructure, and to protect your organization data from threats, you will also get security features on each service including the EC2 instance, guest operating system, EBS volume, storage (S3, EFS, FSx), network, etc. Network security is a very important aspect in the SAP architecture design on AWS. Here, we will discuss how you can secure your network from outer world unwanted traffic.

The security concern at each layer can primarily be categorized into these sections: access and identity provisioning and protection (AIPP) and data protection (DP). And then to keep track of all controls and activities, you require monitoring and logging tools.

On top of all these sits the Governance, Risk, and Compliance to ensure that all the regulatory frameworks such as PCI, GDPR, CCPA, and HIPAA are in place and the organization is abiding by the regulatory and audit requirements.

Some questions that you should be asking when planning the access and data protection are as follows:

1. AIPP: How will the access be provided?

2. AIPP: How will unwanted access be prohibited?

3. AIPP: Who will have access?

4. AIPP: How much access will be provided?

5. DP: How will data at rest be safeguarded?

6. DP: How will data in transit be protected?

Tools

AWS along with its certified security partners provides several services and tools to protect and safeguard each layer.

Tools for Access and Identity Provisioning and Protection

AWS Identity and Access Management (IAM): The IAM service helps you create and manage an identity and its associated permission to use AWS resources. An identity can be a person, an application, an object, or a computer. Through IAM, you can ensure several authentication mechanisms for identities such as password/certificate login, multifactor authentication, and federated access with third-party solutions like Microsoft ADDS.

AWS Single Sign-On (AWS SSO): With AWS SSO, along with the directory that it offers, you can manage the access for users (groups) to AWS services. It is different from AWS IAM in its scope. With the AWS SSO service, you create the users centrally in AWS SSO and manage access to all your AWS accounts and applications. The user just needs to authenticate once with a single set of credentials configured in AWS SSO; all the connected applications can be reached with no additional credentials. This is especially useful in the case of SAP Fiori configuration.

In addition to these plans, appropriately for the operating system–level access that SAP system administrators will need to manage and maintain the systems:

- During installation, the SAP Technical Team will need administrator access (for Windows) or root access (for Linux). Ensure that access is provided using SSH keys rather than a password.

- For the sustained support phase, ensure steps to harden the operating system. You can refer to the vendor-specific guide for OS hardening details.

The OS hardening guide for SUSE Linux Enterprise Server for SAP Applications 15 can be found at the following link:

`https://documentation.suse.com/sbp/all/html/OS_Security_Hardening_Guide_for_SAP_HANA_SLES15/index.html`

The same guide for Red Hat Enterprise Linux 8 is at this link:

`https://access.redhat.com/documentation/en-us/red_hat_enterprise_linux/8/pdf/security_hardening/security-hardening.pdf`

Tools for Data Protection

Protect data at rest. AWS provides data encryption to protect all the locations where SAP data can be stored – EBS, EFS, FSx, S3. Related services offered by AWS are mentioned as follows:

> Key Management Service (KMS): This service helps in key storage, management, and related auditing. The main features of this service are

- It is tightly integrated with AWS services like EBS, EFS, S3, and SQS.

- KMS can generate a key for you, or you can upload your own key.

- The control on who can manage and who can use the keys is governed by IAM users and roles.

- The use of keys can be audited via CloudTrail.

- Compliance: PCI DSS level 1, FIPS140-2 level 2.

> Cloud HSM: Cloud HSM is a dedicated hardware device associated to one customer key management. The main features of this service are

1. It must be located within a VPC.

2. It is not as flexible as KMS in terms of integration with AWS services. You need to write custom script to integrate.

3. It has two versions – classical cloud HSM and current cloud HSM. While classical cloud HSM has upfront cost, current

cloud HSM is chargeable only for usage. Classical cloud HSM is FIPS140-2 level 2, while current cloud HSM is FIPS140-2 level 3.

AWS Secrets Manager: This service helps you manage, rotate, and retrieve the database credentials or keys for file-level encryption, thus eliminating the need to hard-code sensitive information in plain text.

Protect data in transit: The data as it flows in the network is protected through Transport Layer Security (TLS) for HTTPS or with IPsec for VPN connections.

AWS Certificate Manager: It is an AWS managed service that lets you provision, manage, and deploy public and private SSL/TLS certificates. This service is directly integrated with AWS services like EBS, CloudFront, and API Gateway. AWS itself is a CA, so you don't need to register via a third-party CA. You can upload a third-party certificate for use in AWS. AWS Certificate Manager supports a wildcard domain (*<domain_name>.com), thus covering all your subdomains, and automatically takes care of the renewal of certificates periodically.

Monitoring and Logging Tools

To keep track of all controls and activities, AWS offers several monitoring and logging tools:

- AWS CloudTrail

- AWS CloudWatch

- AWS GuardDuty

AWS CloudTrail and AWS CloudWatch have been discussed in Section 4.2. AWS GuardDuty is an intelligent threat protection tool (powered by machine learning) that continuously monitors for suspicious activity and unauthorized behavior to protect your AWS accounts, workloads, and data stored in Amazon S3. It feeds in data from various sources like VPC Flow Logs, AWS CloudTrail Event Logs, and DNS logs and does profiling of what is usual. In case of deviation, raise the alarm. This is a very suitable service to automatically monitor and alert any malicious activity for the SAP setup.

Security Event Response Mechanism

The services and tools mentioned earlier help you prevent a security event. Monitoring and logging tools help detect and alert for one. You should have a robust incident management process to respond to any reported security event in the SAP landscape. Use automation tools, wherever available, to have a swift and speedy investigation and recovery and periodically perform a simulation run for security event handling as well that way you plan for disaster recovery and your business continuity.

The next section covers the security aspects associated to Amazon Virtual Private Cloud Security (VPC) that is one of the first configurations that you need to perform as a preparation for hosting the SAP landscape in the AWS cloud.

Amazon Virtual Private Cloud Security (VPC)

To deploy any instance on AWS, you create a VPC; it's a part of the cloud foundation. A VPC provides you the isolated environment in AWS from the outer world or any other account on AWS or even from any other VPC within the same AWS account as long as you are not enabling the VPC peering. VPCs have an IP range, and you can launch S/4 EC2 instances with private IP addresses that belong to the VPC IP range. Now to provide more security, you need to create a subnet, security group, and Network Access Control List (ACL) to control inbound and outbound traffic. Figure 5-33 provides you an overview about the setup.

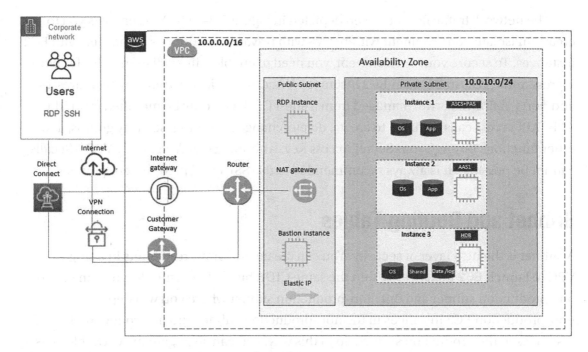

Figure 5-33. *Amazon VPC network architecture*

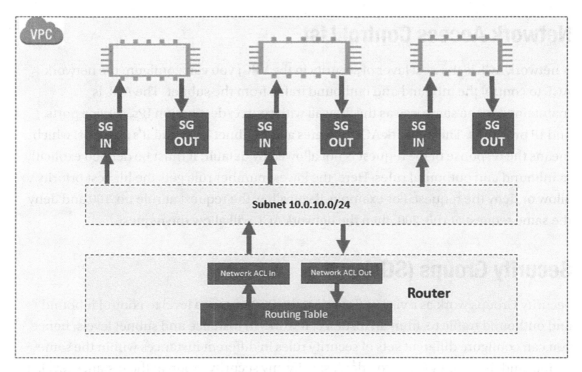

Figure 5-34. *Network security architecture*

The network traffic flow has been depicted in Figure 5-34. The VPC enables you to create an isolated environment within AWS with private IP addresses associated with EC2 instances. To secure your environment, you need to enable a firewall in the VPC for both ingress and egress traffic from EC2 instances. You can restrict the traffic by IP addresses and ports. A firewall is not managed from a guest OS; it can only be modified from VPC APIs. API access calls are used to create, delete, change in routing, security groups, and other functions through your Secret Access Key, without Secret Access Key VPC API calls cannot be possible. It is always recommended to use SSL encrypted API endpoints.

Subnet and Routing Tables

A subnet is the next layer of security. You can create one or more subnets in a single VPC to launch EC2 instances within the same CIDR block. For example, you can create one production subnet and one non-production subnet where you will deploy all non-production EC2 instances in the non-production subnet and all production EC2 instances in the production subnet. So in this way, you can segregate the CIDR block as well as you can control the traffic from/to prod and non-prod systems more granularly.

Network Access Control List

A network ACL is the next layer of security in the VPC; you can configure the network ACL to control the inbound and outbound traffic from the subnet. The ACL is maintained in the same way as the firewall with source/destination IPs, service ports, and IP protocols. The network ACL operates at the subnet level and it's stateless, which means the response of the request is not allowed by default; it must be defined explicitly in inbound and outbound rules. Here, the lowest number rule gets the highest priority to allow or deny the request. For example, if you allow the request at rule no. 100 and deny the same request at rule 200, then the network ACL will allow the request.

Security Groups (SGs)

Security Groups work as a virtual firewall at the EC2 instance level to control inbound and outbound traffic to/from an instance. It works in instance and subnet levels; hence, you can configure different sets of security rules in different instances within the same subnet and the same VPC. If you don't specify any security group at the instance level, it will use the default security group for the VPC.

A Security Group is stateful, which means if you send an outbound request, then the response of that request will get into the instance regardless of inbound rules, and for an inbound request, the response will go out regardless of the outbound rules you set in the security group. When you create an SG, by default it will come with outbound rules which allow all outbound traffic, and you can modify the outbound rules, and with no inbound rules, that means it will deny all inbound traffic. So, when you create an SG, no instances in the same subnet can communicate with each other unless you create inbound rules to allow traffic. SGs are associated with network interfaces (NICs).

Virtual Private Gateway

A virtual private gateway allows you to establish a secured connection between your Amazon VPC and other networks. You can establish a network connection to virtual private gateways from on-premises gateway devices.

Internet Gateway

An Internet Gateway is attached with a VPC and allows you to directly connect to Amazon S3, other services, and the Internet. To allow this kind of request, you need to create an Elastic IP address or NAT Gateway in a public subnet; every Internet-facing request should pass through either an Elastic IP or NAT (Network Address Translation) Gateway.

Hope now you have an idea how you can set up the network security in your SAP environment. To know more in detail, go through the following AWS network guide:

`https://docs.aws.amazon.com/vpc/latest/userguide/what-is-amazon-vpc.html`

Backup and Restore in AWS

A backup is one of the first lines of defense that you must put in place for all AWS resources critical for running the SAP landscape. AWS provides several tools as well as integration options to third-party solutions to back up your operating system and database.

Primary backup entities are

- The EC2s hosting the SAP workload.

- Backup of all the storages where SAP systems' related data is stored.

- Backup of databases operating with SAP systems.

This section summarizes the different ways of taking backups on AWS via AWS Backup, a third-party solution, and the built-in solutions for each of the databases (dump to disk).

Here, we will discuss the AWS-native backup solution which you can design for EC2 instances, file systems, and SAP HANA DB and to be stored in the S3 storage with a proper life cycle. Earlier, we used to take disk-level HANA DB and log backup via the HANA studio or HANA cockpit and then transfer the backup files to S3 via a script. Now to eliminate this operational overhead and additional storage cost for backups, AWS recently introduced its own backup solution through which you configure the HANA DB backup/recovery directly to/from the S3 storage.

SAP HANA DB Backup/Recovery via AWS Backint Agent

AWS Backint agents work in a similar way as other third-party Backint agents. You need to install the AWS Backint agent from the AWS Systems Manager console and then provide the S3 bucket details where data to be backed up, during Backint agent installation. Only S3 buckets which are created after May 2019 are compatible with the AWS Backint agent.

As of now, the AWS Backint agent only supports S3 Standard, S3 Standard IA, and S3 One Zone-IA storage classes. S3 Glacier is not supported by the Backint agent. Once you are done with the agent installation and configuration, you need to update Backint-related parameters in HANA DB (global.ini configuration file) to configure the DB and log backup from HANA studio or HANA cockpit with Backint options instead of file systems. By default, the HANA log backup is scheduled in every 15 mins, but you can adjust the frequency as per your defined RPO. Here, we have to configure the S3 life cycle to store the backup files most economically. Table 5-4 shows an indicative example of storing backups in AWS S3 as per the backup policy in different S3 storage classes in the most cost-optimized way. Plan the life cycle of backups as per the requirements on your side.

Table 5-4. *Backups and Storage Types in AWS*

Backup Type	Retention	Storage Class	S3 Life Cycle
Daily DB and log backups	14 days	S3 Standard	Delete from S3 Standard after 14 days
Weekly full backups	30 days	S3 Standard	Delete from S3 Standard after 30 days
Monthly full backups	12 months	S3 Standard IA	Backups will be moved to S3 Glacier after 30 days and will be deleted from Glacier after one year
Yearly full backups	11 years	S3 Standard IA	Backups will be moved to S3 Glacier after 30 days and will be deleted from Glacier after 11 years

In order to install and configure the AWS Backint agent for SAP, you can simply follow the AWS user guide, accessible at the following link:

```
https://docs.aws.amazon.com/sap/latest/sap-hana/aws-backint-agent-
prerequisites.html
```

EC2 Instance and EBS Volume Backup to S3

To protect your environment, you also need to take a backup of

- EC2 instance

- EBS storage

- EFS file storage

You can take a snapshot backup of EC2 instances and EBS volumes to protect your SAP system from any kind of failure. EBS volumes are backed up individually as a snapshot to S3.

An EC2 snapshot backup includes an AMI (OS configuration) and all the EBS volumes attached to it. So you can create a clone of the existing server or restore the existing server within a few minutes in case of a server crash.

One thing to remember is you cannot move the snapshot to different S3 storage classes; the snapshot is an AWS managed service, and it is always stored in the S3 Standard storage.

Now we will demonstrate how you can take EC2 and EBS snapshots.

Log in to an AWS account, and go to the EC2 dashboard where you can see all the EC2 resources deployed in your AWS region. Figure 5-35 shows you an overview about the deployed instances.

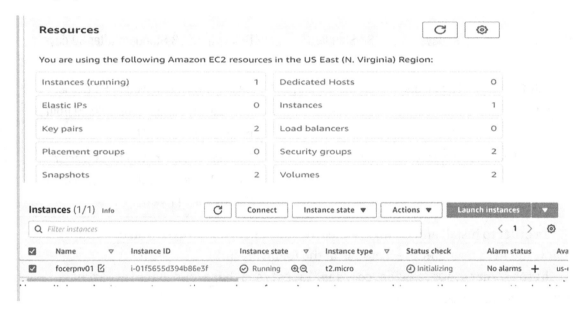

Figure 5-35. *EC2 instance and EBS volume backup to S3*

Now click Instances to see the number of running instances and to see the storage attached to EC2; click the instance ID and go to the storage option. Here, you can see one instance (focerpnv01) running with one root volume and one EBS volume. Now let's see how we can take the EBS volume and EC2 instance snapshot backup.

Snapshot Backup from AWS Console

Click the snapshot option from the EC2 dashboard and create a snapshot.

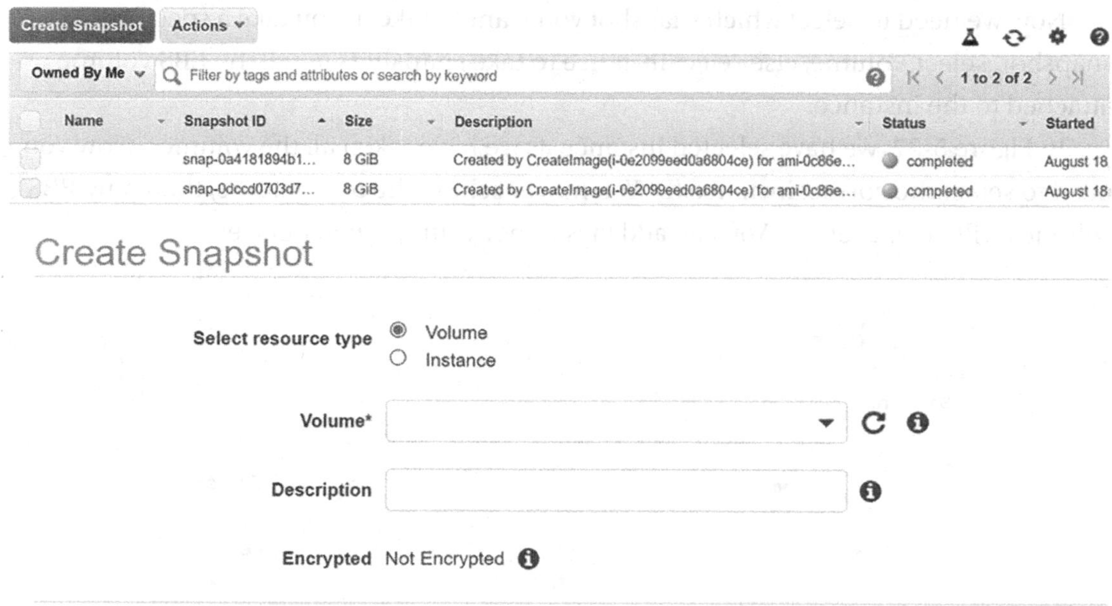

	Name	Snapshot ID	Size	Description	Status	Started
		snap-0a4181894b1...	8 GiB	Created by CreateImage(i-0e2099eed0a6804ce) for ami-0c86e...	completed	August 18
		snap-0dccd0703d7...	8 GiB	Created by CreateImage(i-0e2099eed0a6804ce) for ami-0c86e...	completed	August 18

Create Snapshot

Select resource type	⦿ Volume
	○ Instance

Volume*

Description

Encrypted   Not Encrypted

Figure 5-36. *Snapshot backup from the AWS console – step 1*

Figure 5-36 shows the start screen when creating a snapshot. You can see any snapshots created in the past in the upper half of the screen. Those have been created on August 18.

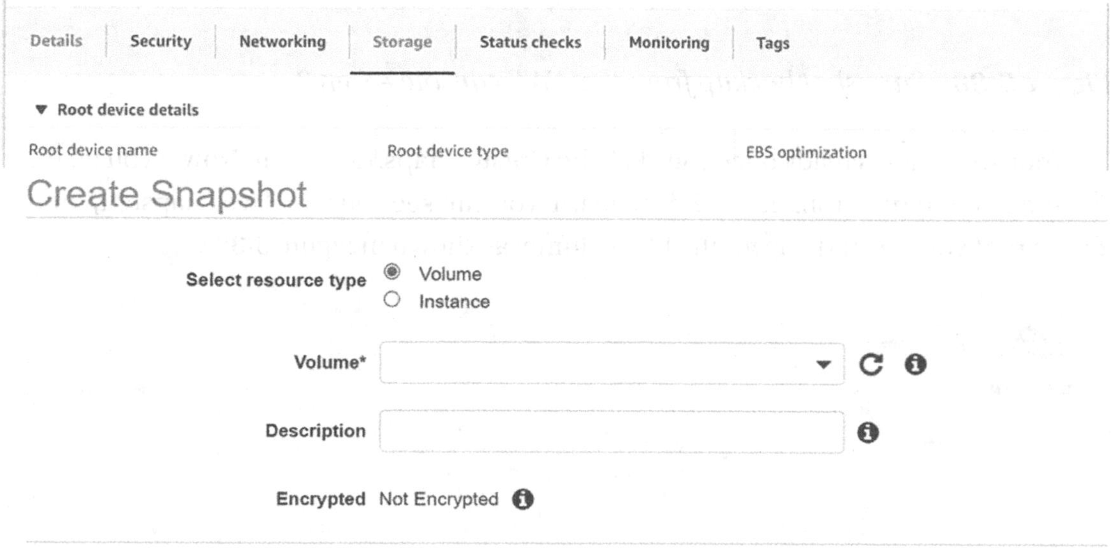

Details	Security	Networking	Storage	Status checks	Monitoring	Tags

▼ Root device details

Root device name	Root device type	EBS optimization

Create Snapshot

Select resource type	⦿ Volume
	○ Instance

Volume*

Description

Encrypted   Not Encrypted

Figure 5-37. *Snapshot backup from the AWS console – step 2*

247

Now we need to select which snapshot you want to take; if you take a specific EBS snapshot, select Volume, else select Instance to take snapshots for all the EBS volumes attached to the instance.

In Figure 5-37, we have selected Instance as we have taken all the volumes. Now you need to select the correct instance ID. You must exclude the root volume, then only EBS volumes will be backed up. You can add tags as per your defined policies.

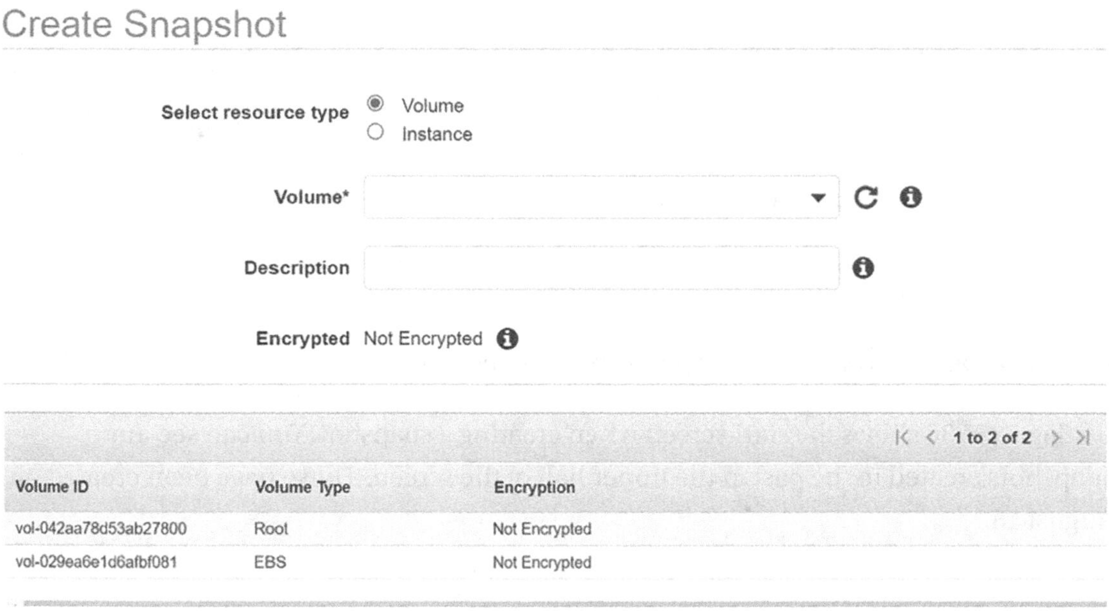

Create Snapshot

Select resource type	● Volume		
	○ Instance		
Volume*		▼ C ⓘ	
Description		ⓘ	
Encrypted	Not Encrypted ⓘ		

			1 to 2 of 2
Volume ID	**Volume Type**	**Encryption**	
vol-042aa78d53ab27800	Root	Not Encrypted	
vol-029ea6e1d6afbf081	EBS	Not Encrypted	

Figure 5-38. *Snapshot backup from the AWS console – step 3*

Your snapshot is ready once you click the Create Snapshot button. Now if you go to the Snapshot option from the EC2 dashboard, you can see your two "testsnapshot," one for the root volume and one for the EBS volume, as shown in Figure 5-38.

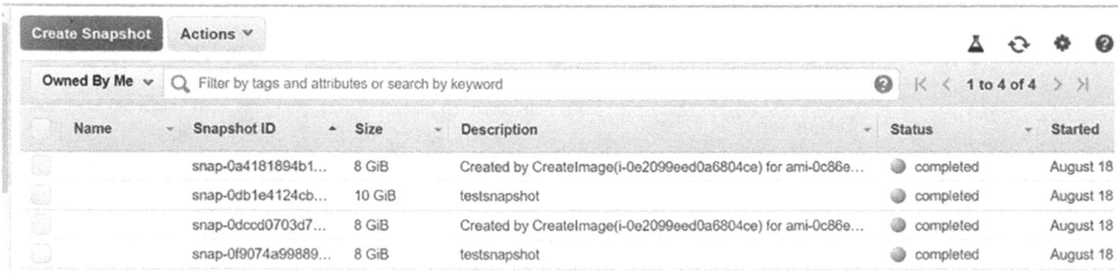

Name	**Snapshot ID**	**Size**	**Description**	**Status**	**Started**
	snap-0a4181894b1...	8 GiB	Created by CreateImage(i-0e2099eed0a6804ce) for ami-0c86e...	● completed	August 18
	snap-0db1e4124cb...	10 GiB	testsnapshot	● completed	August 18
	snap-0dccd0703d7...	8 GiB	Created by CreateImage(i-0e2099eed0a6804ce) for ami-0c86e...	● completed	August 18
	snap-0f9074a99889...	8 GiB	testsnapshot	● completed	August 18

Figure 5-39. *Snapshot backup from the AWS console – step 4*

Once you return back to the overview page, you will see the additional snapshots, which have been created on top of the already existing ones. This is shown in Figure 5-39.

EC2 Image Backup

Select the instance, for which an image shall be created. Go to Actions ➤ Image and templates ➤ Create image, enter the details like the image name and other required details, then click the Create image button as shown in Figure 5-40.

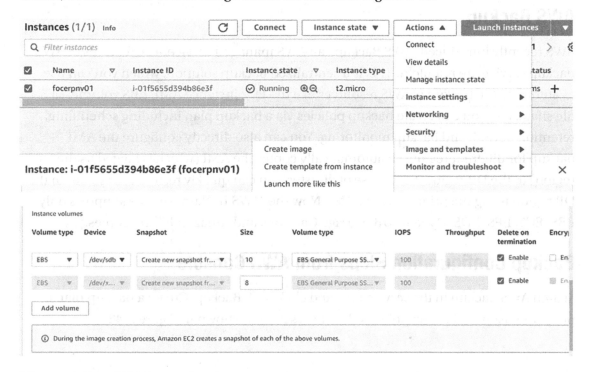

Figure 5-40. *EC2 image backup – step 1*

Now you can see the instance image in Images ➤ AMIs as shown in Figure 5-41.

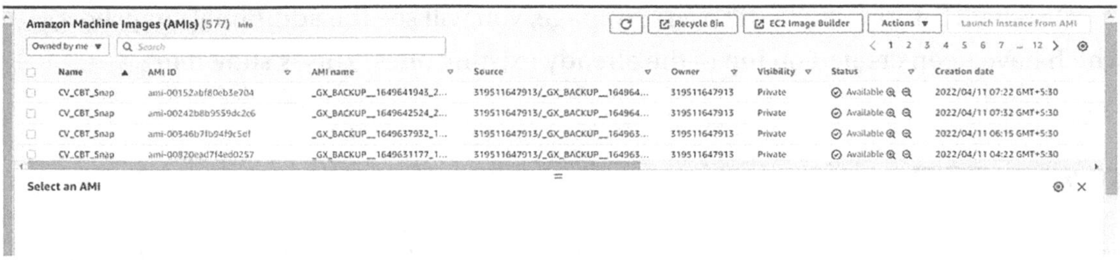

Figure 5-41. *EC2 image backup – step 2*

AWS Backup

AWS recently introduced "AWS Backup," an AWS managed service. The features of AWS backup service are manifold. This is a centralized backup solution, which you can use to automate the backup of AWS resources like the EC2 instance AMI, EBS volume, EFS file share, etc. You can create backup policies via a backup plan including scheduling, retention period, and backup monitoring. You can also directly configure the AMI backup for different regions; it automatically copies the AMI (which is tagged as the DR region) to the DR region. So, in case of disaster, you can quickly restore the system in the DR region using the primary server AMI. Now the "AWS Backup" service supports only EBS, EC2, EFS, RDS, DynamoDB, Storage Gateway, and Amazon FSx resources.

Backup Configuration Steps from AWS Console

Search AWS backup in the service area and click AWS Backup. Create a backup plan as per your customer backup policies. The start screen is shown in Figure 5-42.

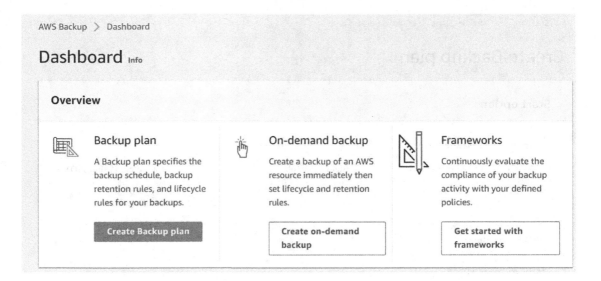

Figure 5-42. *AWS Backup plan – step 1*

Once you start creating the backup plan, you can either start from a template base of build a new plan or you use an existing JSON expression for building the plan as shown in Figure 5-43. In this example, we will go ahead and build a new plan from scratch.

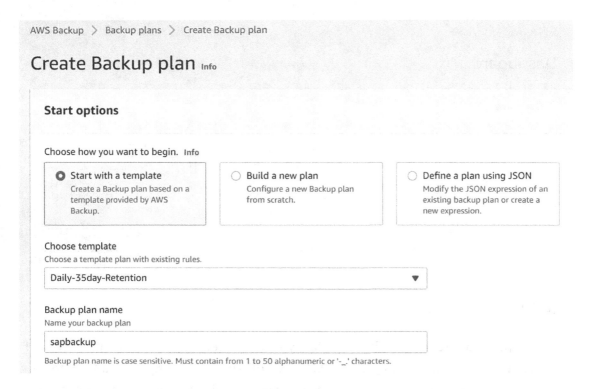

Figure 5-43. *Build a new backup plan*

▼ Tags added to backup plan

Key

🔍 sap ✕

Value - *optional*

🔍 erp ✕   Remove

Add new tag

You can add up to 49 more tags.

Backup rules Info   Add Backup rule   Delete   Edit

Backup rules specify the backup schedule, backup window, and lifecycle rules.

	Name	Backup vault
⦿	DailyBackups	Default

Figure 5-44. *Define the values for the backup plan*

Figure 5-44 shows you the details, which you will need to define for the new backup plan. This includes some important values, like the frequency, but it also includes some values for the movement of backups to cold storage to reduce some costs. This depends on the backup policy of your company or your customer.

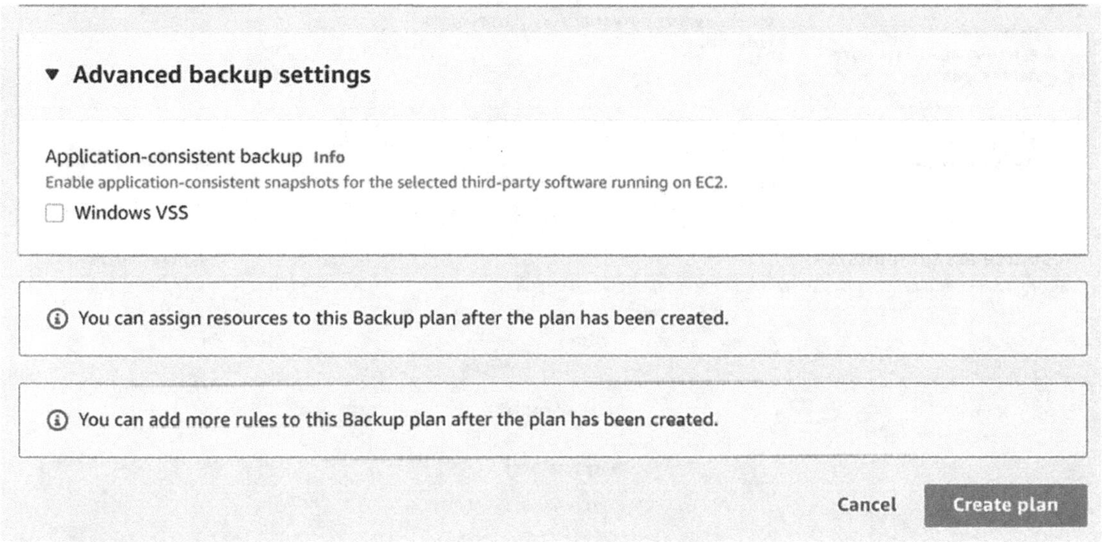

Figure 5-45. *Create the plan*

Click Create plan, and your backup plan is ready (see Figure 5-45); now you need to assign the resources to be backed up. You can assign resources in two ways: via Tags or Resource ID. If you select Tag, then all the resources with the same tag will be included in your policy, and if you select Resource ID, then you have assigned resources to be included in the backup plan. Here in this example, I have selected Resource ID.

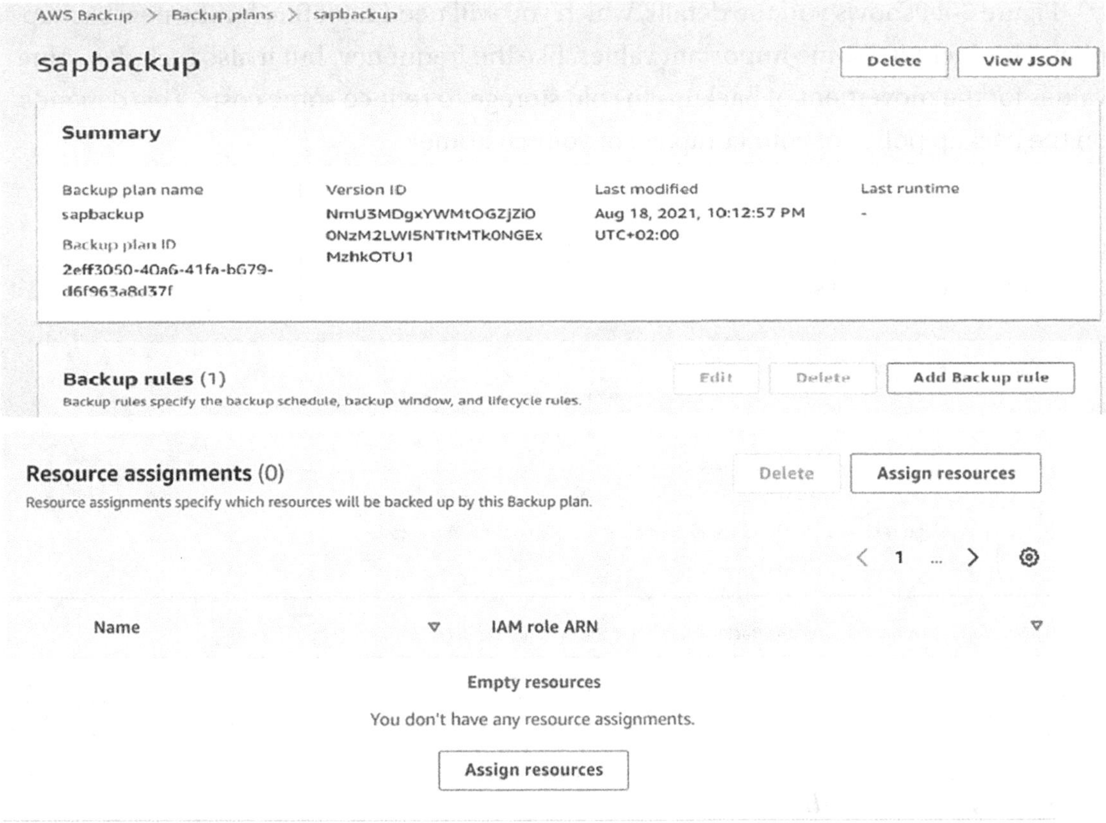

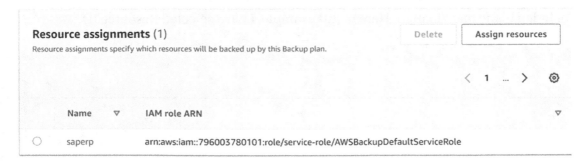

Figure 5-46. *Assign resources to the backup plan*

To select a resource and assign it to the backup plan, click the button "Assign resources," and it will bring you to the next screen as shown in Figure 5-47.

Figure 5-47. *AWS Backup plan – step 6*

Now you can see this resource in your backup plan, which will be backed up and retained as per the policy you set. Create an AWS account to explore all the options as much as you can.

Restore Snapshot from AWS Console

You need to test the restore process for a noncritical environment at least once in a quarter to check if you meet your RPO/RTO. You can restore EC2 instances including all the configurations of your source system, or you can restore only the EBS volume and mount it to any EC2 instance. Here, we will show you how you can restore an EC2 instance AMI.

As shown in Figure 5-48, go to AMIs ➤ Images; here, you have all the images taken into your AWS region. Select the AMI to be restored and launch it.

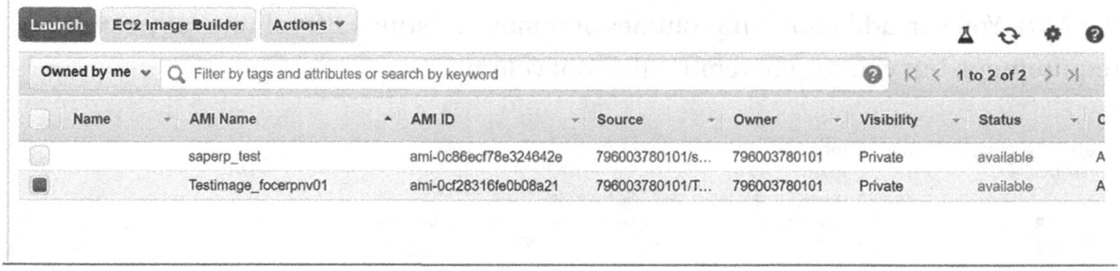

Figure 5-48. *Restore snapshot from the AWS console – step 1*

Select a target instance type, here we have selected t2.micro, and complete the launch wizard with all the details, then review and launch the instance.

Figure 5-49. *Restore snapshot from the AWS console – step 2*

In Figure 5-49, you can see one root and one EBS volume which were included in the AMI. You can add more EBS volumes or remove existing EBS volumes as per your requirement, but you cannot remove the root volume.

Figure 5-50. *Restore snapshot from the AWS console – step 3*

You should have the key pair to log in to the instance after launch. In Figure 5-50, we choose an existing key pair as we already have it. You select the "create key pair" option to launch the instance first time.

Now your new EC2 instance is ready with the image of the existing instance. This is the basic backup-restore process you can do from the AWS console. You can do this from the AWS CLI and automate this process. You just create an AWS account and explore the options as much as you can.

Disaster Recovery via AWS

The reader will learn about the possibilities to implement a proper DR solution based on AWS mechanisms or database-based DR mechanisms. This section will also help in determining the RTO/RPO per solution.

Disaster recovery is a very important aspect in SAP environments and for business continuity. In AWS, you can plan and design your DR solutions for production workloads in a single region with multiple availability zones or in different regions as per customer requirements. Here, we will show you how you can design different types of DR solutions based on a defined RPO (Recovery Point Objective) and RTO (Recovery Time Objective).

Passive DR Architecture – RPO Is More Than Zero and RTO Is Higher

This is the most cost-effective DR solution where you don't need to set up an SAP DR environment in advance; hence, there will not be any running cost for EC2 instances and storage. In the architecture shown in Figure 5-51, you can see how we can achieve passive DR in cross-regions.

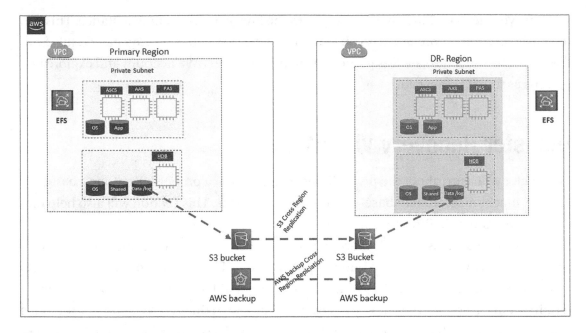

Figure 5-51. *Passive DR solution*

It's very easy and simple to deploy SAP systems in other regions in case of a disaster in the primary region. To do this, you have to configure a backup of DB, EC2 instances, and EFS storage if it's in use.

Steps to Configure the Passive DR

- Configure the HANA DB data and log backup via the AWS Backint agent or any third-party backup tool and store the backup to an S3 storage.

- Enable S3 Cross-Region Replication (CRR).

- Create a backup plan and configure an AWS backup for EC2 instance AMIs (S/4 and HANA DB AMI) and EFS storage.

- The AWS backup will replicate the AMI to the DR region.

Steps to Invoke Passive DR

- Restore the S/4 application and HANA DB server from the AMI backed up through the AWS backup.

- Restore and recover the HANA database from the S3 backup.

- Mount the EFS file system copied to the DR region.

- Start the HANA DB and S/4 application.

If you configure DR in the same region but different availability zones, then Cross-Region Replication and AWS backup need not be configured.

Semi-active DR Solution [RPO Is Near to Zero and RTO Is Medium]

You can go with this DR solution where you need

- RPO is defined near to zero, and RTO is medium.

- Cost-optimized DR solution.

Here, you need to deploy the HANA DB system in the DR region with smaller sizing than primary. Your DR HANA DB server memory sizing would be minimum DB row store table size + 60 GB. You have to configure the HANA System Replication with asynchronous replication mode and log-replay or delta-replay operation mode to replicate the data from the primary to the DR site continuously. As here we are going with the smaller DB DR server compute size to minimize the running DR cost, the preload table option must be turned off during the HSR configuration between primary and secondary:

```
global.ini/[system_replication]-> preload_column_tables=false
```

You need to configure the AWS backup for S/4 application EC2 instance AMIs and EFS storage to restore the SAP application in the DR region. The architecture is shown in Figure 5-52.

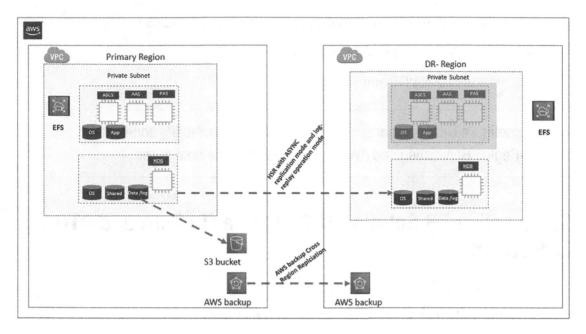

Figure 5-52. *Semi-active DR solution*

Steps to Configure the Semi-active DR

You will need to perform the following steps to create a semi-active DR solution for your SAP system:

- Estimate the DR DB server sizing (row store table size + 60 GB). A minimum of 64 GB memory is required to install HANA DB.

- Calculate the row store size: Select host, round (sum(page_size*USED_BLOCK_COUNT)/1024/1024/1024,2) as "RowStore Size GB" from m_data_volume_page_statistics where page_sizeclass = '16k-RowStore' group by host. Provision the HANA DB VM and install HANA software.

- Configure HANA System Replication with asynchronous replication mode and log-replay operation mode.

- Turn off the preload table option.

- Configure the AWS backup for SAP S/4 instances and EFS storage.

Steps to Invoke DR

In order to invoke the failover in case of a disaster, you will need to perform the following steps:

- Perform a HANA takeover in the DR site.

- Stop the DR HANA database.

- Resize the HANA VM the same as the primary server.

- Start the HANA database.

- Restore SAP S/4 application instances from the AMI backed up in the AWS backup.

- Mount the EFS file system to application servers.

- Start the S/4 application.

If you configure the DR in the same region but different availability zones, you can use a quality server as the DR server to reduce the cost. In case of a disaster, stop the quality system and resize the VM to invoke the DR. No need to configure the AWS backup in the same region.

Active-Active DR Solution [RPO Near to Zero and RTO Is Very Less]

You can go with this DR solution if your requirements meet the following conditions:

- RPO is near to zero, and RTO is very less.

- The DR environment should be in an operating state within a couple of hours.

- This is the most expensive DR solution.

The active-active DR design is the same as semi-active DR; the only difference is here we will provision the HANA DB server the same as the primary one.

Steps to Configure the Active DR

For creating the active DR for your SAP system, you will need to perform the following steps:

- Provision the HANA DB server in the DR region with the same compute and storage as the primary.

- Install HANA DB software.

- Configure HANA System Replication with asynchronous replication mode and log-replay operation mode while enabling the preload option.

- Configure the AWS backup for SAP S/4 application EC2 AMIs for the DR region.

- Configure the AWS backup of the EFS storage for the DR region so that you can mount the same file systems to DR servers.

Steps to Invoke DR

After configuring the DR, you may invoke it as follows:

- Perform a HANA DB takeover.

- Restore SAP S/4 application EC2 instances from AMIs backed up through the AWS backup.

- Mount EFS file systems to DR servers.

- Start the SAP S/4 application.

A DNS update is a mandatory step once you invoke the DR environment in case of a disaster. Your SAP S/4 application server hostname or alias must be the same as the primary server, but the IP would be different. So once your traffic switched to DR servers, you need to just replace the primary server IP with the DR server IP address in the DNS server. So, there are no changes required from the end user and interface perspective in case of an actual disaster.

You can achieve zero RPO and very less RTO if you configure the DR environment in the same region with different availability zones to configure HANA System Replication with synchronous replication mode and log-replay operation mode.

SAP HANA HSR Setup Guide

For setting up the HANA System Replication, there is a comprehensive user guide available from SAP. You can access it at the following link:

```
https://help.sap.com/doc/c81e9406d08046c0a118c8bef71f6bdc/2.0.04/en-US/
SAP_HANA_System_Replication_Guide_en.pdf
```

Summary

Now you have an idea on how to place an SAP S/4HANA system on the AWS public cloud. Here, we will conclude this chapter with AWS core components required to deploy SAP S/4HANA systems on AWS.

Cloud Foundation Design and Implementation

First, you need to assess and design the cloud framework on which your SAP system will be deployed, like as follows:

AWS region: Finalize AWS primary and secondary regions.

Network design: Finalize the network design including

- On-premise to AWS connectivity (site-to-site VPN, Direct Connect)

- Subscription design (Hub ➤ Spoke)

- VPC

- Subnet design

- Resource group policy

- Tagging policy

Security design: Security plays an important role in the public cloud. You need to take proper security measures to protect your SAP system from unknown threats and vulnerabilities:

- IAM service

- OS hardening

- Security group

- Network Access Control List
- Routing table

Once you finalize the design, build the cloud foundation for SAP deployment.

SAP S/4 Architecture Design and Implementation

Assess and understand the customer requirement and design your S/4 architecture on AWS accordingly. It should be a cost-optimized architecture which fulfills customer requirements as well.

Self-healing or default deployment: If no HA DR is required, standard deployment will be on AWS EC2 instance. This is called a single-AZ and single-node architecture.

HANA scale-out deployment: If you have a HANA scale-out environment, then you have to go with single-AZ and multinode deployment. You can add a standby node if you need a HANA HA environment without implementing any additional tool (like Pacemaker).

S/4HANA HA deployment: Here, you need to deploy your S/4 application and HANA DB in multi-availability zones with Overlay IP using Transit Gateway or Network Load Balancer and Pacemaker or the WSFC cluster solution to configure the S/4HANA application–level high availability.

S/4HANA HA and DR deployment: This is an expensive one. Here, you need to deploy S/4HANA in multi-availability zones for HA and different regions for DR server deployment. You can use DR in multi-availability zones as well to optimize the cost. It's totally based on customer requirements.

To minimize the cost, you can also use your QA server as an environment. In this case, you need to deploy your QA in different AZs than production, deploy production HANA DB in a QA environment, and configure async replication with a production system. In case of a disaster, stop the QA system and start HANA DB. (Resize your EC2 instance type if required.)

Now to implement the SAP S/4HANA architecture, you need to go with the following components:

Compute: Based on the sizing, select the right and SAP-certified EC2 instance type.

Storage: Select the AWS standard disk and storage layout for S/4HANA. This is a very important thing because disk throughput depends on the storage configuration.

PAYG or Reserved Instance: Based on the usage, you need to go with PAYG or Reserved Instance. You should always use a reserved instance if it's being used for 24*7 throughout the year. It is always recommended to use with a PAYG model and, after a couple of months' observation, reserve the right instance type for your application.

Backup and restore: A backup is an important aspect as customers have to adhere to several data compliance policies. First, you need to finalize the backup-restore policies with customers during the design phase.

Configure an AWS VM backup and a disk snapshot for instances and file systems and use AWS HANA backup tools to configure the HANA database and log backup as per the defined and agreed backup policies.

## CHAPTER 6

SAP S/4HANA on Microsoft Azure – Concepts and Architecture

This chapter provides an introduction to the basic concepts and functionality of Microsoft Azure Cloud. The aim of the chapter is to provide a detailed introduction to cloud hosting and, in particular, to create a theoretical understanding of the various components and terminology. It thus forms the basis for the practical implementation of the exemplary system architecture in Chapter 7. After a brief introduction to the history of Microsoft Azure, the governance structures are first explained, which enable the mapping of complex corporate structures such as responsibilities and approval processes in Azure. Aspects that are illuminated here concern account management by means of subscriptions and management groups, as well as role concepts and quotas. Finally, the main part of the chapter deals with the actual resource management. For this purpose, all terminologies and provisioning options relevant for SAP hosting are explained. The focus here is on provisioning using virtual computers; alternative offerings such as Hana Large Instances are also briefly addressed. Finally, the chapter concludes with a presentation of an S/4HANA reference architecture presented on the official Microsoft documentation. In particular, the interaction of the components described at the beginning of this chapter is discussed.

© André Bögelsack, Utpal Chakraborty, Dhiraj Kumar, Johannes Rank, Jessica Tischbierek, Elena Wolz 2022
A. Bögelsack et al., *SAP S/4HANA Systems in Hyperscaler Clouds*, https://doi.org/10.1007/978-1-4842-8158-1_6

Historical Overview of Microsoft Azure

Microsoft entered the cloud market several decades ago when the significant impact that the public cloud would have become apparent. Soon, Microsoft set the pace together with AWS. This section paints a picture of the history of Azure and the close collaboration between Microsoft and SAP in hosting SAP systems.

Microsoft Azure launched in the cloud market in 2010 and has been continuously expanding the service offering of the cloud platform since then. Even though the Azure Cloud platform is offered by Microsoft, it is also possible to use Linux servers in addition to Windows servers. Products are offered in the areas of Infrastructure-as-a-Service, Platform-as-a-Service, and Software-as-a-Service. This offers great flexibility in the choice of operating system: SUSE, Debian, Ubuntu, and Windows. There is also a wide range of options for implementing applications from well-known manufacturers, as a large selection of applications from SAP, Oracle, and IBM can be implemented in Azure. Due to the high number of data centers, which are located worldwide, high performance can be offered through short latency times. At the same time, customers have the option to select in which data center resources are obtained. This means that strict data protection requirements can also be met. In addition, it is possible to operate a hybrid cloud, whereby only few applications are operated in Microsoft Azure being integrated into the system landscape of the customer. Figure 6-1 shows an overview of the services offered for the respective areas.

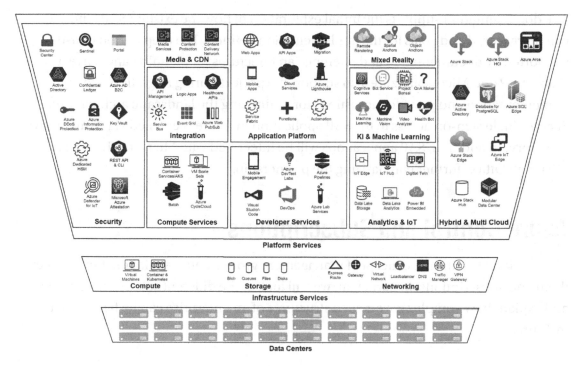

Figure 6-1. *Microsoft Azure product portfolio*

SAP and Microsoft have had a proven partnership for 25 years. In January 2021, Microsoft Azure and SAP announced an even closer cooperation, particularly with regard to the introduction and use of S/4HANA in the cloud. Along with this, Azure became a certified cloud platform provider for SAP applications. The following SAP solutions can be deployed in Azure: SAP HANA, SAP S/4HANA, SAP BW/4HANA, SAP Business Suite, SAP HEC, SAP Business One, SAP Hybris, SAP Cloud Platform. Microsoft Azure can differentiate itself from other cloud providers primarily because of its deployment options in relation to SAP HANA. Here, Microsoft Azure can offer bare-metal hardware, which is why even high resource requirements of up to 24–120 TB of RAM can be covered. Overall, SAP applications can be run in Microsoft Azure as part of development, test, and production scenarios with full support. Azure customers thus gain the ability to migrate SAP legacy infrastructures to Azure with full certification. This made new cloud automation options as well as the simplification of the migration of on-premise structures to the Azure Cloud possible. Provided reference architectures as well as detailed documentation support the customer's plan to migrate to the Azure Cloud. The migration of SAP systems to Microsoft Azure can be broken down into five steps: initial exploration, preparation, migration, operation, and innovation.

The documentation supports the initial exploration of how the existing SAP landscape can be captured and goals for the implementation defined. The preparation phase is supported by documentation and reference architectures for planning and correct sizing. SAP and Microsoft Azure also support the project during migration and implementation and provide suggestions for optimizing the landscape architecture. Secure single sign-on access to the SAP application in Azure is enabled via Azure Active Directory. In addition, SAP applications will be integrated with Microsoft Teams and Microsoft Office, further emphasizing the partnership.

Azure Control and Subscriptions

This section explains the concept of management groups and the relationship between them and subscriptions. In particular, we will look at the different subscription models and explain how complex governance structures of an enterprise can be figured out in Azure.

Azure Organizational Structure

The Azure organizational structure has a total of four levels, as shown in Figure 6-2: management groups, subscriptions, resource groups, and resources.

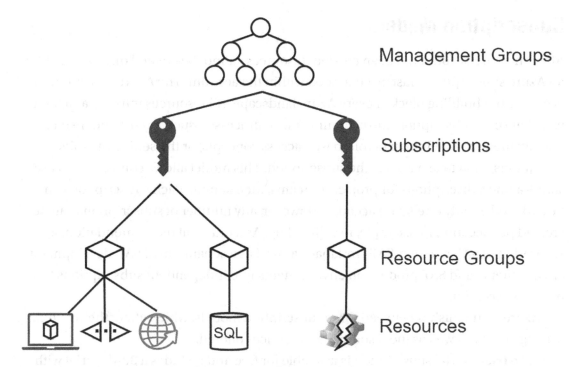

Management Groups

Subscriptions

Resource Groups

Resources

Figure 6-2. *Organizational structure of Microsoft Azure*

Essentially, subscriptions define the user concept, as well as limits and quotas for the resources they contain. In this way, companies can create a logical separation for different business units or projects, for example. A management group is superordinate to the subscriptions and offers the possibility to group them. Some concepts that can be defined at the subscription level, such as role-based access control (RBAC) permissions or Azure Policies, can also be defined at the management group level. In this way, universally valid policies and accesses can be defined, which are automatically inherited by all subordinate subscriptions. It should be noted that even the owner of the subscription cannot override policies defined at the management group level. By creating multiple management groups and subordinate subscriptions, the organizational structure can be mapped, for example, by defining a management group for each department. It can also be used to establish fine-grained cost reporting. Endpoints of the hierarchy are the actual **resources**, which are all services that can be booked: virtual machines, storage, or virtual networks. For simplified management, these are assigned to **resource groups**. This is a container object defined by the customer, which groups all "related" resources. Generally, all resources that are required for a service and/or are subject to the same software life cycle should be added to the same resource group. The concept of subscriptions is described in more detail as follows.

Subscription Models

After an Azure account has been created, resources cannot be created directly. First, an Azure subscription must be generated within the account. The Azure subscription is the central building block of every Azure landscape. All resources must be assigned to exactly one subscription. Most administrative processes, such as cost and invoice management, the definition of role-based access concepts, or the setting of limits and quotas, then take place via the subscription. This model allows companies to use stand-alone subscriptions for projects or teams, for example. Each subscription can be assigned to only one Azure account. However, any number of subscriptions can be created per account, for example, to split billing. As a practical recommendation, a separation of SAP and non-SAP workloads as well as a separation of SAP development environments and SAP production environments into independent subscriptions has proven successful.

Azure distinguishes between three subscription models, which affect the cost billing/ pricing policy, as well as the resources and services offered:

Free trial: A trial subscription is available for free and includes a 30-day trial with a $200 budget (converted to local currency at the time of purchase using the current exchange rate). The free subscription is available to all customers who have not previously used Azure for a fee or have not yet purchased a trial account. A credit card must be provided as part of the registration process. This offer is primarily aimed at Azure newcomers who want to familiarize themselves with the platform and set up a sandbox environment. It should be noted that access to services and resources is also severely limited. Currently, for example, the free trial does not support instances with more than 32 GB of RAM, which means that a HANA Express installation is possible at best. The free subscription can be converted to a usage-based model (PAYG) at any time (upgrade). Regardless of the upgrade, the remaining trial budget always expires after 30 days at the latest.

Pay-as-you-go (PAYG): In the PAYG model, costs for Azure services and resources are incurred on a usage basis and are billed monthly. For example, virtual machines that are shut down and no longer allocated do not incur active "computing costs." However, it should be noted that some services, such as a firewall, or resources, such as managed disks, are still maintained and therefore actively incur costs. The usage-based model also requires a credit card to be specified for standard online registration. Payment by direct debit is also generally possible, but requires a justification and a request to Azure Support. Payment by invoice is not officially supported.

Partner Offers: Microsoft offers a number of attractive offers with high discounts, which can provide cost advantages over the PAYG model. The list of all offers is continuously updated and can be viewed at any time at the following site: `https://azure.microsoft.com/de-de/support/legal/offer-details/`. As with the free trial, offers may come with restrictions on the resources and services that can be booked.

Subscription Management

In the following, the basics of subscription management are taught. The concepts of authorization management are explained, which can be categorized into different administrator roles, as well as limits, budgets, and spending limits. Finally, the implementation options for policies via subscription management are described.

Authorization Management

To ensure that the organizational structure of the company can also be mapped in Azure, Microsoft offers a comprehensive authorization concept to control access to the subscriptions and their associated resources. A distinction can be made between two authorization models "administrator roles for classic subscriptions" and "Azure roles."

Administrator roles for classic subscriptions: This is the original authorization concept, which provides rudimentary control. The concept consists of only three roles. These are the account administrator, the service administrator, and any number of co-administrators (maximum 200 per subscription). With these three roles, access control is simple to implement and easy to understand, but not very flexible and thus not suitable for every company. These roles are thus primarily aimed at small organizational structures or Azure accounts used for non-production application scenarios. The roles are presented individually as follows:

- Account administrator (one per Azure account): The account administrator is the most comprehensive role. It authorizes creating new subscriptions, managing all billing, and assigning service administrator roles for each subscription. There can be only one account administrator per Azure account. The creator of the Azure account automatically becomes the account administrator.

- Service administrator (one per Azure subscription): Each subscription has exactly one service administrator who is authorized to manage the associated subscription. The service administrator has full access to the Azure portal and can manage their services, but also cancel the subscription and appoint co-administrators for the subscription. The account used to register Azure becomes both account administrator and service administrator by default. However, the account administrator can change the service administrator at any time.

- Co-administrator (200 per subscription): Co-administrators are also defined at the subscription level and have identical access rights as the service administrator. However, they cannot change the mapping of subscriptions to Azure directories. Co-administrators can appoint additional co-administrators, but cannot change the service administrator.

Role-based access control (Azure RBAC): To enable granular authorization management, Azure offers role-based access control (Azure RBAC), which is based on the Azure Resource Manager (ARM). This includes numerous "special roles" (currently more than 200) that address different resources and grant predefined permissions for these resources. A list of all roles and their contained authorizations can be found in the Microsoft Docs.[1] Independent of these granular roles, there are three basic roles that apply to all resource types:

- Owner: As an owner, one gets full access to all resources and can delegate access to other users at the same time. For example, service administrators and co-administrators (classic subscription administrator roles) get the owner role for their subscription area.

- Contributor: Contributors can also create and manage all types of Azure resources. However, they cannot further delegate this access.

- Reader: Readers are only authorized to view all Azure resources.

---

[1] https://docs.microsoft.com/en-us/azure/role-based-access-control/built-in-roles

With these basic roles, authorization management is not significantly more flexible than the classic model. Fine-granular control is only made possible by the additional use of the special roles. Furthermore, the role "user access administrator" should be mentioned. This is necessary to manage user access to Azure resources.

Limits, Budgets, and Restrictions

Azure offers numerous limits and thresholds for cost control, which are defined at the subscription level. This allows the use of correct resources as well as the costs incurred to be controlled centrally.

Azure spending limit: The spending limit is enabled for all subscription types that have credit, such as the $200 free trial subscription. The limit acts as a "hard limit" and is always identical to the respective credit balance. It cannot be increased or decreased (but it is possible to remove the limit). Once the incurred costs reach the value of the spending limit, all resources and services are stopped so that no further costs are incurred. This means that running VMs are shut down and their allocation is removed. This does not delete the VM, but it does free up the reservation on the actual hardware. In addition, access to storage accounts is now read-only. Such a "hard shutdown" strategy is not suitable for production use cases. However, spending limits cannot be enabled for regular usage-based subscriptions either.

Azure budgets: Similar to the spending limit, a budget defines a threshold for costs incurred. However, this is a "soft limit" because budgets can be freely defined and only have an alert function by default. In contrast to the expenditure limit, no automatic stop mechanisms are started when the budget is exceeded. Usually, budgets are defined in combination with cost thresholds (e.g., 80%), which send a notification as soon as the incurred costs reach the budget threshold. Using the "Azure Monitor action groups," it is also possible to orchestrate further actions that cause, for example, an orderly shutdown of certain resource groups. Step-by-step instructions for coupling thresholds with an Azure Automation runbook that automatically shuts down VMs can be found in Microsoft Docs.[2]

Resource limits and quotas: Quotas are defined at the subscription level and determine upper limits on resource usage. You can define quotas for specific SKUs such as "vCPUs of the ESv3 family," as well as for specific resource types, for example, number of virtual computers. As part of the "Review+Create" phase during provisioning, the

---

[2] https://docs.microsoft.com/en-us/azure/cost-management-billing/manage/cost-management-budget-scenario

resources you request are then matched against the quotas, and if exceeded, the request is rejected. Raising a quota is done via support request. However, you do not have to create a manual ticket for this, but only request an increase of the quota. The check by the support takes place automatically in the background.

Policies

Azure Policies are a useful tool to establish organizational standards. Especially in Azure environments with multiple teams or subscriptions, it may be necessary to define standards. These include rules on how resources can be configured and used, for example, to ensure security or to meet compliance requirements. To understand the need for Azure Policies, it is worth looking first at the traditional governance approach. The most obvious way, which is used by many customers, is to use dedicated individuals as "Azure administrators." These individuals are then responsible for the complete management of Azure, including all resources and subscriptions, as well as sole access to the Azure portal. Access to the respective resources is then provided by the administrator to the end users such as developers and administrators. In SAP On-Premise hosting, these classic divisions of responsibilities between specialist departments (e.g., Basis and Development) are very prepared and are adopted directly as the governance structure for the cloud. In this way, however, the customer loses a lot of innovation potential, since the actual user group is shielded from the services of the Azure Cloud. This is becoming increasingly important, especially in the context of cloud-native and DevOps scenarios. Policies should not be confused with authorization concepts such as RBAC. RBAC defines which users or roles have access to which resources. Policies, on the other hand, control which properties and configuration resources must have. For example, a policy can define that only VM instance type D may be provisioned. A policy always consists of a definition that describes the desired behavior (restriction to VM instance types) and a parameterization (instance D). Depending on the area to which the policy is applied, it can also be used multiple times with different parameterizations (e.g., in the subscription "SAP HANA Sandbox Systems," only instances of type M may be provisioned). Policies are defined in JSON format and use their own domain language, which is essentially based on the combination of logic operators (and, not, etc.), fields (tag, location, name), and conditions (equal, contains, exist). However, there is no need to define custom policies from scratch. Microsoft Docs offers a wide range of predefined examples for all resources. This also includes policy sets for compliance with international standards such as ISO 27001 (IT security management).

Azure Resource Management

This section explains resource management in Microsoft Azure. The various resource provisioning models and possible provisioning options are discussed. Based on this, the basics for the provision of computing power, storage, as well as network and other services are given. Finally, information on support and licensing is presented.

Resource Provisioning Using Resource Manager

For Microsoft Azure, there are two types of VM resource provisioning models: traditional provisioning and Azure Resource Manager (ARM) provisioning.

Classic vs. ARM Resource Management

Originally, resources could only be created and managed via the classic provisioning model, the so-called Azure Service Manager, whereby a grouping of resources was not possible. As a result, in this deployment model, those resources that belong to an application must be grouped together through appropriate naming or a self-created overview. This is the only way for all parties involved to manually understand the affiliation of resources for the provision of an application. In addition, resources can only be created individually via the Azure Portal. Automation of the steps can only be achieved through the development and use of scripts. The assignment of tags to different resources is only possible using the ARM, which enables better transparency of the resources used.

Since 2014, the ARM can be used, with which computing, network, and storage resources can be managed. Along with this, resource groups were introduced, which group together associated resources. The use of the Resource Manager is recommended by Microsoft, as it enables easier management and provisioning of resources.

Using the Resource Manager, you can create and manage related resources together. This makes resource provisioning much more efficient and offers the possibility of homogeneous resource creation. Furthermore, access control can be applied to all resources in a group, and dependencies between these resources can be defined. By creating an ARM template using the JavaScript Object Notation (JSON), a template can be defined for the resource infrastructure of a particular solution. The assignment of tags to resources has now been made possible for customers within the Resource Manager.

Since the introduction of ARM, all resources are mapped to standard resource groups. This is also the case for resources that have been or will be created via classic provisioning. These are then added to a default resource group of the respective service, even if no resource group was defined during creation. However, you should note that resources created via the classic deployment model are not automatically migrated to the Resource Manager model. This is not the case even if these resources are in a resource group.

In general, resources (compute, network, and storage) created via the classic provisioning model are managed under the classic model. The same applies to the creation of resources via the ARM: if resources are created via this model, they must also be managed via the Resource Manager model. The complexity of resource management increases for the case when resources are created partly via the classic provisioning model and partly via the Resource Manager. You should take this into account during implementation, as both provisioning models support different management operations. As an example, resources created via classic provisioning can be moved to other resource groups using a Resource Manager command. However, this does not mean that other ARM processes are possible with this resource.

Migration of Classic Provisioned Resources to ARM

As of February 28, 2020, Microsoft Azure has begun shutting down Azure Service Manager over a period ending March 1, 2023. It is important to note that after Azure Service Manager is shut down, all VMs created via the classic deployment model will be shut down and no longer usable. Therefore, as of February 2020, VMs can no longer be created via Azure Service Manager. As of March 1, 2023, VMs that were provisioned via Microsoft Azure Service Manager can no longer be started. Virtual instances that are still running will be terminated, and their mappings will be resolved. The planned deletion of these VMs will be communicated to users to allow users to migrate VMs to the remaining ARM deployment model. This will not affect the following services:

- Azure Cloud Services (classic): Represent Microsoft Azure Platform-as-a-Service products created via the classic deployment model

- Storage accounts that are not used by Infrastructure-as-a-Service VMs (classic delivery model)

- Virtual networks that are not used by Infrastructure-as-a-Service VMs (classic deployment model)

- Other resources (classic provisioning model)

When migrating the classically deployed VMs to Azure Resource Manager, you need to consider the following. Since the data structure is the same in Azure Service Manager and Azure Resource Manager, but the representation of the data is different in both deployment models, the data representation of the classic VMs needs to be modified during migration. This means that new APIs, SDKs, and tools are required for the migration. Therefore, you should ensure that resources you want to migrate do not contain unsupported settings and functions. By performing an audit, Microsoft Azure can detect these errors and inform you. Figure 6-3 illustrates the interaction of ARM with the tools, APIs, and SDKs provided. Due to the planned discontinuation of Azure Service Manager, this book focuses on the use of Azure Resource Manager.

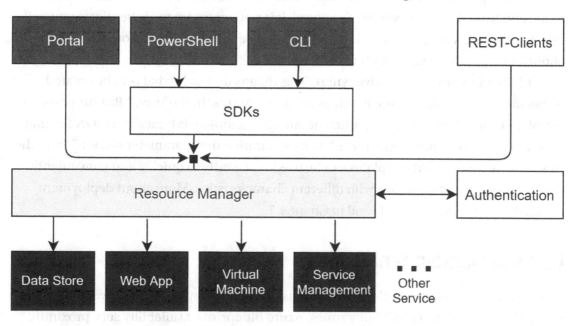

Figure 6-3.   Interaction of ARM within the environment

Provisioning with Azure Resource Manager

ARM acts as a central provisioning service to create, modify, or delete resources. It supports four APIs to accept user requests.

The **Azure Portal** is the common way to interactively manage resources via a graphical front end. Requests are submitted to the ARM using HTTP(s) as REST requests.

However, the **REST API** of the ARM can also be independently accessed directly without using the Azure Portal. For example, custom web-based automation solutions can be developed to manage the Azure landscape.

ARM also supports the **Azure PowerShell** and the **Azure CLI** as **command-line tools**. Both tools are comparable in terms of functionality, although the Azure CLI was developed as a platform-independent tool (Mac/Linux/Windows) that supports PowerShell and Windows Command Prompt as shell environments in addition to Bash. You can install the Azure CLI on Windows, Linux, and macOS. To do this, simply follow the instructions in the Microsoft Docs.[3]

Instead of installing the Azure CLI locally, for example, on a VM, Microsoft also offers the **Azure Cloud Shell**. This can either be called directly via the browser[4] or via a button in the Azure portal. In addition, the cloud shell offers both a PowerShell and a Bash representation. If you access it via the portal, it is not necessary to authenticate yourself first. However, a storage account is mandatory to use the cloud shell. You can read more about using the cloud shell in Chapter 7.

ARM works with a declarative syntax. This means that only what is to be created is specified without describing the steps required for this. In this way, ARM supports template-based deployment in particular. An ARM template is typically a JSON file that fully describes the component assembly. By separating the "parameter section" from the "resource section," ARM templates can be used repeatedly to quickly and conveniently deploy resource compositions with different characteristics. More about deployment using ARM templates can be found in Chapter 7.

General Deployment Options

The basics of the general deployment options can be broken down into several categories: regions and availability zones, Azure Blueprints, availability sets, proximity placement groups, and scale sets. These are outlined in more detail in the next sections.

---

[3] https://docs.microsoft.com/en-us/cli/azure/install-azure-cli
[4] https://shell.azure.com

Regions and Availability zones

Azure offers globally distributed data centers on all five continents. Even if the actual physical location of a service is not transparent to the customer, at least the hosting region must be specified, for example, "Europe West (Netherlands)" or "Germany North (Berlin)." This can be relevant not only for compliance reasons but also affects hosting costs, as regionally increased operating costs (e.g., electricity) are passed on to the customer. Also, certain services are not available in all regions. One of the most important constraints for SAP operations here is the option of availability zones. Availability zones are individual data centers within a region. These are characterized by independent infrastructure supply (power, network, cooling) as well as spatial separation from each other. Redundancy and high availability solutions that are replicated across several availability zones are thus protected against failures within a zone or a data center. However, not all regions have independent availability zones (e.g., "Germany, West-Central" has several availability zones, but Germany North does not). For this redundancy option, you should therefore check whether the desired region supports availability zones. A continuously updated overview of all regions can be found at `https://docs.microsoft.com/en-us/azure/availability-zones/az-region`.

Azure Blueprints

Azure Blueprints enable simple deployments by declaratively defining artifacts via a blueprint. These artifacts can include policies and role-based access restrictions in addition to ARM templates. Azure Blueprints thus do not replace existing ARM templates but rather represent an extension. The focus of the blueprints is, among other things, on the orchestration of complex deployments so that the individual processes within them can be checked and tracked. Furthermore, they enable the compilation of extensive resource configurations, which in particular facilitate the complex interaction between IT governance and IT application by encapsulating the logic for quotas, roles, and access restrictions. In this way, the central cloud architecture team can create blueprints for different roles (e.g., DEV/QAS) or different business units. Blueprints are assigned to a subscription or management group when created and are stored on it. Parameters for an artifact assigned to a blueprint can be either user specific (not defined in the blueprint) or fixed. This ensures that certain values, such as the region, cannot be overwritten.

Availability Sets

Availability sets can be used to distribute virtual machine instances across multiple hardware endpoints, increasing resilience. Hardware in a data center can be divided into update and failure domains. The update domain represents a group of machine instances that share the same hardware and can therefore be started and stopped simultaneously. Fault domains include virtual machines that share the same memory, power, and network switch. To generate high availability, it makes sense to create at least two machines in an availability set. After the virtual machine is created, the availability set cannot be changed because the distribution of hardware components does not make sense. Thus, to change the availability set, the instance must be deleted and recreated. It is important to note that when two machine instances of an availability set are deployed, they may receive the same error domain. To avoid this, the created machine instances should not be terminated or released while the other virtual machines are being created. Before the virtual machines are created, the possible VM sizes can be viewed in the availability set. The possible VM sizes depend on the hardware used in the availability set. This is possible by using the command Get-AZVMSize. It is also possible to provide availability sets within availability zones. However, this requires that additional proximity placement groups are used.

In the context of SAP, all machines within an availability set should have the same role, for example, a separate availability set for the application servers and a separate availability set for the ASCS and ERS.

Proximity Placement Group

A proximity placement group ensures that resources located within this group are provisioned in "physical proximity" to each other. This means that servers are located in the same data center, which ensures that latency between components is kept low. A typical use case scenario for proximity placement groups is to place all instances of an S/4HANA installation (PAS, ASCS, AAS), as well as the database, into one group. Proximity placement groups can also be combined with availability sets. However, since this places additional constraints on the provisioning process, it can fail more easily if the requirements cannot be met.

Scale Sets

A VM scale set is a container object for assembling multiple virtual machines in combination with a scaling policy, load balancing, and various automation features. Based on a fixed initial number of instances, the group can be scaled up to meet higher load requirements. The scale set distinguishes between the scaling policy "manual," where the scaling is done manually by the user, and "user defined" which allows an autoscaling based on a metric. This way, a CPU threshold, for example, 90%, can be set in combination with a time duration, for example, 15 minutes (allowed values are 5–60 minutes). Once the threshold is maintained within the specified time duration, a defined number of virtual machines are added to the scale set, and a maximum number of instances can be defined. A metric for scaling down can also be set in an identical manner. The scale set itself is free of charge, only the provisioning of the virtual instances is charged. Note that instead of a "scale set," you can also manually group multiple VMs and implement scale-out architectures using other components such as load balancing. The strength of the scale set lies in its focus on unified automation such as continuous delivery pipelines. For this reason, the scale set is also more suitable for container-based workloads and less for "hand-maintained" VMs such as those often used in SAP systems.

Computing

This section covers possible sizing options and the available machine types for HANA and non-HANA systems. Since machine types change frequently, this section focuses on VM template classes rather than specific machines. There are several aspects to consider when deploying a VM to run SAP software. Ultimately, all prerequisites for installing SAP software on VM instances in Microsoft Azure must be met to ensure smooth use of the software components. These prerequisites and aspects are described in more detail as follows.

Deployment Models

In general, there are various options for deploying S/4HANA systems in Microsoft Azure. The following subsections describe the deployments via Azure VMs, via Azure Large Instances, and via the SAP Cloud Appliance Library (CAL) in more detail.

Azure VMs

Traditionally, you can use virtual machine instances to implement SAP software in Microsoft Azure. These provide the necessary resources to run the corresponding applications, whereby some Azure tools can additionally be used to enable high availability and scalability. The computer instances can be created and managed via the classic provisioning model or via the Resource Manager. However, there are restrictions regarding the operating system and database system used. In addition, not all system architectures that are supported on-premise can also be implemented in Azure. Table 6-1 provides an overview for unsupported SAP system architectures in Azure. In order to build such system architectures in Azure, a third-party provider is required.

The use of Azure Site Recovery to replicate the virtual instances of the database layer has not yet been tested, so no empirical values exist in this regard.

Table 6-1. *Nonsupported System Architectures*

Scenario	Notes
Storage Software Appliance	Various software appliances are offered in Azure. Support for deployments related to SAP software must be ensured by the third-party vendor (see also SAP Note 2015553)
High Availability Frameworks	Only Pacemaker and Windows Server failover clusters are supported for SAP systems in Azure. Other products, such as DataKeeper from SIOS, must be supported by the respective provider
Cluster with shared disks for database files	Only MaxDB is supported in this scenario. For other databases, only separate storage locations can be used to achieve a high availability scenario supported by Azure

(continued)

Table 6-1. (*continued*)

Scenario	Notes
Scenarios in which there is large network latency between the SAP application layer and the SAP DBMS layer	Examples include • Deploying an S/4HANA system with one of the tiers deployed on-premise and the other tier deployed in Azure • Deploying the application tier and database tier of a system in different regions in Azure • Provisioning virtual network appliances between the application and database tiers • Storage usage for the database or transport directory provisioned in data centers used in parallel with Azure Using two different cloud providers to deploy the application and database tiers
HANA Pacemaker cluster	HANA Pacemaker cluster with multiple instances
Windows cluster	Windows cluster with shared volumes via Azure NetApp Files for supported SAP databases in Windows. It is better to use high availability replication of the databases
SAP databases on Linux with NFS shares	SAP databases with NFS shares in addition to Azure NetApp Files. This does not apply to SAP HANA, Oracle on Oracle Linux, and Db2 on SUSE and Red Hat
Oracle DB neither on Windows nor on Oracle Linux	Implementation of Oracle databases on an operating system other than Windows or Oracle Linux. See also SAP Note 2039619

To deploy a virtual machine instance, several components are required. Table 6-2 gives you an overview of these components.

Table 6-2. *Required Components for Virtual Computer Instances in Microsoft Azure*

Component	Description
Virtual network	The virtual network is made available via the Resource Manager
Storage account	Based on the storage account, the volumes can be backed up for the long term in the BLOB storage
Availability sets	Availability sets distribute the created virtual machines to different hardware endpoints, thus reducing the vulnerability to failures
Load balancer	Load balancing can be enabled via the Azure Load Balancer. The load balancer distributes the incoming data traffic to the virtual machines
Virtual IP address	It is possible to define the public IP address statically or dynamically, and dynamic IP addresses can be provided with a load balancing module. Security groups can be used to protect public IP addresses
DNS name	DNS names can be defined for public IP addresses. The FQDN is <domainlabel>.<region>.cloudapp.azure.com
Network interfaces	Network interfaces reference the IP address of the assigned VM, the subnet of the VM's virtual network, and optionally the VM's network security group

Azure Large Instances for SAP HANA

In addition to using VMs to deploy SAP software, Azure also offers a dedicated offering called "Azure Large Instances (HLI)." In this tailored data center integration (TDI) approach certified for HANA, the customer can deploy an SAP HANA on a bare-metal server. The sizes and sizings provided by this differ from the classic VM templates and offer greater flexibility from 36 cores with 768 GB of memory (smallest unit) to 480 cores and 24 TB of memory (largest unit). In this way, it is possible to implement HANA scale-out deployments with up to 120 TB of RAM. In addition, by eliminating the virtualization layer in HLI, even higher performance is achieved than it is the case with Azure VMs. HLI SKUs typically start with the prefix S*. Since HANA memory requirements typically increase with increasing data capacity, HLI offers, similar to Azure VMs, to start with smaller instances first and switch to larger versions later. Basically, Azure differentiates HLI instances between classes I and II, with I being the entry-level class and class II being suitable for advanced scenarios.

HLI is designed exclusively for provisioning SAP HANA systems and cannot be used for other hosting. For this reason, the choice of available operating systems is also limited to SUSE Linux Enterprise and Red Hat Linux. SAP-specific details such as the SID must already be communicated to Microsoft during provisioning. The instances are directly connected to the Azure backbone and thus offer low latency to the virtual machines in which the SAP application servers are deployed, with the typical RTT within a virtual network usually being lower. UltraPerformance Gateway must be selected as the gateway solution.

Furthermore, when booking HLI instances, no independent memory provisioning is required. HLI instances are provisioned with fixed disk space according to SAP's recommendations. As a rule of thumb, the size of the disks is usually four times the main memory (does not apply to Type II instances). Additional capacity can be added to the instance by means of separate disks in 1 TB increments.

SAP Cloud Appliance Library (CAL)

The SAP Cloud Appliance Library (SAP CAL) provides an online library of configured SAP solutions that can be used immediately in the cloud. This makes it possible to deploy test, demo, and development systems within a very short time.

The SAP Cloud Appliance Library, also abbreviated CAL, makes it possible to create an SAP system in Microsoft Azure with little effort. There are various solutions that can be provided in Azure via the CAL: for SAP S/4HANA, for example, there is the possibility to use the 2020 version (FPS02) with best practice configurations already implemented and core functions provided via the SAP S/4HANA 2020 FPS02 Fully-Activated Appliance. The system can be accessed via SAP Fiori, SAP GUI, SAP HANA Studio, RDP, or at the operating system level. However, a standard installation via S/4HANA 2020 (FPS02) can also be selected, where only SAP Fiori is activated in Client 100 and access is initially only enabled via RDP.

To deploy S/4HANA via CAL, you need to perform several steps. First, log in to SAP CAL using your SAP user. Next, open an SAP CAL account that will be used to provision the S/4HANA system. You also need to select the deployment model accordingly for deployment in Microsoft Azure. Here, you can define the Resource Manager or the classic deployment model. The Resource Manager is recommended here, as the classic deployment model will be phased out. Furthermore, you specify the Azure subscription, taking into account that the CAL account can only be assigned to one subscription. Also, the authorization to provision Azure resources must be given via the CAL for the Azure subscription. To use the SAP CAL, you must sign up for a subscription. The subscription currently costs 750 euros per month for a term of 12 months. At the end of the term, the subscription is automatically renewed for the original term. You can cancel the subscription by giving at least 30 days' notice before the end of the term. You can gain initial insight into SAP CAL and familiarize yourself with it via a free trial version.

Please note that virtual instances are used in various SAP CAL systems, which may not be included in your Azure quota. For example, VMs of the M-series are sometimes required for SAP HANA databases. In this case, an increase of the Azure quota is then necessary. You can read how to increase the Azure quota in Chapter 7.

When deploying SAP systems in Azure via the SAP CAL test version, a limited selection of Azure regions is available. If you want to deploy the system in an Azure region that is not available for selection, you must use a paid CAL subscription with SAP. It may also be necessary to submit a request to SAP to unlock the deployment of the system in the specific region.

Virtual Computers

In the following, the basics of virtual computing instances in Microsoft Azure are taught. The focus is on VM instance types, VM generations, and VM states. Furthermore, the relationships between the resources of an instance as well as the different usage models are described. Spot instances and vCPU quotas are also explained.

Relationships Between Resources

When creating a VM, it is important that you consider the following relationships between resources. All resources are made available within a resource group. The VM is assigned a storage account so that disks can be backed up to BLOB storage. The VM points to a network interface card and an availability group. The network interface card, in turn, points to the IP address of the VM as well as its subnet and the associated network security group, if available. The subnet in the virtual network may also point to a network security group. Load balancing routes requests from a public or private IP address to IP addresses defined within a VM's network interface card.

PAYG vs. Reserved Instances

Microsoft offers customers the option to commit to an instance for a period of time to save money on cloud operations. However, depending on the size of the machine and the purpose of the machine, it may become more cost-effective for some types of machines and systems to use pay-as-you-go options. This issue will be discussed in this section.

When resources are used on a pay-as-you-go basis, the resources that are actually used are billed. For compute resources, for example, this is done on the basis of the runtime in which the VM instance was in the started state. Via the Microsoft Azure peak calculator, the costs can be calculated by selecting a VM instance, as well as the expected runtime. In addition, different prices result depending on which region and which operating system is selected. Moreover, it is possible to reserve instances for a certain period of time, which means that this instance is purchased in advance for this period. The time periods can be set to one or three years and allow a discount of up to 72% compared to usage-based payment for Azure services. If a workload with a long duration and high resource requirements is to be covered in Azure, it makes sense to use a reserved instance to save costs. Instead, the usage-based payment model should be chosen for seasonal workloads that occur in the short term. It makes sense to calculate the costs of both payment models for each case in order to select the more cost-effective alternative. An example calculation has already been carried out in Chapter 2. In principle, some Azure services incur fixed costs regardless of usage-based billing. As an example, the NetApp Files service can only be used from a size of at least 4 TB and must be coupled to the usage period of the virtual machine instances.

VM Instance Types

When deploying a VM-based solution, the most important decision is first to choose the VM type. Azure offers several VM series which are identified by the VM prefix (A, D, M, etc.). Each series in turn offers several sizes which are called VM types (e.g., Standard_D8_v3). Each VM series offers different hardware equipment and thus addresses a different purpose. For example, VMs of the M-series are memory optimized and therefore offer a high ratio of memory to CPU cores. The following are examples of some series that are suitable for SAP hosting (as of 2022):

A-series: Universal VM sizes

These instance types consist of a balanced CPU and memory size, making them suitable for test and development environments, as well as web servers with at most medium workloads. They are less suitable for SAP HANA databases, as they only support small to medium databases.

D-series: Compute optimized

Compute-optimized VM instances are suitable for web services, network appliances and batch operations, and medium-load application servers because they have a high CPU-to-memory ratio.

E-series: Memory optimized

The E-series is well suited for relational database servers and in-memory analytics due to a high memory-to-CPU ratio.

FX-series: Compute optimized

The FX-series is well suited for application servers with medium workloads due to a high CPU-to-memory ratio.

M-series: Memory optimized

Memory-optimized VM sizes consist of a high memory-to-CPU ratio. Therefore, they are well suited for SAP HANA databases as they enable medium to large caches and in-memory analytics.

Furthermore, there are instance series which are memory optimized, GPU optimized, and FPGA optimized as well as series for high-performance computing:

Memory optimized

These instance types enable efficient disk throughput as well as I/O, making them well suited for data warehousing and big data.

GPU: Accelerated compute processes

These VM sizes specialize in compute-intensive, graphics-intensive, and visualization-oriented processes.

FPGA: Accelerated compute processes

These virtual machines enable efficient execution of compute-intensive processes.

High-performance computing

These virtual instances are specifically designed for high-performance computing and enable high scalability, computing power, and cost efficiency.

Most VM series are supported for non-HANA SAP hosting and can therefore be freely selected according to price/performance criteria. Supported VMs include A, D, Das, Dds, DS, Eas, Es, GS, M, and Mds series types. However, it is a prerequisite that the SAP system is implemented as a two-tier or three-tier configuration and any SAP RDBMS that is not deployed based on the A- or D-series uses premium SSD storage (see Chapter 7) for persistence. For more information, see SAP Note 1928533.[5] For SAP HANA hosting, the choice of VMs is much more limited, as only selected VM types have HANA IaaS certification. As of 2021, HANA certified offerings include M-series VM types (from M32*, 192–3892 GB) and some representatives of the Edv4-series (from E20ds, 160–504 GB), as well as the GS5 (448 GB RAM) and DS14v2 (112 GB RAM) types. For an up-to-date and accurate listing of HANA certified Azure instances, the hardware directory[6] should be considered. Especially when choosing the Edv4-series, pay attention to the exact designation, since all series of the E* family are considered memory optimized, but the Eav4-series is based on AMD EPYC and thus does not offer any SAP support.

VM Generations

Microsoft Azure offers virtual machines with two different generations: generation 1 and generation 2. Generation 2 virtual instances support more memory in addition to generation 1 features, as well as virtualized persistent memory, and Intel Software Guard Extensions (Intel SGX). It also enables the use of UEFI boot with second-generation VMs; first-generation VMs use BIOS boot. As a result, second-generation virtual machines have more efficient boot and installation processes. First-generation VMs are supported by all VM sizes except Mv2-series, whereas second-generation VMs have more limitations: B-series, DCsv2-series, DSv2-series, Dsv3-series, Dsv4-series, Dasv4-series, Ddsv4-series, Esv3-series, Esv4-series, Easv4-series, Edsv4-series, Fsv2-series, GS-series, HB-series, HC-series, Ls-series, Lsv2-series, M-series, Mv2-series, NCv2-series, NCv3-series, ND-series, NVv3-series, NVv4-series, NCasT4_v3-series. Please note that once the virtual computer is created, the generation cannot be changed. Due to this, planning ahead is necessary.

VM States

The costs of an Azure VM are billed hourly, but only if it is in the "**Running**" status. If a VM is not actively needed, it can be shut down at any time. If you shut down the machine manually via the operating system, it changes to the "**Terminated**" state. Since a terminated machine continues to reserve the allocated computer resources, the costs

---

[5] https://launchpad.support.sap.com/#/notes/1928533
[6] www.sap.com/dmc/exp/2014-09-02-hana-hardware/enEN/#/solutions?filters=iaas;ve:24

of the VM continue to be incurred even though it is no longer consuming computing power. Regardless of whether the VM is in the "Finished" or "Running" state, you can also click the "Finish" button via the portal at any time to set the VM to the "**Finished (allocation removed)**" state. All reserved resources, such as the assigned dynamic IP, are then removed. VMs in this state no longer incur active costs, although it must be taken into account that costs for reserved memory, backups, etc. continue to be incurred.

Spot Instances

Azure Spot instances use resources that are currently unused in Microsoft Azure. This allows Microsoft Azure to make its offering more efficient by making unused resources usable. These Azure Spot instances are priced lower than instances elsewhere. However, you should be aware that the Azure Spot instances are removed again as soon as the resources are needed elsewhere, and no service-level agreements exist for these instances. There is no entitlement to use the Azure Spot instances; the available resources can differ depending on various aspects such as the region and time of day. Therefore, Spot VMs are best suited for processes where interruptions are not critical, such as development and test environments. Since interruptions are critical in SAP S4/HANA, the use of Spot instances is not recommended. Removal policies can also be defined for Spot instances. These determine the capacity value or price at which a VM is to be removed. The removal policy can initiate the deallocation of the instance or the deletion of the virtual machine. The default setting is to deallocate the VM. The deallocation of the virtual machine only terminates the instance and removes the assignment; there is no guarantee of successful continued assignment upon reprovisioning. Also, costs will continue to be charged for storage services that are allocated to the virtual machines. When the instances are deleted, the associated storage services are also deleted, so no further costs will be incurred for this.

vCPU Quotas

Microsoft Azure has introduced the concept of vCPU quotas. For virtual instances with usage-based billing and reserved VM instances, so-called vCPU standard quotas are allocated, and spot VMs receive a spot vCPU quota. Thereby, the vCPU quota can be considered in two levels: regional vCPUs and VM type family vCPUs. These contingents are assigned to each subscription and region. The vCPU quotas limit VM provisioning in that the virtual instance vCPUs do not exceed the VM type family quota and the regional vCPU quota. The number of virtual machine instances is also regionally limited by quota. The quotas can be viewed in the Azure portal at the subscription level under Usage and Quotas. If a higher number of VMs or vCPUs is required, an increase in quota can be requested. If you request an increase in the vCPU quota for a VM instance type, the quota for the regional vCPUs also increases automatically. An increase in the quota can be initiated in two ways: either via *Help and Support* in the Azure Portal by submitting a support request or by increasing the quota via *Usage and Quotas* in the *Subscriptions* section.

Dedicated Azure Hosts

Microsoft Azure also offers the option of reserving a dedicated host, which is assigned to a physical server. You can host virtual instances on it, which can be flexibly adapted to the respective requirements. Dedicated hosts can be provisioned in a fault domain, availability zone, and region. By using a dedicated host, hosts from other subscriptions and users cannot be placed on the host. Thus, there can be no unforeseen bottlenecks during load spikes of multiple virtual instances. There is also more control during maintenance, as a specific maintenance window can be registered when booking dedicated hosts.

To reserve a dedicated host, create a host group in an availability set and region. After creating the host group, you can add the dedicated host. A host represents a resource that is associated with a physical server. Each host can host different virtual machines that belong to the same size series. The supported size series is defined by the SKU. The SKU, called a stock keeping unit, can be described as a tariff. A host group represents a collection of dedicated hosts.

To ensure high availability of your SAP system, you should use multiple virtual machines distributed across multiple hosts. Using dedicated hosts, you can better control fault-proneness by avoiding bottlenecks during peak loads and avoiding single points of failure by distributing the dedicated hosts across different fault domains and availability zones.

Because a host group is created in an availability zone, all virtual machines in that host group share the data centers in that zone and therefore share the same power, cooling, and networks. To achieve better availability, you should thus create multiple host groups across different availability zones and thus distribute the hosts across these different availability zones.

By distributing dedicated hosts into different fault domains, the virtual machines can be placed in different physical racks within the data center. Thus, availability can be ensured even after a physical rack in the data center fails. When creating the host group, the number of fault domains is defined; it is not necessary to determine the fault domain at the virtual machine level. It is important to note here that no antiaffinity of the fault domains between two different host groups can be assumed. This is only guaranteed if the two host groups are in different availability zones. Additionally, it cannot be assumed that hosts with the same fault domain are physically close to each other in the data center. Antiaffinity in this context means that two or more hosts of both host groups are not in the same fault domain.

Requirements for SAP and Microsoft Azure Support (VM)

To get full support from SAP and Microsoft for the software architecture, you should comply with the published requirements. For this purpose, SAP has published a list of certified hardware for the use of SAP HANA.[7] Here, you can generate a list of VM instances supported by SAP for installing SAP HANA by setting filters.

SAP Note "2015553 – SAP on Microsoft Azure: Support prerequisites" lists general requirements for deploying SAP applications in Microsoft Azure to receive full support from SAP and Microsoft. The note mentions that only VMs from the standard tier are supported, as these ensure that no overuse of resources, that is, resource scarcity, is possible. SAP Note "1928533 – SAP Applications on Azure: Supported Products and Azure VM types" lists these supported VM types. Please pay attention to the actuality of the SAP Note, because the supported VM types are adjusted regularly. In general, machine instances of the instance classes described in Table 6-3 can be used.

---

[7]www.sap.com/dmc/exp/2014-09-02-hana-hardware/enEN/#/solutions?filters=iaas;ve:24

Table 6-3. *Supported Instance Classes for SAP Applications in Microsoft Azure*

Instance Class	Size Range	SAPS	Instance Type
A-series	2–16 vCPU, 14–112 GB	1500–22,000	Universal VM sizes
D-series	2–16 vCPU, 14–112 GB	2325–18,600	Universal VM sizes
DS-series	2–16 vCPU, 14–112 GB	2325–18,600	Universal VM sizes
DSv2-series	2–20 vCPU, 14–140 GB	3530–30,430	Universal VM sizes (faster than D-series)
DSv3-series	2–64 vCPU, 8–256 GB	2178–69,680	Universal VM sizes (with hyperthreading technology)
Easv4-series	2–96 vCPU, 16–672 GB	3022–135,080	Memory optimized
Dasv4-series	2–96 vCPU, 8–384 GB	3022–135,080	Universal VM sizes (more CPUs and memory than DSv2)
Esv3-series	2–64 vCPU, 16–432 GB	2178–70,050	Memory optimized
Ddsv4-series	2–64 vCPU, 8–256 GB	3142–100,550	Universal VM sizes (more local memory and better IOPS on local disks for reads and writes compared to Dsv3)
Edsv4-series	2–64 vCPU, 16–504 GB	3142–100,550	Memory optimized (local high-speed memory, low latency)
GS-series	2–32 vCPU, 28–448 GB	3580–41,670	Memory and mass storage optimized virtual computers
M-series	8–128 vCPU, 219–3892 GB	8616–134,630	Memory optimized (up to 128 vCPU count and up to 3.8 TB memory)
Mv2-series	208–416 vCPU, 2.85–11.4 TB	259,950–488,230	Memory optimized (high memory/CPU ratio, hyperthreading)

(continued)

Table 6-3. (*continued*)

Instance Class	Size Range	SAPS	Instance Type
Msv2-series	32–192 vCPU, 875–4096 GB	42,711–256,750	Memory optimized (only available as generation 2)
Mdsv2-series	32–192 vCPU, 875–4096 GB	42,711–256,750	Memory optimized (only available as generation 2)

Microsoft Azure also offers VM instances with limited vCPUs. The vCPUs can be limited to half or a quarter of the original size. You can use these instances for SAP applications. However, you should calculate the SAPS for the planned system using the following formula:

```
SAPS of the limited VM = (SAPS of the unlimited VM * Number of vCPUs of the
limited VM) / Number of vCPUs of the unlimited VM
```

As a conclusion, you can basically use all instance types offered by Microsoft Azure for provisioning, provided the sizing of the resources is correct. However, no resource scheduling is guaranteed for VMs that are not supported according to the corresponding SAP note. This means that if there is a high demand for resources across VMs, the maximum resource utilization of the VM cannot be guaranteed (noisy neighbor/overcommitment).

At the operating system level, the following limitations apply. Since the use of Azure services is limited to x86-64 or x64 hardware, the system must be built on one of the following operating systems:

- Windows Server 64 bit for the x86-64 platform

- SUSE Linux 64 bit for the x86-64 platform

- Red Hat Linux 64 bit for the x86-64 platform

- Oracle Linux 64 bit for the x86-64 platform

Thus, when migrating the system to Microsoft Azure, you need to switch to one of the preceding operating systems depending on the existing operating system.

Furthermore, the required NetWeaver/ABAP or Java stacks as well as kernel minimum versions depend on the S/4HANA and HANA system to be installed. This must be taken into account in order to guarantee support. In this context, when migrating to Azure, it must be checked whether an update of the SAP kernels will be necessary in the course of the migration. Corresponding information can be found in SAP Note "1928533 – SAP Applications on Azure: Supported Products and Azure VM types."

Storage

Microsoft offers a wide range of different storage types. These differ not only in their performance and their hosting costs but also in their compatibility with regard to the various SAP workload types, as well as in the administrative management options. This section is intended to provide an overview of the various storage options and explain their advantages and possible uses.

Performance Characteristics of Storage Technology

Before going into detail about the individual storage technologies and comparing them with each other, we will first explain the key performance criteria. Three metrics are of particular interest: disk size (in GiB), input/output operations (IOPS), and throughput (MB/sec).

Disk size: Most disks must be booked and paid for in fixed size increments, even if the actual storage used is less. An exception to this is unmanaged disks (see the next section). The sizes available for selection often differ per disk type. While Premium Storage SSD volumes can also be booked as 32 GB versions, for example, the minimum size of Azure NetApp Files (ANF) is 4 TB. Subsequent resizing of the initial size is also not supported by all volume types. For the managed disk family (see Chapter 7), which is mainly used in the context of SAP hosting, the maximum size of a disk is usually 32 TB (exception Ultra Disk with 64 TB). Overall, the disk size plays a subordinate role in the selection of the right storage type, since up to 64 data carriers can be connected depending on the VM type, and thus there is also the flexibility to provide storage in the petabyte range.

IOPS: The IOPS determine the number of read and write accesses per second that are performed on the data carrier. All Azure disk types have predefined IOPS limits. If the application requires more IOPS than the underlying storage provides, a performance loss automatically occurs as the IOPS limit becomes the bottleneck. The IOPS of the memory are influenced by three variables. The first influencing factor is the selected memory type. Higher-value storage, such as "Premium SSD," has higher IOPS limitations than lower-value storage, such as "Standard SSD." However, the size of the data carrier also influences the IOPS number. The IOPS limit usually increases linearly with the size of the data carrier. In addition, the limit can also be increased by using multiple volumes at the same time. In this case, the IOPS limit is cumulative. That is, 2x disks with 10,000 IOPS each result in an IOPS limit of 20,000. Of course, this only applies if the two disks work together, that is, the application writes to both disks at the same time. The IOPS limits can also be differentiated between "cached IOPS" and "uncached IOPS." The "cached IOPS" limits are higher than the "uncached IOPS," but are only taken into account if host caching is enabled for the disk. If host caching has been enabled with the "read-only" strategy, the corresponding volume will have a dedicated cache. Whenever a read access can be answered directly by the cache, the I/O access is counted only for the "cached IOPS limit." If the requested data is not yet in the cache or if a write access was performed, the access is counted for the cached and uncached IOPS limit. If the IOPS limit "read and write accesses" has been activated, write accesses are always first written to the cache, and the changes are written to disk asynchronously and automatically in a background job. There is no change for read access. The write access itself then only counts for the cached IOPS limit.

It is also important that the VM itself has an IOPS limit in addition to the memory. It would therefore not be worth combining an inexpensive VM, for example, Standard_A2_v2 (2000 IOPS), with a high-priced memory, for example, Ultra Disk 64 GB (19,200 IOPS), as in this case the VM itself becomes the bottleneck. Precise planning of the IOPS capacities is therefore essential to achieve the best price-performance ratio.

Throughput: Throughput is usually specified in megabytes per second (MB/s or Mbps) and determines the maximum bandwidth when reading or writing data. This value is particularly important for sequential read or write operations, such as copying large files or updating the database log. Similar to the IOPS, the throughput depends on the data carrier type, the size of the data carrier, and the number. This means that high IOPS automatically result in high throughput. However, it should be noted that not all storage types also achieve their theoretical throughput in practice. In particular, the actual performance of inexpensive standard HDD storage can deviate considerably from the theoretically possible performance. Only more expensive storage types such as "Ultra Disk" also offer performance guarantees.

Managed vs. Unmanaged Volumes

Basically, MS Azure differentiates between managed and unmanaged disks when selecting storage. Managed disks are completely controlled by Microsoft and simplify administration considerably. The range of functions, especially in terms of scalability, reliability, and security, is also greater than for unmanaged disks. For example, managed disks include a role-based access concept with encryption as standard, as well as higher availability and fault tolerance by replicating the data on two additional disks (RAID mirroring). Unmanaged disks, on the other hand, are completely controlled by the customer. For this purpose, a so-called storage account must first be created. This basically provides a namespace through which all storage objects associated with the account can be identified. Volumes can then be created as VHD files in the account. This is then unmanaged storage, as the user must now independently implement concepts to ensure encryption or data recovery. From a technical point of view, VHD files are based on page blobs. In addition to these, other storage objects such as block blobs/append blobs (for unstructured data), tables (NoSQL structured data), queues (message exchange between application components), and files (e.g., network storage based on NFS) can also be provisioned. While nonmanaged volumes are now considered obsolete and should be used instead of managed volumes, the use of other storage objects such as blobs or files is still very important. However, these play a subordinate role in the context of SAP hosting. Both SAP and Microsoft recommend the use of managed data carriers over nonmanaged ones for SAP operation. According to Microsoft, there are no differences between managed and nonmanaged data carriers in terms of pricing strategy. However, it should be noted that managed volumes are generally provisioned in fixed sizes and are always priced at their full capacity (in GiB). The size of nonmanaged standard storage, on the other hand, can be selected flexibly, which can result in a small savings potential, since only the storage actually used is priced. However, this is only the case for standard storage. For premium storage, there are no differences in pricing between managed and nonmanaged storage. Table 6-4 provides a brief overview of the two storage variants.

Table 6-4. *Comparison of Managed and Unmanaged Disks*

Administration and control	Associated storage account must be created by the customer beforehand. Disk can then be manually created as a VHD file. Full control by the customer, but all numerous restrictions that must be considered by the user	Associated storage account is automatically created and managed by Azure Resource Manager. This simplifies design and use for the customer
Size	User-specific size can be selected as long as "Standard" is selected as the performance class	Fixed sizes depending on the memory class. However, subsequent adjustment of the size is possible
Scalability	Only 250 storage accounts possible per subscription/region. Up to 40 VMs possible per storage account. May require distribution to multiple storage accounts	Up to 50,000 volumes per subscription/region
Security	Multiple VHD files are located in one storage account. No standard encryption or role-based access concept	Disks are isolated from each other. Standard encryption and role-based access concept
Performance		
Availability		Disk mirroring to two additional physical disks available by default. Extensive support for availability zones and availability sets

In the following, we will focus on managed disks, as these are mainly used in the context of SAP hosting. We will also look at Azure NetApp Files (ANF). This is a high-performance file server service (NFS/SMB), which is particularly important in the context of high availability scenarios.

Data Carrier Roles

Depending on the purpose of the medium, a distinction can be made between the three roles operating system medium, temporary medium, and regular medium (medium for data). This separation is important because not all volume types (see the next section) can be used for all roles.

Operating system (OS) disk: The operating system is provisioned on this disk as part of the VM creation. The size of the disk is limited to a maximum of 4 TB. The choice of disk types is also limited. For example, the fastest available storage solution (Ultra Disk) cannot be used as an operating system disk.

Temporary disk: Many VMs include an additional temporary disk as standard in addition to the operating system disk. This is primarily used as short-term storage, for example, as swap space for swapping or paging. Unlike the name suggests, this data is not lost during a reboot. However, there are also no warranty claims. Especially during maintenance, resizing, or a reallocation of the VM, the data can be lost. For this reason, the temporary volume should not be used as persistent storage and especially not for SAP applications.

(Regular) data disk: These are classic drives that are used for long-term persistence of application data. In the context of SAP hosting, independent data carriers are usually created and mounted for the various SAP directories such as /hana/data or /hana/log. These reveal themselves to the operating system as SCSI drives and can have a maximum capacity of 32 TB (per disk). The number of disks that can be mounted depends on the selected VM size.

Snapshots and images: Snapshots and images are not independent data media in the classical sense. A snapshot is merely a copy/snapshot of an existing volume and is primarily used for backup purposes. The snapshot exists independently of the source medium. This means that the original medium can be changed or even deleted at any time without affecting the snapshot. Unlike regular disks, snapshots are only priced at their actual size, that is, a snapshot of a 100 GB disk on which only 20 GB are in use is only priced at 20 GB. An extended form of the snapshot is the so-called image. While the snapshot is only a snapshot of a disk, an image includes the complete VM including all assigned disks. In this way, the interaction of several data carriers can also be backed up, for example, in the context of RAID arrays.

Redundancy Options

Microsoft offers four different redundancy options to ensure that stored data is not lost in the event of a physical disk loss:

Locally redundant storage (LRS): Three copies are kept within an Azure data center. Write access is always synchronous, that is, all three copies are written in time. The data is thus protected against failure of individual drives or even an entire server rack. However, a disaster that affects the entire data center (fire/water) could lead to data loss. LRS is supported by all Azure storage services and is also the only redundancy option supported by managed volumes.

Zone redundant storage (ZRS): With ZRS, the three synchronous copies are distributed across three availability zones within the region, that is, the data remains in the primary region, for example, "US West," but is located in different data centers which have independent power supply, cooling, etc. A failure would therefore have to permanently affect all three zones for a potential data loss to occur. ZRS should therefore be used for high availability solutions.

Geo-redundant storage (GRS): With GRS, data is distributed across two regions, for example, "Germany-West" and "US-East." Within one region, the data is kept as LRS. Writes occur in the primary region first and are then replicated to the secondary region asynchronously. If the primary region becomes unavailable in the event of a disaster, a failover must be performed in which the secondary region becomes the primary region; otherwise, the data is unavailable.

Geo-zone redundant storage (GZRS): GZRS is a special form of GRS in which, in addition to asynchronous replication of data across two zones, ZRS is also used within a zone. That is, data is stored within both the primary and secondary regions across three availability zones (six in total). GZRS is the highest redundancy option, but this option is not offered for all regions.

Disk Types

Azure distinguishes between the four data carrier types "HDD Standard," "SSD Standard," "SSD Premium," and "Ultra Disk." These differ in terms of their performance features, their possible data carrier roles, and of course in terms of price.

Ultra Disk: Ultra Disks offer the best performance with transfer rates of up to 2000 MB/s and maximum IOPS of 160,000 (which is however only supported by a few VM sizes such as M128s). A special feature of Ultra Disk is also the ability to dynamically adjust the disk performance (without restarting the VM) to the workload.

However, Ultra Disk also comes with some limitations. For example, only the regular disk role is supported, but not, for example, the operating system disk. Additionally, the use of snapshots is not possible. Only availability zones are offered as a high availability service. However, this is additionally limited to some regions and VM families, for example, in the region "Germany, West-Central," only individual VMs support "Ultra Disk" at all. On the other hand, all application scenarios within SAP hosting are supported without exception, including latency-critical paths such as /hana/log.

SSD Premium: SSD Premium also offers high performance, but does not come close to the performance of Ultra Disk (maximum 900 MB/s throughput and 20,000 IOPS per data carrier). Unlike the Ultra Disk, however, SSD Premium also supports operating system volumes. However, the prerequisite for using SSD Premium is that the selected VM supports "Storage Premium." This is the case, for example, for all M instances (memory optimized), but not for cheaper VMs such as the A- or D-series. SSD Premium also offers guaranteed transfer rates. The "bursting" feature is also offered for smaller data carrier sizes up to 512 GB (P20). Here, each disk is automatically allocated a quota that enables throughput and IOPS to be increased beyond the guaranteed limits. As long as the workload is lower than the guaranteed transfer rates, the credit is replenished. During peak loads, the transfer rates are increased, but the credit is used up. This can result in a considerable performance advantage, especially for smaller sizes. For example, a P4 data carrier actually only has a throughput of 25 MB/s. With bursting, however, this can be increased to up to 170 MB/s. Bursting is enabled by default and does not need to be enabled manually. SSD Premium should ideally be used as an operating system data medium, since faster variants like Ultra Disk or ANF cannot be used. Furthermore, the use of SSD Premium is recommended for almost all SAP application scenarios. Only as HANA log volume (/hana/log), the usability is limited because the I/O latencies required for HANA cannot be achieved. For this reason, only the VM families M and Mv2 are supported under the premise that Azure write acceleration is enabled. This is an exclusive feature of the M-series which can be used in combination with SSD Premium. The write acceleration is optimized for writing log files. It should therefore only be enabled in this context, but not for classic data volumes, for example, /hana/data. The write acceleration is also associated with some restrictions. With acceleration enabled, no snapshots can be taken from the disk from now on. In addition, disk caching must be disabled or in write-protected mode.

SSD Standard: SSD Standard is the cheaper version of SSD Premium. The performance theoretically is similar to Premium, but it can be subject to greater fluctuations. SSD Standard also supports bursting, but the burst throughput of 150 MB/s is usually 20 MB/s lower than SSD Premium. SSD Standard is also supported throughout by all VM instances. SSD Standard is only suitable to a limited extent for SAP hosting. For non-productive instances, SSD Standard should only be used for the SAP system mount directory /sapmnt and as an operating system data carrier. Other application purposes such as a global transport directory are no longer supported.

HDD Standard: HDD Standard is the cheapest but also the slowest data carrier type. The theoretical throughput of up to 4 TB (S4 to S50) of 60 MB/s is not even half that of standard SSDs. Bursting is also not offered. HDD is therefore only suitable as mass storage when performance plays a subordinate role or the network is the bottleneck (e.g., archive or file server). In other cases, it is almost always worthwhile to invest the surcharge for SSD. For SAP hosting, HDD Standard can only be used as an operating system data carrier and for the SAP system mount directory or backup storage, although even these application scenarios are not recommended. Figure 6-4 shows the hierarchical allocation of storage to subscriptions, accounts, and pools.

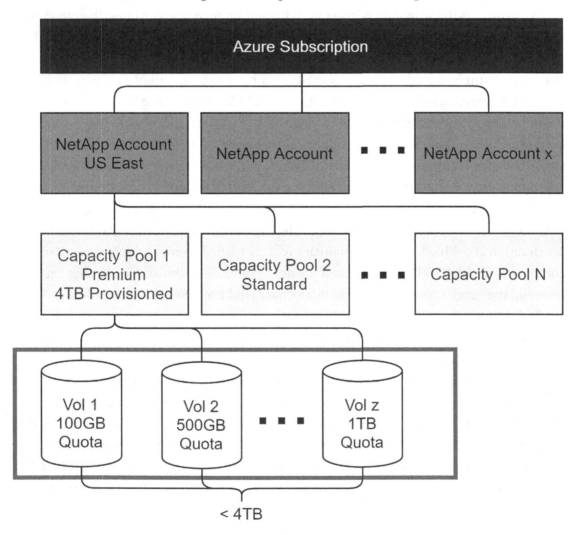

Figure 6-4. *Hierarchical structure of storage to subscriptions*

Azure NetApp Files (ANF): ANF is an Azure NFS service that can provide high-performance network storage. As shown in Figure 6-4, a NetApp account must first be created. This account is region dependent and can therefore only be used in the region in which it was created.

Based on this account, capacity pools can be created, which in turn provide the individual data carriers/quotas. These are integrated as network storage in the form of NFS or SMB data carriers. As of 2021, ANF is the only shared file system that is SAP HANA certified. ANF is therefore particularly suitable if large storage capacities in combination with high performance are required. The minimum size for creating an ANF capacity pool is 4 TB and can be increased in 1 TB steps up to 400 TB. ANF thus offers the highest scalability of all storage solutions. A minimum quota of 100 GiB up to a maximum of 100 TB must be allocated per data carrier. This has an impact on the costs. When using SAP HANA, NFS is only supported in protocol version 4.1. ANF offers three service levels: Standard (16 MB/s), Premium (64 MB/s), and Ultra (128 MB/s). These throughputs apply cumulatively per TiB contingent. That is, the larger the contingent, the higher the throughput, for example, a 4 TiB Premium storage offers 4 x 64 MB/s = 256 MB/s and would thus be more performant than 1 TiB Ultra storage. It should be noted that ANF throughput is always counted against the network bandwidth and not against the memory bandwidth. ANF is suitable for all types of SAP volumes that occur in the context of S/4HANA. The only restriction is that both /hana/data and /hana/log are provided on ANF. ANF is particularly suitable in the context of HA scenarios as a solution for providing highly available shared NFS storage, for example, for /sapmnt or the transport directory /usr/sap/trans.

Network and Services

This section describes the concept of the hub-spoke topology and explains other relevant services and tools for network configuration.

Hub-Spoke Topology and Network Peering

The hub-spoke topology is a standard concept that is used in almost all Azure network architectures. The hub serves as the central point of contact from the on-premise network and comprises several subnets. As shown in Figure 6-5, the gateway subnet forms the gateway to the enterprise network. The gateway subnet is a dedicated network type that cannot be used for normal VM deployments, but can only be used to deploy a gateway component. It connects to the corporate network using one of two methods. A site-to-site (S2S) VPN allows a VPN connection to be established by pairing a dedicated VPN device from the on-premise network with an Azure VPN gateway. In contrast, there is the ExpressRoute variant. Here, a private connection with agreed bandwidths can be established between the corporate network and Azure in cooperation with the Internet service provider. The gateway network often leads to a DMZ network, which hosts central services and, if necessary, a firewall. Finally, the management subnet provides one or more jumpboxes, also called bastion hosts. These are remote systems that serve to administer the SAP landscape and have a hardened operating system. Furthermore, corresponding client tools are provided and preconfigured, such as SAP Logon, HANA Studio, or HANA Cockpit. In addition, the hub network is set up in such a way that for administrative accesses such as SSH, a further connection to the adjacent spoke networks is only enabled from there. This is made possible by appropriate settings in the network security groups (NSG). Thus, one does not connect directly to the target systems but establishes a connection to the jump server from which one can then connect to the respective target machine. In principle, every VM can be configured as a jump server. Azure alternatively offers the in-house "Azure Bastion" PAS service, which is already preconfigured with RDP and SSH, among other things, and can also be called directly via the Azure portal.

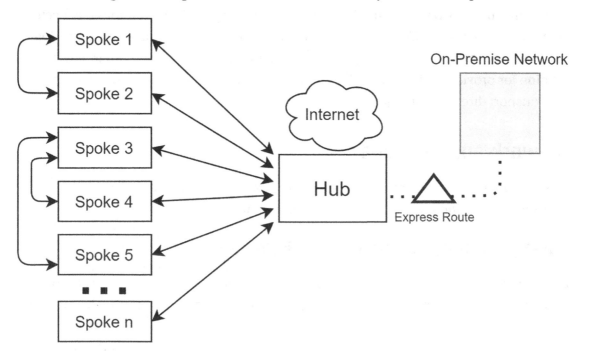

Figure 6-5. *Hub-and-spoke network*

Finally, the spoke network hosts the actual SAP workload. Typically, different workload types (e.g., productive vs. development) are split between different storage networks. User access is also set up accordingly so that developers and end users are enabled for different spoke networks, with extensive management access only enabled from the management subnet, the hub.

VNet peering: To implement the concept of the hub-spoke network, the concept of VNet peering is required. Each virtual network in Azure defines a private address space by default. VNet peering is required to allow instances of one VNet to access instances of another VNet without communicating over a public IP. Peered networks appear as if all VMs are part of the same network. The prerequisite for implementation is that both VNets have non-overlapping IP ranges. VNets from different regions or subscriptions can also be peered together. From a performance perspective, peered networks get the same throughput as if they were on the same network, but only as long as they are in the same region. In this case, the data transfer is also internal to Microsoft and is not routed over the public network, but peered networks incur transfer costs which can cause high data volumes and thus costs, especially in SAP hosting. For this reason, it is usually recommended not to isolate the application server and database of an SAP installation in VNets, but to use subnets instead.

SAP support restrictions: The distribution of the SAP workload to the respective virtual networks should be carefully planned and carried out in consideration of the SAP recommendations from SNOTE 2015553.[8] SAP generally recommends not separating application layers and database layers by means of different VNets, but instead defining separate subnets. However, separation at the virtual network level is supported as long as these are peered. A hybrid cloud layer separation, where, for example, only the application server or database layer is hosted in the cloud and the other layer is hosted on-premise, is explicitly not supported. In all cases, latency between the Azure region and the corporate network should also be considered. A careful evaluation of ExpressRoute or site-to-site VPN should be performed, especially for production workloads.

ExpressRoute vs. S2S VPN

The implementation of a hybrid network that couples an existing corporate network with the virtual Azure network is the norm in the context of SAP hosting. There are two options available for this which are explained in more detail as follows.

---

[8] https://launchpad.support.sap.com/#/notes/2015553

S2S VPN: A site-to-site VPN connection can be implemented quickly and is easy to configure. Here, the data traffic between the Azure VPN gateway and the on-premise gateway device is encrypted using IPsec and routed regularly via the public network. However, no statement can be made about latency and maximum bandwidth here. Due to the criticality of SAP workload, Microsoft's official recommendation is to use an express route to ensure better performance (throughput and latency), as well as security and reliability. In practice, however, an S2S VPN connection is sufficient for many use cases (including SAP). SAP itself supports both connection scenarios (SNOTE 2015553[9]):

1. For implementation, a VPN gateway must first be created in the Azure Gateway subnet. This component comes in six different price classes (Basic + VpnGw1 - VpnGw5), as well as several AZ subvariants that offer additional zone redundancy. The bandwidth ranges from 100 Mbit/s to 10 Gbit/s, depending on the price class. Here, the base costs are calculated per hour (e.g., $3.65/hr). This price includes up to ten tunnels. Additional tunnels are charged separately (also per hour and for the duration of use) whereby a gateway supports a maximum of 30 tunnels in total. It should be noted that a single tunnel provides a maximum of 1 Gbit/s bandwidth. The price class of the gateway can usually be changed dynamically, unless the basic price class has been selected, and it is not possible to change a Gen1 gateway to Gen2.

2. Then the on-premise VPN device has to be set up. In addition to configuring a shared key and the public IP of the Azure VPN gateway, the recommended configuration settings of the device manufacturer or Microsoft should also be taken into account. Microsoft does not support all VPN devices, but a large number which can be found at the following site: `https://docs.microsoft.com/en-us/azure/vpn-gateway/vpn-gateway-about-vpn-devices`. For Cisco, Juniper, and Ubiquiti devices, there are also configuration scripts available which simplify the setup and can be downloaded from the Azure portal.[10] If no hardware

---

[9] `https://launchpad.support.sap.com/#/notes/2015553`

[10] `https://docs.microsoft.com/en-us/azure/vpn-gateway/vpn-gateway-download-vpndevicescript`

VPN is available, software-based VPNs can also be used, such as OpenSWAN (Linux) or MS Routing and Remote Access Service (Windows).

ExpressRoute: The ExpressRoute is a private connection between the corporate network and Azure which is provided by an external network provider. Packets sent via the ExpressRoute are not routed via the public network, which means that higher performance can be achieved and greater security and reliability can be ensured. When setting up an express route, a distinction can be made between four modes:

- Cloud Exchange composition: The Cloud Exchange mode is particularly suitable if the company already uses a Cloud Exchange. A Cloud Exchange provider (usually well-known carriers such as AT&T or Verizon) is a service provider that has connected its network to common cloud providers and passes this access on to the company via a WAN access. In this case, the packets are passed directly to the Cloud Exchange without being routed over the public network. In this case, another cross-connection to the MS Cloud can simply be set up. As a rule, these are layer 2 or layer 3 connections.

- Point-to-Point Ethernet connection: PPPoE is also offered by Azure, but requires support from the Internet service provider. As with Cloud Exchange, both layer 2 connections and managed layer 3 connections can be set up this way.

- Any-to-Any IPVPN connection (MPLS): Any-to-Any IPVPN connections are usually based on MPLS VPN. In this case, the private WAN of a carrier is used. This requires that the carrier is registered as an ExpressRoute provider. In this constellation, a managed layer 3 connection is used.

- ExpressRoute Direct: Finally, Microsoft offers globally distributed peering sites which can be connected via ExpressRoute Direct. Peak transmission rates of up to 100 Gbit/s can be realized here.

Global Reach and FastPath: Microsoft Azure also offers a way to reduce latency through ExpressRoute Global Reach and ExpressRoute FastPath. If you use two or more ExpressRoute connections in your landscape, ExpressRoute Global Reach is a possible option to reduce latency. Since this involves bridging the Border Gateway Protocol

(BGP) route between two ExpressRoute routing domains, latency reduction can only be achieved when multiple ExpressRoute circuits are traversed. Currently, ExpressRoute Global Reach can only be used for private peering and does not provide the ability to change network access. Because of this, you should implement local network data filtering to limit resource access appropriately. ExpressRoute FastPath is implemented by default on newly created ExpressRoute connections. For existing connections, FastPath can be enabled through Azure Support. ExpressRoute FastPath is also defined as Microsoft Edge Exchange v2 and reduces network hops for many data packets. However, it should be noted that VNet peering cannot be combined with FastPath. If peering is implemented for other VNets, you must link all VNets directly to the specific ExpressRoute line. Otherwise, the traffic will go to the VNet gateway instead of the ExpressRoute.

Network Security Groups and the Azure Firewall

Network security groups (NSGs) control which data traffic is allowed and can be defined both at the level of a virtual (sub)network and at the level of a VM interface. The concept of NSGs is similar to packet filters such as IPtables. An NSG consists of any number of individual rules which define an action (Allow or Deny) based on the five-tuple information source IP, source port, destination IP, destination port, and protocol. Here, each rule is prioritized with a number between 100 and 4096, with lower priority rules applied first. Each incoming or outgoing packet is compared to the rule collection according to their priority, and the first match according to the five-tuple information is applied. Other potentially valid rules with higher priority are not considered further. In the context of SAP, a whitelisting approach is usually recommended. That is, first all necessary accesses are defined as a rule with the action "Allow," for example, an SSH access from the management network. Finally, a "Deny All" catch rule is set with the highest priority. This ensures that no access is possible unless it is explicitly allowed. An NSG is managed as a stand-alone resource and can also be defined without being assigned to a network or interface (but as long as it is, the NSG is not active). NSGs can also be reused, for example, an NSG can be assigned to multiple resources.

Azure Firewall and Network Virtual Appliances (NVA): While configuring appropriate NSGs is mandatory, optionally deploying a firewall can also be worthwhile. These are offered both by third parties as "Network Virtual Appliance" (NVA) or by Microsoft as Azure Firewall. The differences between the respective offerings must be compared individually. The key advantage of using a firewall over NSGs is that it can be deployed centrally in the DMZ subnet as part of a hub-spoke topology, thus securing all of the Azure landscape's own VNets at this point. Also, the feature set of NVAs is far greater than that of NSGs. As a rule, NVAs operate stateful and offer more advanced rule configurations and analysis functions such as intrusion detection. A firewall should always be used in addition to NSGs, but not instead of them.

Network Interfaces

All VMs in an Azure landscape are based on a common software-defined network. This is also accompanied by a uniform network fabric, which is why there is no added value from a performance point of view in defining multiple network interfaces (NICs) for a VM. By default, an Azure NIC also supports multiple IP addresses, which also enables the use of virtual hostnames (for usage, see SNOTE 962955). The manual creation of additional NICs is therefore only suitable if the data traffic is to be split, for example, for monitoring reasons.

Network Performance

The bandwidth of a virtual machine is always calculated based on the outgoing network traffic from the entire machine. Incoming data is not counted toward the bandwidth. This means that regardless of the communication destination (including VMs in the same subnet) and regardless of the number of network interfaces, the cumulative overrun value is offset against the available bandwidth, for example, 1 Gbit/s, and throttled to the maximum bandwidth if exceeded.

In addition, accelerated network operation can be activated for virtual machines. This is based on the SR-IOV technology which bypasses the virtual switch of the virtualization layer and takes a large part of the network load away from the CPU and shifts it to the FPGA-accelerated network interfaces. This extra performance is particularly noticeable when other VMs in the virtual network also have this feature enabled. In the context of SAP hosting, it is recommended to activate the feature for the VMs of the database layer as well as for those of the application layer. To do this, the VM must be stopped and the assignment must be removed.

Load Balancing

A load balancer can accept any TCP- or UDP-based requests and distributes them to the respective back-end systems based on a configured set of rules. For SAP hosting, load balancing is therefore an essential component and is used in particular in high availability scenarios where there must be a fixed virtual IP which is to be forwarded dynamically to the primary instance. Essentially, a load balancer consists of four components:

1. Front-end IP(s): Defines one or more IPs (IPv4 and IPv6 supported) over which the load balancing is addressed. When creating a load balancer, you must define whether it is to be an internal or public load balancer. A public load balancer can be provided with public front-end IPs and thus be addressed from outside. A typical example would be a server cluster for a customer service desk. An internal load balancer, on the other hand, can only be given private IP addresses, for example, to connect a highly available HANA cluster to the S/4HANA application servers.

2. Back-end pool(s): A back-end pool is a collection of target systems to which the load balancer should forward incoming requests. Either machines or a VM scaling group can be included in a pool. Multiple pools can also be defined.

3. Integrity test(s): An integrity test determines which instances of a back-end pool are eligible as load balancing targets. The test defines a kind of heartbeat mechanism determined by a protocol (TCP/UDP), a destination port, an interval (in seconds), and an error threshold. The integrity test then periodically checks the connectivity to the target port of the back-end system. If this test fails more times than the error threshold allows, the instance is no longer considered as a possible load balancing target. On the back-end instance side, this requires that a service is listening on the specified port (e.g., netcat, socat, or azure-lb).

4. Load balancing rule: Finally, the load balancing rule combines
    the front-end IP, back-end pool, and integrity test into one rule.
    By assigning a front-end IP, you first define for which IP address
    the load balancing rule should be applied, so different rules can
    be defined for at the IP level. The port and protocol (UDP/TCP)
    determine for which types of requests the rule is valid. The back-
    end port and back-end pool finally define the destination to which
    the load balancing request should be forwarded. In addition,
    the integrity test to be applied to check the appropriate back-
    end systems must be defined. This makes it possible to define a
    separate test for each rule. By defining a session persistence, it
    is also possible to configure whether for a client the traffic of a
    session should always be forwarded to the same back-end system
    ("Client IP" or "Client IP and Protocol") or whether this can be
    done by any VMs ("None"). Finally, the idle timeout determines
    how long a TCP or HTTP connection should be kept open even if
    no corresponding message is sent by the client. Figure 6-6 shows
    how outbound rules can be used to configure the behavior of
    outbound Source Network Address Translation connections.

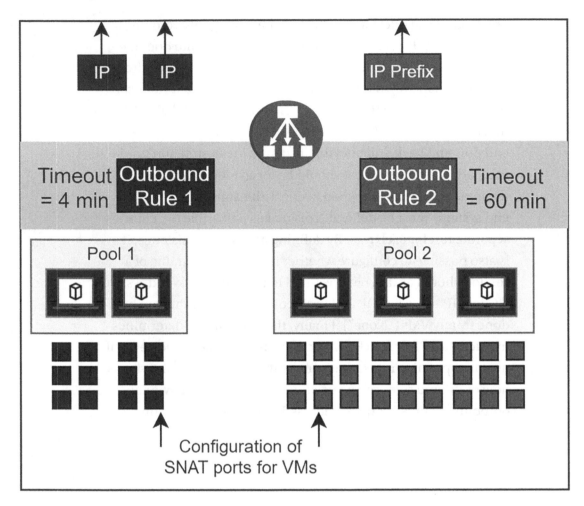

Figure 6-6. *Load balancer rules*

Basic vs. standard: Load balancing is available both as a free "basic" variant and as a chargeable "standard" variant. In principle, most use cases such as SAP-HA can also be implemented with a basic load balancing. However, the standard variant offers an extended range of functions, such as the use of HA ports, which enables a 1:1 mapping from front-end ports to back-end ports, as well as larger back-end pools with up to 1000 instances. For more differences between the two SKUs, see the official documentation.[11]

---

[11] https://docs.microsoft.com/en-us/azure/load-balancer/skus

Support and Licensing

Licensing of SAP products must be performed by the customer. Orders placed via the Azure Marketplace always specify how licensing is handled. When selecting the operating system image, for example, there are separate "bring-your-own-subscription" (BYOS) templates.

When moving to the Azure Cloud, the booking of additional support services should also be considered in addition to the classic SAP support. Microsoft offers a range of support plans. The Basic plan is included free of charge by default for all customers and basically allows support tickets to be created. For non-productive SAP landscapes, the Standard support plan can be considered. For €84.33/month, this already includes 4h*7 support with response times of less than one hour in case of severe impairments. SAP recommends as a minimum for all Azure customers to book the Professional Direct Support (approx. €843.3/month) which is aimed at companies with business-critical landscapes. In addition to the support services covered in Standard, this includes additional offerings such as webinars and program-controlled management of support tickets via the Microsoft Support API. In the case of SAP hosting based on Windows Server or MS SQL Server, Microsoft also recommends booking Premium Support. When operating Linux (SLES/RHEL), a valid support contract is a prerequisite. Here, too, different support performance classes are offered, for example, Standard vs. Priority Support at SUSE. With regard to Azure, however, there are no special conditions compared to on-premise hosting.

Azure Disaster Recovery Services

This section introduces the disaster recovery services available in Azure. First, the service "Azure Backup" is explained, which is the generic term for the respective backup services. Then we will introduce the two types of vaults, which are the central building blocks of the Azure Backup concept. We will also explain the backup of disks, virtual machines, and SAP HANA databases. Finally, we will introduce the Azure Site Recovery service, which supports cross-region replication and migration scenarios.

Azure Backup

Azure Backup is a SaaS service that allows to perform backups for various resources such as virtual machines, applications (e.g., MS SharePoint or databases), and even on-premise systems. Among other things, the service also offers seamless support for SAP HANA databases. Backups are created based on a **backup policy**. This defines the planning parameters such as the frequency of automatic backups, as well as retention times (retention policy). For storage, Azure uses so-called vaults. This resource is divided into two types, the so-called "Recovery Services vaults" and the backup vaults. The central entry point for managing backups and creating vaults is the "**Microsoft Backup Center**" service. This is used to create vaults and policies and to monitor backup operations.

Backup Vault

The backup vault is a storage entity and is required to perform backups and snapshots for Azure blobs, Azure volumes, or Azure databases for PostgreSQL servers. In the context of SAP hosting, backup of managed volumes is a common usage scenario. For this, a volume can first be selected and a backup frequency defined. This can be selected between 4 hours and a maximum of 24 hours. In addition, a retention period must be specified, which can be between 1 and 30 days. However, it should be noted that the maximum number of snapshots is limited. Theoretically, up to 200 incremental backups can be kept per data carrier. However, Azure limits these backups to 180 to reserve capacity for on-demand backups. Based on these scheduled values, Azure will now perform regular and automatic incremental snapshots. These will be stored in the backup vault. The backup vault data can be stored both geo-redundantly (default setting) and locally redundantly. However, the redundancy must be configured before the first backup, as it cannot be changed afterward. Azure Backup works without an agent installation and does not slow down the system. Costs when using backups are only incurred for storing the incremental data. Only the delta between the last two backups is priced.

Recovery Services Vault

Similar to the backup vault, the Recovery Services vault is also a storage entity. However, this is required for backing up other components, for example, virtual machines, databases, or Azure Files. In addition, the Recovery Services vault is required for disaster recovery using Azure Site Recovery.

Azure VM Backup

For the regular backup of a VM, a frequency (daily or weekly + time) as well as a retention period (7–9999 days) can be defined, similar to the disk backup. In addition to the retention of daily backups, the retention of weekly, monthly, and yearly backup points can also be configured. By default, when a VM backup is performed, a snapshot of all disks except the temporary disk is taken. The "Backup OS disk only" option can be used to specify that only the OS disk should be backed up. Adding a VM to the regular backup works without any manual effort. When configuring for the first time, only the VM needs to be selected and associated with a backup policy that defines the mentioned scheduling parameters. In the background, Azure automatically installs the necessary extension on the VM's operating system. With the backup process set up, an on-demand backup can now also be performed manually at any time. Note that backing up a VM can take several hours.

HANA DB Backup

Based on the Recovery Services vault, a backup of an SAP HANA database can also be performed based on the Backint interface. Azure Backup promises an RPO of 15 minutes here, offering a great alternative if you don't want to build your own backup infrastructure. To manage a HANA using Azure Backup, two phases need to be performed. First, as part of "Discovery" (Phase1), the database is discovered on the available VMs. After the discovery is started, all available virtual machines are listed. These must be in the same region as the vault. You will then be offered a script to download, which you must run on all VMs with HANA DB. The script requires root privileges and requires you to specify a "system key." The key is a hdbuserstore key for the SYSTEM user. This way, Azure Backup gets the necessary permissions to access the HANA database. Afterward, the respective VMs can be selected, and the discovery phase can thus be completed. Now the actual backups can be configured. For each individual (system) database or tenant, you can store a separate backup policy. Similar to the backup of virtual machines, you can differentiate between daily, weekly, monthly, and annual backups. In addition, backup policies are created according to the backup type, that is, you can create your own policies for full, differential, and incremental backups.

Azure Site Recovery

Site Recovery is an Azure disaster recovery service which is also based on the Recovery Services vault. It supports not only replication of entire Azure landscapes (e.g., virtual machines, disks, virtual networks, resource groups, etc.) but also on-premise systems based on VMware and Hyper-V. In this way, Azure Site Recovery can be used not only for disaster recovery but also for migrating workloads to the cloud. When using Site Recovery for Azure VMs, the vault must be located in a different region than the source; otherwise, only replication within availability zones (within a region) is possible. After a VM is added, all VM metadata (e.g., size, connected network components, etc.) is stored in the vault. In the context of a failover, it is sufficient to create these resources based on the metadata definition in the target region. The volumes, on the other hand, are actually replicated. Data modifications (after initial replication) are first written to the storage account cache and then replicated to the target region. This ensures that the productive workload is not affected. The replication itself can be configured individually, for example, individual volumes can be excluded and the subscription of the replicated resources can be changed. Recovery plans can be defined for the failover of resources. In these, disaster recovery can be orchestrated to map dependencies between resources. For example, for an S/4HANA three-tier architecture, the order could be defined that first the VMs of the HANA database, then the ASCS instance, and finally the VMs of the application servers are booted. Recovery plans also offer test failover for testing purposes. In this case, the replicated machines are booted without shutting down the primary site.

S/4 on Azure Architecture

This section presents a complete architecture that meets the service-level agreements of the Azure environment and the availability offered for Azure components. This architecture includes a discussion of high availability, disaster recovery, backup and recovery, and the security measures that must be taken to secure the environment. The section also covers scale-out and scale-up scenarios.

Basic Reference Architecture

The reference architecture presented here consists of virtual machines with an installed Linux operating system. It includes high availability strategies in the environment of S/4HANA systems and supports disaster recovery in the Microsoft Azure environment.

In this context, this architecture can be seen as a standardized basic framework that can be adapted according to context and company requirements.

The architecture is visualized in Figure 6-7 and comprises the components described as follows.

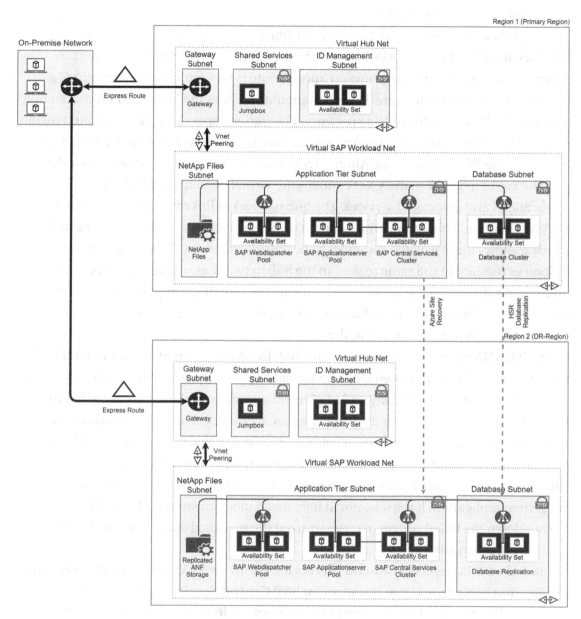

Figure 6-7. *Basic reference architecture*

The **Azure Virtual Network (VNet)** is the starting point. It connects the required Azure resources and prevents unauthorized access to them. In this architecture, the resources can be accessed from outside via the gateway. In this context, the gateway represents a hub, and the VNet represents the spoke of the hub-and-spoke model described in a previous section.

The **gateway** is used to link the networks from outside the VNet; it represents the interface between the networks. You can choose from several options to connect to Azure resources through the gateway. ExpressRoute is recommended for creating secure connections from Azure. Here, you should consider the latency when connecting between the VNet and the outside network. This varies depending on the selected region of Azure resources. To reduce latency, you can use the ExpressRoute Global Reach and ExpressRoute FastPath services. Alternatively, you can use a virtual private network.

The spoke network in the **VNet** contains the virtual instances with the SAP applications and associated services. The hub network is linked to the spoke network via VNet peering. This enables the isolation of different Azure resources from each other. Peering allows these isolated resources to be linked without performance degradation as long as they are in the same region. In the hub network as well as the spoke network, additional subnets are implemented to separate the individual applications from each other. Three subnets exist in the hub network, as in the spoke network. The virtual computing instances are located in the subnets.

SAP HANA forms the foundation of the S/4HANA deployment and is implemented with high availability using two Linux instances. By clustering the two instances, you can also scale the database centrally and implement automated failover in case of failures. For high availability, note that the two instances are deployed in different **availability sets**. This approach prevents system failures when individual Azure resources fail. If one database instance fails due to system errors or maintenance, the other database still remains functional. Redundancy between the two HANA databases is ensured via system replication. It must be noted here that a mechanism must be implemented to shut down the failed system in order to avoid the so-called split-brain state, which enables data inconsistencies.

Based on this, several **front-end servers** are set up, two **SAP Web Dispatchers**, two **application servers,** and two instances for **SAP Central Services**. The two instances of each SAP component are localized into different **availability sets** in order to realize better availability.

The third subnet of the spoke network contains the **network file sharing service**. To meet the high availability requirements, there are several options: Azure NetApp Files, an NFS cluster server, or SIOS DataKeeper provides the necessary features. Using the Pacemaker cluster enables high availability for shared Azure volumes.

When using Red Hat Enterprise Linux, you can use GlusterFS for a highly available file share.

The **jumpbox** is located in the **hub network** and is used to establish a secure connection with the other virtual instances in the VNet. One "jumps," so to speak, from the outer network first to the jumpbox in order to gain access to the other virtual computers via it. For example, services such as **SAP HANA Studio**, **SAP GUI**, and **SWPM**, which are needed to install and manage the SAP landscape, are run on the jumpbox. The **Azure Bastion** service is a good option as a jumpbox should you only use **Remote Desktop** or **Secure Shell services** for deployment.

Network security groups (NSGs) can be used to additionally restrict subnet-internal as well as outbound and inbound data transactions. In the example reference architecture, NSGs are implemented in all subnets except for the gateway and file sharing service.

Load balancing modules are placed in front of the SAP Web Dispatcher pool, the central services cluster, and the two HANA databases in this architecture. This allows traffic to be distributed among the instances. However, you should note that the virtual instances behind the load balancing modules have no outbound connection via default.

Proximity placement groups can still be used to optionally allow virtual machines to be co-located in the same data center.

Application security groups can be used to group instances and allow only filtered traffic for applications.

Virtual Private Network Reference Architecture

To implement a virtual private network, a local network and a hub-and-spoke network are created. The two networks are separated from each other by different resource groups. AVN gateways are used to link the two networks together. This type of linking is technically similar to connecting the network outside Azure to the networks inside Microsoft Azure. Through the Microsoft Azure Portal, provisioning can be automated (approximately 45 minutes of provisioning time). Figure 6-8 illustrates the system architecture.

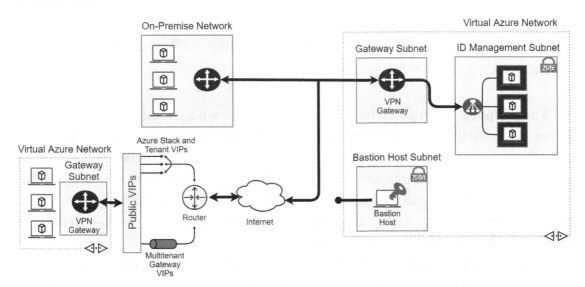

Figure 6-8. *Virtual private network reference architecture*

The architecture includes the following components. The Azure Stack Network VPN gateway sends encrypted data over a public connection. It consists of a dedicated gateway subnet, a network gateway, and a site-to-site tunnel. The virtual network is where the applications and gateway are located, as well as the Azure Bastion. The Azure Bastion enables an SSH or RDP connection to the virtual instances without the instances being freely available over the Internet connection. Thus, in the event of a VPN connection failure, the instances are still accessible via the SSH or RDP connection. When creating such an architecture, you should take care to define the address space of the virtual network accordingly, since it must not overlap with that of the local network. Also, you should place the gateway subnet at the top of the virtual network address space. Please note not to locate any virtual instances in the gateway subnet and not to define any network security group there; otherwise, the gateway will not remain functional.

Summary

Microsoft Azure is one of the largest hyperscaler providers, and many customers run the SAP environments based on Azure. This chapter has shown you which key components are important for such SAP environments. Starting with a brief history of MS Azure, the key points before starting a deployment have been described. These include the points of subscriptions and key user groups.

The chapter showed you the core components of MS Azure for building an SAP S/4HANA system, such as compute, storage, and network components, as well as their integration with the company's own services.

To secure SAP systems, MS Azure provides you with important basic features, such as Azure DR for disaster recovery, and can also support with a basic backup and recovery feature.

For productive SAP S/4HANA systems, Microsoft offers Premium Support, which should be used in any case. Through this, customers receive important support and timely support in case of errors. This is elementary for productive SAP S/4HANA systems.

In the following chapter, we will show the concrete implementation and the steps for deploying a new SAP S/4HANA system in the MS Azure Cloud.

## CHAPTER 7

SAP S/4 on Microsoft Azure – Deployment

This chapter will deepen the theoretical foundations from the previous chapter in a practice-oriented manner by deploying an S/4HANA system based on Azure VM step by step. Firstly, we will present the example architecture demonstrating how the system resources will be implemented to receive the end result. After that, we will deploy the basic network architecture, the HANA HA cluster, and the S/4HANA HA cluster in order. We will show how to provision resources manually as well as how to create and use custom ARM templates. Finally, we will shortly look at alternative deployment automations based on SAP CAL, as well as Ansible and Terraform.

Azure S/4HANA Reference Architecture

As shown in Figure 7-1, we will provide a lightweight S/4HANA high availability architecture with its own management network (hub network), as well as a workload network (spoke). For this, we will highlight different alternatives. Thus, the example should be considered as an exercise scenario and not as a best practice recommendation for a production implementation. The configuration steps on the operating system level are based on SUSE Linux Enterprise 12 SP5. Instructions for Windows and Red Hat Linux are linked at the appropriate place.

For the sample implementation, we use the specifications in Table 7-1.

© André Bögelsack, Utpal Chakraborty, Dhiraj Kumar, Johannes Rank, Jessica Tischbierek, Elena Wolz 2022
A. Bögelsack et al., *SAP S/4HANA Systems in Hyperscaler Clouds*, https://doi.org/10.1007/978-1-4842-8158-1_7

Table 7-1. *Naming Conventions*

Component	Designation
SID – HANA	**HA1**
HANADB (HA1) – Instance number	03
SID – NetWeaver	**S4H**
ASCS – Instance number	00
ERS – Instance number	02
PAS – Instance number	01
AAS – Instance number	04

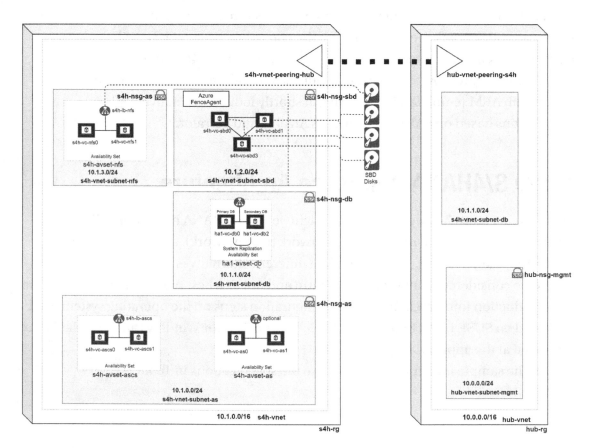

Figure 7-1. *Reference architecture*

High availability aspects: For fencing, Azure offers two alternatives based on STONITH Block Devices (SBD) and the Azure Fencing Agent. We will use SBD for fencing all Pacemaker clusters, but will cover the creation of a fence agent including STONITH configuration as part of a digression. For highly available shared storage, it is possible to either deploy an own HA-NFS cluster or rely on the Azure NetApp Files SaaS service. We use the NFS cluster as SAP mount directory /sapmnt and use ANF for the transport directory /usr/sap/trans. In practice, it is recommended to stick to only one variant.

Deploying a Basic Network Configuration via Azure Cloud Portal

We first start the deployment of our target architecture with a basic configuration. As shown in Figure 7-2, this includes the resource group as well as the hub-spoke network architecture including peering, subnet configuration, and network security policies. Deployment and configuration are explained in the following using the Azure Cloud Portal as an example.

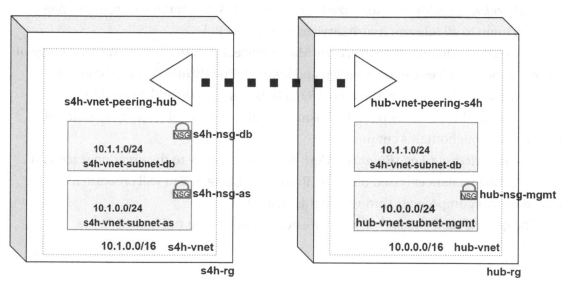

Figure 7-2. *Basic network configuration*

Azure Cloud Portal

The Azure Cloud Portal is the central tool for all management processes also enabling the creation of resources via a graphical interface. The portal is only one of a total of four interfaces. The Azure CLI, Azure PowerShell, and REST API are particularly important for deployments using ARM templates or for automatic resource management processes. However, the portal is particularly suitable as an entry point because it firstly provides an insight into the extensive offerings of the Azure platform, such as the Azure Marketplace, which also includes third-party offerings, and secondly contains entry aids and supplementary descriptions.

Navigation: The Azure Portal offers a hashtag navigation which allows to navigate to the corresponding Azure service by simply adding the hashtag to the URL. For example, the URL `https://portal.azure.com/#home` points to the home directory. In the context of this chapter, we will specify the target hashtag at the appropriate place to facilitate navigation. If you can't find the corresponding service, you can always use the central search. Useful hashtags include the following:

#home: Points to the home directory. From here, you can jump directly to recently used resources, central Azure services, and information offers.

#allservices: Provides a categorized overview of all Azure services. From this page, you can jump to all relevant Azure services with a few clicks.

#create/hub: Direct link to the Azure Marketplace. From this point, the wide range of resources and services can be browsed and jumped directly into resource creation.

#create/Microsoft.VirtualMachine-ARM: Navigates directly to the creation screen of a virtual machine based on Azure Resource Manager. You will create a few virtual machines throughout this chapter.

#create/Microsoft.LoadBalancer-ARM: Navigates directly to the creation screen for creating a load balancer based on Azure Resource Manager. You will create at least two load balancer components throughout this chapter.

The general look and feel of the Azure portal can be seen in Figure 7-3.

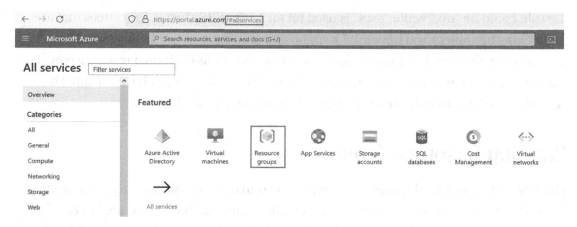

Figure 7-3. *Azure Cloud Portal*

Naming Conventions and the Resource Concept

All objects that you create in Azure, such as virtual machines, networks, or disks, are listed under the collective term "resources." Many of these objects are merely part of a configuration in on-premise hosting, but are explicitly managed as resources in Azure. For example, on-premise you would simply configure a public IP or network restrictions based on iptables. In Azure, there are separate resources for this, such as "public IP addresses" or "network security groups." As a result, you will be working with a large number of resources in Azure which need to be identified by unique names. Due to the large number of these objects, it is advisable to establish a naming scheme in advance in order to be able to describe resources and their relationships to each other unambiguously. To allow flexibility in naming, at least a prefix scheme should be defined. The scheme we use in the context of this book is the following (names in [] are optional components):

```
<sid>-<resource type>-[<role>[nr]]-[<child resource type>[nr]-
[<designation>]]
```

The minimum designation of a resource thus consists of <sid> and <resource type>. The <sid> is derived from the future SAP system, so in our example "s4h" or "ha1" for the database. The resource type is an abbreviation for the type of the respective resource. For an availability set, for example, this could be "avset," and in the case of a load balancer, "lb." The <role> optionally specifies the purpose of the resource, if there can be multiple resources of the same type. For example, if an availability set is used for the database, the role could be "db," while "ascs" is used for an ASCS/ERS cluster. Resources that are part of another object and have a 1:1 relationship to it, such as a subnet or a disk, have the resource name of the parent object as a prefix, as well as their own resource type. For example, a managed disk of the virtual computer h41-vc-db0 might have the label h41-vc-db0-disk-data0 to indicate that it is mounted under /hana/data.

Creating Resource Groups

The first step in this deployment is to create a resource group. All resources required for the S/4HANA system, such as the virtual machines and load balancers, are later added to this group and are subject to the same life cycle. It is also possible to use multiple resource groups, for example, to manage the application servers and database in separate groups.

Navigate to **#allservices** and select the "General" category and then "Resource groups." You are now in the "Resource Groups" service view.[1] Click the "Create" button to add a new group. Select the subscription to be used for billing and a region. Also, set a name for the resource group such as **s4h-rg**.

Next, click "Verify+Create." Azure will now check if the resources you requested can be provisioned. On the one hand, these are checked against the quotas you have set. On the other hand, the availability in the target region is also checked. However, checking the resource group should only take a few seconds as there are only a few dependencies in this case. Finally, click "Create." Now select the resource group you created in the previous step. First, familiarize yourself with the left navigation bar. Click one of the functions to open a new detail view that displays the corresponding information. We would like to briefly introduce the following views:

- Overview: The overview shows you all resources contained in the group. It is also where most administrative operations are triggered, such as creating or moving a resource and deleting a group.

- Activity log: All operations within the resource group are logged in the activity log. This includes operations such as stopping or deleting a virtual machine and the initiator of the operation.

---

[1] https://portal.azure.com/#blade/HubsExtension/BrowseResourceGroups

- Access control: Here, you can view current role assignments and add new accesses.

- Resource quick view: When you select resources in the overview, you can use the resource quick view to create a graph that shows you the resources and their dependencies in a graphical tree view.

- Deployments: Similar to the activity log, the deployments of new resources are listed here, but no other management operations. However, this is not a simple log. The ARM templates of all past deployments are kept here and can be redeployed at any time.

- Repeat the steps for another resource group "**hub-rg**."

Network Configuration

Based on the resource group, we want to create the virtual networks next. Basically, you don't have to create the virtual network separately, but you can also add it directly during the creation of the first VM. For better planning, we will perform the network configuration as a separate step. To do this, first navigate to the overview of the "**hub-rg**" resource group and click the "Create" button. Enter "**virtual network**" in the search (at the time of writing this book, the English term must be used for the search). First, click the object name. You will now see a detail view with a brief description of the resource. You should see a note about deployment using the Resource Manager. Now click the "Create" button.

You are now in the configuration mask for creating a virtual network. Make sure that the top description of the mask is "Create virtual network" and does not have the suffix "(classic)." Otherwise, the object would be provisioned as part of the classic resource provisioning and not through Azure Resource Manager.

Derived from your resource group, most fields should already be prefilled. First, check the region and the selected subscription in the basic settings. Then set "**hub-vnet**" as the network name. Click "Next: IP addresses" and set the IP range to **10.0.0.0/16**. Now add a subnet with the name "**hub-vnet-subnet-mgmt**" and the IP address range **10.0.0.0/24** (no NAT gateway). Then navigate to the "Security" tab. Here, you have the option to include a bastion host as well as a firewall and DDoS protection in the deployment. The bastion host is a PaaS offering for managing virtual machines in the Azure landscape. A bastion host defines a public IP through which you can connect to the respective target machines based on SSH or RDP. In the context of our hub/ spoke network architecture, this is a classic service you could deploy into the hub. Alternatively, you can classically define a virtual computer as a "jumpbox." Note that in all three cases, these are fee-based services. Next, complete the provisioning process.

Now navigate to your resource group "**s4h-rg**" and repeat the provisioning for the virtual network "**s4h-vnet**" [10.1.0.0/16]. Make sure that the region is specified correctly and that the address range does not overlap with the address space of "hub-vnet." This is a mandatory requirement for peering which we will do in the next step. Also, delete the default subnet and replace it with the following two networks:

- **s4h-vnet-subnet-as** [10.1.0.0/24] # Subnet for the application servers and central instances

- **s4h-vnet-subnet-db** [10.1.1.0/24] # Subnet for the database servers

Complete the deployment and switch to the newly created VNet resource. As already known from the resource groups, you will find a navigation bar with numerous settings on the left side of the screen. Via the menu items "Address range" and "Subnets," you can adjust the IP ranges and manage subnets at any time. Select "Peerings" to switch to the peering configuration view.

The hub network "**s4h-hub**" provides the central access to the spoke networks. However, at this time, both are internal networks between which routing is not possible. To enable data traffic, we now create a peering between the two networks. Click the "**Add**" button. The peering resource will be created twice – once as a node of the network "**s4h-vnet**" and once as a node of the network "**hub-vnet**." Therefore, you have to define two names. Select "**s4h-vnet-peering-hub**" and "**hub-vnet-peering-s4h**." Leave the default settings and select "**hub-vnet**" as the target network. Then click "*Add*."

Creating Network Security Groups

Now that we have created the network areas, it is time to set the port rules. For this purpose, we will assign each subnet its own network security group (NSG). Navigate to your resource group again (via #allservices and then "resource groups") and select "**hub-rg**." Search the Marketplace for "network security group" and create it with the name "**hub-nsg-mgmt**."

Repeat the steps first for the NSG "s4h-nsg-as" in the resource group "**s4h-rg**." After you create them, wait until the deployment is complete and they are in the Deployments view (alternatively, navigate over the "**s4h-rg**" resource group and select *Deployments*).

To add the remaining NSG "**s4h-nsg-db**," we will now navigate over the deployment template. Click the "*Deploy again*" button. You will now see the familiar input screen, but this time the fields are prefilled with the original parameter values. Note, however, that for some fields, input helpers (drop-down) are no longer available, only free text is offered. Template staging has virtually no input validation and for this reason should always be edited carefully. Check the prefilled values and set the name for the database NSG. Even though the effort savings for creating an NSG using a template is small, this principle can basically be done for any resource.

Now it is time to assign the NSGs to the respective subnets, as well as to configure the port rules. First, navigate to the "**s4h-nsg-db**" resource and select "*Subnets*" from the left navigation bar. Click Assign and first select the VNet "**s4h-vnet**" and then the subnet "**s4h-vnet-subnet-db**."

Now select the menu item "*Inbound Rules*" in the left navigation bar. Security rules basically consist of a four-tuple information. The **priority** specifies the order in which the rules are applied, with the lowest value being executed first. The **name** simply defines a label for the rule. The combination of **port**, **protocol**, **source**, and **destination address** must be satisfied together for the rule **action** (Allow or Deny) to be executed. Classically, NSGs are configured according to the whitelisting principle, that is, all types of connections are prohibited unless they are explicitly allowed. The default settings after creating a new NSG reflect this principle. Health probes of the Azure Load Balancer as well as traffic with the service tag "VirtualNetwork" are generally allowed on all ports. Other connection requests, such as requests from the public network, are prohibited. Note that you cannot remove the default rules, but you can override them with lower priority rules.

Which rules for which NSG? How free you want to make access to your landscape is basically enterprise dependent. In the context of a hub-spoke architecture, however, it is advisable to design the releases for any SAP workload networks (spokes) restrictively. Extensive access should only be possible from the management subnet (part of the hub). The following considerations could be relevant here:

s4h-nsg-db: The database network should generally be designed in a particularly restrictive manner, especially if the HANA platforms it contains are only used as databases for S/4HANA instances. The rules in Table 7-2 can be relevant for this task.

Table 7-2. *NSG Rules for the Database Network*

Priority	Source IP	Source Port	Target IP	Target Ports	Protocol	Action	Description
100	subnet-as	*	Any	3<nr>13, 3<nr>15, 3<nr>40, 3<nr>41, 3<nr>42	Any	Allow	SAP HANA ports
101	subnet-mgmt	*	Any	22, 3389	Any	Allow	SSH, RDP
102	subnet-mgmt	*	Any	7630	Any	Allow	Hawk (Pacemaker)

s4h-nsg-as: The application servers should only be available from the corporate network via SAP GUI or Fiori. Table 7-3 shows the network security groups for the subnet of the application server.

Table 7-3. *NSG Rules for the Application Server Subnet*

Priority	Source IP	Source Port	Target IP	Target Ports	Protocol	Action	Description
100	Servicetag = Virtual Network	*	Any	32<nr>, 33<nr>, 80<nr>, 443<nr>	Any	Allow	SAP Dispatcher, SAP Gateway, ICM HTTP, ICM HTTPS
101	subnet-mgmt	*	Any	22, 3389	Any	Allow	SSH, RDP
102	subnet-mgmt	*	Any	4237	Any	Allow	SWPM
103	subnet-mgmt	*	Any	7630	Any	Allow	Hawk (Pacemaker)

In addition to IP addresses, NSGs also support so-called service tags and application security groups for specifying the destination or source. Service tags are predefined address ranges that apply to a specific application purpose and are maintained by Microsoft. The service tag "Virtual Network," for example, covers all IPs from the connected on-premise address range, as well as peered virtual networks and networks that are connected to a network gateway. A list of available service tags can be found in the Azure documentation.[2]

Application security groups[3] (ASGs) allow individual network interfaces to be added to a group and NSG rules to be set on that basis. In principle, similar control can also be defined based on IP addresses, but ASGs allow greater flexibility because, unlike IP addresses, they generally do not change.

Note   : For most productive SAP systems, it is recommended that they are only available over the intranet and not over the public network. However, for a VM to gain access to public endpoints, such as those required for repositories, the Azure Fencing Agent, or Azure Backup, it is necessary that they either have a public IP address or that Internet access is provided by means of load balancing for outbound communication or an Azure Firewall. For this purpose, please read Microsoft's guidance[4] on how to implement such a scenario. From an IT security perspective, the latter two alternatives are preferable. In the context of this example architecture, we will work with public IP addresses for each VM to simplify matters.

Deployment of a HANA HA Cluster

In the following, the provision of a HANA HA cluster is discussed in more detail. First, the HANA cluster architecture is outlined, and then the provision of the necessary HANA cluster resources is discussed. Finally, the configuration of the Pacemaker cluster and the setup of the HANA HA cluster are described in more detail.

---

[2] https://docs.microsoft.com/en-us/azure/virtual-network/service-tags-overview
[3] https://docs.microsoft.com/en-us/azure/virtual-network/application-security-groups
[4] https://docs.microsoft.com/en-us/azure/virtual-machines/workloads/sap/high-availability-guide-standard-load-balancer-outbound-connections

HANA Cluster Architecture

Now that the basic configuration is complete, we want to deploy a HANA high availability cluster. For this purpose, we extend our architecture with the components illustrated in Figure 7-4.

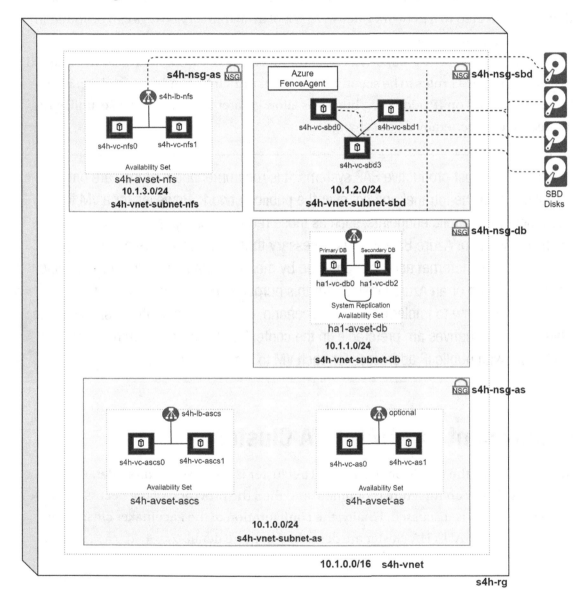

Figure 7-4. *HANA cluster architecture*

Virtual computers and availability sets: In the database subnet "**s4h-vnet-subnet-db**," we deploy two virtual computers "**ha1-vc-db0**" and "**ha1-vc-db2**." Both instances are part of the availability set "**ha1-avset-db**." System replication is also set up between the two HANA systems so that the secondary node also receives the changes of the primary node.

Load balancing: To ensure that the application servers are not affected in the event of a node failure, internal load balancing is implemented upstream. The load balancing provides a static IP address to the outside which does not change even if an account fails. The application servers communicate with the IP of the load balancer, while the load balancer forwards the requests internally to the corresponding primary HANA accounts, based on an integrity test.

iSCSI target VMs: To avoid a split-brain scenario in the Pacemaker cluster, a fencing mechanism is needed. One way to implement this is by using the Azure Fencing Agent which we will discuss in more detail in the section "Excursion Azure Fencing Agent." The classic way is to use STONITH Block Devices (SBD). For this purpose, a shared volume must be made available on the nodes of the cluster. In contrast to the on-premise area where such a scenario can usually be configured based on a SAN, in Azure we use the iSCSI protocol. Here, SCSI commands can be exchanged based on IP networks to enable data transfer between distributed systems. iSCSI is based on a client/server architecture where the server (the so-called "target") provides SBD devices and the clients (the so-called "initiators") access them via IP. For the clients, the iSCSI devices appear as if they were locally connected. The iSCSI target VM is a stand-alone virtual machine and can be shared by multiple Pacemaker clusters. For this reason, we deploy the iSCSI VMs in a stand-alone virtual subnet. For a basic configuration, one iSCSI VM is sufficient. However, this requires that the SBD device is always available. For productive operation, it is therefore recommended to work with three iSCSI targets (three SBD devices). In this case, one target VM can also be shut down/stopped for maintenance reasons. Note that two SBD devices do not provide you with additional protection, since in this case Pacemaker is unable to perform automatic fencing if one SBD device fails.

Provisioning HANA Cluster Resources

To keep the manual effort as low as possible, we use a so-called quick start template for the provision of the HANA database. Azure offers numerous ARM templates for various deployment scenarios. An overview of all templates can be found on the Microsoft website.[5] Search for the keyword "sap" to see all SAP-specific deployment templates. We will then take a closer look at the manual provisioning of a virtual machine based on the iSCSI target VM.

Azure Quick Start Templates

In the following, we will first explain the structure of a quick start template before adapting the template for our own needs. This is the best way to learn the process and how ARM templates work.

In preparation for deployment, we first need the ID of the database subnet we created, as well as our network security group. Navigate to the "**s4h-rg**" resource group, click the "**s4h-vnet**" resource, and in the "Overview" section, click the "JSON View" button at the top right of the screen. The JSON view fully describes the configuration of the object including all ID references to other resources. Search for the subnet name "**s4h-vnet-subnet-db**" and note the ID below it. Repeat this step for the network security group "**s4h-nsg-db**." Instead of the JSON view, you can also open the "Properties" view via the navigation bar and then display the resource ID. Now switch back to the resource group "**s4h-rg**" and create the resource "Template deployment (deploy with custom templates)." Select "Quick Start Template" as the template source and select "sap-3-tier-marketplace-image-multi-sid-db-md."

We now want to build a deeper understanding of how ARM templates work. Therefore, first click "Edit template."

You are now in an edit mode. Azure templates are based on JSON syntax and basically consist of three areas – parameters, variables, and resources:

- Parameters: These are the fields that are displayed to the user as part of a deployment as a form to fill out. The template we have chosen has a total of 12 parameters. Click the parameter "osType" to learn more about it. In the right JSON view, you can see that this field is an enumeration which accepts only one of eight allowed values. The default value is "Windows Server." Make a note of the allowed values, for example, "SLES 12 BYOS." Now navigate to the parameter "sapSystemSize" and note the values allowed there (e.g., Demo,

---

[5] https://azure.microsoft.com/en-us/resources/templates/

Small). As you can see from this example, parameters usually have a user view and do not encapsulate the detailed technical information. We cannot yet identify which VM instance will be created with the value "Small" on this basis.

- Variables: Variables contain the actual (technical) information used for deployment. The parameters set by the user usually only refer to background variables. Now select the variable "images" and check the values in the JSON tree. Here, again, the values are listed which we have already noted for the parameter "osType." Now check which "sku" is defined, for example, for "SLES 12 BYOS." In our case, this is "12-SP3," which is an obsolete SLES version. You are free to make the first adjustments here. In our case, we change the SKU to "12-SP5." Make sure that the combination of "offer" and "sku" actually exists and is available in its version. Otherwise, you will receive an appropriate error message during the verification step. How to check the availability of images for your region is described in the following article. Then select the variable "sizes." The structure here is a bit more complex. Under "Demo," the value "HANA" should appear first before the actual "vmSize" is specified as "standard_e8s_v3." If you scroll down further, you will find the value "SQL." This is because the template uses different VM sizes for HANA and non-HANA databases. The "standard_e8s_v3" size for about $0.64/hour uses 8 vCPUs as well as 64 GB of RAM, so it is suitable for a bare NetWeaver installation at best. If you want to stay true to the template and install a true S/4HANA system, you must therefore choose at least the "Small" size (standard_E32s_v3 with 32 vCPUs and 256 GB of RAM) which, however, costs four times as much (about $2.56/hour). Alternatively, you are welcome to customize the "vmSize" yourself. In our view, the following VM sizes serve the price middle ground between "Demo" and "Small" well, with the FX-series offering a particularly good price/performance ratio at the expense of fewer cores. Note, however, that in this case you will also need to adjust "offer" and "sku" in the "imageReference" node of the deployment template. Suitable VM templates for SAP are listed in Table 7-4.

Table 7-4. *Suitable VM Sizes*

VM Size	vCPUs	RAM	Costs (West Europe)	Available Image Offers (SUSE)	Available SKUs
Standard_E16s_v3	16	128	$1.28/hr	sles-sap-12-sp5-byos	gen1/gen2
Standard_E20s_v3	20	160	$1.6/hr	sles-sap-12-sp5-byos	gen1/gen2
Standard_FX4mds	4	80	$0.45/hr	sles-sap-12-sp5-byos	gen2
Standard_FX12mds	12	256	$1.35/hr	sles-sap-12-sp5-byos	gen2

- Resources: The resources define the objects that are to be provided within the framework of the template. In this file, the combination of parameters and variables is then applied to uniquely specify the resources. Firstly, select the resource node of the virtual machine.

The interaction between parameters and variables can be seen in the "storageProfile" area. See Figure 7-5 for an illustration.

Figure 7-5. *Storage profile area*

The resource identifies the "sku" by passing the parameter entered by the user (referenced by the "osType" field) and the variable "images" as a key and returning the associated value. If you have already made adjustments to the VM size, you must ensure that "sku" and "offer" are available for the VM size you have chosen.

Note : The semantics of sku and offer are not always applied consistently by all providers in Azure. For the offer "SLES-SAP," for example, SUSE offers the skus "12-sp4" and "12-sp4-gen2." Gen2 stands for the hypervisor version. Some VM sizes such as the FX-series are only offered as a Gen2 variant. In this case, the sku "12-sp4" could not be used. However, SUSE also offers the "sles-12-sp5" offer with the "gen1" and "gen2" skus. Therefore, when creating a template, note what the exact combination of sku and offer must be to get a valid deployment.

Customizing the DB Quick Start Template

The template currently does not quite meet the requirements of our sample architecture. First, we want to adapt the names of the resources so that they correspond to our naming scheme.

Note : Editing a template can easily lead to problems during deployment. In addition to semantic errors (invalid JSON file), there may be inconsistencies in version dependencies or components in particular. We recommend that you still follow the steps in this chapter to build an understanding of template deployments. If problems arise later, you can always deploy the original template or perform the necessary steps manually.

Select the virtual machine resource node and remove the separator between variable name and copyIndex(). To do this, change the "name" value to "[concat(variables('vmNameDB'), copyIndex())]", as demonstrated in Figure 7-6.

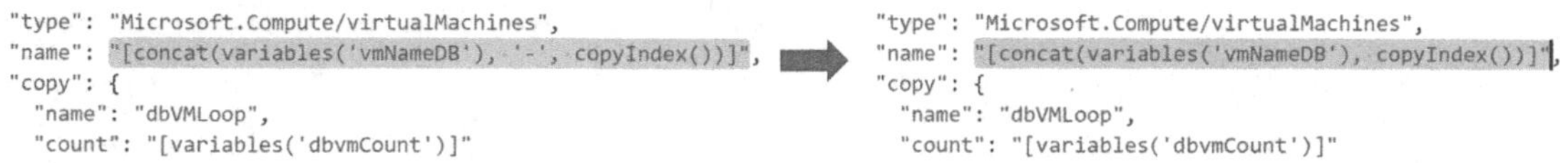

```
"type": "Microsoft.Compute/virtualMachines",          "type": "Microsoft.Compute/virtualMachines",
"name": "[concat(variables('vmNameDB'), '-', copyIndex())]",   "name": "[concat(variables('vmNameDB'), copyIndex())]",
"copy": {                                             "copy": {
  "name": "dbVMLoop",                                   "name": "dbVMLoop",
  "count": "[variables('dbvmCount')]"                   "count": "[variables('dbvmCount')]"
```

Figure 7-6. *Adaptation of the VM resource node name*

Repeat this step for the network interface, as well as for the public IP address. Then open the variable "vmNameDB" and change its value to

```
"vmNameDB": "[concat(variables('sidlower'), '-vc-db')]"
```

341

The name generation for the availability set as well as the load balancing does not need to be adjusted. The resources created by the template currently contain eight objects, including a virtual network and an NSG. Both resources have already been created as part of our basic configuration and therefore should not be created again. Therefore, in the next step, we customize the template to deploy to our existing subnet and reuse existing NSGs.

Switch to the "Resources (8)" node and delete the "networkSecurityGroups" and "virtualNetworks" objects in the JSON view. When deleting, make sure that the JSON file is correctly bracketed as shown in Figure 7-7.

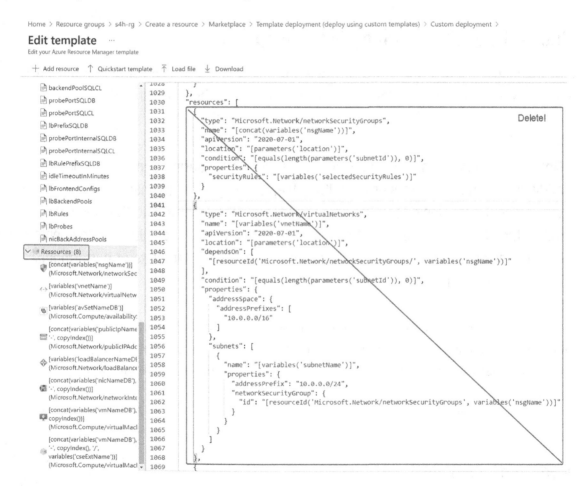

Figure 7-7. *Deletion of "networkSecurityGroups" and "virtualNetworks" resources*

The resource node in the left navigation bar should then update to (6). The parameter "subnetId" already exists for specifying the subnet. For the specification of the NSG, we define a new parameter "nsgId." Select the "subnetId" node in the navigation bar and copy its parameter definition. Then change the ID to "nsgId" and the description to "The id of the nsg you want to use." Figure 7-8 illustrates the result of this step.

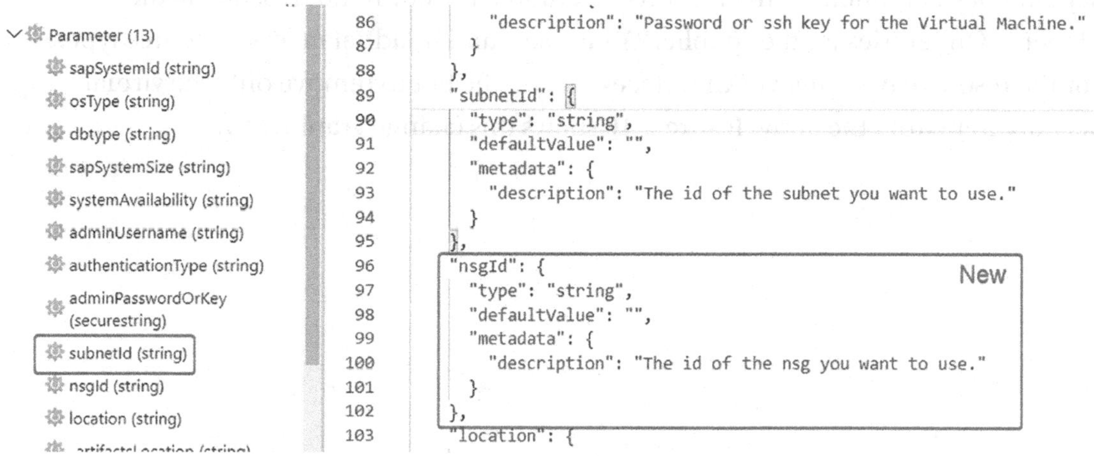

Figure 7-8. *Definition of the "nsgId" parameter*

We also need to adjust the "_artifactsLocation" parameter. This is a URI that allows other external files to be included in the deployment. In the context of this template, for example, online scripts are included which automatically partition and mount the created volumes of the VM. The scripts are available in the template's associated Git repository. We enter the URL to the repository as "defaultValue." Be sure to reference the "raw" and not the HTML representation of the resource. The URL must also end with "/". Enter the URL "`https://raw.githubusercontent.com/Azure/azure-quickstart-templates/master/application-workloads/sap/sap-3-tier-marketplace-image-multi-sid-db-md/`" and compare its result with Figure 7-9.

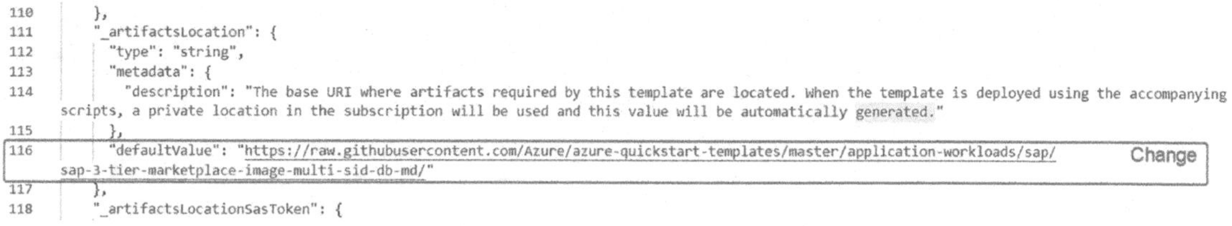

Figure 7-9. *Modification of the "_artifactsLocation" parameter*

Due to possible dependencies between individual resource objects, for example, a network interface requires a public IP, these can also be defined as part of template provisioning. This ensures that provisioning for the subsequent resource is aborted if its prerequisite is not met or could not be provisioned. Since we have deleted the virtual network as well as the NSG in the template, we need to adjust the corresponding dependency definitions in the resource definition as well. To do this, delete the "dependsOn" entries for the "publicIPAddresses" and "loadBalancers" resource types. For the resource type "networkInterfaces," it is sufficient to remove only the virtual network item from the array. Figure 7-10 shows this change graphically.

```
{
  "type": "Microsoft.Network/publicIPAddresses",
  "name": "[concat(variables('publicIpNameDB'), '-', copyIndex())]",
  "apiVersion": "2020-07-01",
  "condition": "[equals(length(parameters('subnetId')), 0)]",   Delete!
  "dependsOn": [
    "[resourceId('Microsoft.Network/virtualNetworks/', variables('vnetName'))]"
  ],
  "location": "[parameters('location')]",
  "copy": {
    "name": "dbpipLoop",
    "count": "[variables('dbvmCount')]"
  },
  "properties": {
    "publicIPAllocationMethod": "Dynamic"
  }
},
{
  "type": "Microsoft.Network/loadBalancers",
  "name": "[variables('loadBalancerNameDB')]",
  "apiVersion": "2020-07-01",
  "location": "[parameters('location')]",
  "condition": "[greater(variables('dbvmCount') , 1)]",        Delete !
  "dependsOn": [
    "[resourceId('Microsoft.Network/virtualNetworks/', variables('vnetName'))]"
  ],
  "properties": {
    "frontendIPConfigurations": "[variables('lbFrontendConfigs')[parameters('dbtype')]
ariables('internalOSType')]]",
    "backendAddressPools": "[variables('lbBackendPools')[parameters('dbtype')]
~iables('internalOSType')]]",
    "loadBalancingRules": "[variables('lbRules')[parameters('dbtype')][variables
nternalOSType')]]",
    "probes": "[variables('lbProbes')[parameters('dbtype')][variables
nternalOSType')]]"
  }
},
{
  "type": "Microsoft.Network/networkInterfaces",
  "name": "[concat(variables('nicNameDB'), '-', copyIndex())]",
  "apiVersion": "2020-07-01",
  "copy": {
    "name": "dbNICLoop",
    "count": "[variables('dbvmCount')]"
  },
  "dependsOn": [
    "dbpipLoop",                                               Delete!
    "[resourceId('Microsoft.Network/virtualNetworks/', variables('vnetName'))]",
    "[resourceId('Microsoft.Network/loadBalancers/', variables('loadBalancerNameDB'))
```

Figure 7-10. *Modification of the NSG template*

For the "networkInterface" resource, we also define a reference to the new "nsgId" parameter in the "properties" section to define the network security group. Since we have changed the naming convention for public IP addresses, we also need to remove the hyphen in "publicIPAddress." Figure 7-11 summarizes these changes.

```
{
    "type": "Microsoft.Network/networkInterfaces",
    "name": "[concat(variables('nicNameDB'), copyIndex())]",
    "apiVersion": "2020-07-01",
    "copy": {
        "name": "dbNICLoop",
        "count": "[variables('dbvmCount')]"
    },
    "dependsOn": [
        "dbpipLoop",
        "[resourceId('Microsoft.Network/loadBalancers/', variables('loadBalancerNameDB'))]"
    ],
    "location": "[parameters('location')]",
    "properties": {
        "ipConfigurations": [
            {
                "name": "ipconfig1",
                "properties": {
                    "privateIPAllocationMethod": "Dynamic",
                    "publicIPAddress": "[if(equals(length(parameters('subnetId')), 0), json(concat('{\"id\": \"', resourceId
('Microsoft.Network/publicIPAddresses', concat(variables('publicIpNameDB'), [⬚] copyIndex())) ,'\"}')), json('null'))]",       Delete!
                    "subnet": {
                        "id": "[variables('selectedSubnetId')]"
                    },
                    "loadBalancerBackendAddressPools": "[if(greater(variables('dbvmCount') , 1), variables('nicBackAddressPools')
[parameters('dbtype')][variables('internalOSType')], json('null'))]"
                }
            }
        ],                                         New
        "networkSecurityGroup": {
            "id": "[parameters('nsgId')]"
        },
        "enableAcceleratedNetworking": "[variables('sizes')[parameters('sapSystemSize')][parameters('dbType')].useFastNetwork]
```

Figure 7-11. *Modification of the "networkInterface" resource*

Finally, use the browser search to remove the remaining four occurrences of "-". For the "virtualMachines" resource, the hyphen must be removed three times in the "osProfile," "networkInterfaces," and "osDisk" sections. Additionally, the name for the "virtualMachines/extensions" resource needs to be adjusted.

This concludes our changes to the template. Click the "Download" button to save the customized version of the template locally on your PC. You can restore the template at any time later by clicking "Load file." Finally, click the "Save" button to apply the changes and switch to the deployment screen.

Customized Template Deployment

In the "Custom Provisioning" view, you get to select the subscription, as well as the resource group, as usual. First, make sure that the values entered here are correct. The parameters listed under "Instance Details" correspond to the values we have already seen in the context of the pre-algorithm editing. Under the entry "Subnet Id," you should also see the newly defined parameter "Nsg Id" including tooltip. Just fill the parameter "SAP System Id" with the value "HA1" and then click the button "Visualize" to get an overview of the resources to be created. The resource quick view should now display a graph with five resource nodes, with the arrows representing the "dependsOn" dependencies. Since the sixth "resource" is a "VM extension object" that is not created independently, but only defines post-processing steps, it is not displayed in the visualization. Also, pay attention to the resource name to ensure that the naming conventions have been observed.

Close the quick view again and select the value "HA" in the input mask for the parameter "System Availability." Then click the "Visualize" button again. You should now see three additional resources consisting of another virtual machine, a network interface, and a public IP address. Close the view and set the following input parameters:

- Region: <Your region>

- SID: HA1

- Os Type: <HANA supported Linux version such as SLES 12 (BYOS = bring-your-own-subscription)>

- Dbtype: HANA

- Sap System Size: <Size of the SAP system>

- System Availability: HA

- Admin Username: <Name for administrator user, e.g., cloudadm>

- Pw or Key: <Password>

- Subnet Id: <Noted ID of your virtual subnet>

- Nsg Id: <Noted ID of your NSG>

- For the remaining fields, you can accept the default values. Now click "Check + create" and wait until the deployment is complete.

Note   : If there are errors in the deployment, click Details for more information about the problem. If the errors are due to problems in the template (e.g., "invalid JSON"), click "Deploy again" and upload your template again. Then make the appropriate adjustments. Remember to delete any previously created resources before attempting a new deployment. Alternatively, you can deploy the original template (in which case you may need to adjust or delete the basic configuration) or deploy the resources manually. We will explain manual provisioning of a VM in the next step in the context of the iSCSI target VM.

As a result, your resource group should now contain 24 new objects consisting of 18x disks (2x OS disks + 16 HANA disks), 2x virtual machines, 2x network interfaces, as well as an availability set and a load balancer. Most of the objects like the load balancer are already preconfigured and do not need to be adjusted further as long as the HANA installation is done with instance number 03; otherwise, adjust the ports of the load balancer rules.

Adjust IP configuration: First, check the IP settings of your resources (virtual machines + load balancing). All IP addresses must be changed to static. We have left the dynamic setting in the template so that valid values are automatically chosen from the pool of unused IP addresses. For both virtual machines, we also want to define a public IP address to have access to the repositories. To do this, select the network interface of your VM in the resource view and click "IP configurations" in the left navigation bar. Now select the IP configuration and assign a public IP address by clicking "Create new." Select "**s4h-pip-db0**" as name, "Basic" as SKU, and "Static" as assignment. Then change the assignment of the private IP to "Static" and save. If you want to access the VM via SSH from the public network, you must first enable the network security group for SSH access from the Internet. Please note that this is a significant security risk and should not be considered a permanent solution under any circumstances. Instead, prefer to use a jump server or a bastion host as part of your "**hub-vnet**."

Check script post-processing: To ensure that the post-processing scripts have been executed correctly, now connect to their virtual machine. Check the memory availability with "df -h". As you can see, the 8x HANA volumes have already been mounted under / hana/data, /hana/log, and /hana/backup. For this purpose, three LVM volume groups consisting of two volumes each were configured. The script-based post-processing was therefore performed correctly.

Manual Provision of the iSCSI Target Servers

Before we start creating the virtual machine, we need a new subnet in which the iSCSI target VM(s) will be deployed. Select the virtual network "**s4h-vnet**" and add a new one under "Subnets." We select "**s4h-vnet-subnet-sbd**" as the name and 10.1.2.0/24 as the address range. If necessary, create a new network security group "**s4h-nsg-sbd**" with port shares for 860 and 3260 (iSCSI).

Note   : The steps for creating an iSCSI target server are based on the recommendation of Microsoft and are presented in abbreviated form in the following. For detailed instructions, see `https://docs.microsoft.com/en-us/azure/virtual-machines/workloads/sap/high-availability-guide-suse-pacemaker`.

Creating the Virtual Machine

Navigate to their resource group "s4h-rg" and create a new virtual machine (#create/ Microsoft.VirtualMachine-ARM). Make the following specifications in the **basic settings**:

- Name: s4h-vc-sbd0

- Region: <Your region>

- Availability option: Availability set

- Availability set: Create new -> "s4h-avset-sbd", Error domain=2, Update domain=20

- Image: SLES Linux for SAP (BYOS)

- No spot instance

- Size: Small VM sufficient for our example architecture, for example, "Standard_DS1_v2"

Navigate further to the **Disk** tab and select SSD Premium with Standard Encryption as the operating system disk.

Under Network, make the following specifications and complete the deployment:

- Virtual network: s4h-vnet

- Subnet: s4h-vnet-subnet-sbd

- Public IP: Create new (basic, static)

- Network security group: s4h-nsg-sbd

iSCSI Target Server Configuration

We will now present the configuration steps to create an iSCSI-based SBD device using the HANA database HA1 as an example. However, the iSCSI target server can provide basic SBD devices for other Pacemaker clusters such as ASCS/ERS and NFS. If you want to implement this, repeat the appropriate steps. In this case, replace all occurrences of "**ha1**" with the appropriate designation (e.g., **nfs** or **s4h**). First, connect to your new target server via SSH, license your operating system in the case of BYOS, and install the iSCSI target service.

```
# To be executed once
sudo SUSEConnect --url=https://scc.suse.com  -e <user> -r <key>
sudo zypper update
sudo zypper install targetcli-fb dbus-1-python
sudo systemctl enable targetcli
sudo systemctl start targetcli
```

Now create the directory /sbd and create the so-called "**backstores**" in it. This is the local storage area on the target server which is to be used for the iSCSI exports. The backstore objects should be used file-based (FILEIO). For SBD, we also have to disable the file system cache by setting "write_back=false". We then define a so-called "**iSCSI Qualified Name (IQN)**" for each Pacemaker cluster that we want to serve with an SBD device, via which the SBD devices can be uniquely identified in the network.

```
sudo mkdir /sbd
# Repeat the following commands for additional clusters
sudo targetcli backstores/fileio create sbdha1 /sbd/sbdha1 50M write_
back=false
sudo targetcli iscsi/ create iqn.2006-04.ha1.local:ha1
```

By creating the IQN, a so-called "**Target Portal Group (TPG)**" with the name **tpg1** is automatically created. The portal uses port 3260 by default and listens for all incoming IPv4 requests there. Additional TPGs can be created, but in most cases this is not necessary. We want to export the backstores as SCSI Logical Units (LUNS). For this purpose, we link the backstore objects with the respective IQNs in the first step. For each initiator/client, we have to allow access by configuring the ACL. For this, we have to add each host individually. We do this using the example of the HANA hosts "**ha1-vc-db0**" and "**ha1-vc-db1**."

```
# Repeat the following command for additional clusters
sudo targetcli iscsi/iqn.2006-04.ha1.local:ha1/tpg1/luns/ create /
backstores/fileio/sbdha1
# Replace ha1-vc-db0 with the corresponding hostnames
# Example: s4h-vc-ascs0 or s4h-vc-nfs0
sudo targetcli iscsi/iqn.2006-04.ha1.local:ha1/tpg1/acls/ create
iqn.2006-04.ha1-vc-db0.local:ha1-vc-db0
sudo targetcli iscsi/iqn.2006-04.ha1.local:ha1/tpg1/acls/ create
iqn.2006-04.ha1-vc-db1.local:ha1-vc-db1
```

Finally, save your changes. This sets up the iSCSI target server.

```
sudo targetcli saveconfig
```

Configuration of the Pacemaker Cluster

In this section, we cover the necessary steps to set up a basic Pacemaker cluster based on SBD and SLES 12 SP5 for the future HANA VMs "ha1-vc-db0" and "ha1-vc-db1." If you are using SLES version <= 12 SP4[6] or Red Hat Linux,[7] we recommend you to follow the instructions according to the official Microsoft documentation.

Some of the following steps must be performed on all machines [A] or only on "ha1-vc-db0" [db0] or "ha1-vc-db1" [db1]. We use the designations **[A]**, **[db0]**, and **[db1]** to indicate which host the subsequent steps should be performed on.

---

[6] https://docs.microsoft.com/en-us/azure/virtual-machines/workloads/sap/high-availability-guide-suse-pacemaker

[7] https://docs.microsoft.com/en-us/azure/virtual-machines/workloads/sap/high-availability-guide-rhel-pacemaker

Mounting the iSCSI Disk

[A] First, we need to make the iSCSI-based SBD device of our target server available locally to enable fencing. Connect to both machines via SSH and make the services "iscsi," "iscsid," and "sbd" available. Also, configure the initiator name in "/etc/iscsi/."

```
# ssh <ha1-vc-db0 / ha1-vc-db1>
sudo systemctl enable iscsid
sudo systemctl enable iscsi
sudo systemctl enable sbd
sudo vi /etc/iscsi/initiatorname.iscsi
# [db0] Change the value to
      InitiatorName=iqn.2006-04.ha1-vc-db0.local:ha1-vc-db0
# [db1] Change the value to
      InitiatorName=iqn.2006-04.ha1-vc-db1.local:ha1-vc-db1
```

[A] After restarting the iSCSI service, the SBD devices can be mounted. To do this, a discovery must first be performed using sendtarget (st). A list of available targets is sent to the initiator. The internal IP of the iSCSI server can be used as the target, for example, 10.1.2.0. The default port of the TPG is 3260.

```
sudo systemctl restart iscsid
sudo systemctl restart iscsi
sudo iscsiadm -m discovery --type=st --portal=<IP of s4h-vc-sbd0>:3260
```

[A] We then perform a login to the portal (TPG) by specifying the IQN. In order to avoid the need to manually perform the login again after a reboot, we also configure an automatic login. Finally, check whether the new SCSI device has been mounted by the initiator!

```
sudo iscsiadm -m node -T iqn.2006-04.ha1.local:ha1 --login --portal=<IP of
s4h-vc-sbd0>:3260
sudo iscsiadm -m node -p =<IP of s4h-vc-sbd0>:3260 -T iqn.2006-04.ha1.
local:ha1 --op=update --name=node.startup --value=automatic
# Check if the disk "sbdha1" is available
Lsscsi
```

Using the iSCSI Disk As an SBD Device

[A] Now we want to use the SCSI device as SBD. In order to do so, we first need to identify the ID of the disk. Use "lsscsi" to check which logical device the iSCSI disk was provisioned as. If you used template provisioning, this is usually /dev/**sdk**. To identify the ID, then run the following command:

```
ls -l /dev/disk/by-id/scsi-* | grep sdk
```

[A] The disk is available through three paths. Azure recommends that you copy the path that starts as the ID with the prefix "/dev/disk/by-id/scsi-3". Afterward, we define the SBD device specifying the path and with a "msgwait" timeout of 120 seconds:

```
sudo sbd -d <device-ID> 60 -4 120 create
```

Now that the SBD device has been created, you have to include it in the Pacemaker configuration. You can specify up to three SBD devices as a list separated by semicolons:

```
sudo vi /etc/sysconfig/sbd
# Set the following values:
        SBD_DEVICE="<device-ID1>;<device-ID2>;<device-ID3>"
        SBD_PACEMAKER="yes"
        SBD_STARTMODE="always"
```

Only the "softdog" is supported as watchdog in this setup. Activate the module on both database VMs:

```
echo softdog | sudo tee /etc/modules-load.d/softdog.conf
sudo modprobe -v softdog
```

Initialization of the Pacemaker Cluster

In order for the Azure load balancer to be able to identify later which HANA VM is acting as primary and should therefore receive all database requests, SUSE relies on the "**socat**" tool. This is a further developed netcat program that is only started on the primary node. The load balancer uses an integrity test, which checks if a defined port (socat) is reachable on the VMs in the back-end pool. By ensuring that socat is only running on the primary node, or on the former secondary node in case of failover, we ensure that load balancing always forwards requests to the correct HANA. Depending on the version of your SUSE system, you can also use azure-lb instead of socat. In addition to socat,

353

we also need the so-called resource agent. These are collections of scripts that enable the instances to be started and stopped and define return values that Pacemaker can react to.

```
sudo zypper install -y socat
sudo zypper in -y resource-agents
```

Microsoft also recommends increasing the default resource limit "DefaultTasksMax." This number specifies the maximum number of processes or threads a service can create. The default value of 512 can in some cases be exceeded by Pacemaker which leads to problems with heartbeat mechanisms. Also, when using SLES 12/11, the size of the change cache should be reduced to prevent a known performance bug.

```
sudo vi /etc/systemd/system.conf
# Change the DefaultTasksMax from 512 to 4096
        DefaultTasksMax=4096
sudo systemctl daemon-reload
sudo vi /etc/sysctl.conf
# Set the following values:
        vm.dirty_bytes = 629145600
        vm.dirty_background_bytes = 314572800
```

There are a couple of changes to be made on the cluster nodes and then individually on one node of the cluster only. In order to distinguish between the operations, we will use the following notation:

- **[A]** stands for an activity to be carried out on both nodes.

- **[db0]** stands for an activity to be carried out on the first database node.

- **[db1]** stands for an activity to be carried out on the second database node.

[A] Before we can initiate the cluster initialization, we must first enable passwordless SSH communication within the cluster and install the Azure Python SDK. For this, we need to enable the SLES Public Cloud module on all hosts. Make sure you specify your SUSE version correctly here (12/15). We also configure the internal naming solution using /etc/hosts:

[A]

```
sudo SUSEConnect -p sle-module-public-cloud/12/x86_64
sudo zypper in -y python-azure-mgmt-compute
sudo vi /etc/hosts
# Add both VMs to the hosts-file -> <priv IP> <Hostname>
        10.1.1.1 ha1-vc-db0
        10.1.1.2 ha1-vc-db1
sudo ssh-keygen
# 3x Enter (Standard path, no password, no password)
sudo cat /root/.ssh/id_rsa.pub
# Copy the public key for [db0-pubkey] and [db1-pubkey]
```

[db0]

```
echo "[db1-pubkey]" >> vi /root/.ssh/authorized_keys
```

[db1]

```
echo "[db0-pubkey]" >> vi /root/.ssh/authorized_keys
# Insert the public key you copied into the authorized keys file # on the
first server
sudo vi /root/.ssh/authorized_keys
```

[db0] Now we can start the initialization of the cluster. If you are asked to overwrite the private key /root/.ssh/id_rsa, deny with "n"; otherwise, accept the default suggestions, whereby we do not configure an administration IP for Hawk:

```
sudo ha-cluster-init -u
# ! NTP is not configured to start at system boot.
# Do you want to continue anyway (y/n)? y
# /root/.ssh/id_rsa already exists - overwrite (y/n)? n
# Address for ring0 <IP-[db0]> Press ENTER
# Port for ring0 [5405] Press ENTER
# SBD is already configured to use <SBD Device> overwrite? n
#WARNING: Not configuring SBD - STONITH will be disabled.
# Do you wish to configure an administration IP (y/n)? n
```

[db1] Now that the cluster has been initialized, we can add the second node:

```
sudo ha-cluster-join
# IP address of hostname of existing node (e.g.: 192.168.1.1)[] <IP-[db0]>
```

[A] Some post-processing steps are now necessary on both nodes. First, we adjust the Corosync settings. The default values are optimized for on-premise installations and specify a quorum timeout (token) of five seconds. For Azure, this value is too low. Due to maintenance work, it happens that VMs are migrated between servers, which leads to short timeout scenarios. Experience has shown that the default timeout is set too low and that this results in "more frequent" scenarios where a node is marked as faulty, although it is available again within a few seconds. This makes the cluster unstable, which is why a value of 30 seconds is now recommended. By adjusting the token, we also have to change the "consensus" value. This should always be 1.2 times token. We also set a password for the new user "hacluster" created during the cluster initialization:

```
passwd hacluster
vi /etc/corosync/corosync.conf
        token: 30000
        consensus: 36000
sudo service corosync restart
```

[db0] Finally, on the primary node, we configure the default values recommended by Azure when using Pacemaker based on SBD. We set the timeout for STONITH activities to 144 seconds (default 60) and set the fencing to 15 seconds:

```
sudo crm configure property stonith-timeout=144
sudo crm configure property stonith-enabled=true
sudo crm resource stop stonith-sbd
sudo crm configure delete stonith-sbd
sudo crm configure primitive stonith-sbd stonith:external/sbd \
    params pcmk_delay_max="15" \
    op monitor interval="15" timeout="15"
```

[db0] Optionally, it is advisable to configure Azure events for Pacemaker. Azure services are not free of scheduled maintenance events. To enable the customer to react to such events, Azure provides a metadata service called "Scheduled Events," which informs about upcoming maintenance events. The resource agent "azure-events" can monitor these events and react accordingly, for example, to migrate resources to another node before the corresponding event occurs. This is done by putting the node affected by the maintenance event into standby mode. The "azure-events" agent should have already been installed with the installation of the "resource-agents" package. On the main node (ha1-vc-db0), you only need to configure the corresponding Pacemaker resources. To do this, we first put the cluster into "maintenance mode" and then configure the resource:

```
sudo crm configure property maintenance-mode=true
sudo crm configure primitive rsc_azure-events ocf:heartbeat:azure-events op monitor interval=10s
sudo crm configure clone cln_azure-events rsc_azure-events
#Exit maintenance mode -> warnings can be ignored
sudo crm configure property maintenance-mode=false
```

Excursus on Azure Fencing Agent

Instead of the SBD setup based on iSCSI target servers, fencing can alternatively be enabled via the Azure Fencing Agent. However, answer the cluster initialization (ha-cluster-init -u) question about using SBD with "n". Also, install the "fence-agents" package:

```
sudo zypper install fence-agents"
```

Next, we will create our Fence Agent. For this, we will use the Azure Cloud Shell which we access via the portal. Alternatively, you can also use the Azure CLI by installing the necessary packages on your jump server.[8] First, look for the service "Azure Active Directory." Now open the menu item "Properties" in the left navigation bar and copy your "**Client ID.**" Then select the "App Registration" menu item and click the "**New Registration**" button. Choose a name, for example, "**S4HFenceAgent,**" and select "Only accounts in this organization directory" in the supported account types. Also, specify a redirect URI of type "Web" and with URL http://localhost (the URL is not actually used). Now select the created "S4HFenceAgent." In the "Overview" section, copy the "**Application ID**" and then click "**Certificates & Secrets**" in the left navigation bar. In it, create a new secret key "**ClientSecret0**" with a validity of 24 months. Once this has been created, copy the cell in the "**Value**" column; this will be needed as the password for the service principal. Finally, navigate to the "Subscriptions" service and copy the displayed **subscription ID**.

---

[8] https://docs.microsoft.com/en-us/cli/azure/install-azure-cli

Now open the "Cloud Shell" by clicking the console icon to the right of the search bar in the Azure Portal. The Cloud Shell requires an Azure file share. If you do not have a storage account yet, you will get a message asking if you want to create a new storage. Note that having a storage account will incur additional fees. Although the file share is only about 6 GiB in size, the file service is created with a share capacity of 5 TiB. We will use the following Cloud Shell to create a user-specific role for the Azure Fencing Agent. This should allow to start/stop virtual machines as well as to read information:

```
vi customRoleFenceAgent.json
# Add the following lines
{
        "Name": "Custom Role Fence Agent",
        "description": "Allows to power-off and start virtual machines",
        "assignableScopes": [
                "/subscriptions/<Subscription-ID>"
        ],
        "actions": [
                "Microsoft.Compute/*/read",
                "Microsoft.Compute/virtualMachines/powerOff/action",
                "Microsoft.Compute/virtualMachines/start/action"
        ],
        "notActions": [],
        "dataActions": [],
        "notDataActions": []
}
```

Now create the new role with the call:

```
New-AzRoleDefinition -InputFile "customRoleFenceAgent.json"
```

We have now defined the new role. Now we have to link the Fence Agent with the role in the access control of the respective virtual machines (for which the Fence Agent is responsible). To do this, navigate to the virtual computer, for example, "**s4h-vc-db0**," and select the item "Access Control (IAM)" in the left navigation bar. Then click the "Add" button and "Add role assignment." Make the selection in the mask as follows:

- Role: Custom Role Fence Agent

- Assign access to: User, Group, or Service Principal

- Select: S4HFenceAgent

Then click "Save" and repeat the steps for further virtual computers. Finally, to use the Fencing Agent as a STONITH device, we need to extend the cluster configuration:

```
sudo crm configure property stonith-enabled=true
sudo crm configure property concurrent-fencing=true
sudo crm configure primitive rsc_st_azure stonith:fence_azure_arm \
  params subscriptionId="<Subscription-ID"" resourceGroup="<Resource
group z.B. s4h-rg>" tenantId="<Client-ID>" login="Application-ID"
passwd="<Password value>"\
  pcmk_monitor_retries=4 pcmk_action_limit=3 power_timeout=240 pcmk_reboot_
timeout=900 \
  op monitor interval=3600 timeout=120
sudo crm configure property stonith-timeout=900
```

Setting Up the HANA HA Cluster

After setting up the Pacemaker cluster, we will set up the HANA cluster in this section. In order to do this, we will first install two HANA databases and set up HANA System Replication between the two nodes. Then, we will set up Pacemaker to allow automatic failover between the nodes.

Installation of HANA Database

If you used the quick start template, ten volumes + optionally other SBD devices should be mounted. In addition, mount points should already be set for the paths /mnt, /usr/sap, /hana/shared, /hana/backup, /hana/data, and /hana/log.

For data, backup, and log, a separate LVM volume group was set up with 2x physical disks each (6x in total). The remaining four disks are used for root, /hana/shared, /mnt, and /usr/sap.

If you want to configure your file system layout manually, use either the graphical partitioning help via "yast -> partitioner" or the corresponding terminal commands (pvcreate, vgcreate, lvcreate, mkfs.xfs, mkdir, mount, sudo vi /etc/fdisk). When doing so, make sure that the disks you use meet the performance requirements of HANA:

- **/hana/log** at least 250 MB/sec read/write for 1 MB I/O

- **/hana/data** at least 400 MB/sec read and 250 MB/sec write for 16 MB and 64 MB I/O

For HANA System Replication, it is necessary that both HANA systems are installed with identical SID (HA1) and instance number (03). Make the HANA installation files available and run "hdblcm" to perform the HANA installation. No special components are required for our setup. In this example, we only use "server," "client," and "afl" for the server installation.

Setting Up the System Replication

[A] In order for the primary HANA dataset to be transferred to the secondary, the next step we need to take is to set up HANA System Replication. First, we create a database for the future S/4HANA system. For the tenant name, we use the SID of the future S/4 system. Then, we need to back up the system database and all tenants of the HANA system. This is a prerequisite to set up the system replication.

Note   : The default path for backups is /hana/shared/<SID>/HDB<instance no.>/backup/data/.

Thus, the mount point /hana/backup is not used by default.

```
su - ha1adm
hdbsql -u SYSTEM -p "<Password>" -i 03 -d SYSTEMDB 'CREATE DATABASE S4H
SYSTEM USER PASSWORD "<Password>"
hdbsql -d SYSTEMDB -u SYSTEM -p "<Password>" -i 03 "BACKUP DATA USING FILE
('initialSYS')"
hdbsql -d HA1 -u SYSTEM -p "<Password>" -i 03 "BACKUP DATA USING FILE
('initialHA1')"
hdbsql -d S4H -u SYSTEM -p "<Password>" -i 03 "BACKUP DATA USING FILE
('initialS4H')"
```

[db0] Since the system replication is encrypted, we also need to transfer the PKI system data of the primary node to the secondary:

```
su - ha1adm
scp /usr/sap/HA1/SYS/global/security/rsecssfs/data/SSFS_HA1.DAT  ha1-vc-
db1:/usr/sap/HA1/SYS/global/security/rsecssfs/data/
scp /usr/sap/HA1/SYS/global/security/rsecssfs/key/SSFS_HA1.KEY  ha1-vc-
db1:/usr/sap/HA1/SYS/global/security/rsecssfs/key/
```

Next, we define the location name. Here, we should not use terms like "primary/secondary" or "master/slave," because these roles can change at any time. We use "DB0" and "DB1" as the name (according to the hostnames of our systems). First, we enable system replication for db0 and then register db1 with the primary node:

```
[db0]
hdbnsutil -sr_enable --name=DB0
[db1]
sapcontrol -nr 03 -function StopWait 600 10
hdbnsutil -sr_register --remoteHost=ha1-vc-db0 --remoteInstance=03
--replicationMode=sync --name=DB1
```

[db0] Finally, check the status of replication. DB0 should be detected as "primary" and "source system." Also, DB1's replication mode should be labeled "sync." Optionally, you can view more details about the replication with the Python script "systemReplicationStatus.py":

```
hdbnsutil -sr_state
HDBSettings.sh systemReplicationStatus.py
```

[A] As of HANA 2.0, it is also recommended to configure the Python system replication hook, which allows for better integration of HANA into the Pacemaker cluster. To do this, we first create a new directory under /hana/shared where we store the Python script and enable sudo access for the <sid>adm user. Then we make an entry in the "global.ini" to use the hook and finally restart both HANA systems:

```
mkdir -p /hana/shared/myHooks
cp /usr/share/SAPHanaSR/SAPHanaSR.py /hana/shared/myHooks
chown -R ha1adm:sapsys /hana/shared/myHooks
sapcontrol -nr 03 -function StopSystem
```

```
cat << EOF > /etc/sudoers.d/20-saphana
ha1adm ALL=(ALL) NOPASSWD: /usr/sbin/crm_attribute -n hana_ha1_site_
srHook_*
EOF
vi /hana/shared/HA1/global/hdb/custom/confi/global.ini
        # Fügen Sie folgende Zeilen hinzu
         [ha_dr_provider_SAPHanaSR]
        provider = SAPHanaSR
        path = /hana/shared/myHooks
        execution_order = 1
         [trace]
        ha_dr_saphanasr = info
sapcontrol -nr 03 -function StartSystem
```

[db0] Finally, verify that HANA is installed correctly:

```
cdtrace
 awk '/ha_dr_SAPHanaSR.*crm_attribute/ \
 { printf "%s %s %s %s\n",$2,$3,$5,$16 }' nameserver_*
```

Defining HANA Cluster Resources in Pacemaker

[db0] All of the following steps in this section can be performed on any VM as long as they are part of the cluster. First, we need to create the HANA topology as a cluster resource. To do this, we need to put the cluster into maintenance mode:

```
sudo crm configure property maintenance-mode=true
sudo crm configure primitive rsc_SAPHanaTopology HA1 HDB03
ocf:suse:SAPHanaTopology \
  operations \$id="rsc_sap2_HA1_HDB03-operations" \
  op monitor interval="10" timeout="600" \
  op start interval="0" timeout="600" \
  op stop interval="0" timeout="300" \
  params SID="HA1" InstanceNumber="03"

sudo crm configure clone cln_SAPHanaTopology HA1 HDB03 rsc_
SAPHanaTopology_HA1_HDB03 \
  meta clone-node-max="1" target-role="Started" interleave="true"
```

We now create the HANA resources. If necessary, adjust the SID and instance number according to their configuration. Make sure that the Azure load balancer port is derived from the instance number (62503 in this example) and that you specify the front-end IP of the load balancer correctly:

```
sudo crm configure primitive rsc_SAPHana_HA1_HDB03 ocf:suse:SAPHana \
  operations \$id="rsc_sap_HA1_HDB03-operations" \
  op start interval="0" timeout="3600" \
  op stop interval="0" timeout="3600" \
  op promote interval="0" timeout="3600" \
  op monitor interval="60" role="Master" timeout="700" \
  op monitor interval="61" role="Slave" timeout="700" \
  params SID="HA1" InstanceNumber="03" PREFER_SITE_TAKEOVER="true" \
  DUPLICATE_PRIMARY_TIMEOUT="7200" AUTOMATED_REGISTER="false"

sudo crm configure ms msl_SAPHana_HA1_HDB03 rsc_SAPHana_HA1_HDB03 \
  meta notify="true" clone-max="2" clone-node-max="1" \
  target-role="Started" interleave="true"

sudo crm configure primitive rsc_ip_HA1_HDB03 ocf:heartbeat:IPaddr2 \
  meta target-role="Started" \
  operations \$id="rsc_ip_HA1_HDB03-operations" \
  op monitor interval="10s" timeout="20s" \
  params ip="<IP Load Balancer>"
```

As explained before, the Azure load balancing integrity test makes TCP requests to a defined port (e.g., 62503) to verify that the machine is suitable as a load balancing target. Depending on your SUSE version, you should use either "socat" or the newer "azure-lb" as a service. In this example, we are working with "socat" and adding it as a cluster resource. Pacemaker must ensure that the service is only ever active on the primary node. The rest of the cluster configuration follows the recommendations from SUSE and Microsoft. Complete the configuration by checking the status of the cluster resources:

```
sudo crm configure primitive rsc_nc_HA1_HDB03 anything \
    params binfile="/usr/bin/socat" cmdline_options="-U TCP-LISTEN:62503,bac
klog=10,fork,reuseaddr /dev/null" \
    op monitor timeout=20s interval=10
sudo crm configure primitive rsc_nc_HA1_HDB03 azure-lb port=62503 \
```

```
  meta resource-stickiness=0
sudo crm configure group g_ip_HA1_HDB03 rsc_ip_HA1_HDB03 rsc_nc_HA1_HDB03
sudo crm configure colocation col_saphana_ip_HA1_HDB03 4000: g_
ip_HA1_HDB03:Started \
  msl_SAPHana_HA1_HDB03:Master
sudo crm configure order ord_SAPHana_HA1_HDB03 Optional: cln_
SAPHanaTopology_HA1_HDB03 \
  msl_SAPHana_HA1_HDB03
sudo crm resource cleanup rsc_SAPHana_HA1_HDB03
sudo crm configure property maintenance-mode=false
sudo crm configure rsc_defaults resource-stickiness=1000
sudo crm configure rsc_defaults migration-threshold=5000
sudo crm_mon -r
```

This completes the configuration. We now have a highly available HANA cluster and can proceed with the deployment of the S/4HANA system.

Deploying an S/4HANA HA Cluster

In this section, we conclude the deployment of the sample architecture by setting up a highly available S/4HANA system. We will first provision the outstanding resources for this and go deeper into how Azure load balancing works. We will then take a closer look at highly available shared storage in Azure by first provisioning an NFS cluster and then introducing Azure NetApp Files as an alternative. Building on this, we will create the ASCS cluster using Enqueue Replication Server 2. Finally, we will conclude with the installation of the application servers.

SAP S/4HANA Cluster Architecture

As shown in Figure 7-12, the "**s4h-vnet**" is extended by another subnet "**s4h-vnet-subnet-nfs**" in which we provide two NFS servers in a Pacemaker cluster including an availability group. The cluster uses the existing iSCSI target servers for SBD fencing. We need NFS as a highly available solution to ensure that even in the event of a node failure, the shared directories /usr/sap/<SID>, /usr/sap/trans, as well as /sapmnt remain available, and there is no impact to the S/4HANA cluster. We will also introduce ANF as a highly available SaaS offering. You are free to provision all directories over an NFS or ANF. Finally, we will deploy the ASCS and ERS instance in the existing "**s4h-vnet-subnet-as**" including the other application servers. Unlike the ASCS and ERS instance, the application servers (AAS/PAS) do not require a Pacemaker cluster, but we will also deploy them as part of an availability group to prevent a simultaneous failure of both instances.

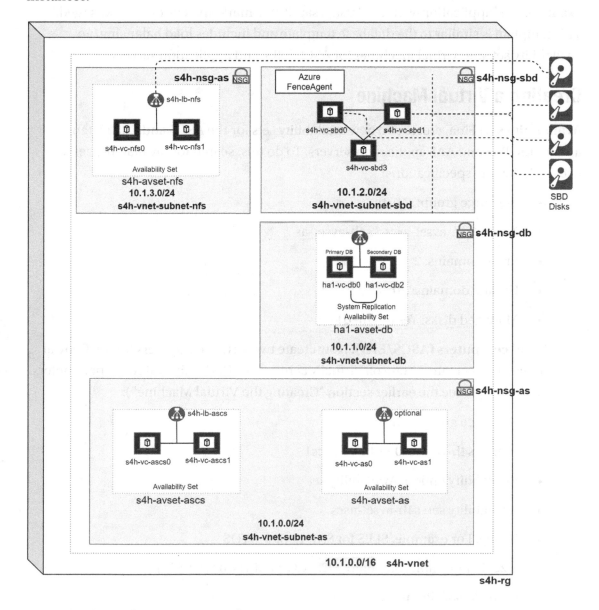

Figure 7-12. *S/4HANA HA architecture*

Provisioning SAP S/4HANA Cluster Resources

In contrast to the HANA deployment using a quick start template described in the section "Deployment of a HANA HA Cluster," in this section we will create and configure the Azure resources manually. If you prefer to use a template again, you can use, for example, the "application-workloads/sap/sap-3-tier-marketplace-image-converged." This template is similar to the database template and includes load balancing, an availability set, and virtual machines for ASCS, ERS, and application servers.

Creating a Virtual Machine

Availability set: First, create two new availability sets for the ASCS and ERS instances and for the PAS and AAS application servers. To do this, search for "availability set" and use the following specifications:

- Resource group: s4h-rg

- Name: s4h-avset-ascs / s4h-avset-as

- Error domains: 2

- Update domains: 20

- Managed disks: Yes (aligned)

Virtual computers (ASCS/ERS): Now create two virtual computers for the Central Services cluster (#create/Microsoft.VirtualMachine-ARM). Use the following parameters (for detailed steps, see the earlier section "Creating the Virtual Machine"):

- Resource group: s4h-rg

- Name: s4h-vc-ascs0 / s4h-vc-ascs1

- Availability option: Availability set

- Availability set: s4h-avset-ascs

- Image: For example, SLES for SAP 12 SP5-BYOS

- Size: For example, Standard_D2s_v3 (2 vCPUs, 8 GB RAM)

- OS disk: SSD Premium

- Additional disk: None

- Virtual network: s4h-vnet

- Subnet: s4h-vnet-subnet-as

- IP: Static internal IP (e.g., 10.1.0.1/10.1.0.2) + static public IP (basic)

- Network security group: s4h-nsg-as

- Accelerated network operation: Yes

- Load balancing: No

Virtual computers (PAS/AAS): Also create two virtual computers for the application server pool (for detailed steps, see the earlier section "Creating the Virtual Machine"):

- Resource group: s4h-rg

- Name: s4h-vc-as0 / s4h-vc-as1

- Availability option: Availability set

- Availability set: s4h-avset-as

- Image: For example, SLES for SAP 12 SP5-BYOS

- Size: For example, Standard_DS4_v2 (8 vCPUs, 28 GB RAM)

- OS disk: SSD Premium

- Additional disk: 128 GB SSD Premium (P10)

- Virtual network: s4h-vnet

- Subnet: s4h-vnet-subnet-as

- IP: Static internal IP (e.g., 10.1.0.3/10.1.0.4) + static public IP (basic)

- Network security group: s4h-nsg-as

- Accelerated network operation: Yes

- Load balancing: No

Creation and Configuration of the Load Balancer

Load balancer: The load balancer is available in two SKUs, "Standard" and "Basic." The Basic load balancer is free of charge, but is subject to some restrictions, such as that "only" up to 300 instances can be connected and that all back-end systems must be in a single availability set or scale set. Therefore, for the example we use, it is possible to use Basic load balancing. However, to make configuration easier, we use the Standard version, which is also recommended by Microsoft.

ASCS/ERS Load Balancer

Create a load balancer for the ASCS/ERS cluster (#create/Microsoft.LoadBalancer-ARM). Make the following values for the basic settings:

- Resource group: s4h-rg

- Name: s4h-lb-ascs

- Type: Internal

- SKU: Standard

- Tariff: Regional

Then add two front-end IP addresses through which the load balancer will accept requests:

- Name: s4h-lb-ascs-fip-ascs / s4h-lb-ascs-fip-ers

- Virtual network: s4h-vnet

- Subnet: s4h-vnet-subnet-as

- Assignment: Static

- IP address: For example, 10.1.0.5/10.1.0.6

- Availability zone: Zone redundant

Then define two back-end pools. These each contain the same virtual computers (ASCS and ERS instances):

- Name: s4h-lb-ascs-backend-ascs / s4h-lb-ascs-backend-ers

- Virtual network: s4h-vnet

- Configuration of the back-end pool: Network interface

- IP version: IPv4

- Virtual computers: [s4h-vc-ascs0,s4h-vc-ascs1]/[s4h-vc-ascs0,s4h-vc-ascs1]

Finally, we configure the actual load balancing rules. If you have used load balancing in the "Standard" SKU, it is sufficient to select "HA ports." In the case of "Basic," we need to manually configure the respective ports for the ASCS and ERS based on the instance number (IN). These are for the ASCS instance (32<IN>, 36<IN>, 39<IN>, 81<IN>, 5<IN>13, 5<IN>14, 5<IN>16) and for the ERS instance (32<IN>, 33<IN>, 5<IN>13, 5<IN>14, 5<IN>16):

- Name: s4h-lb-ascs-inbrule-ascs / s4h-lb-ascs-inbrule-ascs

- IP version: IPv4

- Front-end IP address: s4h-lb-ascs-fip-ascs / s4h-lb-ascs-fip-ers

- HA ports: Yes

- Back-end pool: s4h-lb-ascs-backend-ascs / s4h-lb-ascs-backend-ers

- Integrity test ASCS: Create new -> s4h-lb-ascs-probe-ascs, Port=621<InstNr. ASCS> (62100), Interval=5, Error threshold=2

- Integrity test ERS: Rebuild -> s4h-lb-ascs-probe-ers, Port=621<InstNo. ERS> (62102), Interval=5, Error threshold=2

- Session persistence: None

- Idle timeout (minutes): 30

- TCP reset: Disabled

- Floating IP: Enabled

Load Balancer for the Application Server Pool

Optionally, you can also create a load balancer for the application server pool. This is not necessary for a high availability scenario based on SAP GUI, but if your application servers also use web services such as an embedded Fiori front-end server. Note that this is an active/active configuration (as opposed to the HANA active/passive scenario), which means that the integrity test must be successful for all Fiori front-end servers (Pacemaker socat control). Also, consider the use of a session persistence. The "Client IP" setting should be sufficient for most scenarios. This will forward all requests from one IP to the same back-end server.

Highly Available NFS Storage in Azure

The classic way to provide highly available shared network storage for an SAP system is to use an NFS cluster (or SMB failover cluster in Windows). However, Azure also offers the SaaS service ANF, which allows you to create highly available SMB or NFS shares without having to administer the necessary infrastructure. In the following, we will briefly examine both options to help you make your decision.

Alternative 1: NFS Server Cluster

For the NFS cluster, we will create two virtual machines. Some of the following configuration steps must be performed on either all or only one of the two nodes. We denote this with the labels **[nfs0]** for "**s4h-vc-nfs0**," **[nfs1]** for "**s4h-vc-nfs1**," and **[A]** for all.

Create Azure Resources

First, create a new subnet "**s4h-vnet-subnet-nfs**" [10.1.3.0/24] and place two new virtual computers (**s4h-vc-nfs0, s4h-vc-nfs1**) as well as an availability set (**s4h-avset-nfs**) in it. Use the section "Provisioning SAP S/4HANA Cluster Resources" as a guide for the parameters. Since we use the virtual computers exclusively as NFS for our demo system, a small SKU such as "Standard_DS1_v2" (1 vCPU, 3.5 GiB RAM) is sufficient. Also, mount another disk, for example, 128 GB SSD Premium (P10).

Create an **internal** load balancer "**s4h-lb-nfs**." For our example architecture, the SKU "basic" is sufficient. Create a front-end IP (s4h-lb-ascs-fip-nfs) and a back-end pool (**s4h-lb-nfs-backend**) with the two virtual machines you just created. For the integrity test (**s4h-lb-nfs-probe**), we use a TCP probe on port 61000 with an interval of five seconds and an error threshold of two. Finally, create the load balancing rules. We create the rule "**s4h-lb-nfs-inbrule-tcp**" for port 2049 as a TCP connection using the previously configured settings (IP, pool, and probe) and with an idle timeout of 30 minutes and floating IP enabled. Since old protocol versions (esp. NFSv2) still use UDP as protocol, we also create the rule "**s4h-lb-nfs-inbrule-udp**" identical to the previous rule, but with UDP as protocol.

Configuration of the NFS Cluster

After the required resources have been created, we first create the basic Pacemaker cluster configuration. To do this, first configure a new SBD device on your target iSCSI server (see the section "iSCSI Target Server Configuration") and finally initialize the cluster as described in the earlier section "Configuration of the Pacemaker Cluster."

[A] **File system layout:** Our NFS service will serve files via the /srv/nfs/ directory. As background storage, we will create an LVM over the SCSI mounted additional volume. As a volume group, we use "vg-NFS," and as a logical volume, we use "lv-S4H":

```
mkdir /srv/nfs
sudo sh -c 'echo /srv/nfs/ *\(rw,no_root_squash,fsid=0\)>/etc/exports'
sudo sh -c 'echo -e "n\n\n\n\n\n\nw\n" | fdisk /dev/disk/azure/scsi1/lun0'
sudo vgcreate vg-NFS /dev/disk/azure/scsi1/lun0-part1
sudo lvcreate -l 100%FREE -n lv-S4H vg-NFS
```

"drbd" is used to replicate the files between the two NFS servers. Install the necessary packages and then make the following configuration settings:

```
sudo zypper install drbd drbd-kmp-default drbd-utils
sudo vi /etc/drbd.conf
    # Make sure that the following lines are included
    include "drbd.d/global_common.conf";
    include "drbd.d/*.res"
sudo vi /etc/drbd.d/global_common.conf
    # Modify the „handlers" section as follows
    global {
        usage-count no;
    }
    common {
        handlers {
            fence-peer "/usr/lib/drbd/crm-fence-peer.sh";
            after-resync-target "/usr/lib/drbd/crm-unfence-peer.sh";
            split-brain "/usr/lib/drbd/notify-split-brain.sh root";
            pri-lost-after-sb "/usr/lib/drbd/notify-pri-lost-after-
sb.sh; /usr/lib/drbd/notify-emergency-reboot.sh; echo b >
/proc/sysrq-trigger ; reboot -f";
        }
```

```
    startup {
        wfc-timeout 0;
    }
    options {
    }
    disk {
        md-flushes yes;
        disk-flushes yes;
        c-plan-ahead 1;
        c-min-rate 100M;
        c-fill-target 20M;
        c-max-rate 4G;
    }
    net {
        after-sb-0pri discard-younger-primary;
        after-sb-1pri discard-secondary;
        after-sb-2pri call-pri-lost-after-sb;
        protocol     C;
        tcp-cork yes;
        max-buffers 20000;
        max-epoch-size 20000;
        sndbuf-size 0;
        rcvbuf-size 0;
    }
}
```

We now create the drbd device /dev/drbd0 which uses the logical volume lv-S4H as the volume:

```
sudo vi /etc/drbd.d/S4H-nfs.res
#
    resource S4H-nfs {
        protocol     C;
        disk {
            on-io-error      detach;
        }
```

```
    on s4h-vc-nfs0 {
        address    10.1.3.0:7790;
        device     /dev/drbd0;
        disk       /dev/vg-NFS/lv-S4H;
        meta-disk internal;
    }
    on s4h-vc-nfs1 {
        address    10.1.3.1:7790;
        device     /dev/drbd0;
        disk       /dev/vg-NFS/lv-S4H;
        meta-disk internal;
    }
}
```

We can now take the drbd resource online, but before that we need to initialize the metadata store:

```
sudo drbdadm create-md S4H-nfs
sudo drbdadm up S4H-nfs
```

[nfs0] We now shorten the initial resynchronization and set the primary. Then we wait until the drbd devices are synchronized and create the file system layout:

```
drbdadm new-current-uuid --clear-bitmap S4H-nfs
drbdadm primary --force S4H-nfs
drbdsetup wait-sync-resource S4H-nfs
# Wait until the synchronization finished
sudo mkfs.xfs /dev/drbd0
sudo mkdir /srv/nfs/S4H
sudo chattr +i /srv/nfs/S4H
sudo mount -t xfs /dev/drbd0 /srv/nfs/S4H
sudo mkdir /srv/nfs/S4H/sidsys
sudo mkdir /srv/nfs/S4H/sapmntsid
sudo mkdir /srv/nfs/S4H/trans
sudo mkdir /srv/nfs/S4H/ASCS
sudo mkdir /srv/nfs/S4H/ASCSERS
sudo umount /srv/nfs/S4H
```

[**nfs0**] Finally, we include the NFS drbd devices in the cluster configuration. Make sure that you specify the correct load balancing IP address and the port for the integrity test:

```
sudo crm configure rsc_defaults resource-stickiness="200"
sudo crm configure property maintenance-mode=true
sudo crm configure primitive drbd_S4H_nfs \
  ocf:linbit:drbd \
  params drbd_resource="S4H-nfs" \
  op monitor interval="15" role="Master" \
  op monitor interval="30" role="Slave"
sudo crm configure ms ms-drbd_S4H_nfs drbd_S4H_nfs \
  meta master-max="1" master-node-max="1" clone-max="2" \
  clone-node-max="1" notify="true" interleave="true"

sudo crm configure primitive fs_S4H_sapmnt \
  ocf:heartbeat:Filesystem \
  params device=/dev/drbd0 \
  directory=/srv/nfs/S4H  \
  fstype=xfs \
  op monitor interval="10s"
sudo crm configure primitive nfsserver systemd:nfs-server \
  op monitor interval="30s"
sudo crm configure clone cl-nfsserver nfsserver
sudo crm configure primitive exportfs_S4H \
  ocf:heartbeat:exportfs \
  params directory="/srv/nfs/S4H" \
  options="rw,no_root_squash,crossmnt" clientspec="*" fsid=1 wait_for_
leasetime_on_stop=true op monitor interval="30s"

sudo crm configure primitive vip_S4H_nfs \
  IPaddr2 \
  params ip=10.1.3.2 cidr_netmask=24 op monitor interval=10 timeout=20
sudo crm configure primitive nc_S4H_nfs azure-lb port=61000
sudo crm configure group g-S4H_nfs \
  fs_S4H_sapmnt exportfs_S4H nc_S4H_nfs vip_S4H_nfs
sudo crm configure order o-S4H_drbd_before_nfs inf: \
```

```
  ms-drbd_S4H_nfs:promote g-S4H_nfs:start
sudo crm configure colocation col-S4H_nfs_on_drbd inf: \
  g-S4H_nfs ms-drbd_S4H_nfs:Master

sudo crm configure property maintenance-mode=false
```

Alternative 2: Azure NetApp Files

Unlike most other services, ANF cannot be booked from the Azure Portal by default. In order to gain access to ANF, a so-called waitlist request must first be sent. This step is necessary because Azure has very strict SLA requirements for the ANF service and therefore has to perform checks based on your planning values first. Only when you receive an email confirmation, you can book ANF via the portal. Before that, you can select ANF, but all options are grayed out when you create the NetApp account.

Registering for ANF

Firstly, fill out the waiting list request. The questions include the usual customer contact information, as well as ANF usage information. We would like to briefly highlight the following six pieces of information as they may require additional advance planning or coordination:

- Workload for ANF: Here, for example, a distinction is also made between SAP File Share (e.g., /sapmnt) and SAP HANA (e.g., /hana/data). Select the options that most closely match your setup. You can also select multiple application scenarios at the same time.

- Use of HANA on ANF: This yes/no question is an extension to the general workload question. If you answer "Yes" to this question, you will also be asked to fill out another form in which you should specify, among other things, the expected CPU cores as well as the VM size of the HANA.

- Use cases: Here, you have the choice between "production environment," "development/test environment," "disaster recovery," and "synchronization." Multiple answers are also possible here.

- Which regions for ANF: Here, you have to select the region you use. Since ANF subscriptions are region dependent, Microsoft must ensure that the planning parameters you send can be implemented in the target region.

- Subscription: Enter the GUID of your subscription here. You can also enter an additional ID if you want to activate ANF for two subscriptions. For additional subscriptions, you have to fill out the form again.

- Subscription environment: Select "Azure Commercial" here if you are not a US government agency subject to special security requirements.

After you submit the form, wait for a mail confirmation. Then create a new NetApp account. Create a new resource and search for "Azure NetApp Files" in the Marketplace. Enter a name, the subscription to be assigned, the region, and the resource group.

Creating a Capacity Pool

After the ANF account has been created, you can now create a capacity pool. This is only a container object which will later provide the actual volumes, also called quota. You have to make the following settings when creating the pool:

Name: Use a unique name for your capacity pool.

Service level: Here, you select the performance layer that will be applied to all volumes of the pool. You can choose between Standard (16 MiBs/TB), Premium (64 MiBs/TB), and Ultra (128 MiBs/TB). Note that for /hana/data, a minimum of 400 MB/sec read access (or 250 MB/s write access) is recommended. Microsoft recommends using the Ultra performance level for all types of SAP workload. However, by choosing a larger quota, the performance requirements can also be achieved with a lower service level. So, to get to the target performance of 400 MB/sec, you can alternatively provision 3.125 TiB of Ultra storage, 6.25 TiB of Premium storage, or 25 TiB of Standard storage.

Size (in TB): The minimum pool size is 4 TiB and is regionally limited to 25 TiB per subscription. The 25 TiB limit can be further increased by submitting a support request. However, it is not possible to go below the 4 TiB limit. Note that costs are calculated by pool size, not for actual used storage. Prices are charged per GB and at the time of writing are approximately €0.124 for Standard, €0.248 for Premium, and €0.331 for Ultra storage. After the pool has been created, you can now create individual volumes.

Creating and Mounting ANF Volumes

Basic configuration: In addition to the quota level, you must also specify a virtual network here. Since ANF volumes are mounted as NFS or Samba shares, you should select the network of the future clients, for example, the ASCS or HANA instances. This way, the traffic stays within one network which is worthwhile both from a cost and performance point of view. Then specify an existing subnet or create your own. Note that you cannot create network security groups for an ANF network.

Protocol: Here, you specify if the volume should be mounted as SMB or NFS share. You also specify the protocol version. If the volume is used for HANA, note that you must use NFS v4.1 to mount /hana/data and /hana/log over ANF. For /hana/shared, you can use NFS v3. For the transport directory, you can use either SMB or NFS. For the sapmount directory, it is recommended to use SMB for Windows systems or NFS for Linux systems. For NFS, you can additionally restrict the access to certain IP addresses in the "Export Policy" area, whereas the default settings allow all accesses. If you use SMB, you also have to create an Active Directory connection and a name for the share (you can maintain Active Directory connections in the root directory of your ANF account).

After the volume has been created, you can select it and view instructions for mounting the share under "Mounting instructions." The ANF volume behaves like a regular Samba or NFS share. In the case of NFS, the mount instructions also list the required packages such as nfs-common/nfs-utils. You can also mount NFS shares under Windows using the Windows NFS client. To do this, however, you must first mount the share under Linux and enable unrestricted read and write access using chmod 777 or 775.

Installation of ASCS and ERS

In the following, we use the designation **[A]** for steps that must be executed on all nodes and use **[ASCS]** for "**s4h-vc-ascs0**" or **[ERS]** for "**s4h-vc-ascs1**" if an operation is to be performed only on a specific virtual computer.

Preparing the File System and Mounting NFS

[A] First, create an entry for the NFS cluster in the /etc/hosts file. Use the front-end IP of the NFS load balancer "**s4h-lb-nfs**." Then, add the front-end IPs of the load balancer s4h-lb-ascs:

```
vi /etc/hosts
      # Add the following entry
      10.1.3.2 s4h-nfs
      10.1.0.5 s4h-ascs
      10.1.0.6 s4h-ers
```

If you are using Azure NetApp Files or NFS version 4.1, make sure that the domain configuration in the /etc/idmapd.conf file is identical to ANF. Otherwise, all files will be set with the ownership **nobody:nobody**. Also, the /sys/module/nfs/parameters/nfs4_disable_idmapping parameter must be set to "Y."

Now create the directories:

```
sudo mkdir -p /sapmnt/S4H   &&   chattr +i /sapmnt/S4H
sudo mkdir -p /usr/sap/trans  &&   chattr +i /usr/sap/trans
sudo mkdir -p /usr/sap/S4H/SYS   &&   chattr +i /usr/sap/S4H/SYS
sudo mkdir -p /usr/sap/S4H/ASCS00  &&   chattr +i /usr/sap/S4H/ASCS00
sudo mkdir -p /usr/sap/S4H/ERS02   &&   +i /usr/sap/S4H/ERS02
```

Instead of static mounts via fstab, we use autofs to dynamically mount NFS files. Add the NFS entries and then start the autofs service. We also configure the Azure Linux Agent to use the SWAP:

```
sudo vi /etc/auto.master
      # Add the following two entries
      +auto.master
      /- /etc/auto.direct
sudo vi /etc/auto.direct
      # Add the following entry
      /sapmnt/S4H -nfsvers=4,nosymlink,sync s4h-nfs:/S4H/sapmntsid
      /usr/sap/trans -nfsvers=4,nosymlink,sync s4h-nfs:/S4H/trans
      /usr/sap/S4H/SYS -nfsvers=4,nosymlink,sync s4h-nfs:/S4H/sidsys
sudo systemctl enable autofs
sudo service autofs restart
sudo vi /etc/waagent.conf
      # Make the following settings
      ResourceDisk.EnableSwap=y
      ResourceDisk.SwapSizeMB=2000
sudo service waagent restart
```

Installation of the ASCS Cluster

[ASCS] First, we install the SUSE Cluster Connector. This is a link between "sapcontrol" for starting and stopping the SAP instances and Pacemaker. Then we include the ASCS instance in the Pacemaker configuration:

```
sudo zypper install sap-suse-cluster-connector
sudo crm node standby s4h-vc-ascs1
sudo crm configure primitive fs_S4H_ASCS Filesystem device='s4h-nfs:/S4H/
ASCS' directory='/usr/sap/S4H/ASCS00' fstype='nfs4' \
  op start timeout=60s interval=0 \
  op stop timeout=60s interval=0 \
  op monitor interval=20s timeout=40s
sudo crm configure primitive vip_S4H_ASCS IPaddr2 \
  params ip=10.1.0.5 cidr_netmask=24 \
  op monitor interval=10 timeout=20
sudo crm configure primitive nc_S4H_ASCS azure-lb port=62000
sudo crm configure group g-S4H_ASCS fs_S4H_ASCS nc_S4H_ASCS vip_S4H_ASCS \
  meta resource-stickiness=3000
```

Now we can start the ASCS installation. Start the SWPM with the "SAPINST_USE_ HOSTNAME" option specifying the virtual hostname "s4h-ascs":

```
sudo <SWPM Verzeichnis>sapinst SAPINST_USE_HOSTNAME=s4h-ascs
# In SWPM, select the high availability option and then ASCS
```

Installation of the ERS (ENSA2) Cluster

[ERS] Now create the cluster configuration for the ERS instance and install the SUSE Cloud Connector there as well:

```
sudo zypper install sap-suse-cluster-connector
sudo crm node online s4h-vc-ascs1
sudo crm node standby s4h-vc-ascs0
sudo crm configure primitive fs_S4H_ERS Filesystem device='s4h-nfs:/S4H/
ASCSERS' directory='/usr/sap/S4H/ERS02' fstype='nfs4' \
  op start timeout=60s interval=0 \
  op stop timeout=60s interval=0 \
```

```
  op monitor interval=20s timeout=40s
sudo crm configure primitive vip_S4H_ERS IPaddr2 \
  params ip=10.1.0.6 cidr_netmask=24 \
  op monitor interval=10 timeout=20
sudo crm configure primitive nc_S4H_ERS azure-lb port=62102
sudo crm configure group g-S4H_ERS fs_S4H_ERS nc_S4H_ERS vip_S4H_ERS
```

Now install the ERS instance with the SWPM using the virtual hostname "**s4h-ers**":

```
sudo <SWPM directory>/sapinst SAPINST_USE_HOSTNAME=s4h-ers
# In SWPM, select the high availability option, and then select
```

Final Configuration

[**ASCS0**] Change the settings in the /sapmnt/S4H/profile/S4H_ASCS00_s4h-ascs profile of the ASCS instance:

```
# Replace "Restart_Program_01 = local $(_EN) pf=$(_PF)" with
Start_Program_01 = local $(_EN) pf=$(_PF)
# Add the following entries
service/halib = $(DIR_CT_RUN)/saphascriptco.so
service/halib_cluster_connector = /usr/bin/sap_suse_cluster_connector
```

[**A**] On both nodes, set the keepalive settings according to SAP Note 1410736 and add s4hadm to the haclient group:

```
sysctl -w net.ipv4.tcp_keepalive_time = 300
sysctl -w net.ipv4.tcp_keepalive_intvl = 75
sysctl -w net.ipv4.tcp_keepalive_probes = 9
sudo usermod -aG haclient s4hadm
```

Make sure that the /usr/sap/sapservices file on both nodes contains an entry for the ASCS as well as for the ERS:

```
cat /usr/sap/sapservices | grep ASCS00 | sudo ssh s4h-vc-ascs1 "cat >>/usr/
sap/sapservices"
sudo ssh s4h-vc-ascs1 "cat /usr/sap/sapservices" | grep ERS02 | sudo tee -a
/usr/sap/sapservices
```

We finally add the Pacemaker configuration for ENSA2:

```
sudo crm configure property maintenance-mode="true"
    sudo crm configure primitive rsc_sap_S4H_ASCS00 SAPInstance \
    operations \$id=rsc_sap_S4H_ASCS00-operations \
    op monitor interval=11 timeout=60 on-fail=restart \
    params InstanceName=S4H_ASCS00_s4h-ascs START_PROFILE="/sapmnt/S4H/
    profile/S4h_ASCS00_s4h-ascs" \
    AUTOMATIC_RECOVER=false \
    meta resource-stickiness=5000

    sudo crm configure primitive rsc_sap_S4H_ERS02 SAPInstance \
    operations \$id=rsc_sap_S4H_ERS02-operations \
    op monitor interval=11 timeout=60 on-fail=restart \
    params InstanceName=S4H_ERS02_s4h-ers START_PROFILE="/sapmnt/S4H/
profile/S4H_ERS02_s4h-ers" AUTOMATIC_RECOVER=false IS_ERS=true

    sudo crm configure modgroup g-S4h_ASCS add rsc_sap_S4H_ASCS00
    sudo crm configure modgroup g-S4H_ERS add rsc_sap_S4H_ERS02
    sudo crm configure colocation col_sap_S4H_no_both -5000: g-S4H_ERS
g-S4H_ASCS
    sudo crm configure order ord_sap_S4H_first_start_ascs Optional: rsc_sap_
S4H_ASCS00:start rsc_sap_S4H_ERS02:stop symmetrical=false
    sudo crm node online s4h-vc-ascs0
    sudo crm configure property maintenance-mode="false"
```

Installation of PAS and AAS

First, customize their /etc/hosts on all application server instances. For "s4h-nfs," "s4h-ascs," "s4h-ers," and "s4h-db," use the front-end IP of the respective load balancer:

10.1.3.2 s4h-nfs
10.1.0.5 s4h-ascs
10.1.0.6 s4h-ers
10.0.0.2 s4h-db
10.1.0.3 s4h-vc-as0
10.1.0.4 s4h-vc-as1

Then mount the NFS directories /sapmnt/S4h and /usr/sap/trans. Proceed as described in the section "Preparing the File System and Mounting NFS."

Now install the Primary Application Server on "**s4h-vc-as0**" and the Additional Application Server on "**s4h-vc-as1**." If you are using an embedded Fiori front-end server, you can use the load balancer "**s4h-lb-as**" as a virtual hostname:

```
sudo <SWPM Verzeichnis>/sapinst SAPINST_USE_HOSTNAME=virtual_hostname
```

This completes the installation of the sample architecture. Please note that testing all HA components is essential for a productive setup. For more information, please refer to the official Microsoft documentation[9] and the SUSE ER2 HA Setup Guide.[10]

Excursus: Automated SAP Provisioning

Until now, we have largely deployed and configured our systems manually. Template-based deployments based on ARM templates offer a minimum level of automation, but this only covers resource provisioning. In this section, we will take a brief look at other automation options in the context of Azure Cloud deployment.

Ansible and Terraform in Azure

Ansible and Terraform are widely used cloud automation tools whose interaction allows to perform a "full stack deployment" (resources + application). A particular advantage here is that this form of automation is cloud agnostic, meaning it can be reused across all hyperscalers without customization. In addition, this form of deployment offers the highest level of user configuration.

The **Terraform module's** job is to provision the actual infrastructure components, such as virtual networks, VMs, and disks, similar to an ARM template. After successful provisioning, the module also calls the respective **Ansible playbook**, which in turn uses various **Ansible roles** to perform software installations and configurations. SAP systems can thus be deployed with only a few command lines. Terraform modules are written

---

[9] https://docs.microsoft.com/en-us/azure/virtual-machines/workloads/sap/high-availability-guide-suse

[10] https://documentation.suse.com/sbp/all/pdf/SAP_S4HA10_SetupGuide-SLE15_color_en.pdf

in HCL or optionally in JSON. For Azure, Microsoft offers a Git repository[11] that covers numerous deployment scenarios for SAP. To do this, clone the Git repository using

```
git clone https://github.com/Azure/sap-hana.git
```

A service principal is required to create the resources. First, create this[12] and also create a "Key Vault Resource." Then follow the instructions to deploy a sample system.[13]

SAP Cloud Appliance Library

With its SAP Cloud Appliance Library (SAP CAL), SAP offers a repository of preconfigured SAP solutions that can be deployed directly on GCP, AWS, and of course MS Azure. A major strength of the SAP CAL is that it includes fully configured appliance solutions that are ideal for evaluating the latest SAP innovations. In addition, there are some solutions that are CAL exclusive and not available through the classic SAP download portal. One example of such a solution is the SAP Model Company (MC). These are customized industry solutions, for example, "Model Company Core Retail," in which SAP has incorporated over 20 years of industry experience. These systems thus function as a kind of collection of industry-specific best practice processes which customers can evaluate on the basis of the MC and adapt for their productive system.

The provision of a solution by means of CAL takes place directly via the SAP website https://cal.sap.com/ on the basis of the customer's own S-User. After logging in, you will find a list of possible systems and their availability in the "Solutions" section. Select a solution and click "Create instance." Then accept the general terms and conditions. Select "Microsoft Azure" as the cloud provider and enter your subscription ID. Leave the authorization type at "Standard Authorization."

Now click Authorize to connect to your Azure account. You will now be presented with a cost estimate in the upper right-hand area of the screen. You can also now configure the instance details.

---

[11] https://github.com/Azure/sap-hana

[12] https://github.com/Azure/sap-hana/blob/master/documentation/SAP_Automation_on_Azure/Process_Documentation/readme.md

[13] https://github.com/Azure/sap-hana/blob/master/documentation/SAP_Automation_on_Azure/Process_Documentation/Getting_started_with_the_SAP_Deployment_Automation_cloudshell.md

During deployment, you have the option to switch between **standard mode** and **advanced mode**. The default mode only requires your subscription ID, as well as SID, region, and password as input values. All other parameters are populated with default values, for example, a new virtual network is created by default.

Via the advanced mode, you have the possibility to further configure the deployment. For example, you can deploy the instance to an existing (sub)network, assign a public static IP address, and change the default values for VM size and memory size. Make the appropriate entries and finally click "Create."

Save the private key in the SAP Cloud Application Library or optionally download it. Note the warning about provisioning. This takes about 60 minutes, and you should not attempt to connect to the instance during activation. You can monitor the progress of the deployment in the CAL in the "Instances" tab. Once the status changes to "Active," the instance is ready. You now have the option to access the instance directly via the CAL using the "Connect" button. In the case of the "S/4HANA 2020 FPS 02" solution, for example, an RDP connection is available. Now connect to the instance; use the master password specified during creation as the password. As shown in Figure 7-13, as soon as you have connected to the instance, you will receive a welcome message with further information about the provided solution and its access IDs.

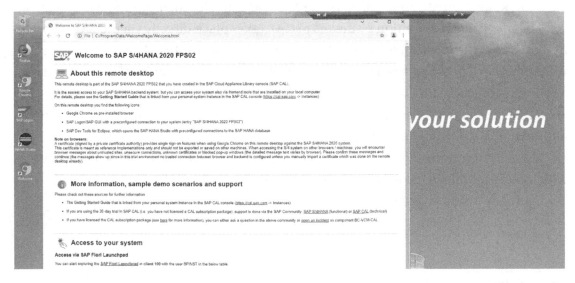

Figure 7-13. *SAP CAL landing page*

Summary

This chapter has shown you how to create a new SAP S/4HANA system on the MS Azure Cloud. For this purpose, the exemplary architecture was first explained, which has to be implemented. To start provisioning, it is necessary to first create the basic network configuration. After that, the provisioning of the resource groups and other components can be started.

High availability clusters are used to secure productive SAP S/4HANA systems. For this, the chapter showed you the steps on how to set up and use such clusters with SAP S/4HANA systems. Thus, you know all the steps to deploy SAP S/4HANA systems on Azure Cloud.

The chapter has also given an outlook on the automated procedures, such as Ansible and Terraform, as well as the SAP Cloud Appliance Library. Just as in the chapter on the other hyperscalers, there is an opportunity for you to standardize and significantly accelerate provisioning.

CHAPTER 8

SAP S/4HANA on Google Cloud – Concepts and Architecture

History of Google Cloud

Google launched the Google Cloud Platform with the first service called App Engine in preview in April 2008. Two years later, Google Cloud Storage was offered as the next service. Further service developments and releases continued steadily over the years with, among others, Google Compute Engine in preview in 2012 and Google Kubernetes as a fully managed service on the Google Cloud in Alpha in 2014, when Kubernetes was also released to the market as an open source project by Google.

Many Google Cloud services followed, and as of September 2021, Google Cloud offers more than 100 different cloud services and products, which range from IaaS to PaaS to the SaaS category. The entire list can be found on the website. Google is known for its many publications and contributions to the open source community over the past two decades. Google's whitepapers influenced technologies such as Beam, Hadoop, and many other frameworks and technologies that are now established as industry standards in IT. In fact, Google has contributed more than 2000 open source projects. Among the largest projects on GitHub are Kubernetes and TensorFlow, both of which were also invented by Google.

© André Bögelsack, Utpal Chakraborty, Dhiraj Kumar, Johannes Rank, Jessica Tischbierek, Elena Wolz 2022
A. Bögelsack et al., *SAP S/4HANA Systems in Hyperscaler Clouds*, https://doi.org/10.1007/978-1-4842-8158-1_8

For several years in a row, analysts such as Forrester and Gartner have confirmed that Google Cloud leads the market with many of the cloud platform services, including the following:

- Google: A Leader in Magic Quadrant for Cloud Infrastructure and Platform Services (Gartner, 2021)

- Google BigQuery: A Leader in The Forrester Wave: Cloud Data Warehouse (Q1 2021)

- Google Cloud: A Leader in Magic Quadrant for Cloud Database Management Systems (DBMS) (Gartner, 2020)

- Google Cloud: A Leader in The Forrester Wave: Infrastructure as a Service (IaaS) Platform Native Security (Q4 2020)

- Google (Apigee): A Leader in the Magic Quadrant for Full Life Cycle API Management (Gartner, 2020)

- Google Apigee: A Leader in The Forrester Wave: API Management Solutions (Q3 2020)

- Google Cloud: A Leader in The Forrester Wave: Unstructured Data Security Platforms (Q2 2021)

- And many more…

Development of the Partnership Between SAP and Google

In March 2017, the major partnership between SAP and Google was officially announced. SAP HANA was generally available on Google Compute Engine VMs and certified by SAP from that day on.[1] In addition, the SAP HANA Express Edition was offered via the Google Cloud Marketplace from this date.

---

[1] https://news.sap.com/2017/03/just-google-it-cloud-has-arrived/

Many other joint activities and achievements of this partnership were announced and published in the following years, strengthening the partnership between SAP and Google and providing many helpful opportunities and services for enterprise customers. The highlights are described chronologically as follows:

- June 2018: The new SAP Data Custodian product was available on Google Cloud as the first public cloud.[2]

- May 2019: In order to develop extensions for SAP C/4HANA, SAP has published the Kyma project, also called SAP Cloud Platform Kyma Runtime. It is based on Knative and was offered directly from the beginning on the Google Cloud.[3]

- September 2019: Google Cloud was the first hyperscaler to offer 6 TB and 12 TB virtual machines certified by SAP and fully virtualized (no bare metal).[4] At that time, other hyperscalers had these sizes available only as a bare-metal service.

- June 2020: The very first "SAP Data Center powered by Google Cloud," operational in Frankfurt, Germany, has been announced. It is a service that can only be used by SAP.[5] Also, during SAPPHIRE 2020, a co-innovation project between Google Cloud Visual Inspection and SAP Digital Manufacturing Cloud was presented with two reference customers: Kaeser Compressors and AES.

- January 2021: Official announcement of the new SAP program called "RISE with SAP" in partnership with Google Cloud and the other major hyperscalers.

---

[2] https://news.sap.com/2018/06/general-availability-sap-data-custodian-google-cloud-platform/

[3] https://blogs.sap.com/2019/05/20/getting-started-with-the-sap-cloud-platform-extension-factory/

[4] https://cloud.google.com/blog/products/sap-google-cloud/announcing-the-general-availability-of-6-and-12tb-vms-for-sap-hana-instances-on-gcp

[5] www.linkedin.com/pulse/sap-google-cloud-partnership-our-joint-journey-continues-gary-slater/?trackingId=KOfUM2yTQbSWZnmaReCBBg%3D%3D

- April 2021: Alphabet, Google Cloud's parent company, migrated from Oracle ERP to the entire SAP S/4HANA stack and announced a successful go-live.[6] The public announcements about this strategy and project were made earlier in 2019.[7]

- July 2021: An updated announcement was made on the "RISE with SAP" partnership with SAP, which has since been so detailed only between Google[8] and SAP.[9] SAP and Google Cloud are working together in this expanded strategic partnership to accelerate their customers' business process and cloud migrations. Google Cloud's reliable, scalable, and high-performance network and real-time integrations with Google Cloud's AI and ML services will serve this purpose. Deep integrations will also continue, and SAP solutions such as SAP Analytics Cloud, SAP Data Warehouse Cloud, and SAP Business Technology Platform (BTP) will run on Google Cloud. Together, SAP and Google Cloud have established very innovative projects such as SAP HANA Fast Restart[10] with Google Cloud's Memory Poisoning Recovery[11] capabilities for SAP S/4HANA landscapes.

During these few years from 2017 to 2021, Google Cloud has gained and established a large global customer base in all major industries: retail, engineering, banking, financial services, healthcare, pharmaceutical and life sciences industries, and many more. Some of these customers are official references and can be viewed on the website; a selection of SAP on Google Cloud customers in October 2021 is: Vodafone, Schlumberger, Siemens Energy, Deutsche Börse, Metro, MediaMarktSaturn, PayPal, Otto Group, Kaeser Compressors, The Home Depot, McKesson, Carrefour, Cardinal Health, Loblaw, and many more.

---

[6] www.heise.de/news/Google-migriert-Finanzsoftware-von-Oracle-zu-SAP-6005704.html

[7] www.asug.com/events/alphabets-sap-s-4hana-journey-and-partnering-for-innovation

[8] https://cloud.google.com/blog/products/sap-google-cloud/sap-and-google-cloud-expand-their-partnership

[9] https://news.sap.com/2021/07/google-cloud-and-sap-accelerate-business-transformations-cloud/

[10] https://cloud.google.com/blog/products/sap-google-cloud/protect-hana-uptime-with-fast-restart-on-google-cloud

[11] https://cloud.google.com/blog/products/sap-google-cloud/mitigating-memory-errors-for-your-sap-environment

Reasons for Choosing SAP on Google Cloud

There are many reasons why customers should decide to migrate and run their SAP landscape on Google Cloud. These include, in summary, the following main areas outlined: innovation, risk and downtime minimization, flexibility through simplified deployment, and sustainability.

Innovation

As explained at the beginning of the chapter, Google is known for its achievements and services in the areas of data analytics, big data, and machine learning, which is also confirmed by the many open source projects and analyst evaluations.

For SAP landscapes, modernization is the way forward. In particular, maximizing the insights you can gain from your SAP data with Google's AI, ML, and Advanced Analytics is a key future building block for staying competitive. Easily integrate Google's ML services for vision, translation, and text-to-speech, for example, while leveraging intelligent decision making to automate processes, make predictions, and optimize business processes and operations. You can extend SAP processes with Google-provided datasets, cloud-native and container-based services and extensions, and Apigee API management.

Risk and Downtime Minimization

You can reduce risk and minimize downtime with mechanisms for increased granular security and high availability, which are fully supported with Google Cloud services and brought to the most forward-thinking and modern state of the art. Increase security and performance with Google's premium global network, where your data is not transmitted over public networks and is encrypted at rest and in transit by default. Google has one of the largest private networks in the world, with more than 100 points of presence (PoPs). Here, the network works like a global network, and no VPN or peering needs to be established between regions or zones.

Significantly reduced downtime is what you get for your SAP applications through Google's global distribution with zone and region concept, as well as native live migration, which enables hardware-side configuration changes without delay and continuous hardware maintenance without required planned outages and reboots.

Flexibility and Cost Optimization Through Simplified Deployment

Leverage Google Cloud Migration Support for both traditional projects and "RISE with SAP" to minimize duplicate infrastructure costs during migration. Deploy OLTP and OLAP environments with the largest VM sizes in the industry, even certified for custom VM configurations (custom machines). Easily manage thousands of VMs with VM Manager and optimize storage costs and performance with Google Cloud's multiple storage types. With Anthos, multicloud and hybrid cloud landscapes are simplified, and not only their flexibility is increased but also their security. Automation as a basic building block of modern cloud deployments is enabled and simplified by a wide variety of Google Cloud services.

In the IDC Business Value Report[12] (August 2020), it was confirmed that SAP deployments on Google Cloud lead to the following optimizations:

- 31% lower cost of IT infrastructure

- 65% less staff time to deploy/migrate

- 56% more efficient IT teams, including

  - 66% more efficient IT infrastructure teams

  - 39% more efficient database administration teams

  - 60% more efficient IT security teams

Further, the Forrester TEI Report (August 2020) confirmed that SAP upgrades are 35% more efficient, improving agility and flexibility for the business.[13]

Another study by Forrester in 2020[14] confirms that running SAP on Google Cloud generates 160% return on investment (ROI) and requires a payback period of only six months or less. This can be explained on the basis of savings in legacy infrastructure costs, prevention of downtime, and performance and productivity improvements.

---

[12] https://inthecloud.withgoogle.com/sap-roi/dl-cd.html

[13] https://cloud.google.com/blog/products/sap-google-cloud/reports-examine-business-value-of-running-sap-on-google-cloud

[14] https://services.google.com/fh/files/misc/forrester_tei_for_sap_on_google_cloud_infographic.pdf

Sustainability

Instantly reduce your IT emissions by moving SAP applications to Google's efficient and intelligent data centers. With data-driven innovation and the use of Google data and services, new business models can be developed, and your sustainability goals can be advanced.

Google has been fully carbon neutral (CO2 neutral) since 2007, and in 2017 Google became the first company of its size to offset 100% of its annual global electricity consumption with renewable energy. Today, Google is the world's largest commercial purchaser of renewable energy on an annual basis and one of the "cleanest" clouds in the industry. Google's goal is to move completely to zero-carbon energy by 2030 and to use it everywhere, 24/7.[15]

The following Google Cloud services, among others, are offered to support customers around sustainability: Asset Inventory and Machine Config Benchmark, Cloud Value Tool CO2 Calculator, Data Center Carbon Footprint Estimate, Environmental Insights Explorer, and Sustainable Value Chain Assessment.

Google Cloud Organizations and Resources

This section explains the structure of the Google Cloud and the services. Resources play a fundamental role here. First, the resource hierarchy is described, and then the properties of resources are explained.

Google Cloud Resource Hierarchy

Google Cloud organizations are the starting point for all activities performed on the Google Cloud and are described in this section. All resources in the Google Cloud hang in a resource hierarchy, which consists of the top node of the organization as the root node, then one or more levels of folders, and below that the projects. The resources of Google Cloud services hang directly on projects and thus make up the lowest level of the hierarchy. The advantages of such a hierarchy are that there is an affiliation and binding between the elements and their parent elements, and thus they are also related to the

---

[15] https://sustainability.google/intl/de/

life cycle of the respective upper hierarchy. As a result, the levels and resources inherit all access controls and organizational policies from their upper level, hence from top to bottom.

The organization node represents an organization, for example, a company, and is the top node. It has an organization ID and is directly linked to the Cloud Identity account. This account can be the email address of the IT manager, for example. There can only be one organization ID for a Cloud Identity account. The organization node contains folder resources and/or project resources.

Benefits of an organization resource

- Resources (like projects, etc.) belong to the organization; if an employee leaves, the resources will not be deleted.

- Organization admins have access to all resources that belong to the organization.

- Granting roles at the organization levels means they will be inherited by the resources below, and this makes the management of access control easier.

The folder resource is a level that provides a grouping mechanism and can isolate the different projects. Folders can be seen as suborganizations within the organization, like different departments, legal entities, and/or teams. Folders can contain both further folders and projects.

Project resources are the base-level organizing entity. The project is required to be able to create any resource with the Google Cloud services available. Projects are isolated from each other. Network communication between projects does not take place by default, but can be enabled.

All projects have the following properties:[16]

- Two identifiers

  - Project ID, which is a unique identifier for the project.

  - Project number, which is automatically assigned when you create the project. It is read-only.

---

[16] https://cloud.google.com/resource-manager/docs/cloud-platform-resource-hierarchy#projects

- One mutable display name

- The life cycle state of the project, for example, ACTIVE or DELETE_
  REQUESTED

- A collection of labels that can be used for filtering projects

- The time when the project was created

Cloud billing accounts are required to bill Google Cloud resources; these are linked to one or more projects.

Figure 8-1 illustrates an example resource hierarchy of a company.

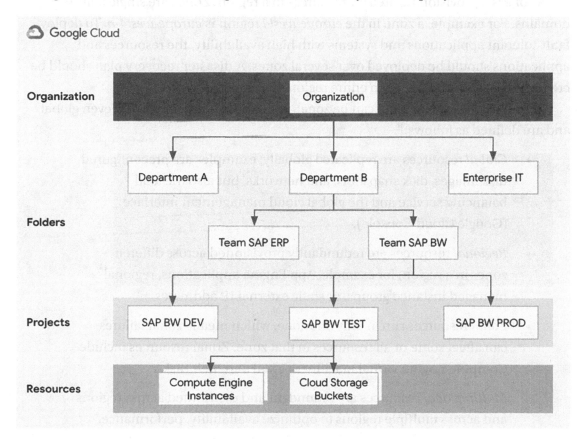

Figure 8-1. *Google Cloud resource hierarchy*

The recommended best practices for creating resource hierarchies should be viewed in advance on the Google Cloud website.[17]

Properties of Google Cloud Resources

Resources can be created in different Google Cloud regions. A *region* is an independent geographical location and consists of at least three different zones. An example of a region is *europe-west4* (Google Cloud region in the Netherlands). As of September 2021, there are 27 global Google Cloud regions, which are constantly expanding.[18]

A *zone* is a provisioning area for resources in a region. Zones are single failure domains. For example, a zone in the *europe-west4* region is *europe-west4-a*. To deploy fault-tolerant applications and systems with high availability, the resources and applications should be deployed over several zones. A disaster recovery plan should be created to cover the failure of an entire region due to disasters.

Resources in Google Cloud can be zonal, regional, multiregional, and even global and are defined as follows:[19]

- *Global* resources are replicated globally; examples are preconfigured disk images, disk snapshots, and networks, but also the load balancing service and the global cloud management interface (Google Cloud Console).

- *Regional* resources are redundantly provisioned across different zones in a region, for example, App Engine applications, regional managed instance groups, or static external IP addresses.

- *Zonal* resources run in only one zone, which means zonal failures can affect some or all resources in that zone. Zonal resources include Compute Engine virtual machines (VMs) and their disks.

- *Multiregional* resources are redundant and distributed across regions and across multiple regions to optimize availability, performance,

---

[17] https://cloud.google.com/iam/docs/resource-hierarchy-access-control#best_practices

[18] https://cloud.google.com/about/locations

[19] https://cloud.google.com/compute/docs/regions-zones/global-regional-zonal-resources

and resource efficiency. Examples include Google Cloud Storage, Cloud Key Management Service, and BigQuery.

Google Cloud Offered Services Important for SAP S/4HANA

This section will provide a detailed overview about the possible services of Google Cloud which are relevant for SAP S/4HANA deployments and that are important to know before starting the provisioning. It will also help to understand the needed core components for deploying S/4HANA systems and the interdependencies. All the services are the basis for the architecture and deployment later on.

Google Cloud Compute Engine

Compute Engine is Google's customizable compute service that makes it possible to create and manage virtual machines (VMs) on Google's infrastructure in the data centers spread over the different regions.

With Compute Engine, it is possible to use predefined machine types with a predefined number of vCPU (virtual central processing unit) and RAM (random access memory). However, it is also possible to create user-defined machine types consisting of a self-selected number of vCPU and RAM. In addition, there are so-called preemptive machine types (instances on demand), which can be used at a lower price than the normal instances. However, these can be shut down at any time by Compute Engine and are therefore only suitable for batch jobs or fault-tolerant applications. They are therefore not recommended for SAP systems and are not SAP certified.

Compute Engine is split into different groups of machine types where not all are SAP certified (as of September 2021):

- General-purpose machine type: *E2, N2, N2D, N1* – SAP certified

- Ultra-high memory machine type: *M1, M2* – SAP certified

- Compute-intensive machine type: *C2* – not SAP certified

- Scale-out machine type: *T2D* – not SAP certified

- Most demanding applications and workloads: *A2* – not SAP certified

- Bare Metal machine type: *O2* – SAP certified

Up to 12 TB of memory size, all Google Compute Engine machines are virtualized. Certified machines for SAP HANA are based on an Intel CPU platform; some are Intel Broadwell and Intel Skylake, and most of the machine types are Intel Cascade Lake (n2, m2, o2). The certified machines for SAP applications are based on the previously mentioned Intel CPU platform types or based on minimum AMD EPYC Rome (n2d).

The Google Cloud Bare Metal machine types (o2) are designed for specialized workloads, for example, for extra-large, high-performance SAP HANA workloads (which need to be bigger than 12 TB memory) or also other workloads that need to run on nonvirtualized machines due to license matters or other reasons. These o2 machine types are based on Intel Cascade Lake and go up to 24 TB of memory and are fully managed from a full hardware, storage, and network perspective and offer integrated Google Cloud support and billing and of course an enterprise SLA. A difference to the Google Cloud Compute Engine service is that they are dedicated and single-tenant systems and are placed in a co-location with very low latency to the Google Cloud data centers.[20]

In an SAP S/4HANA setup, the SAP database, SAP application servers, SAP Web Dispatcher, and also jump hosts are being installed and deployed on Compute Engine machines. The SAP-certified machine types are documented in the Google Cloud website under Certifications for SAP HANA[21] and Certifications for SAP Applications[22] and as well in the SAP HANA Hardware Directory and the following SAP Notes:

- SAP HANA Hardware Directory[23]

- 2456432 – SAP Applications on Google Cloud: Supported Products and GCP VM types[24]

Google Cloud is currently the only Hyperscaler that is offering custom machine sizes certified by SAP. These underlie the rules and conditions of the following table to be supported by SAP (see SAP Note linked previously and Certifications for SAP Applications).

---

[20] https://cloud.google.com/solutions/sap/docs/sap-hana-on-bms-planning

[21] https://cloud.google.com/solutions/sap/docs/certifications-sap-hana

[22] https://cloud.google.com/solutions/sap/docs/certifications-sap-apps

[23] www.sap.com/dmc/exp/2014-09-02-hana-hardware/enEN/#/solutions?filters=iaas;ve:29

[24] https://launchpad.support.sap.com/#/notes/2456432

As of today, Google Cloud is the only hyperscaler that offers custom machine types certified by SAP. These are subject to the sizing rules and conditions formulated in the following table in order to be supported by SAP (see also SAP Note in the previous section and Certifications for SAP Applications). Note: Any custom machine type must first be analyzed by SAP via a SAP Support Ticket before SAP will support them for your systems.[25] Table 8-1 shows the standard machine types, which are available for SAP workloads in Google Cloud.

Table 8-1. *Compute Engine Custom Machine Size Rules*

Machine Type	vCPU Requirement	Standard Memory Usage Requirement	High Memory Usage Requirement
n1	1 or any even number up to 96	3.75 GB per vCPU	6.5 GB per vCPUUp to a total of 624 GB per VM
n2	Any even number up to 32 After 32 up to 80 vCPUs, the number must be divisible by 4	4 GB or more per vCPU	8 GB or more per vCPUUp to a total of 640 GB per VM
n2d	2 up to a maximum of 96 in the following Increments: 2, 4, 8, or 16 vCPUs. After 16, you can increment the number of vCPUs by 16, up to 96 vCPUs	Select between 1 GB and 16 GB per vCPU	Up to a total of 768 GB per VM

The built-in AI functionality called "Rightsizing Recommendation" gives users the ability to optimize the resource utilization with automatic recommendations to resize the VMs depending on the usage behavior and statistics of the machines. Therefore, users can adapt the VM instances and consume resources in a more efficient and cost-saving way.

---

[25] https://cloud.google.com/solutions/sap/docs/certifications-sap-apps#sap-certified-vms-custom

Business Continuity Features

A unique feature in comparison to the available public clouds is Google's Live Migration functionality. Besides that, Google Compute Engine offers host auto-restart. Both mechanisms are relevant for high availability and will be explained in a later section.

Service-Level Agreements (SLA) for Compute Engine

If instances are set up in a high availability setup, meaning over at least two zones of a region, and supported by a load balancer, then Compute Engine provides a monthly uptime of >=99.99%. The load balancing service also provides an SLA of >=99.99%. The default SLA for individual Google Compute Engine instances is >=99.5%, which means the instance is deployed in a single zone without high availability (as of September 2021).[26]

Operating Systems on Compute Engine

Almost all of the aforementioned components of an SAP S/4HANA architecture require an installed operating system. Certified for SAP HANA are SUSE Linux Enterprise Server (SLES) and Red Hat Enterprise Linux (RHEL). On Compute Engine, you can either use the operating system with your own operating system image (bring-your-own-image, BYOI) and your own license (bring-your-own-license, BYOL) or use and pay for it directly via Google Cloud Images in Compute Engine. The Google Cloud operating system images provide high availability features specifically configured for Google Cloud. It is recommended to check the documentation for both SAP HANA[27] and SAP NetWeaver[28] beforehand.

The following operating systems are supported for SAP HANA by Google Cloud Compute Engine and by SAP (September 2021):

- RHEL 8: 8.1 for SAP and pending: 8.2, 8.4

- RHEL 7: 7.4, 7.6, and 7.7 for SAP

- SLES 15: SP1, SP2 for SAP and pending: SP3

- SLES 12: SP3, SP4, SP5 for SAP

---

[26] https://cloud.google.com/compute/sla

[27] https://cloud.google.com/solutions/sap/docs/sap-hana-os-support

[28] https://cloud.google.com/solutions/sap/docs/netweaver-os-support

See SAP documentation in SAP Note:

- SAP HANA Supported OS – 2235581[29]

The following operating systems are supported for SAP NetWeaver by Google Cloud Compute Engine and by SAP (September 2021):

- RHEL 8: 8.1, 8.2, and 8.4 for SAP

- RHEL 7: 7.4, 7.5, 7.6, and 7.7 for SAP

- SLES 15: SP1, SP2, and SP3 for SAP

- SLES 12: SP3, SP4, and SP5 for SAP

- Windows Server 2019, 2016, and 2012 R2

See SAP documentation and SAP Note:

- SAP Applications on Google Cloud Platform: Supported Products and Google VM types – 2456432[30]

- Product Availability Matrix[31]

In addition to SAP HANA, other certified databases for SAP landscapes are also available and supported on Google Cloud (see SAP Note as before – 2456432), including

- IBM DB2

- Microsoft SQL Server

- SAP ASE

- SAP MaxDB

Storage Considerations

SAP systems require different types of storage: disks, distributed file systems, and storage for backups. The Google Cloud services described in the following cover all the required components.

---

[29] https://launchpad.support.sap.com/#/notes/2235581

[30] https://launchpad.support.sap.com/#/notes/2456432

[31] https://userapps.support.sap.com/sap(bD1lbiZjPTAwMQ==)/support/pam/pam.html#ts=0

Google Cloud Disks

Persistent disks are a persistent and high-performance block storage for Compute Engine instances. This storage is equivalent to hard disks in on-premise landscapes. Persistent disks are available in three classes, namely, standard, SSD, and extreme format, whereby the SSD type is divided into SSD and balanced block storage. The three classes differ in their performance characteristics[32] vs. prices:

- Standard persistent disks (pd-hdd): Low-cost block storage

- SSD-based persistent disks (pd-ssd and pd-balanced): Fast and reliable block storage, with high IOPS and low latency

- Extreme persistent disks (pd-extreme): Designed for high-end database workloads with consistently high performance

Block storage can be created either zonally or regionally, with zonal drives only available in one zone and regional drives replicated synchronously across two zones in a region. As a result, regional nonvolatile storage offers very low risk of data loss and high availability. They can be used for disaster recovery. On the other hand, zonal disks offer higher performance.

Furthermore, there are local SSDs that are physically connected to the hardware on which the VM instance is running. While these provide higher throughput and lower latency, there is no guarantee that the VM instance will always run on the same hardware. Therefore, the connection of the local SSD disk to the VM may be deleted if the VM is migrated to a different hardware. This may be the case when the VM instance is restarted, or a live migration is performed. Local SSDs should therefore only be used for temporary data and are hardly relevant for SAP systems.

Snapshots can be created from the disks, and new disks can be created from them. When an instance is terminated, the nonvolatile memory retains the data and can be allocated to another instance. More about snapshots in the area of backups is explained in a later section.

Drives are used to store the various file directories and subfolders of the SAP system. Table 8-2 gives recommendations on the disk storage types per SAP file directory type:[33]

---

[32] https://cloud.google.com/compute/docs/disks#introduction

[33] https://cloud.google.com/solutions/sap/docs/architectures/sap-s4hana-on-gcp#recommended_linux_directory_structure_for_sap_hana

Table 8-2. *Storage Type Recommendation for SAP Directories*

SAP HANA Directory Structure	Storage Type
/usr/sap	SSD PD
/hana/data	SSD PD, zonal[34]
/hana/log	SSD PD, zonal
/hana/shared	SSD PD, zonal
/hanabackup	HDD Standard PD

Table 8-3 shows which mount points can be hosted on the HDD Standard PD, which is more cost-efficient than SSD storage.

Table 8-3. *Storage Type Recommendation for ABAP Directories*

ABAP Directory Structure	Storage Type
/sapmnt	HDD Standard PD
/usr/sap/	HDD Standard PD
Boot and exe files	HDD Standard PD or Balanced PD

For SAP HANA, only SSD-based disks are currently certified for /hana/data and /hana/log directories.

The performance of SSD-based disks increases the larger the storage and the larger the number of vCPUs. Google Cloud provides a recommendation for the minimum disk size per category and per certified machine type for SAP HANA in the documentation. The following formulas are recommended for SAP HANA directories, where the

---

[34] https://cloud.google.com/solutions/sap/docs/checklist-sap-hana

"memory" mentioned here is the memory of the Compute Engine instance (in GB). The following rules apply to scale-up and not horizontal, scale-out usage:

- /hana/data: 1.2 x memory

- /hana/log: Either .5 x memory (adjusted to be a multiple of 64, if necessary) or 512 GB, whichever is smaller

- /hana/shared: Either 1 x memory or 1024 GB, whichever is smaller

- /usr/sap: 32 GB

- /hanabackup: 2 x memory, optional allocation

It is also recommended to create fewer and therefore larger disks and to partition them logically in the operating system into several file systems. For SAP HANA, it is recommended to map /hana/data, /hana/log, /usr/sap, and /hana/shared into one disk. Using larger and fewer disks overall also allows for easier resizing and simplified management and operation, as well as higher performance.

File Sharing Solutions for SAP on Google Cloud

Google Cloud supports several file sharing solutions for SAP deployments; the selection depends on the required region and zone requirements as well as performance. The following solutions are currently recommended (as of September 2021):

- Google Filestore: Google Cloud's high-performance, fully managed file storage

- NetApp Cloud Volumes Service (CVS) Performance (Standard and Extreme) for Google Cloud: NetApp's high-performance and fully managed file storage that can be provisioned, configured, and billed directly in the Google Cloud Console

- NetApp Cloud Volumes ONTAP: A full-featured, smart storage solution that you deploy and manage yourself on a Compute Engine virtual machine

The differences between these three solutions are listed in Table 8-4.

Table 8-4. *Comparison of File Sharing Solutions for SAP on Google Cloud*

Feature	Google Filestore	NetApp CVS-Performance	NetApp Cloud Volumes ONTAP
Managed service	Yes	Yes	No
SLA	99.5%	99.99%	99.99% for only the Google Cloud Compute Engine
High availability	No	99.99% SLA	Multi-zone HA solution
Disaster recovery	Manual	Multiregion replication	Automated with SnapMirror
Local snapshots	Yes	Yes	Yes
Regional replication	No	Yes	With SnapMirror
Regional availability	All regions	See NetApps region map[35]	All regions
RPO	N/A	As low as 15 minutes	As low as 15 minutes
RTO	N/A	As low as 30 minutes	As low as 15 minutes
Protocols	NFSv3	NFSv3, v4.1, SMB	NFSv3, v4.1, SMB iSCSI
Minimum storage size	1 TB	1 TB	100 GB volume with 638 GB system disk
Support provider	Google Cloud	Google Cloud	NetApp for NetApp software and Google Cloud for infrastructure
Throughput performance	100 MB/s R/W	128 MB/s R/W	Depending on the configuration[36]

In which use case which of the three solutions is recommended can be determined under the following categories:

Interface directory

- For use as a general storage location by SAP and other software systems to pass files between servers

- NetApp Cloud Volumes ONTAP

- NetApp CVS-Performance, Extreme

---

[35] https://cloud.netapp.com/cloud-volumes-global-regions
[36] www.netapp.com/pdf.html?item=/media/9090-tr4816pdf.pdf

SAP transport directory

- For use as an SAP storage location by SAP systems to hold shared application files in distributed or high availability deployments or to transport SAP files and updates between different operational environments

- NetApp Cloud Volumes ONTAP

- NetApp CVS-Performance, Standard

Backup directory

- For use by SAP or other systems as a centralized storage location for backups

- NetApp Cloud Volumes ONTAP

- NetApp CVS-Performance, Extreme

SAP HANA scale-out system directory

- For use within a single zone by SAP HANA scale-out systems to share binaries and configuration files between the SAP HANA nodes

- Google Filestore

- NetApp Cloud Volumes ONTAP

- NetApp CVS-Performance, Extreme

Google Cloud Storage

The object storage of Google Cloud is a fully managed service for storing objects, so files of any format, in the cloud. Objects are stored in containers which are called buckets and are linked to a project. In on-premise landscapes, Google Cloud Storage corresponds to backup application and storage, among other things.

Google Cloud Storage has the following features:

- Unlimited storage with no minimum object size

- A high annual durability of 99.999999999%

- Worldwide accessibility and worldwide locations

- Low latency (time to first byte typically tens of milliseconds)

- Automatic geo-redundancy when a multiregion or dual-region location type is selected

Google Cloud Storage is available in several storage classes[37] which define differences in the object's availability and the pricing model associated. The four storage classes are

- Standard storage: Recommended for frequently accessed files – minimum duration none

- Nearline storage: Recommended for less than once per month accessed files – minimum duration 30 days

- Coldline storage: Recommended for infrequently accessed data less than every 90 days

- Archive storage: Recommended for less than once a year used files – minimum storage duration 365 days

Cloud storage can be deployed locally (regional), dual-regionally, or multiregionally. The choice depends on the requirements for data location and constraints, latencies for backups and recovery, and regional resilience requirements. Choose dual- or multiregional buckets in the same regions or close to the regions where the Compute Engine instances (SAP systems) are running. Storage bucket locations can be found in the documentation.[38]

Availability SLAs differ based on the storage class and storage location type. For example, for the standard storage class, the SLAs are

- Multiregion: 99.95% SLA – >99.99% typical monthly availability

- Dual-region: 99.95% SLA – >99.99% typical monthly availability

- Region (local): 99.9% SLA – 99.99% typical monthly availability

For SAP deployments, Google Cloud Storage is especially relevant for backups with persistent disk snapshots and SAP HANA backups because it is SAP HANA Backint certified. This means that a configuration in the SAP HANA database is possible for

---

[37] https://cloud.google.com/storage/docs/storage-classes#available_storage_classes
[38] https://cloud.google.com/storage/docs/bucket-locations#location-r

Google Cloud Storage as the saving point for HANA backups. See the documentation: Cloud Storage Backint Agent for SAP HANA[39] and SAP Note 2031547.[40] Furthermore, there is a detailed best practice overview for Google Cloud Storage in general.[41]

Google Cloud VPC and Networking

This section provides an overview of the services required to build all network components in an SAP on Google Cloud deployment. The network design has a major impact on availability, performance, and resilience of the SAP landscape. Most of the network services in Google Cloud are virtual (software-defined networking), which simplifies the design of complex landscapes for administrators while still meeting organizational and security requirements.

Google Cloud VPC Setup

A Virtual Private Cloud (VPC) network[42] is a virtual version of a physical network that, in Google Cloud, is based on Google's own implemented and privately owned Andromeda network. The VPC connects all Google Cloud services and the different regions (sites) without communicating over the Internet, but remains in Google's private network cables. VPC networks are global resources and consist of regional virtual subnets (subnets) connected via a global wide area network (WAN). Subnets that belong to a VPC connect zones in a region. VPC networks are logically separated from each other and belong to projects.

Figure 8-2 shows a VPC network, which spans across two regions (europe-west4 and europe-west1). Both regions have one/two subnets for respective zones, in which you will deploy VMs.

---

[39] https://cloud.google.com/solutions/sap/docs/sap-hana-backint-overview#:~:
text=Backint%20for%20SAP%20OHANA%20certification

[40] https://launchpad.support.sap.com/#/notes/2031547

[41] https://cloud.google.com/storage/docs/best-practices

[42] https://cloud.google.com/vpc/docs/overview

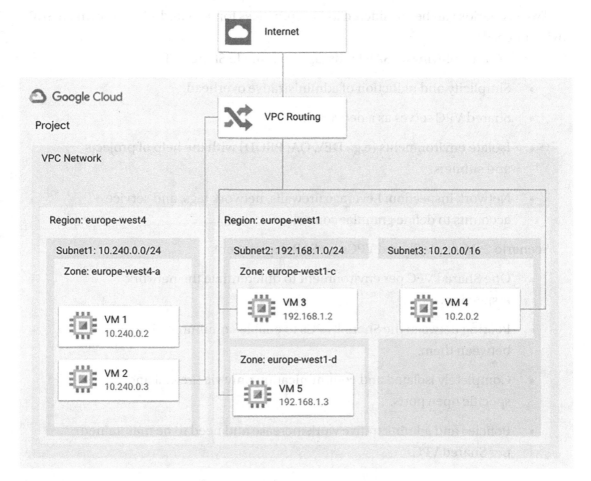

Figure 8-2. *Google Cloud VPC concept*

A project can have several different VPCs, and a VPC network can also be shared between several projects in an organization. This concept is called Shared VPC. VPCs from different projects can be connected to each other via VPC network peering.

VPC networks provide TCP/UDP and HTTP(S) load balancing and connect the Google Cloud to on-premise landscapes via Cloud VPN or Cloud Interconnect (see the next section).

Google Cloud's private network offers network bandwidths of 32 Gbps and low latencies for instances in the same zone. For SAP landscapes, it is recommended to deploy the database instances and application servers in the same zone for maximum performance.

Two scenarios can be considered as best practices for a Shared VPC setup in an SAP environment:[43]

Scenario 1: Deploying an SAP landscape on a single Shared VPC

- Simplicity and reduction of administrative overhead.

- Shared VPC serves as a network hub.

- Isolate environments (e.g., DEV, QA, PROD) with the help of projects and subnets.

- Network inspection: Leverage firewalls, network tags, and service accounts to define granular control.

Scenario 2: Multiple Shared VPCs for SAP deployment

- One Shared VPC per environment to differentiate the network inspection.

- Peering between the Shared VPCs to enable communication between them.

- Completely isolated and communication only via firewall and specific open ports.

- Policies and administrative work increase and need to be maintained per Shared VPC.

Cloud VPN, Partner, or Dedicated Interconnect

The connection between the on-premise and Google network can be established via the Internet or via a private network. Since a private network offers more security, this is the only option for most SAP customers. There are three options for connecting on-premise enterprise networks and landscapes (hybrid cloud concept) and other hyperscalers (multicloud concept) to the Google Cloud: Cloud VPN, Partner Interconnect, Dedicated Interconnect.[44] These are described in more detail with their advantages and disadvantages as follows:

---

[43] https://cloud.google.com/blog/products/sap-google-cloud/set-up-your-network-for-a-seamless-sap-cloud-deployment

[44] https://cloud.google.com/network-connectivity/docs/how-to/choose-product

Cloud VPN

- Connects the peer network to the Google Cloud VPC via an IPsec VPN connection (tunnel) over the Internet. The bandwidth is limited by the Internet connection and the number of tunnels (see the following). The advantage of the Cloud VPN over a direct Internet connection is not the bandwidth, but the encryption and the possibility to use private IP addresses.

- Two-way tunnel.

- Dynamic routing.

- Traffic is encrypted by one VPN gateway and encrypted by the other VPN gateway.

- Each Cloud VPN tunnel can support 1.5 Gbps up to 3 Gbps for a sum of ingress and egress traffic.

- Two types of Cloud VPN gateways: HA VPN and Classic VPN.

- HA VPN: SLA 99.99%.

- Classic VPN: SLA 99.9% – deprecated as of October 31, 2021

Advantages

- Easy and fast to set up

- No further contracts or hardware and configurations needed

Disadvantages

- Limited bandwidth

- Tunnel over the Internet

- Recommendation in SAP environments only for proof of concepts, pilots, or short-term connections

Dedicated Interconnect[45]

- A direct physical connection between the on-premises network and the Google Cloud network as shown in Figure 8-3.

---

[45] https://cloud.google.com/network-connectivity/docs/interconnect/concepts/dedicated-overview

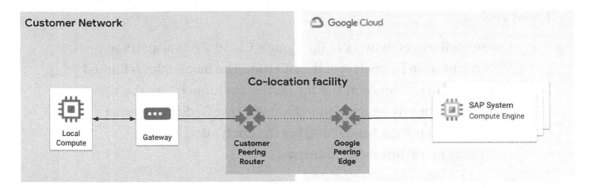

Figure 8-3. *Google Cloud Dedicated Interconnect*

- The connection to the Google network is established in a co-location facility where the customer provides its own routing equipment.

- Connections with 10 Gbps, 100 Gbps, or link bundles are possible.

- SLA of 99.9% and 99.99% (with redundancies, recommended) possible.

Partner Interconnect[46]

- Also a physical connection between the on-premises network and the Google Cloud network, but through a supported services partner as shown in Figure 8-4

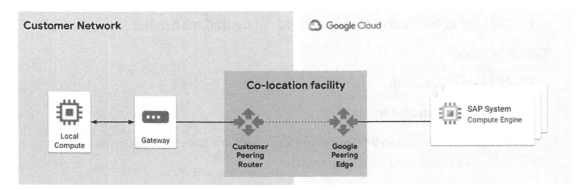

Figure 8-4. *Google Cloud Partner Interconnect*

---

[46] https://cloud.google.com/network-connectivity/docs/interconnect/concepts/partner-overview

- Connections from 50 Mbps to 10 Gbps possible

- Recommendation to use it as a choice if you can't meet the Google Cloud colocation facility location to connect or if customer does not need a 10 Gbps connection, but a smaller connection (50 Mbps to 10 Gbps)

- SLA of 99.9% and 99.99% (with redundancies, recommended) possible

Inbound (Ingress) and Outbound (Egress) Traffic

Within Google Cloud, inbound network traffic (ingress) is free, while outbound network traffic (egress) incurs costs. These costs depend on the amount of traffic, the source services and region, destination services and region, and the type of connection.

The different connection types are

- Data traffic within Google Cloud via internal IP addresses

- Data traffic from Google Cloud to other Google services (such as YouTube and Maps)

- Data traffic from Google Cloud to the Internet

- Traffic from Google Cloud to a Cloud VPN

- Traffic from Google Cloud to a Partner or Dedicated Interconnect

- And more

The documentation provides a precise overview and further details, for example, the prices.[47]

Routing and Forwarding Rules

Routes define for the VM instances and the VPC network how traffic should flow from an instance to the defined destination inside or outside the Google Cloud. Each VPC network has automatically generated routes to define traffic between subnets and forwarded by instances, for example, to the Internet.

---

[47] https://cloud.google.com/vpc/network-pricing

Compared to routes that define traffic leaving an instance, forwarding rules define how traffic should flow from outside to a Google Cloud resource on the VPC network (based on the IP address, protocol, and port). Forwarding rules can direct traffic to the destination either from outside or inside the same network. Destinations can be instances, load balancers, or cloud VPN gateways.

Firewalls

Each VPC network implements a distributed virtual firewall that can be configured as desired. Firewall rules control which data packets and communications are allowed to which destinations in the VPC network. Each VPC network has two firewall rules that are automatically set up and included by default; the first blocks all incoming connections, and the second allows all outgoing connections.

Cloud DNS

Cloud DNS is a fully managed, high-performance, resilient, and global domain name service (DNS) that publishes domain names mapped to the respective IP address to a global DNS. DNS forwarding rules can be inbound or outbound. The best practices[48] for Cloud DNS should also be viewed.

Cloud NAT

In production landscapes and enterprise environments, VM instances usually do not have public external IP addresses with a direct connection to the Internet due to security risks. Therefore, Network Address Translation (NAT) services are used. With Cloud NAT, Google offers a distributed, software-defined, and fully managed service with which VM instances can establish outbound connections to the Internet and also receive inbound feedback over it. An alternative would be to set up a Compute Engine VM instance manually as NAT, but then it is not a managed service.

---

[48] https://cloud.google.com/dns/docs/best-practices

In an SAP landscape, Internet connections over Cloud NAT are used for a variety of reasons, a common one being the registration and activation of operating system licenses with SUSE or Red Hat.

Cloud Load Balancing

The Google Cloud Load Balancing service is a fully managed, software-defined, high-performance, and scalable load balancer. Cloud Load Balancer can automatically distribute user access and traffic across multiple instances of the application in a scalable manner. There is global and regional load balancing; if the applications are spread across multiple regions, then global load balancing should be selected, otherwise regional load balancing. The Cloud Load Balancer (LB) is not instance or hardware based, so customers do not have to worry about high availability, scaling, or management.

The following options are available on Google Cloud and can be selected based on your landscape requirements using a decision tree in the documentation:[49]

- Global external load balancing (including HTTP(S) LB, SSL Proxy LB, TCP Proxy LB)

- Regional external Network LB

- Regional internal TCP/UDP LB

The Google Cloud Load Balancer is integrated with the Cloud DNS and guarantees a 99.99% SLA. In SAP on Google Cloud landscapes, load balancers are typically used to represent a single IP address for redundant web dispatchers.

Google Cloud Security

Google Cloud is a secure infrastructure by design, built on Google's own private network (Google Backbone).[50] Standard encryption for storage (at rest) and transmission (in transit) protects personal, application, service, and other data, as well as instances and systems.

---

[49] https://cloud.google.com/load-balancing/docs/choosing-load-balancer#flow_chart
[50] https://cloud.google.com/infrastructure

A long list[51] of security and IT security services and functions is available on the Google Cloud. A selection of relevant services for SAP landscapes is the following, but most of these are not considered in detail here and can be found in the documentation.

Security Solutions

Access Transparency, Cloud Intrusion Detection System, Cloud Key Management, Firewalls, Secret Manager, Security Command Center, VPC Service Controls, and many more.

Identity and Access Solution

Certificate Authority Service, Cloud Identity, Identity and Access Management, Managed Service for Microsoft Active Directory, Policy Intelligence, Resource Manager, and many more.

Identity Provider and Authoritative Source

During the onboarding process and before you use Google Cloud or other Google services, you must decide which system to use as your identity provider (IdP) and which system to use as your authoritative source. The following options are possible:[52]

- Google as IdP and authoritative source

- Google as IdP and Human Resources Information System (HRIS) like SAP SuccessFactors or Workday as authoritative source

- Active Directory as IdP and authoritative source

- Azure AD as IdP and Active Directory as authoritative source

- External IDaaS (third party) as IdP and authoritative source

With Active Directory as the IdP and authoritative source, the distribution can be implemented, as illustrated in Figure 8-5.[53]

---

[51] https://cloud.google.com/products/security-and-identity

[52] https://cloud.google.com/architecture/identity/reference-architectures

[53] https://cloud.google.com/architecture/identity/reference-architectures#external_idaas_as_idp_and_authoritative_source

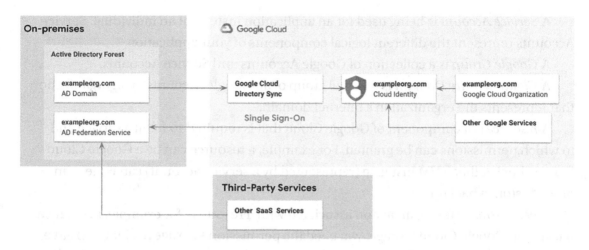

Figure 8-5. *Federation with Active Directory as IdP for Google Cloud*

Google Cloud Directory Sync is a free service provided by Google that replicates user data and groups from Active Directory to Google Cloud Identity or Google Workspace. The synchronization always takes place in one direction only, so that Active Directory remains the authoritative source. The Active Directory can be in the on-premise landscape, as illustrated in the figure. Customers can alternatively also use the fully managed Active Directory service in Google Cloud. For single sign-on, Google Cloud Identity uses Active Directory Federation Services. Other on-premises enterprise applications or third-party cloud solutions also use Active Directory Federation Services as IdP.

Google Cloud Identity and Access Management (IAM)

With Google Cloud Identity and Access Management (IAM), access control to all resources can be managed through so-called *policies*. These are

> A definition of *who* (an identity, such as a user, Google group, or service account) has *what kind of access* (roles such as viewer, editor, or owner) to *what resources*.[54]

A *Google Account* is a representation of a person who interacts with Google Cloud, for example, an administrator or a developer. The Google Account is associated with an email address as the identity and can be of any domain.

---

[54] https://cloud.google.com/iam/docs/overview

A *Service Account* is being used for an application instead of an individual. Service Accounts represent the different logical components of your application.

A *Google Group* is a collection of Google Accounts and Service Accounts.

A *Cloud Identity Domain* is a virtual group of all Google accounts in an organization that represents the organization's Internet domain.

A *resource* is a component of Google Cloud that is required to fulfill a service and to which permissions can be granted. For example, a resource can be a Google Cloud Storage bucket that a VM instance (represented by a service account) can write to in order to store a backup.

A *permission* refers to an action associated with a resource, for example, to create a backup on Google Cloud Storage, you need the permission `storage.objects.create`.

A *role* is a collection of permissions, because permissions are not granted directly to the user but should first be grouped. If you grant a role to a user, also all permissions that are contained in this role are being granted to the user. Roles are divided into the following categories:

- Basic roles: Owner, editor, viewer – not recommended for productive landscapes!

- Predefined roles: These allow for more fine-grained control than the basic roles.

- Custom roles: These roles can be created by the user in order to assign only the necessary permissions according to the least privilege principle and thus to meet the requirements of the organization when a predefined role does not meet the needs.

There are a lot of security best practice guides available by Google Cloud,[55] and it is recommended to read them through in detail. A short summary is provided as follows:

- Always use least privilege and grant only the smallest scope of access that is needed.

- Use service accounts and service account keys which should be rotated regularly.

---

[55] https://cloud.google.com/iam/docs/using-iam-securely

- Audit all access, logs, changes, and more with the help of Google Cloud Audit Logs.

- Work with IAM policies and set them on the organization level.

- Grant roles to groups and not individual users.

Google Cloud Operations

With Google Cloud Operations (formerly called Stackdriver), Google delivers a full operations suite as a managed service to monitor, troubleshoot, and improve the application performance of your cloud environment.[56]

General Features of Google Cloud Operations

Monitoring: With features of monitoring, you receive an overview on performance, health, status, etc. of the landscape and all systems and collect metrics, events, and metadata from all Google Cloud services.

Logging: With the logging features, you can analyze all collected logs and accelerate application troubleshooting, and, furthermore, you can ingest application and system log data from many different other sources.

Alerting: Automate alerting when an unforeseen event occurs, like email or SMS alerts, and trigger further action points by automation.

Application Performance Management (APM): Cloud Trace, Cloud Debugger, and Cloud Profiler are available for managing and optimizing performance.

Google Cloud Monitoring and Logging Agent for SAP HANA and SAP NetWeaver

The Cloud Logging agent provides you with a solution for system activity logging, including operating system events and, if you are using SAP HANA, also SAP HANA events. The Cloud Logging agent is an optional but recommended component.

The monitoring agent for SAP HANA (V2.0)[57] collects metrics from SAP HANA with the help of SQL queries. It is a fully refactored agent with changes in metrics, installation

---

[56] https://cloud.google.com/products/operations

[57] https://cloud.google.com/solutions/sap/docs/sap-hana-monitoring-agent-planning-guide

method, configuration, and directories than V1.0. In general, a set of default queries are used, but you can also create custom queries. The SQL syntax and system views are defined by SAP here and defined in the documentation.[58] The main usage scenarios for monitoring metrics and dashboards are

- Use the SAP HANA memory utilization metrics for capacity planning.

- Help to manage memory-based SAP HANA licensing.

- Correlating SAP HANA metrics with Compute Engine metrics can help to identify usage and performance trends.

- Definition of custom queries to capture additional metrics, for example, for more insight into your SAP HANA installation.

- Create dashboards to visualize your SAP HANA metrics and set up alerts based on metric thresholds.

To view the monitoring data for SAP HANA, you can use or create new dashboards in Google Cloud Monitoring and search for `sap_hana` in the metric field.

The Google Cloud Monitoring agent for SAP NetWeaver though is required for SAP support of SAP NetWeaver on Google Cloud.[59] When installing the agent on a Compute Engine VM, the monitoring agent for SAP NetWeaver combines monitoring data from Monitoring and Compute Engine APIs and provides this data to the SAP Host Agent. The agent is also required for running SAP NetWeaver on Google Bare Metal instances.

Google Cloud Customer Care

Google Cloud offers several different support offerings (Customer Care[60]) which are offering an integrated experience for customers and can be upgraded with value-added services. Four support classes are available:

---

[58] https://help.sap.com/viewer/4fe29514fd584807ac9f2a04f6754767/2.0.02

[59] https://cloud.google.com/solutions/sap/docs/netweaver-operations-guide#the-monitoring-agent-for-sap-netweaver

[60] https://cloud.google.com/support

Basic Support

- Always included

- Support only for billing issues – not recommended for productive enterprise workloads

Standard Support

- SLO of 4 hours (for P2 cases)

- 8 hours/5 days (Mo–Fr) of support for high-impact issues

Enhanced Support

- SLO of 1 hour (for P1 cases)

- 24 hours/7 days of support for high- and critical-impact issues

Premium Support

- SLO of 15 minutes (for P1 cases)

- 24 hours/7 days of support for high- and critical-impact issues

- A named Technical Account Manager (TAM)

- Support for third-party technologies

- Training offers and credits

- Costs are calculated based on the net monthly spend and are calculated using the official Google Cloud Calculator or your Google Cloud Sales contact

For SAP landscapes on Google Cloud, which are mission critical in almost all cases, it is recommended to choose Enhanced or Premium Support, because the other two Google support classes are not accepted by SAP in a support case. These and other support notes are described in SAP Note 2456406[61] and in the Google documentation.[62,63] SAP and Google Cloud work closely together in the context of support.

---

[61] https://launchpad.support.sap.com/#/notes/2456406

[62] https://cloud.google.com/solutions/sap/docs/getting-support

[63] https://cloud.google.com/solutions/sap/docs/getting-support-from-sap

Furthermore, Google Cloud offers many other services, for example, Mission Critical Services (Premium Support) or Technical Account Advisor Service (Enhanced Support), or with Google Consulting Services, also consulting packages for SAP migrations (e.g., the Cloud Sprint for SAP[64]).

Further Google Cloud Services Relevant for SAP S/4HANA Deployments

Especially with regard to innovation and expansion projects as well as implementation of new SAP-related solutions and applications, the following Google Cloud services can be used:

Google BigQuery

- Google's Enterprise Data Warehouse, which is serverless and managed, also highly scalable and cost-effective.

- Consists of features like BigQuery Machine Learning (ML), BigQuery Omni (for multicloud setups), BigQuery BI Engine, and BigQuery GIS (Geographic Information Systems).

- Integration of SAP systems with BigQuery is possible in three ways: via SAP integration solutions (such as SAP Data Services, SAP SLT, SAP Data Intelligence, and many more), Google Cloud solutions (such as Cloud Data Fusion), or via partner solutions (such as Qlik, Informatica, and many more).

Google Vertex AI Platform

- Fully managed choice of AI solutions with pretrained and custom tools to build, deploy, and scale ML models.

- The extension and optimization of SAP business processes with Google AI solutions is possible and has already been implemented by Google Cloud reference customers, for example, for visual inspection.

---

[64] https://services.google.com/fh/files/misc/gc_consulting_cloud_sprint_sap.pdf

Google Kubernetes Engine (GKE)

- Google's fully managed Kubernetes container platform.

- SAP Data Intelligence (formerly SAP Data Hub) and SAP Hybris are supported by SAP on GKE – there are existing Google Cloud reference customers running these SAP solutions on GKE.

Google Apigee API Management

- Google's fully managed API Management platform with full API life cycle capabilities

- For designing, securing, analyzing, monetizing, and scaling APIs

Google Industry Solutions[65]

Relevant to several industries

- Advanced marketing analytics

- Contact Center AI

- Remote productivity and collaboration

- Procurement DocAI

- Demand forecasting

Retail

- Recommendation AI

Consumer packaged goods

- Vision API product search

Manufacturing

- Production quality control with Visual Inspection AI

- Connected Vehicle Telematics

---

[65] https://cloud.google.com/solutions?hl=de#section-2

Automotive

- Connected Car Telemetry Platform

- Connected vehicle solution

- Infotainment solutions by Google (Android Automotive)

Financial services

- Open Banking API

- Lending DocAI

Healthcare and life sciences

- Cloud Healthcare API

Google Cloud Front End

Google Cloud offers different ways to interact with the services and resources depending on the role of the user. In this section, firstly, the front-end tools of Google Cloud are presented and then the use of these tools according to typical user roles.

Google Cloud Front-End Tools

The *Google Cloud Console* is a web interface in the browser with very good search functionality, where users can perform the main tasks around the typical Google Cloud services, such as creating Compute Engine VM instances, creating Cloud DNS records, and much more. The console is shown in Figure 8-6.

Figure 8-6. *Google Cloud Console*

The *gcloud* command-line tool, which is part of the Cloud SDK, can be used to perform many of the platform tasks on Google Cloud, either directly from the command line or via automation scripts. For example, Compute Engine VM instances and other resources can be created; clusters, networks and subnets, Cloud DNS managed zones, and datasets can be created and edited; and much more. The command-line tool is shown in Figure 8-7.

Figure 8-7. *Google Cloud command-line tool gcloud (in Cloud Shell)*

There are two ways to use the command-line tool, either via Cloud SDK or via Cloud Shell:

- *Cloud SDK* is downloaded and installed on the user system. From the computer or system, the gcloud tool can then be used via a terminal window to manage the Google Cloud resources via commands.

- *Cloud Shell* is your admin machine in the cloud. It is accessible in the Google Cloud Console directly in the browser and runs on an instant-on Linux box. It is being used to quickly handle power tasks as it is fully equipped with a lot of admin tools. The Cloud SDK is preconfigured, authenticated, and ready to go.

The *Cloud SDK* includes client libraries that enable you to easily create and manage resources. Google Cloud client libraries expose APIs for two main purposes: Admin APIs offer resource management functionality, and App APIs provide access to services.

Typical User Roles in an SAP on Google Cloud Landscape

In SAP environments, different users and user roles work on different levels of the system and thus also have different access to the SAP systems. All users, groups, roles, responsibilities, and policies can be configured and defined using Google Cloud Identity and Access Management features, as described in the previous section:

Infrastructure administrators

- Work primarily with the Google Cloud Console in the service areas of Compute Engine, Networking, Identity and Access Management, and with the command-line gcloud via Cloud Shell/SDK and also with automation scripts and bash scripts

- Depending on the deployment and landscape, also use Google Operations for monitoring and logging purposes, as well as Cloud Build, Cloud Scheduler, and Cloud Functions

Operating system administrators

- Work mainly with the Google Cloud via gcloud command line or via SSH on the Compute Engine instance directly in the system

- Depending on the deployment and landscape, also use Google Operations for monitoring and logging purposes

Network administrators

- Work mainly with the Google Cloud Console in the Network services section or via the command-line tool gcloud

- Depending on the deployment and landscape, also use Google Operations for monitoring and logging purposes

SAP application developers and SAP customizing

- Work mainly in the SAP system itself, namely, via SAP GUI, via SAP HANA Studio, or via extension platforms and additional services from SAP or from Google Cloud

End user

- Work mainly on the SAP system directly, which means either with SAP transactions via SAP GUI or on the SAP Fiori launchpad (mostly the case in SAP S/4HANA environments)

SAP S/4HANA on Google Cloud Architecture

All components for the deployment of an SAP S/4HANA architecture on Google Cloud are described in the following sections. The first section gives a quick guidance to the licenses and sizing, and then the entire architecture is explained. Based on this architecture, the planning and the decisions to be made for the setup of high availability, the disaster recovery setup, and the criteria for the selection of storage solutions are considered in detail. Finally, there are two excursus sections, one on SAP S/4HANA scale-out deployments and the other on SAP HANA Fast Restart and Memory Poisoning Recovery mechanism.

Licenses and Sizing

SAP customers can use and provide their existing SAP Business Suite or S/4HANA licenses for SAP on the Google Cloud under the BYOL model (bring-your-own-license model). The operating system licenses can be provided and billed via Google Cloud Compute Engine, or customers can bring their own operating system images and licenses.

The required sizing of the SAP landscape is best done with the SAP Quick Sizer program. It is important to note that the SAP components, mainly the database and the application servers, which are also presented in the following section, are installed on SAP-certified Compute Engine instances. Otherwise, support from SAP cannot be guaranteed. The relevant documentation on the certifications can be found in a later section.

SAP S/4HANA Architecture Overview

The following components are part of an SAP S/4HANA architecture in a distributed and noncentralized deployment (a centralized deployment, meaning an SAP S/4HANA application and SAP HANA database on one Compute Engine instance, is not recommended for production environments but only for sandbox and development environments and is therefore not considered further here, but can be found in the documentation):[66]

- SAP HANA database

- PAS: SAP S/4HANA Primary Application Server

- AAS: SAP S/4HANA Additional Application Server(s)

- SAP S/4HANA ASCS

- SAP Fiori Front-End Server

- SAP Web Dispatcher or Load Balancer

- SAP Router

- Jump server/bastion host

A load balancer is mandatory in a distributed deployment. These components are illustrated in Figure 8-8's high-level architecture overview. Also illustrated are some other Google Cloud services that are relevant for SAP deployments and that have been described in the previous section. These include Google Cloud Storage, Cloud DNS, Cloud NAT, firewall rules, and the VPC network.

---

[66] https://cloud.google.com/solutions/sap/docs/architectures/sap-s4hana-on-gcp

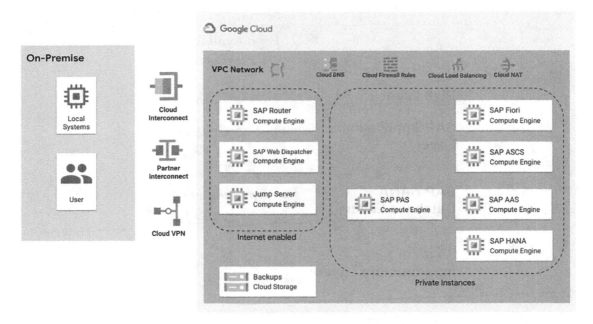

Figure 8-8. *SAP S/4HANA on the Google Cloud overview of architecture components*

Setup for High Availability

Google Cloud offers various mechanisms for implementing and ensuring high availability in SAP landscapes. The mechanisms are divided into four different levels, which are illustrated in Figure 8-9. These include mechanisms at the infrastructure, database, SAP application, and on the web level.[67]

---

[67] https://cloud.google.com/solutions/sap-on-google-cloud-high-availability.pdf

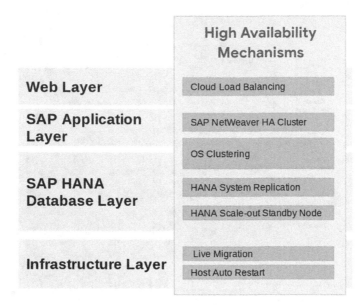

Figure 8-9. High availability mechanisms for SAP on Google Cloud

It is important to note that the infrastructure mechanisms described, such as Live Migration and automatic restart, do not apply to the installed components on the VM instances. These include the operating system, the SAP database, and the application layer. To build a high availability architecture, operating system clustering is used between the SAP components: at the SAP HANA database level, SAP HANA System Replication can be used, and at the SAP NetWeaver application level, the Linux Pacemaker cluster can be used. Within this setup, the Google Cloud region selected as primary for your landscape is being used to distribute the cluster across two zones of that region. In scale-out scenarios, for example, for SAP Business Warehouse or very large SAP S/4HANA systems with scale-out configuration, the SAP HANA scale-out standby nodes can be used to implement high availability.

The top level, the web layer, uses the Google Cloud Load Balancer to route and distribute traffic between the zones if one zone should fail.

Infrastructure Layer

At the lowest level, the infrastructure level, Google Cloud is already highly available by design due to the redundant infrastructure with globally distributed data centers. These regions each contain at least three zones, which are also set up to be independent of each other. Each zone has its own power, cooling, and network supply and is isolated from the other zones. To build a highly available cluster for an SAP landscape, at least two different zones of the primary selected region should be used, and the VM instances should be distributed across them. In addition, Google Compute Engine VMs provide two other important built-in mechanisms relevant to high availability: Live Migration and host auto-restart.

Live Migration

With Live Migration, the virtual machine instances keep up and running even if a host system event, like a hardware, security, or software maintenance, is happening. Live Migration is a Compute Engine built-in feature and comes with no additional cost. As defined on the Google Cloud website

> *Live migration keeps your instances running during:*
>
> *Regular infrastructure maintenance and upgrades.*
>
> *Network and power grid maintenance in the data centers.*
>
> *Failed hardware such as memory, CPU, network interface cards, disks, power, and so on. This is done on a best-effort basis; if a hardware fails completely or otherwise prevents live migration, the VM crashes and restarts automatically and a hostError is logged.*
>
> *Host OS and BIOS upgrades.*
>
> *Security-related updates, with the need to respond quickly.*
>
> *System configuration changes, including changing the size of the host root partition, for storage of the host image and packages.*[68]

Live Migration does not change any attributes, configurations, or properties (e.g., IP addresses, network, block storage like disks, etc.) of the virtual machine and is by default turned on when starting a virtual machine. You have the possibility to turn it off, though this is not recommended. During a Live Migration event, the installed

---

[68] https://cloud.google.com/compute/docs/instances/live-migration

application and database on this instance continue to run and do not require any manual activity. A great unique Google Cloud feature is that Live Migration is applicable to all Compute Engine virtual machine types, so even the SAP HANA–certified large machines. This helps of course in uptime and business continuity for critical SAP S/4HANA systems.

Host Auto-Restart

Another functionality is host auto-restart. If activated for a Compute Engine VM, host auto-restart will automatically restart a host (VM only) if it was shut down due to an unplanned event. It will not directly restart the application on it, but references to startup scripts which can be attached to the VMs and that will be executed after the start of the VM. Host auto-restart does not require any additional setup and comes as a built-in feature with no additional cost.

High Availability of the SAP HANA Database Layer

High availability for the SAP HANA database works with the SAP HANA database native mechanism called SAP HANA System Replication (HSR) and the Linux operating system clustering Pacemaker with the STONITH fencing mechanism. Data is replicated continuously and synchronously from the primary system, which is located in one zone, to the secondary system, which is located in another zone of the same region. The secondary system is running, and the data is completely preloaded in memory. SQL commands for processing data (DML, such as insert, update, delete) can be performed only in the primary system. Thus, in the event of a zonal failure, synchronous data replication results in no data loss and minimal downtime. Since each SQL transaction in the primary database is not fully processed until it is also fully processed in the secondary system, a Recovery Point Objective (RPO) of zero can be achieved here (meaning no data loss). Both systems are in the same Google Cloud region, but in two different zones to achieve the 99.99% SLA for the infrastructure layer with Compute Engine. Deployment also configures the internal TCP/UDP load balancer and VIP (virtual IP address) for routing traffic in case of failures. Static VIP or Alias IP deployments are no longer recommended by Google Cloud.

More information can be found in the planning documentation. The architecture in Figure 8-10 shows the SAP HANA layer with SAP HANA System Replication and the operating system cluster.

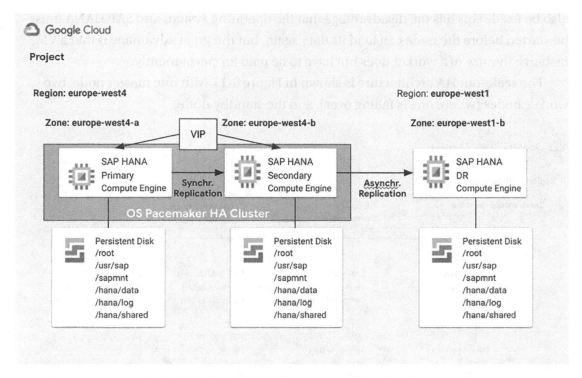

Figure 8-10. *SAP HANA high availability on Google Cloud*

SAP HANA Scale-Out Node Host Auto-failover

SAP HANA also provides a native mechanism for failure recovery for scale-out deployments supported by the Google Cloud infrastructure. The host auto-failover mechanism uses one or more standby hosts, which are powered on, to take over in the event that a primary or worker node is shut down due to an unforeseen failure. When the standby node takes over, the recovery time is determined by the size of the SAP HANA data of the downed node, since it must first be loaded into memory. After the failover is performed, the previously shutdown node is restarted and takes over as the new standby host.

SAP supports up to three standby nodes on Google Cloud in a scale-out system. These standby nodes do not count toward the maximum sum of 16 possible active nodes, but in addition.

It is important to note that SAP HANA host auto-failover does not protect against a zonal failure or failures because all nodes are created in the same zone. In Google Cloud, instead of host auto-failover, the Google Cloud Compute Engine feature auto-restart can

433

also be used. This has the disadvantage that the operating system and SAP HANA must be started before the node can load its data again, but the great advantage is that a VM instance the size of a worker does not have to be paid for permanently.

The scale-out HA architecture is shown in Figure 8-11 with one master node, two worker nodes (where one is failing over), and the standby node.

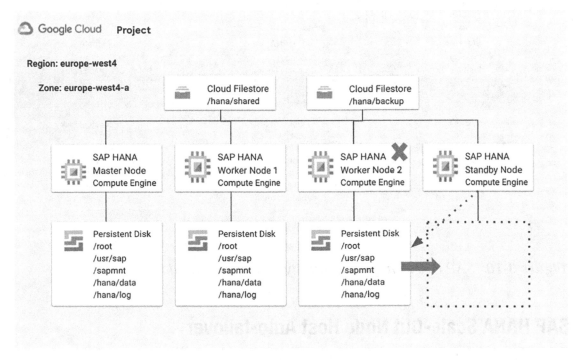

Figure 8-11. *SAP HANA scale-out high availability on Google Cloud*

High Availability of SAP NetWeaver Application Servers

To guarantee high availability at the SAP NetWeaver application server level, the setup can be chosen with at least four VM instances:[69] one instance with activated ABAP SAP Central Services (ASCS) in the primary zone of the primary region and one instance with activated Standalone Enqueue Replication Server (ERS) in the secondary zone of the same primary region. The application servers are distributed across the two zones. The cluster for the SAP ASCS and ERS components includes the Linux operating system

---

[69] https://cloud.google.com/solutions/sap/docs/netweaver-ha-planning-guide

high availability cluster (based on Pacemaker) and a STONITH fencing mechanism. The cluster is configured with an automatic restart (host auto-restart) for all systems as new secondary instances.

The deployment also configures the internal TCP/UDP load balancer and VIP (virtual IP address) for routing traffic in case of failures. Static VIP or Alias IP deployments are no longer recommended by Google Cloud.

The SAP NetWeaver global file system must be available for all SAP NetWeaver instances in your system landscape and is therefore a potential single point of failure. To ensure the availability of the global file system in Google Cloud, use either highly available file share storage or replicated zonal nonvolatile storage (persistent disks).

Figure 8-12 shows the dependencies between the different components of the SAP application layer:

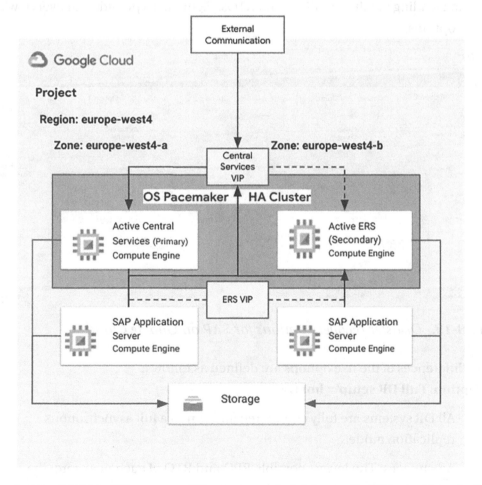

Figure 8-12. *SAP NetWeaver application server high availability in Google Cloud*

Disaster Recovery Setup

A disaster recovery (DR) setup requires several decisions and can be set up in many different ways. More general information on this has already been described in an earlier chapter.

The first decision that should be made is the region selection. A disaster recovery scenario on Google Cloud is based on a primary region and another, secondary region, which are many kilometers apart with the state of the regions as of September 2021. For example, a pair of regions in Europe might be europe-west3 (Frankfurt, Germany) and europe-west1 (St. Ghislain, Belgium).

The second decision that should be made is to determine the required Recovery Point Objective (RPO) and Recovery Time Objective (RTO). In general, there are five different strategies to build a disaster recovery scenario for SAP systems on Google Cloud, each leading to different RPOs and RTOs. Figure 8-13 provides an overview of these five options.

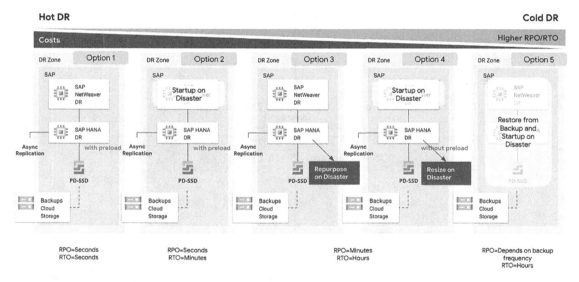

Figure 8-13. *Disaster recovery options for SAP on Google Cloud*

The differences of the five options are defined as follows:

1. Option: Full DR setup = hot DR

- All DR systems are fully configured and run in a full asynchronous replication mode.

- Advantages: The lowest possible RPO and RTO of each near zero; the disaster systems are available in a few seconds.

- Disadvantages: Highest costs, as the DR systems are always running.

- Recommendation: Switching from a primary region in case of a disaster to the secondary region for the users should be done manually; this may result in RTO in the range of minutes.

2. Option: Full DR setup only for the database

- The database layer is fully configured and running – lowest RPO of almost zero.

- The application servers are switched off and are directly reprovisioned from snapshot backups with automation; however, due to the small size, these do not take long – RTO is in the minute range.

- Advantages: The running instance costs for the application servers can be saved in the secondary region and are then only billed in the event of a disaster.

- Disadvantages: RTO increases compared to Option 1 (hot DR), not by hours, but by several minutes – redeployed application servers need to be tested if the deployment is fully functional.

3. Option: Repurpose in a disaster case

- With this option, the QA/test system is generally located in the secondary region and is converted in the event of a disaster, that is, the delta logs since the last backup are reloaded.

- RPO is in the minute range, and the RTO is in the hour range.

- Advantages: High cost savings, as no extra DR systems have to be paid for.

- Disadvantages: The QA/test system unavailable during a disaster; increased traffic costs (egress) due to constant communication between regions; increased RTO and RPO as there is no continuous asynchronous system replication, but delta logs are loaded in case of a disaster.

4. Option: Half-size database

- The database in the secondary region is only half the size of the productive database, and all changes are continuously loaded asynchronously via SAP HANA System Replication.

- In the event of a disaster, the DR system restarts and is scaled up to the size of the source databases, but the data must then be loaded into memory.

- Advantages: Cost savings and minimal data loss (RPO) in the range of minutes; RTO is in the range of hours and less than a day.

- Disadvantages: Restart of the SAP HANA database required and therefore high RTO, since the data must be loaded into memory; it is also not guaranteed that the actual size required is available in the secondary region if there is no reservation of the machines.

5. Option: Turn on/deploy systems in a disaster case = cold DR

- In the event of a disaster, the SAP systems in the secondary region are completely rebuilt with the SAP HANA backups and application server snapshots from the Google Cloud Storage – highest RPO and RTO.

- Instances should be set up using automation (scripts) to keep RTO as low as possible.

- Advantages: The highest cost savings are possible with this method, but the availability of the Compute Engine instances is not guaranteed in case of a disaster; therefore, reservations are necessary, which though do not lead to any cost savings.

- Disadvantages: The loading time of the SAP HANA data into memory takes several minutes per TB of SAP HANA size – this affects the RTO, which is thus in the range of hours in most cases.

Primary and Secondary Storage Considerations and Recommendations

Each layer of the SAP architecture has different requirements for the storage needed. Table 8-5 provides an overview of the layers and the respective recommendation for primary and secondary storage. The secondary storage recommendation corresponds to the backup storage.

Table 8-5. *Storage Considerations and Recommendations*

SAP System Layer	Primary Storage Recommendation	Secondary Storage Recommendation
Instance boot disk and application binaries	Persistent disks	Persistent disk snapshots
SAP HANA database	Persistent disks	Persistent disk snapshots, Google Cloud Storage buckets with HANA Backint
SAP NetWeaver application servers	Persistent disks, managed NFS (e.g., Google Filestore or NetApp Cloud Volumes)	Persistent disk snapshots, Filestore, Google Cloud Storage buckets

For backups, so the secondary storage recommendations, several options are available and are described in Figure 8-14.

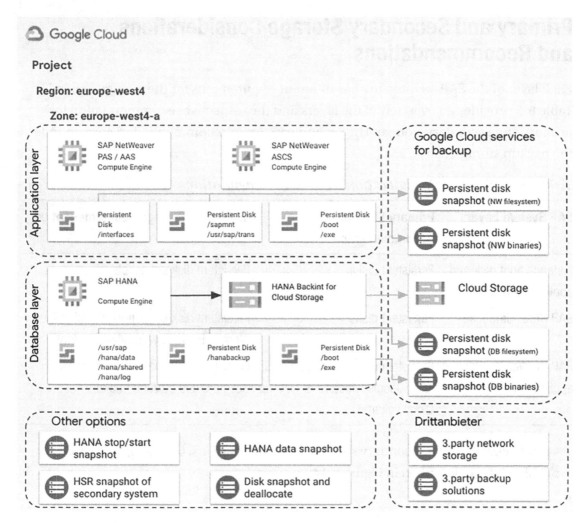

Figure 8-14. *Overview of backup solutions for SAP on Google Cloud*

A recommendation on which of these options have which advantages and disadvantages and in which use cases they should be used (e.g., for productive systems or non-productive ones) is contrasted in Table 8-6.[70]

---

[70] https://cloud.google.com/solutions/sap-on-google-cloud-backup-strategies. pdf, page 17

Table 8-6. *Comparison of Advantages and Disadvantages of Storage Solutions and Recommendations*

Storage Method/ Strategy	Features	Considerations	Environment Suitability	Recommendation
Persistent disk snapshots (complete disks)	Straightforward tooling, crash consistent, globally addressable	File and application-level consistency is not ensured	Production and non-production	For system clones. It complements the other options for production
Volume snapshots (database backup volumes)	Straightforward tooling, crash consistent, reasonably fast, globally addressable	Not application-aware, quiesce file system for correct snapshots, no rule-based life cycle management	Production and non-production	For production
SAP HANA Backint Agent for Cloud Storage	No egress, application-aware, free, streaming with inherent consistency checks	Compression not effective, extra steps for system copy	Production and non-production	Specific to SAP HANA databases
Third-party NFS	Multi-zone availability	Cost/managed trade-off, slower than native storage, egress charges	Production and non-production	For SAP NetWeaver high availability installations
Third-party backup agent and managed service	Enterprise-grade, centralized management, industry-specific retention and compliance requirements	Cost vs. managed service trade-off, possible egress charges	Production	For specific customers and industries that require long retention periods

(continued)

441

Table 8-6. (*continued*)

Storage Method/ Strategy	Features	Considerations	Environment Suitability	Recommendation
SAP HANA data snapshot	SQL based, application consistent, database-level tooling	Not supported for multitenant database, extra configuration required	Only non-production	Specific to SAP HANA databases. Not recommended for multitenant SAP HANA
Stop and start snapshots	Trivial way to help ensure consistency	VM restarts required	Only non-production	Suitable for quick non-production clones
Snapshot and deallocate	Allocate storage only for taking snapshots	Extra scripting required	Only non-production	Use cases with stringent cost considerations

Persistent Disk Snapshots

Snapshots can be used to incrementally back up data from nonvolatile storage, that is, persistent disks. Snapshots are incremental and are automatically compressed, which optimizes costs. They work as follows. The first successful snapshot of nonvolatile storage is a complete snapshot that contains all of the nonvolatile storage's data. The second snapshot contains only new data or data that has changed since the first snapshot. Data that has not changed since the first snapshot is not included. Instead, for the unchanged data blocks, the second snapshot simply contains references to the first snapshot. The third snapshot then includes the data that has been newly added or changed since the second snapshot, but again does not include unchanged data from the first and second snapshots, but instead includes references to those snapshots.[71]

Snapshots are global resources and can therefore be shared and used across projects.[72] Since snapshots are also stored in Google Cloud Storage, the storage buckets can be regional or multiregional (with the closest region being the default).

---

[71] https://cloud.google.com/compute/docs/disks/snapshots

[72] https://cloud.google.com/compute/docs/images/sharing-images-across-projects

As a best practice, you should consider disk decommissioning when creating snapshots, which means freezing file systems or application writes interruption. It is also recommended to automate snapshots and schedule them directly.[73]

The trade-offs for using snapshots for backups in SAP landscapes are

Advantages

- Fast and cost-efficient

- No need for further replication between regions, as Google Cloud Storage is globally addressable and handles replications directly (depending on storage class)

- Crash consistent

Disadvantages

- No consistency guaranteed at the file or application level, only consistency at the block level

In the SAP application server environment, the following disks and binaries can be backed up using snapshots:[74]

- Set of SAP NetWeaver binaries and configuration files

- Common files that are used to share (or transport) customer developments or other transports between systems in a single SAP landscape

- Folders that are required by a highly available system (e.g., to restore locking table if an instance fails over)

- Folders containing interfaces to surrounding systems

In the SAP HANA environment, snapshots of persistent disks are crash consistent, but they do not provide consistency at the application level or file level and are therefore not recommended in the production environment for the SAP HANA data in /hana/ data. Instead, it is recommended to back up the SAP HANA backup volumes. Snapshots are recommended in the SAP HANA environment for the following volumes:

---

[73] https://cloud.google.com/compute/docs/disks/scheduled-snapshots
[74] https://cloud.google.com/solutions/sap-on-google-cloud-backup-strategies. pdf, page 10

- Application binary directories.

- Database configuration files.

- Directories containing data or database transactions.

- Shared files such as binaries, logs, and configurations. For a multiple-host SAP HANA system, this must be an NFS-shared file system.

- Recent redo logs. For a multiple-host SAP HANA system, a shared NFS volume is required to enable SAP HANA multiple-host cluster functionality.

- Files or file systems containing database, file interfaces, and application configuration backups.

It is recommended to work with machine images in the snapshot environment, since most SAP systems consist of multiple disks. These images store all configurations, metadata, permissions, and data from one or more disks needed for a fully functioning VM instance. The image is also stored in Google Cloud Storage in a regional or multiregional bucket. Therefore, no replication is needed. The IP addresses and the data in the RAM are not stored.[75]

Machine images are being used for several use cases:

- Instance creation

- Instance cloning

- Instance backup

- Instance sharing

- Disaster recovery

Google Cloud Storage Buckets with SAP HANA Backint

Google Cloud Storage provides a free and SAP-certified Backint agent for SAP HANA.[76] When SAP HANA Backint is used for backups, the native SAP HANA database tools are used to configure backups and properties. SAP HANA Backint can be used in scale-up and scale-out landscapes and must be installed and configured on all nodes.

---

[75] https://cloud.google.com/compute/docs/machine-images

[76] https://cloud.google.com/solutions/sap/docs/sap-hana-backint-overview

The Backint agent provides a high throughput average and is also multistream capable, so large databases can also be backed up quickly. SAP HANA Backint can act in three different backup modes: full, incremental, and differential.

Advantages

- Elimination of persistent disks for the backup volume

- Application consistency aware

Disadvantages

- Compression is not effective.

- Only specific to an SAP HANA database.

Other backup solutions that can be used include Actifio, NetApp, Commvault, and many other partner and third-party solutions.

Actifio

Actifio is part of Google Cloud and provides functionality for application-consistent and incremental backups. The benefits are very low RPO due to the more frequent smaller backup windows as well as RTO which can be minimized from hours to minutes. This is made possible by Actifio's unique functionality in that multi-TB databases can be restored instantly. Actifio stores backups in native format. Drives can then be mounted directly from the backup appliance. Databases supported include SAP HANA, Oracle, Microsoft SQL Server, PostgreSQL, and MongoDB. Actifio can perform backups at all different application levels, as well as in on-premise landscapes and in a wide variety of private and public clouds: Google Cloud, Azure, AWS, IBM, Oracle, and more.[77]

The latest product, Actifio GO for Google Cloud, is a fully managed solution (SaaS) that serves for enterprise backups, disaster recovery deployments, rapid database cloning, and more. Here, Actifio GO for Google Cloud consists of two main components:

Actifio Global Manager (AGM): The management control plane that is automatically deployed in Google Cloud. You use AGM to set up backup SLAs, recover files/folders/VMs, and DR in Google Cloud. AGM is also used to administer, monitor, and manage one or more Actifio Sky data movers.

---

[77]`www.actifio.com/`

Actifio Sky data mover: A VM appliance that is deployed in your data center to protect on-premises workloads or in your Google Cloud projects to protect Compute Engine VMs. Sky is the core data mover engine that performs incremental forever backups, instant recoveries, and instant database cloning.

Other features of Actifio

- The ***incremental forever technology*** allows multiple datasets (snapshots) to be kept without increasing memory consumption beyond a charge.

- Data states can be mounted directly from the appliance in read/write mode and used with SAP HANA. This means that in the event of data loss, operations can be resumed without the need for a restore. The restore step can be very time-consuming, depending on the database size. Restore times of eight hours or more are not uncommon for large databases. And large databases are typically particularly mission critical.

- The ability to mount snapshots makes it possible to isolate a logical error. For example, if a table was accidentally deleted, it is possible to mount multiple snapshots on a non-production system to see between which snapshots that table was deleted. This also makes it conceivable to repair the database.

- The ability to mount snapshots read/write also allows productive database environments to be transferred to preproduction, quality assurance, test, and development environments via anonymization and SID rename.

Advantages

- Enterprise solution that supports many platforms and setups such as hybrid and multicloud

- Meet industry-specific retention and compliance requirements

- Point-in-time recovery

- Instant recovery capability

- Virtual copies without extra storage

Disadvantages

- Weighing the additional service costs vs. benefits of fully managed service.

- Complex setups may incur minimal outbound traffic costs in special cases.

NetApp

NetApp Cloud Volumes (CVS) are integrated with Google Cloud Console as a fully managed data storage service.

They provide distributed file systems that are typically needed in the SAP environment for

- Interfaces, which are files written by one application and read by one or more others

- The transport directory for propagating changes across environment boundaries (typically `/usr/sap/trans`)

- The SAPMNT directory, which is accessed by multiple application servers

- The executables, profiles, and traces shared across multiple HANA scale-out nodes, typically in `/hana/shared`

NetApp Cloud Volumes also offer many options for migrating and deploying SAP landscapes:

- Snapshot scheduling

- Storage of snapshots in Google Cloud Storage buckets

- SAP NetWeaver high availability setups

- And more

Currently, only multi-zone availability is offered, but no multiregion disaster recovery functionality. CVS should not be used for persistence of SAP HANA installations (`/hana/data` and `/hana/log`) as of September 2021.

CommVault

Another backup and recovery solution that is natively integrated with Google Cloud is Commvault. It is agentless and a popular enterprise-grade offering for industries where the data retention guidelines and regulations are quite stringent. It also offers some niche security features and features that support the long-term retention of the backup data. One feature is its self-adjusting backup with the help of AI that improves performance.

Excursus: SAP S/4HANA Scale-Out (SAP Innovation Award 2021)

This section provides an overview on the topic SAP S/4HANA in a scale-out architecture which Google and SAP proved together in a joint project with customer PayPal.[78]

The mission of this project was to prove the scalability and performance of the cloud for the SAP S/4HANA Financial Products Subledger (FPLS). SAP HANA is able to handle and improve mixed workloads and parallel processing of large datasets – it supports both OLTP and OLAP transactions on a single platform. The first tests were conducted by a cluster of eight nodes with 4 TB each (m1-ultramem-160) so a total of 32 TB DRAM, and the second tests were then using eight nodes with 12 TB each (m2-ultramem-416) VM which is a total of 96 TB DRAM scale-out cluster that has been deployed and tested.

Facts about the data used in the SAP system

- Started with 27 TB of real financial data

- 10 million current accounts and daily postings of 40 million business payment transactions

- A total of 12 billion payments and more than 200 billion subledger items intended for end-of-year accounting

The following is a summary of the important lessons learned and successes achieved through this project:[79]

---

[78] www.sap.com/documents/2020/11/86745fb6-c67d-0010-87a3-c30de2ffd8ff.html
[79] https://cloud.google.com/blog/products/sap-google-cloud/google-cloud-and-sap-demonstrate-scalability-for-financial-services-customers

- Touching 200 billion records for year-to-date balances was reduced in the *runtime of this query from 20 minutes down to 30 seconds* compared with performance levels for scale-up systems of similar size.

- *40x acceleration in query runtime speed* through parallelization.

- *Reduced runtime by 2.7X – from 2 hours down to 44 minutes* compared with performance levels for on-premise scale-up systems.

- Loads were increased progressively from 40 million transactions to 160 million, *quadrupling the number of line items per posting date from 500 million to 2 billion per day.*

- Enabling new optimizations like HANA data tiering resulted in a *78% memory footprint reduction.*

- Engineers consistently measured *speeds faster than 5 GB/second for backups* to a multiregion-replicated cloud storage bucket (16.97 TB at 5.39 GB/second = 54 minutes).

- The application management (maintenance window) time for redistributing SAP HANA scale-out nodes (from eight to ten nodes) was *decreased by 50% in time.*

With this project, the participating companies PayPal and Google Cloud won the SAP Innovation Award 2021.[80, 81]

Excursus: SAP HANA Fast Restart and Memory Poisoning Recovery Capabilities for SAP S/4HANA

A brand-new unique feature that Google Cloud presented in September 2021 is Memory Poisoning Recovery (MPR)[82] in combination with SAP HANA Fast Restart.[83] Background

---

[80] www.sap.com/idea-place/sap-innovation-awards/submission-details-2021.html?idea_id=2376

[81] www.sap.com/bin/sapdxc/inm/attachment.11189/pitch-deck.pdf

[82] https://cloud.google.com/blog/products/sap-google-cloud/mitigating-memory-errors-for-your-sap-environment

[83] https://cloud.google.com/blog/products/sap-google-cloud/protect-hana-uptime-with-fast-restart-on-google-cloud

for this are memory errors which are the most common type of hardware failure that is happening. These can have major impact resulting in a complete SAP system like the SAP HANA database to crash and to be restarted, which can take a long time depending on the database size that needs to be loaded into memory.

How does MPR work and how does it help address this challenge? The solution is based on several layers, some existing Google Cloud capabilities like Live Migration and then capabilities on the CPU level (by Intel) and SAP HANA level. Two main processes are happening:

Memory error isolation

- The hardened VM technology of Compute Engine is intercepting and analyzing errors coming from the system; the signaled region of the memory DIMM will be marked as poisoned.

- Then processes are triggered to keep track of the errors and the poisoned areas.

Memory error recovery

- A notification to the guest OS and the memory-check exception (MCE)–aware applications that a memory error has been recorded

- A direct communication to Live Migration of Compute Engine to trigger a Live Migration move event of the affected host

As it currently stands, MPR will be available for memory-optimized Compute Engine machines (m1- and m2-machine-types) in the last quarter of 2021 and will be rolled out to other Google Cloud machine types on a continuous basis in the future.

Summary

This section provides a summary of the previous sections with all the main points and considerations that should be kept in mind when planning an SAP S/4HANA landscape on Google Cloud in terms of architecture and concepts.

After an overview of the history of Google Cloud and the development over time of the partnership with SAP, which has existed since 2017, the reasons for SAP's decision in favor of Google Cloud were examined in more detail. The main reasons include the innovation, the risk and failure minimization, the flexibility through simplified provisioning, and the sustainability of the Google Cloud.

The general concepts and relevant Google Cloud services for an SAP S/4HANA deployment were then explained. The Google Cloud organizational hierarchy with folders, projects, and resources formed the basis. Then the Compute Engine services, the relevant storage services such as block storage, file sharing, and Google Cloud Storage were explained. After that, the network concept was described, which consists of the VPC network, the subnetworks, routes and forwarding rules, firewall rules, the Cloud Load Balancer, Cloud DNS, and Cloud NAT. The network connection is deployed through either a Cloud VPN, Partner Interconnect, or a Dedicated Interconnect. Then the basics of Google Cloud Security and Identity and Access Management were given. Finally, an overview of Google Cloud Operations with monitoring and logging services as well as Google Cloud support and the Google Cloud front-end tools used such as the Cloud Console and gcloud command line followed.

The remaining sections explained the architectural components of SAP S/4HANA on Google Cloud and the deployment considerations and decisions for high availability, disaster recovery, and data management based on the Google Cloud concepts and services described earlier.

Finally, two special excursion chapters in the environment of co-innovation were shown: first, the results of a project for a 96 TB SAP S/4HANA scale-out project together with SAP and the reference customer PayPal, which was awarded the SAP Innovation Award 2021. On the other hand, the benefits of SAP HANA Fast Restart with Google Memory Poisoning Recovery were explained. These two projects showed, among other things, that Google Cloud offers unique innovations here compared to other providers.

In summary, Google Cloud provides a modern infrastructure for SAP systems. Virtual machines are mapped as Google Compute Engine instances, which offer similar controllability with higher flexibility. Unlike other instance types, the controllability extends across the entire operating system. The Google Cloud infrastructure provides high availability mechanisms, and there are many services to choose from for backups and storage.

What is new compared to on-premise landscapes is the elasticity. It makes no difference how many machines a user provisioned. There is also flexibility: instead of weeks of procurement time, instances can be provisioned in minutes and billed by the second. Users can also opt for other billing models, more on this in the following chapter.

## CHAPTER 9

SAP S/4HANA on Google Cloud – Deployment and Setup

This chapter talks about deployment and setup on the Google Cloud Platform. Topics covered include planning and deployment, the Google Cloud account setup, and the compute setup including the deployment of NetWeaver application servers. We also cover pricing and billing and some best practices around managing your costs.

Example Architecture for SAP S/4HANA on Google Cloud

This section introduces an example SAP S/4HANA architecture on Google Cloud, which will be used for the following sections. With this architecture, the main components are shown and named (e.g., size of the application servers and hard disks, region selection, network name, etc.).

The deployment will include a full high availability cluster and a full disaster recovery setup for both the database and the application server. The operating system chosen is SLES for SAP 15 SP2, yet RHEL would also be a possible alternative and is also fully supported, certified, and recommended by SAP and Google Cloud.

All the components of the architecture can be found in the architecture, starting with the selection of the two regions for the disaster recovery strategy, namely, *europe-west1* (Belgium) as the primary region and *europe-west4* (Netherlands) as the secondary region, then the selection of the two zones for the high availability distribution, namely,

© André Bögelsack, Utpal Chakraborty, Dhiraj Kumar, Johannes Rank, Jessica Tischbierek, Elena Wolz 2022
A. Bögelsack et al., *SAP S/4HANA Systems in Hyperscaler Clouds*, https://doi.org/10.1007/978-1-4842-8158-1_9

zone c (*europe-west1-c*, Belgium) as the primary zone and zone d (*europe-west1-d*, Belgium) as the secondary zone.

The VPC is called *demonetwork* and the subnets are *subnet-europe-west1* and *subnet-europe-west4*.

The selected Compute Engine machines are three n1-highmem-32 (with 32 vCPUs and 208 GB RAM) for the SAP HANA databases named *primaryhana*, *secondaryhana*, and *disasterhana*. Each SAP HANA Compute Engine instance is allocated the following disk space, respectively:

- SSD persistent disk (pd-ssd) with 834 GB for /hana/data, /hana/log, /hana/shared, and /usr/sap

- Standard persistent disk (pd-hdd) with 30 GB as boot disk

- Standard persistent disk (pd-hdd) with 416 GB for /hana/backup

For the SAP NetWeaver application servers, three n2-standard-4 instances (with 4 vCPUs and 16 GB RAM) named *nw-ha-vm-1*, *nw-ha-vm-2*, and *nw-ha-vm-3* are set up for the ASCS/ERS component with the Linux cluster. The application servers themselves are three n2-standard-16 (with 16 vCPUs and 64 GB RAM) named *nw-app-srv-vm-1, nw-app-srv-vm-2, and nw-app-srv-vm-3*. Each application server instance is allocated the following disk space:

- Standard persistent disk (pd-hdd) with 54 GB

Another VM instance is added as an RDP client for SAP HANA Studio (n1-standard-4, with 4 vCPUs and 15 GB RAM) and another as a jumpbox/SAProuter (n1-standard-4, with 4 vCPUs and 15 GB RAM). The architecture is shown in Figure 9-1's architecture diagram with all associated components.

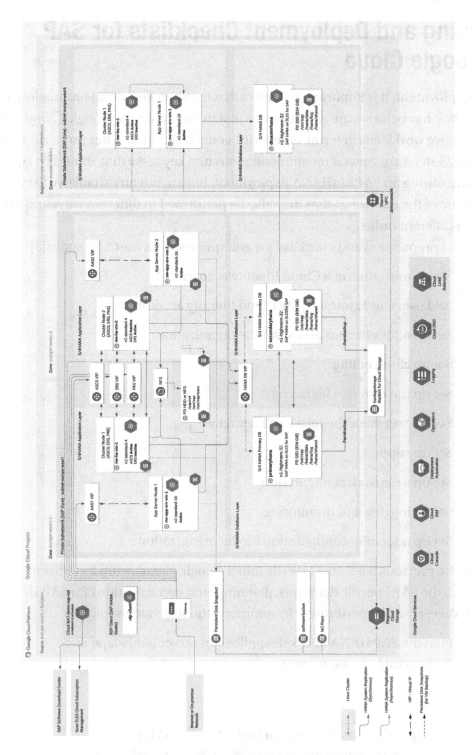

Figure 9-1. *Example architecture for SAP S/4HANA on Google Cloud*

Planning and Deployment Checklists for SAP on Google Cloud

Before deployment, it is important to ensure that the so-called cloud foundation or landing zone has been set up, which means that the setup on the Google Cloud is ready for productive workloads in terms of security, compliance, and other properties. The following 25 steps are general recommendations and key tasks that should be completed before and during an SAP S/4HANA deployment, but are not an exhaustive list in all cases. Some of the following steps may also be performed in different ways and in some cases in a different order.

General preparation and checklist[1] for enterprise setups (not SAP specific)

1.   Set up and confirm a Cloud Identity account.

2.   Add users and groups to the Cloud Identity account.

3.   Set up administrator access for the organization.

4.   Set up cloud billing.

5.   Set up the resource hierarchy.

6.   Set up access for the resource hierarchy.

7.   Set up support.

8.   Set up a network configuration.

9.   Set up logging and monitoring.

10.   Set up a security configuration for the organization.

After the previous basic steps for the initial Google Cloud setup have been performed, the SAP-specific decisions, planning, and configurations for SAP HANA[2] and SAP NetWeaver[3] can be performed. In summary, the steps are as follows:

11.   Plan the SAP HANA and SAP application server landscape and architecture (versions, etc.).

---

[1] https://cloud.google.com/docs/enterprise/setup-checklist

[2] https://cloud.google.com/solutions/sap/docs/checklist-sap-hana

[3] https://cloud.google.com/solutions/sap/docs/checklist-sap-netweaver

12. Follow migration recommendations and plan the migration concept.

13. Select regions and zones for the architecture.

14. Select a deployment model for SAP systems (manual installation vs. automation).

15. Select appropriate and certified machine types and operating systems.

16. Plan and design network requirements.

17. Plan and design a security concept.

18. Select storage, disk space, file system, and configurations.

19. Recommended: Implement SAP HANA Fast Restart.

20. Select a backup strategy for the SAP landscape.

21. Plan a high availability concept for the SAP landscape.

22. Plan a disaster recovery concept for the SAP landscape.

23. Use monitoring and alerting for the SAP landscape.

24. Activate integration interfaces for SAP NetWeaver.

25. Set up load balancing and scaling.

By completing all the preceding steps, you are ready to get your SAP system provisioned on the Google Cloud.

Google Cloud Account, Network, and Security Setup

Before the SAP components of the planned landscape can be set up in the Google Cloud, the basic configurations such as the Google Cloud account, the organizational hierarchy, the projects, and the network concept must be set up with all the required security policies (Identity and Access Management). The steps for an exemplary setup are explained in the following subsections.

Google Account, Cloud Billing, and Identity and Access Management Setup

To set up the correct billing and account information, please follow these steps in Google Cloud:

1. Set up a Google Account (Identity Account).

2. The Identity Account creation requires an email address, a user account for the first super admin user, and the organization's domain. After login, Google Cloud creates the root node of the resource hierarchy, also called the organizational resource.

3. Add users and groups to the Identity Account.

4. This is where you create the users and groups that will be involved in the following checklist activities and systems deployment.

5. Set up administrator access for the organization.

6. Administrator access is set up here to give the administrator a centralized view and control of the organization's cloud resources.

7. Configure cloud billing.

8. Make sure that billing is enabled for your project. The navigation in the Console will take you directly to "Billing." If you have only one cloud billing account, you will go directly to the overview page. If you have more than one cloud billing account, a window opens with the text which account is linked. If you do not have an account, you will get the message to link an account.

9. Set up the resource hierarchy.

10. A resource hierarchy for your organization with folders and projects is created here. The projects and folder structure required for the SAP landscape should directly be created.

11. Set security policies and access for the resource hierarchy.

12. Access control is then created for the IAM resource hierarchy, and roles and policies are assigned to the relevant users and groups.

13. Configure the support.

14. Here, you should select and set up an option for support for your
     Google Cloud projects.

Before performing the subsequent steps in the next sections, you should always
ensure that all configurations and deployments are implemented in your target
project(s) that you defined for the SAP landscape.

Shared VPC, Subnets, Firewall Rules, Cloud NAT, and Cloud DNS Setup

In the following, all network components are configured with a Shared VPC, subnets,
firewall rules, the Cloud NAT, and the Cloud DNS.

Shared VPC and Subnet Setup

First, create a Shared VPC network, either through the Google Cloud Console or from the
command line using the following commands:[4]

1. Create the network *demonetwork* with this command:

    ```
    gcloud compute networks create demonetwork --subnet-
    mode=custom
    ```

2. Create the subnet in the primary region named *subnet-
    europe-west1* and one in the secondary region named *subnet-
    europe-west4*.

3. An example command for the subnetwork of the primary region is
    as follows:

    ```
    gcloud compute networks subnets create subnet-europe-
    west1 --network=demonetwork --region=europe-west1 --range=
    10.128.0.0/20
    ```

---

[4] https://cloud.google.com/solutions/sap/docs/netweaver-deployment-linux-
dm#creating-a-network

Firewall Rule Setup

Create firewall rules that allow only the access that is needed and block any external access that is not needed. An example of firewall rules that can be created with the following commands in the Cloud Shell is

1. ```
   gcloud compute firewall-rules create icmp --network=
   demonetwork --action=allow --target-tags=icmp,
   sap-ports --source-ranges=10.128.0.0/20 --rules=
   tcp,icmp,udp
   ```

2. ```
   gcloud compute firewall-rules create rdp --network=
   demonetwork --action=allow --target-tags=rdp --source-
   ranges=<ip.range.ihrer.admins> --rules=tcp:3389
   ```

3. ```
   gcloud compute firewall-rules create sap-ssh --network=
   demonetwork --action=allow --target-tags=sap-ssh --source-
   ranges=<ip.range.ihrer.admins> --rules=tcp:22
   ```

In a production enterprise landscape, much more firewall rules are needed, and these are defined by your organization's security policies. For SAP landscapes, there are also some recommendations that can be taken from the documentation.[5]

Specify network tags for the VM instances. This allows firewall rules and routes to be applied to specific VM instances. If Deployment Manager templates are used, then they can be defined as follows: networkTag: [TAG].[6]

If you are creating VMs without an external IP address, then in Deployment Manager templates, specify the parameter publicIP: No.

---

[5] https://cloud.google.com/solutions/sap/docs/netweaver-deployment-linux-dm#adding_firewall_rules

[6] https://cloud.google.com/vpc/docs/add-remove-network-tags
   ```

Setup of Cloud NAT

It is recommended to use a Cloud NAT gateway to not expose VM instances to the Internet and set them up without external IP addresses, but still have the ability for software updates or OS registrations over the Internet. Follow these steps[7] to set up Cloud NAT for your landscape:

1. Open the Cloud Console and the left navigation menu and select Network Services ➤ Cloud NAT.

2. Click "Create NAT Gateway."

3. Enter the desired NAT gateway name.

4. Choose the previously created VPC network *demonetwork*.

5. Choose the Google Cloud region for the gateway.

6. Select or create a cloud router in the region.

Figure 9-2 shows the different options for configuring a new NAT gateway.

---

[7] https://cloud.google.com/nat/docs/using-nat

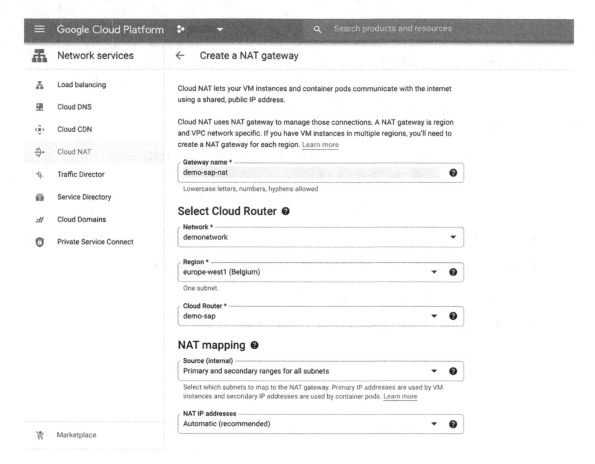

Figure 9-2. *Console screenshot: create Cloud NAT Gateway*

7. Under "NAT mapping," the IP ranges of the subnets that want to access public IP addresses are mapped to source NAT IP addresses.

8. Click "Advanced Configurations."

9. Select "Translation and errors" under "Stackdriver Logging."

10. Define the "Minimum ports per VM instance" and "Timeouts for protocol connections" if needed.

11. Click "Create."

The next step will be the creation of the Cloud DNS.

Setup of Cloud DNS

In this section, the Cloud DNS entry for the virtual IP address (VIP) of the SAP landscape is configured so that the systems can each be addressed via the DNS name:

1. Before the entry can be configured, a metadata entry must be created in the project so that the DNS is replicated globally. The command for gcloud is

    ```
    gcloud compute project-info add-metadata --metadata=VmDns
    Setting=GlobalOnly
    ```

2. Open the navigation menu in the Console and select Network Services ➤ Cloud DNS.

3. In the displayed window named Zones, click "Create Zone" to create a new DNS zone for your project.

4. Enter the configuration as displayed in the console screenshot in Figure 9-3 and click "Create."

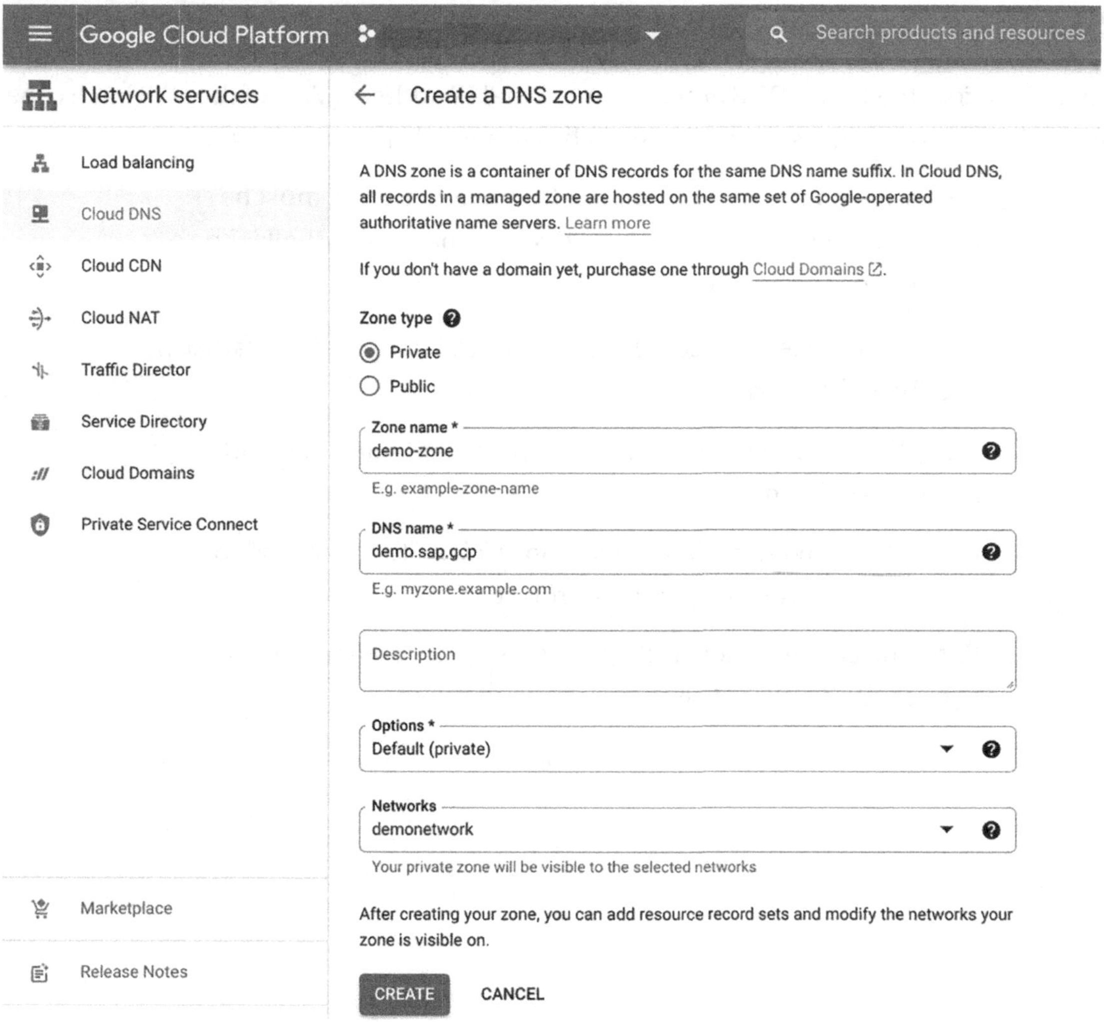

Figure 9-3. *Console screenshot: create a DNS zone*

5. In the following window, click "+ Add record set."

6. Set the configuration values as shown in Figure 9-4.

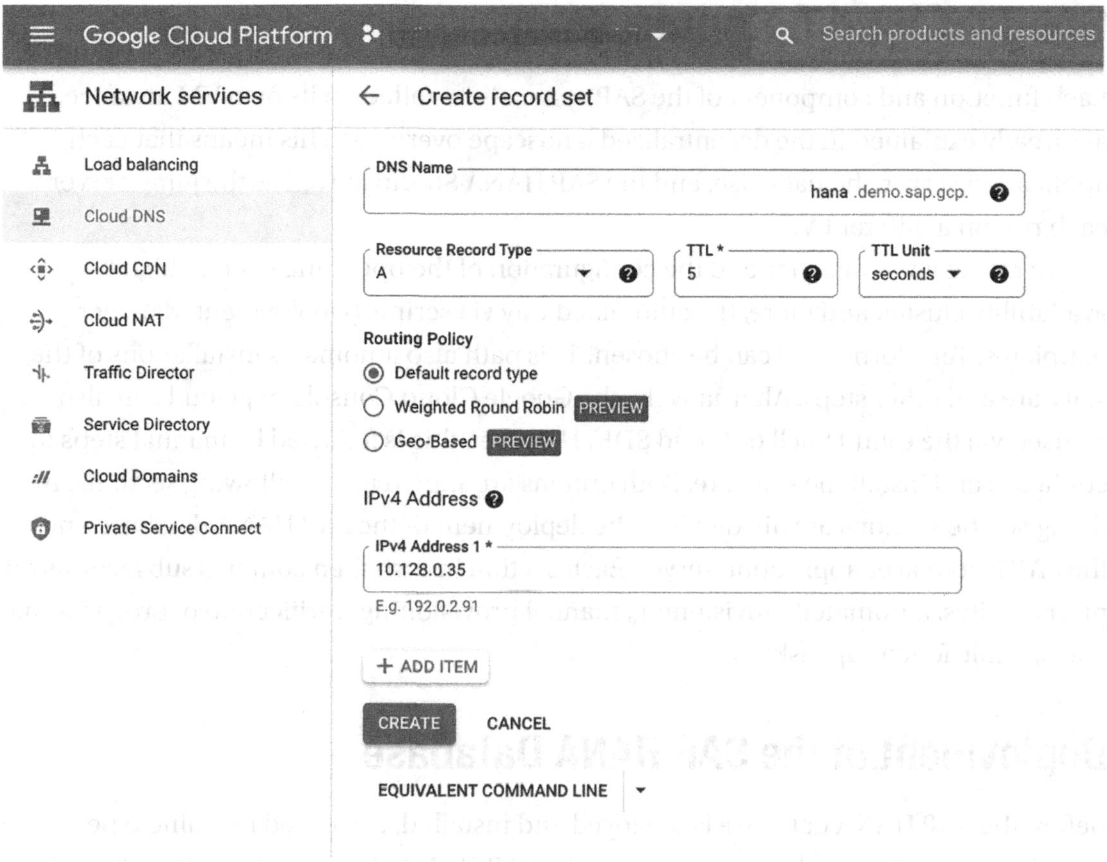

Figure 9-4. Console screenshot: create a DNS record set

7.   Click "Create."

After the Cloud DNS configuration is finished, you can reserve the floating IP to avoid that it will be assigned to another VM instance during deployment. The command for gcloud is

```
gcloud compute addresses create alias01 --project=[YOUR
PROJECT ID] --subnet=subnet-europe-west1 --region=
europe-west1 --addresses=10.128.0.35
```

Google Cloud Compute Setup

Each function and component of the SAP system is installed on its own VM instance, as already explained in the decentralized landscape overview. This means that each application server, the database, and the SAP HANA Studio as well as the jump server each run on a different VM.

To create a VM instance and the configuration of the operating system, high availability cluster, and more, the automated way via scripts (Deployment Manager templates, Terraform, etc.) can be chosen. This path also automates installations of the software and other steps. Alternatively, the Google Cloud Console or gcloud can also be used via the Cloud Shell or Cloud SDK. However, this is followed by manual steps to configure and install the software. Both options are shown in the following sections. In doing so, the sections are divided into the deployment of the SAP HANA database and the SAP NetWeaver application server. Each section in turn then contains subsections on prerequisites, automated provisioning, manual provisioning, verification of provisioning, and specific follow-up tasks.

Deployment of the SAP HANA Database

Before the SAP HANA database is deployed and installed, a certified machine type must be selected in the documentation or the SAP HANA Hardware Directory. In the architecture example of the previous section, the machine type n1-highmem-32 was selected for the SAP HANA instances.

Prerequisites for the Deployment of SAP HANA with High Availability

Before deploying the VM instances, verify that the following configurations have been made:

1. Check that the quotas are large enough for the project and for the size of the planned deployment of the entire landscape.

2. The Google Identity Account, the organizational resource hierarchy, and the projects are created and configured.

3. The Shared VPC network, subnets, Cloud NAT, and Cloud DNS have been set up.

4. The firewall rules have been created.

5. Download the SAP media files for installing the software (SAP HANA and others) and upload them to a Google Cloud Storage bucket with the required permissions. The name *sap-software-bucket* was defined for this bucket.

6. To do this, go to "Cloud Storage" under Storage in the Console menu.

7. In the Cloud Storage Browser, click "Create Bucket" and enter the bucket name (sap-software-bucket).

8. Set the storage location as multiregional in European regions as illustrated in Figure 9-5.

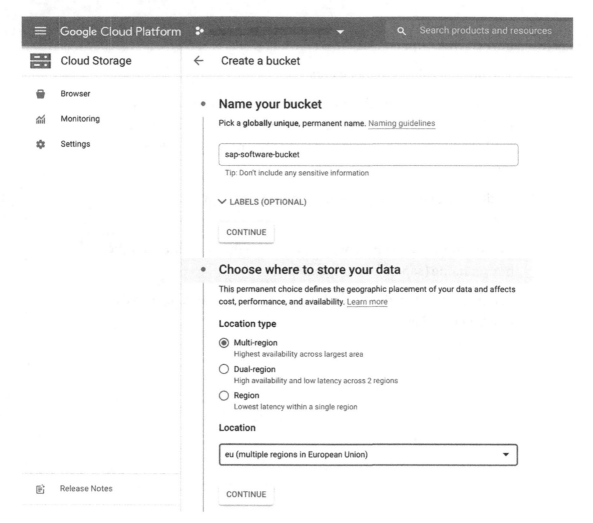

Figure 9-5. *Console screenshot: create a Google Cloud Storage bucket*

9.   Then define the storage class and the accesses as needed.

10.   Click "Create."

11.   Once the bucket has been created, the media files can be uploaded into it.

12.   Create a VM with SAP tools such as SAP HANA Studio installed for possible access to the database after installation. For this, you can use the following gcloud command, which can use an image you

preconfigured earlier that already provides the installation media
for SAP HANA Studio:

```
gcloud compute instances create rdp-client --zone=$PRIMARY_
ZONE --machine-type=n1-standard-4 --image-project=<ihr.
projekt> --image=<ihr.sap.rdp.image> --network=
demonetwork --subnet=subnet-$PRIMARY_REGION --tags=rdp,
http-server,https-server --boot-disk-type=pd-ssd
```

13. After a successful deployment of the VM instance, an RDP
    connection to this Compute Engine instance can be made from
    the Console by resetting the Windows password of this VM, saving
    it somewhere safe, and then logging in with the username and
    password.

14. Create another VM as a SAProuter or jumpbox, either manually
    via the Compute Engine menu in the Console or via gcloud. More
    information about the installation and setup of the SAP Support
    Channel can be found in the documentation.[8]

Automated Deployment of SAP HANA High Availability Systems

The SAP HANA high availability systems can be set up using the templates provided for
Google Cloud Deployment Manager or Terraform. Automated deployment is one of the
best practices of SAP and Google Cloud and saves time and effort. The stored scripts
can be reused at any time, which is necessary for highly available and failure-resistant
landscapes to enable fast recoveries. In the following steps, the following components of
the landscape are set up and configured automatically:

- VM instances with the required persistent disks for each SAP HANA
  instance

- SAP HANA installation on the VM instances with an enabled
  configuration for synchronous system replication and
  memory preload

- Automatic failover cluster

---

[8] https://cloud.google.com/solutions/sap/docs/sap-hana-operations-guide#setting_
up_your_sap_support_channel_with_saprouter

- Automatic restart enabled (host auto-restart)

- A reservation of VIP specified by you

- Failover support using internal TCP/UDP load balancing

- Firewall rules that allow Compute Engine health checks, enabling monitoring of VM instances in the cluster

- Pacemaker high availability cluster resource manager

- Google Cloud fencing mechanism

The following steps must be performed for this setup:[9]

1. Open the gcloud command line.

2. Load the YAML template into your working directory:

   ```
   wget https://storage.googleapis.com/cloudsapdeploy/
   deploymentmanager/latest/dm-templates/sap_hana_ha_ilb/
   template.yaml
   ```

3. Edit the template with your specific settings and naming and change the file name if desired. The example here shows the SAP HANA instances with the machine sizes and regions selected as introduced earlier:

   ```
   imports:
   - path: https://storage.googleapis.com/sapdeploy/dm-templates/
   sap_hana_ha/sap_hana_ha.py

   resources:
   - name: sap_hana_ha
     type: https://storage.googleapis.com/sapdeploy/dm-templates/
     sap_hana_ha/sap_hana_ha.py
     properties:
       primaryInstanceName: primaryhana
       secondaryInstanceName: secondaryhana
       primaryZone: europe-west1-c
   ```

---

[9]https://cloud.google.com/solutions/sap/docs/sap-hana-ha-dm-deployment#creating_a_high-availability_linux_cluster_with_sap_hana_installed

```
secondaryZone: europe-west1-d
instanceType: n1-highmem-32
subnetwork: subnet-europe-west1
linuxImage: family/sles-15-sp2-sap
linuxImageProject: suse-sap-cloud
sap_hana_deployment_bucket: sap-software-bucket
sap_hana_sid: GCP
sap_hana_instance_number: 00
sap_hana_sidadm_password: testpw
sap_hana_system_password: testpw
sap_vip: 10.128.0.35
networkTag: icmp,sap-ports,sap-ssh
```

4. After you save your configuration file customizations, you can run
   the deployment script:

   ```
   gcloud deployment-manager deployments create hanaha  --config
   hana_ha_na.yaml
   ```

It will take around 20–30 minutes to complete the automated provisioning,
installation of the SAP HANA databases, and configuration of the high availability cluster.

Then follow the steps in the section "Verification of the SAP HANA High Availability
Systems Deployment."

Manual Deployment of SAP HANA High Availability Systems

If you choose not to follow the recommended path via automated deployment scripts,
you can perform a manual deployment in the Google Cloud Console and with the
gcloud command line. To do this, you need to perform the following steps, which are not
explained in detail here but can be found in full detail in the documentation:[10]

1. Create the required Compute Engine VM instances.

2. Install SAP HANA.

3. Verify the deployment in the SAP HANA system (see the section
   "Verification of the SAP HANA High Availability Systems Deployment").

---

[10] https://cloud.google.com/solutions/sap/docs/sap-hana-ha-config-sles

4. Install the Google Cloud Monitoring Agent v2.0.

5. Disable SAP HANA Autostart (because Pacemaker will start SAP HANA).

6. Allow an SSH connection between the primary and secondary SAP HANA machines.

7. Enable and configure SAP HANA System Replication (HSR).

8. Configure the Google Cloud Load Balancer failover.

9. Deploy the Pacemaker cluster.

10. Test a failover.

Verification of the SAP HANA High Availability Systems Deployment

After a successful manual or automated setup, the SAP HANA HA cluster must be verified in Cloud Logging and on the VM instances in SAP HANA itself. The following steps should be performed for this purpose:

Check Google Cloud Logging:

1. Navigate via the menu to Operations and here in Cloud Logging under Logging. In the Log Explorer, select "Global" as the resource type and click "Run Query."

2. As soon as you see the line "INSTANCE DEPLOYMENT COMPLETE" in the logs for both instances, *primaryhana* and *secondaryhana*, the setup and configuration of SAP HANA on these Compute Engine instances has been successfully performed and completed (see Figure 9-6).

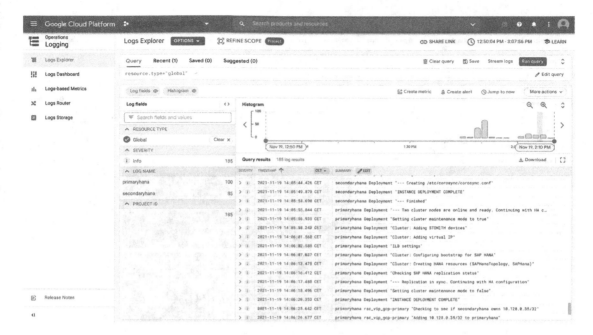

Figure 9-6. *Console screenshot: Google Cloud Logging*

Verify VM configuration and SAP HANA installation:

3. You can now navigate to your Compute Engine instances via the menu in the Console and log in to the *primaryhana* via SSH. Now enter the following command in the SSH Console:

```
top
```

4. Now check if the "hdbindexserver" is visible. As soon as this entry appears, the installation is finished and the clustering is set up. You can check the status as illustrated in Figure 9-7.

473

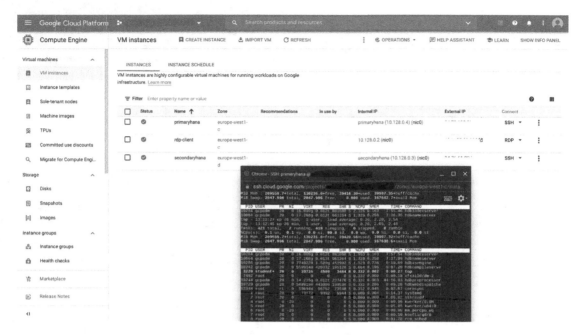

Figure 9-7. *Console screenshot: check the SAP HANA status in Google Cloud Compute Engine*

Check the Load Balancer and the instance groups:

5. From the Console menu, navigate to Network Services and then to Load Balancing. A TCP load balancer should be configured for your HA cluster. In the instance groups, check the VMs and whether their status is shown as error-free. One instance group shows 1/1, and the current secondary (failover) instance group shows a 0/1.

   Check the SAP HANA database in SAP HANA Studio:

6. Log in to the VM instance *rdp-client* via RDP. To operate SAP HANA Studio and check the SAP HANA database, you can follow the documentation.[11]

   Run a failover test:

---

[11] https://cloud.google.com/solutions/sap/docs/sap-hana-ha-dm-deployment#checking_the_sap_hana_system_using_sap_hana_studio

7. The following command, shown executed in Figure 9-8, allows
    you to check the status of the SUSE Pacemaker cluster, as well as
    which server is the primary and which is the secondary:

    ```
    crm status
    ```

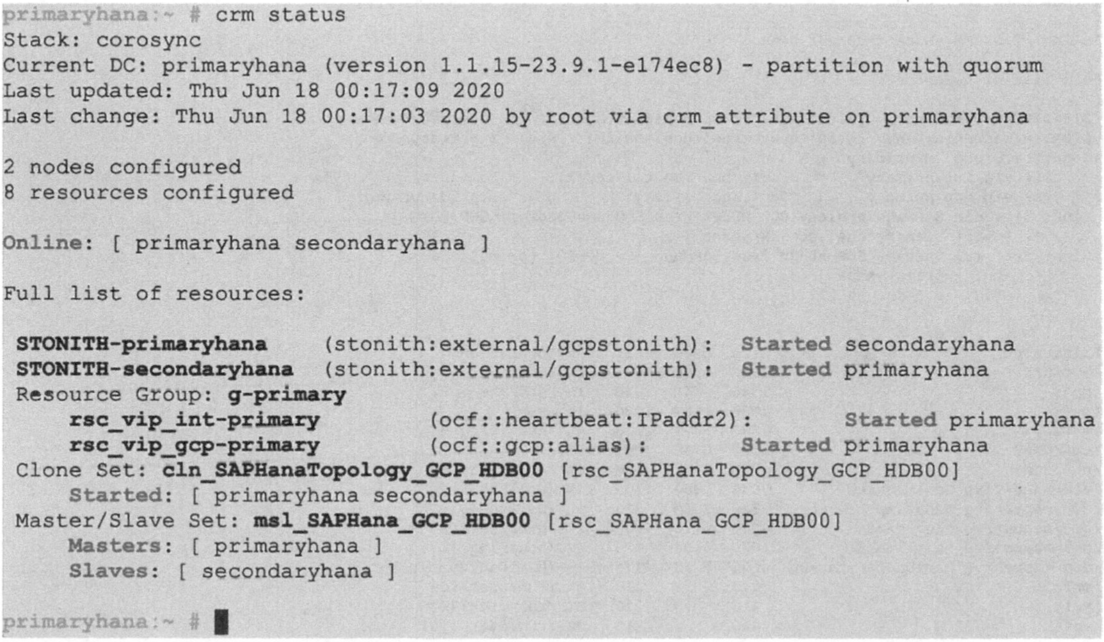

```
primaryhana:~ # crm status
Stack: corosync
Current DC: primaryhana (version 1.1.15-23.9.1-e174ec8) - partition with quorum
Last updated: Thu Jun 18 00:17:09 2020
Last change: Thu Jun 18 00:17:03 2020 by root via crm_attribute on primaryhana

2 nodes configured
8 resources configured

Online: [ primaryhana secondaryhana ]

Full list of resources:

 STONITH-primaryhana       (stonith:external/gcpstonith):   Started secondaryhana
 STONITH-secondaryhana     (stonith:external/gcpstonith):   Started primaryhana
 Resource Group: g-primary
     rsc_vip_int-primary           (ocf::heartbeat:IPaddr2):        Started primaryhana
     rsc_vip_gcp-primary           (ocf::gcp:alias):        Started primaryhana
 Clone Set: cln_SAPHanaTopology_GCP_HDB00 [rsc_SAPHanaTopology_GCP_HDB00]
     Started: [ primaryhana secondaryhana ]
 Master/Slave Set: msl_SAPHana_GCP_HDB00 [rsc_SAPHana_GCP_HDB00]
     Masters: [ primaryhana ]
     Slaves: [ secondaryhana ]

primaryhana:~ # █
```

Figure 9-8. *Console screenshot: check the SAP HANA high availability cluster*

The df-h command in Figure 9-9 shows that the deployment requires a default disk
configuration for SAP HANA. Each disk size is based on the amount of memory allocated
to the machine during installation.

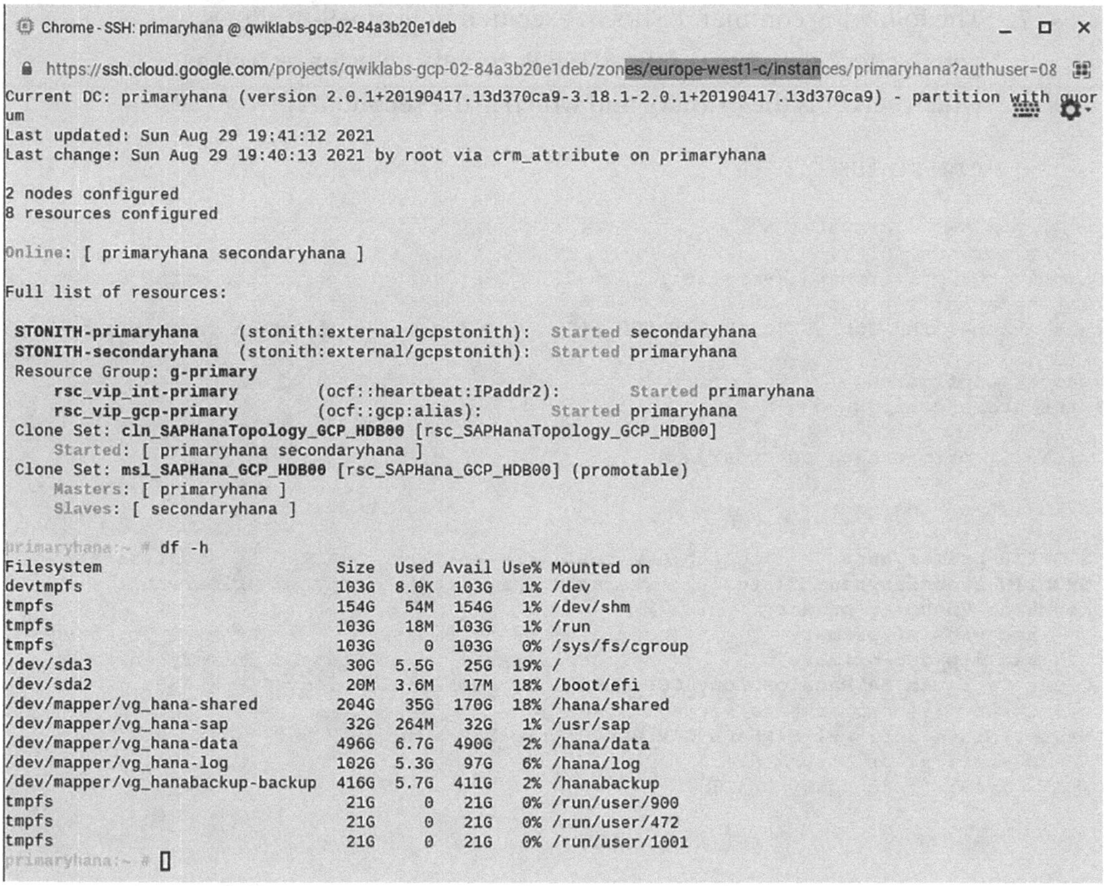

```
Chrome - SSH: primaryhana @ qwiklabs-gcp-02-84a3b20e1deb                                    _  □  ×

   https://ssh.cloud.google.com/projects/qwiklabs-gcp-02-84a3b20e1deb/zones/europe-west1-c/instances/primaryhana?authuser=0
Current DC: primaryhana (version 2.0.1+20190417.13d370ca9-3.18.1-2.0.1+20190417.13d370ca9) - partition with quor
um
Last updated: Sun Aug 29 19:41:12 2021
Last change: Sun Aug 29 19:40:13 2021 by root via crm_attribute on primaryhana

2 nodes configured
8 resources configured

Online: [ primaryhana secondaryhana ]

Full list of resources:

 STONITH-primaryhana      (stonith:external/gcpstonith):  Started secondaryhana
 STONITH-secondaryhana    (stonith:external/gcpstonith):  Started primaryhana
 Resource Group: g-primary
     rsc_vip_int-primary        (ocf::heartbeat:IPaddr2):        Started primaryhana
     rsc_vip_gcp-primary        (ocf::gcp:alias):           Started primaryhana
 Clone Set: cln_SAPHanaTopology_GCP_HDB00 [rsc_SAPHanaTopology_GCP_HDB00]
     Started: [ primaryhana secondaryhana ]
 Clone Set: msl_SAPHana_GCP_HDB00 [rsc_SAPHana_GCP_HDB00] (promotable)
     Masters: [ primaryhana ]
     Slaves: [ secondaryhana ]

primaryhana:~ # df -h
Filesystem                          Size  Used Avail Use% Mounted on
devtmpfs                            103G  8.0K  103G   1% /dev
tmpfs                               154G   54M  154G   1% /dev/shm
tmpfs                               103G   18M  103G   1% /run
tmpfs                               103G     0  103G   0% /sys/fs/cgroup
/dev/sda3                            30G  5.5G   25G  19% /
/dev/sda2                            20M  3.6M   17M  18% /boot/efi
/dev/mapper/vg_hana-shared          204G   35G  170G  18% /hana/shared
/dev/mapper/vg_hana-sap              32G  264M   32G   1% /usr/sap
/dev/mapper/vg_hana-data            496G  6.7G  490G   2% /hana/data
/dev/mapper/vg_hana-log             102G  5.3G   97G   6% /hana/log
/dev/mapper/vg_hanabackup-backup    416G  5.7G  411G   2% /hanabackup
tmpfs                                21G     0   21G   0% /run/user/900
tmpfs                                21G     0   21G   0% /run/user/472
tmpfs                                21G     0   21G   0% /run/user/1001
primaryhana:~ # □
```

Figure 9-9. *Console screenshot: check persistent disks and file system configuration of SAP HANA*

Now, log in to the primary VM instance via SSH and run the following commands:

- `sudo su -`

- `zypper install net-tools-deprecated`

- `ifconfig eth0 down`

Then navigate to Google Cloud Logging in the menu. In the Cloud Log Explorer, as shown in Figure 9-10, you should now be able to see how the *secondaryhana* instance takes over as the primary instance.

Figure 9-10.   *Console screenshot: check the failover in Cloud Logging*

If these verification steps have been performed successfully, then the deployment has finished without errors.

Follow-Up Tasks After the Installation of the SAP HANA Systems

Before using the SAP HANA instances, the following tasks should be completed after deployment:[12]

- Change temporary passwords.

- Update SAP HANA software and patches.

- Install additional components or perform configurations as needed.

- Configure a backup and recovery.

- Configure a SAProuter for the support channel with SAP.[13]

---

[12] https://cloud.google.com/solutions/sap/docs/sap-hana-ha-dm-deployment#performing_post-deployment_tasks

[13] https://cloud.google.com/solutions/sap/docs/sap-hana-operations-guide#setting_up_your_sap_support_channel_with_saprouter

Deployment of SAP NetWeaver Application Servers

For the SAP NetWeaver application servers, the required sizes must also be checked against the certified sizes. The following section focuses on the setup of SAP NetWeaver systems on Linux[14] (the Windows installations can be found in the official documentation[15]).

Prerequisites for the Deployment of SAP NetWeaver Application Servers

Before going ahead with the installation of the SAP NetWeaver application servers, you should take some time to consider the following preparation tasks:

- Check that the quotas are large enough for the project and for the size of the planned deployment of the entire landscape.

- The Google Identity Account, organizational hierarchy, and projects are created and configured.

- The Shared VPC network, subnets, Cloud NAT, and Cloud DNS have been set up.

- The firewall rules have been created.

- Upload the SAP media files for installing the software to a Google Cloud Storage bucket with the required permissions.

Automated Deployment of SAP NetWeaver Application Servers

The SAP NetWeaver application servers can be set up using the templates provided for Google Cloud Deployment Manager or Terraform. Automated deployment is one of the best practices of SAP and Google Cloud and saves time and effort. The stored scripts can be reused at any time, which is necessary for highly available and fail-safe landscapes to enable fast recoveries. In the following steps, the following components of the landscape are set up and configured automatically:

- Two host VMs for the SAP NetWeaver application servers

---

[14] https://cloud.google.com/solutions/sap/docs/netweaver-deployment-guide-linux
[15] https://cloud.google.com/solutions/sap/docs/netweaver-deployment-guide-windows

- Two host VMs, one with an active SAP Central Services (ASCS) and one with an active Standalone Enqueue Server (ERS)

- Pacemaker cluster resource manager for high availability

- STONITH fencing mechanism

- Automatic restart of a failed instance as a new secondary instance

The following steps must be performed for this setup:

1. Open the gcloud command line.

2. Download the YAML template to your working directory:

   wget https://storage.googleapis.com/cloudsapdeploy/
   deploymentmanager/latest/dm-templates/sap_nw/template.yaml

3. Edit the template with your specific settings[16] and naming and change the file name if desired. The example here shows the ASCS and ERS instances with the machine sizes and regions as introduced in the previous section:

```
 resources:
- name: sap_nw_node_1
  type: https://storage.googleapis.com/cloudsapdeploy/
deploymentmanager/latest/dm-templates/sap_nw/sap_nw.py
  properties:
    instanceName: nw-ha-vm-1
    instanceType: n2-standard-4
    zone: europe-west1-c
    subnetwork: subnet-europe-west1
    linuxImage: family/sles-15-sp2-sap
    linuxImageProject: suse-sap-cloud
    usrsapSize: 15
    sapmntSize: 15
    swapSize: 24
    networkTag: cluster-ntwk-tag,allow-health-check
```

---

[16] https://cloud.google.com/solutions/sap/docs/netweaver-ha-config-sles#nw-ha-example-config-file

```
      serviceAccount: limited-roles@example-project-123456.iam.
      gserviceaccount.com
- name: sap_nw_node_2
  type: https://storage.googleapis.com/cloudsapdeploy/
  deploymentmanager/latest/dm-templates/sap_nw/sap_nw.py
  properties:
    instanceName: nw-ha-vm-2
    instanceType: n2-standard-4
    zone: europe-west1-d
    subnetwork: subnet-europe-west1
    linuxImage: family/sles-15-sp2-sap
    linuxImageProject: suse-sap-cloud
    usrsapSize: 15
    sapmntSize: 15
    swapSize: 24
    networkTag: cluster-ntwk-tag,allow-health-check
    serviceAccount: limited-roles@example-project-123456.iam.
    gserviceaccount.com
```

4. As can be seen in the script, two VMs of the n2-standard-4
    machine type are created here, each with 4 vCPUs and 16 GB RAM
    with the SLES 15 SP2 operating system.

5. Now the automated provisioning of the two application servers
    itself is described; this must also be defined twice in succession.
    Here is the example for *nw-app-srv-vm-1*:

```
resources:
- name: sap_nw_app
  type: https://storage.googleapis.com/cloudsapdeploy/
  deploymentmanager/latest/dm-templates/sap_nw/sap_nw.py
  #
  # By default, this configuration file uses the latest release of
  the deployment
  # scripts for SAP on Google Cloud.  To fix your deployments to a
  specific release
```

```
# of the scripts, comment out the type property above and
uncomment the type property below.
#
# type: https://storage.googleapis.com/cloudsapdeploy/
deploymentmanager/202103310846/dm-templates/sap_nw/sap_nw.py
properties:
  instanceName: nw-app-srv-vm-1
  instanceType: n2-standard-16
  zone: europe-west1-c
  subnetwork: subnet-europe-west1
  linuxImage: family/sles-15-sp2-sap
  linuxImageProject: suse-sap-cloud
  usrsapSize: 15
  sapmntSize: 15
  swapSize: 24
```

6. Create both deployments with the two templates using the
    following command:

    ```
    gcloud deployment-manager deployments create [DEPLOYMENT_NAME]
    --config sap_nw_app.yaml
    ```

After the deployment, perform the steps in the sections "Verification of the
Deployment of SAP NetWeaver Application Servers" and "Configuring the High
Availability Cluster."

Manual Deployment of SAP NetWeaver Application Servers

If you do not choose the recommended automated deployment path, you can also
perform a manual deployment of the VM instances. This is done in the Google Cloud
Console or in gcloud.

In the Google Cloud Console, navigate to Compute Engine in the menu:

1. Click "Image" in the left menu bar.

2. Select the image here (SLES for SAP 15 SP2 in this architecture
    example) and click "Create Instance," then enter the
    following values.

3. Enter the name of the VM instance.

4. Select the region and zone.

5. Select the machine type, in this example n2-standard-4.

6. Configure a boot disk (here with 20 GB) and the operating system SLES 15 SP2.

7. Select the service account and access scopes (if you are using a custom service account that restricts access to Google Cloud resources, select full access to all APIs).

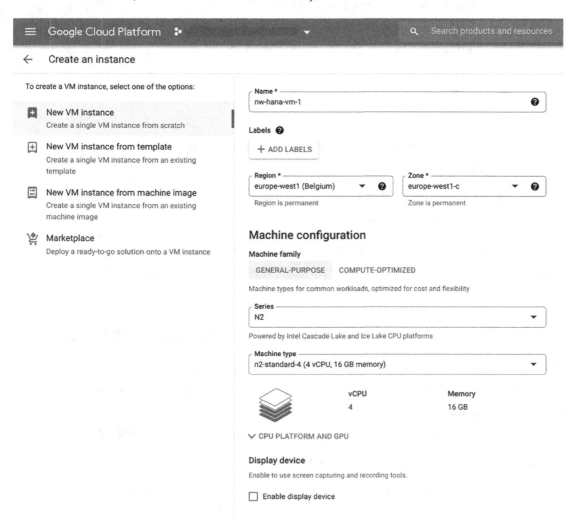

Figure 9-11. *Console screenshot: create an instance*

1. Expand the section "Management, disks, networking, sole tenancy."

2. In the Networking tab, select the network and the subnetwork.

3. If a NAT Gateway is being used, add the tag that directs traffic to the gateway under "Network" ➤ "Network Tags."

4. In Management ➤ "Availability Policy," select

   - Preemptibility ➤ Off (recommended)

   - Host Maintenance ➤ Migrate VM Instance (recommended)

   - Automatic Restart ➤ On (recommended)

5. In the disks tab under "Additional Disks," select "Add new disks."

6. Add SAP NetWeaver binaries and swap disk.

7. Set the name, disk type (as Standard-PD, HDD), source type (as blank disk), and the size.

8. Click "Create" to create the instance.

Alternatively, the command-line equivalent for the gcloud command line can be displayed and copied in the Cloud Console to the right of the "Create" button. For the system described here, the command would look like this:

```
gcloud compute instances create nw-ha-vm-1 --project=<ihr.project.
name> --zone=europe-west1-c --machine-type=n2-standard-4 --network-
interface=network-tier=PREMIUM,subnet=subnet-europe-west1 --maintenance-
policy=MIGRATE --service-account=<ihr.automatischer.service.account>-
compute@developer.gserviceaccount.com --scopes=https://www.googleapis.
com/auth/devstorage.read_only,https://www.googleapis.com/auth/logging.
write,https://www.googleapis.com/auth/monitoring.write,https://www.
googleapis.com/auth/servicecontrol,https://www.googleapis.com/auth/
service.management.readonly,https://www.googleapis.com/auth/trace.
append --create-disk=auto-delete=yes,boot=yes,device-name=nw-ha-
vm-1,image=projects/suse-sap-cloud/global/images/sles-15-sp2-sap-v2021060
4,mode=rw,size=20,type=projects/<ihr.project.name>/zones/europe-west1-c/
diskTypes/pd-balanced --create-disk=device-name=nw-disk,mode=rw,name=nw-
disk,size=54,type=projects/<ihr.project.name>/zones/europe-west1-c/
```

```
diskTypes/pd-balanced --no-shielded-secure-boot --shielded-vtpm --shielded-
integrity-monitoring --reservation-affinity=any
```

After the VM instance is deployed, log in to the VM via SSH. Now, the disks and nonvolatile storage must be configured and mounted. The following commands must be repeated for all the disks that are to be created:[17]

1. Log in as a super user: `sudo su -`

2. Create a physical volume for the disk: `pvcreate /dev/disk/by-id/google-[DISK]`

3. Create a volume group for the disk: `vgcreate vg_usrsap /dev/disk/by-id/google-[DISK]`

4. Create a logical volume for the disk: `lvcreate -l 100%FREE -n vol vg_usrsap`

5. Format the disk with a file system, for example, single xfs: `mkfs -t xfs /dev/vg_usrsap/vol`

6. Update the file systems table (fstab): `echo "/dev/vg_usrsap/vol /usr/sap xfs defaults,discard,nofail 0 2" >>/etc/fstab`

7. Create a mount point: `mkdir -p /usr/sap`

8. Mount the disk to a VM: `mount -a`

9. Confirm that your disks are mounted properly: `df -h`

Format and mount the swap disk:

10. Create a physical volume for the swap disk: `pvcreate /dev/disk/by-id/google-[DISK]`

11. Create a volume group: `vgcreate vg_swap /dev/disk/by-id/google-[DISK]`

12. Create a logical volume for the swap disk: `lvcreate -l 100%FREE -n vol vg_swap`

13. Format the swap disk: `mkswap /dev/vg_swap/vol`

---

[17] https://cloud.google.com/solutions/sap/docs/netweaver-deployment-linux-manual#formatting_and_mounting_disk_drives

14. Update fstab: `echo "/dev/vg_swap/vol none swap defaults,nofail 0 2" >>/etc/fstab`

15. Mount the disk to the VM: `swapon /dev/vg_swap/vol`

Finally, prepare the operating system according to the SAP Note documentation.[18]

Verification of the SAP NetWeaver Application Server Deployments

After the deployment is completed, you should verify the correct deployment by following these steps:

1. Verify the deployment in Cloud Logging ➤ Log Explorer under Resource Type ➤ Global and connect to the VM instance via SSH.

2. Check the file systems/directories with the command: `df -h`

3. Check if the swap directory has been created as well: `cat /proc/meminfo | grep Swap`

4. Install the Cloud Logging Agent and the Monitoring Agent for SAP NetWeaver.

5. Then install SAP NetWeaver – for more information, see SAP Help Portal[19] and the SAP NetWeaver Master Guide.[20]

Configuring the High Availability Cluster

If the SAP NetWeaver application servers are to be set up in a high availability cluster, the setup is more complex and requires additional steps to configure the Linux Pacemaker cluster, load balancing, and more. In the following, the steps[21] after the creation of the VM instances of the previous section are roughly explained; the details can be taken from the documentation:

---

[18] https://cloud.google.com/solutions/sap/docs/netweaver-deployment-linux-manual#preparing_the_operating_system

[19] https://help.sap.com/viewer/p/SAP_NETWEAVER_750

[20] https://help.sap.com/doc/18cb1a50b9924bc3b94c2988cc8c51d9/7.5/en-US/mg_nw_75.pdf

[21] https://cloud.google.com/solutions/sap/docs/netweaver-ha-config-sles

1. Create firewall rules that allow access to host VMs, for example, between all cluster VMs and also between them and the jump server.

2. Enable load balancer communication between VMs.

3. On each VM in the cluster, log in via SSH, switch to the root user, and run the following command to enable local routing:

```
echo net.ipv4.conf.eth0.accept_local=1 >> /etc/sysctl.conf
sysctl -p
```

4. Create a startup script on each VM for communication between VMs; see a sample script in the documentation.[22]

5. Configure the SSH keys between the hosts, that is, the primary and secondary VM instances.

6. Set up the file sharing solution (NFS) and configure the directories shared between VMs.

7. Configure failover support for Cloud Load Balancing.

8. The internal TCP/UDP load balancer with failover support forwards data traffic from ASCS and ERS systems to the active instances (application servers) in an SAP NetWeaver cluster. The internal TCP/UDP load balancer uses virtual IP addresses (VIP), back-end services, instance groups, and system diagnostics to forward this traffic accordingly.

9. Setup of Pacemaker.

10. Configure the cluster resources of the high availability cluster for the infrastructure.

11. Install ASCS and ERS.

12. Configure SAP services.

13. Configure cluster resources for ASCS and ERS.

---

[22] https://cloud.google.com/solutions/sap/docs/netweaver-ha-config-sles#enable-back-end-comms

14.   Test the cluster.

Pricing and Billing Concepts with Best Practices

This section covers the pricing and billing concepts on demand (also called pay-as-you-go) and with discounts called committed use discounts. The possibilities of reservations and quotas are also explained. Finally, the architecture example from the previous section is calculated using the official Google Cloud price calculator.

On-Demand vs. Committed Use Discounts

Google Cloud offers the possibility to assure the use of specific services and workloads, thus confirming to Google an assurance of need. This commitment of usage leads to significant cost reductions for the customer in the form of discounts. Discounts for committed use are available on Compute Engine resources such as vCPUs, RAM, and local SSDs, among others. These discounts are up to 57% for most resource types and up to 70% for memory-optimized machines (m1 and m2 machine types). The decision is made based on the Compute Engine machine types and usage types. This section helps to decide which systems should be provided with committed use.

Discounts for committed use are stored and assured in the Google Cloud Console in the menu on the left under "Compute Engine ➤ Committed Use Discounts ➤ Purchase Commitment." These must be created separately for each machine type (n1, n2, n2d, and memory-optimized machine type). The total amount of vCPU and RAM that is to run on schedule with this machine type is also given here, as illustrated in Figure 9-12.

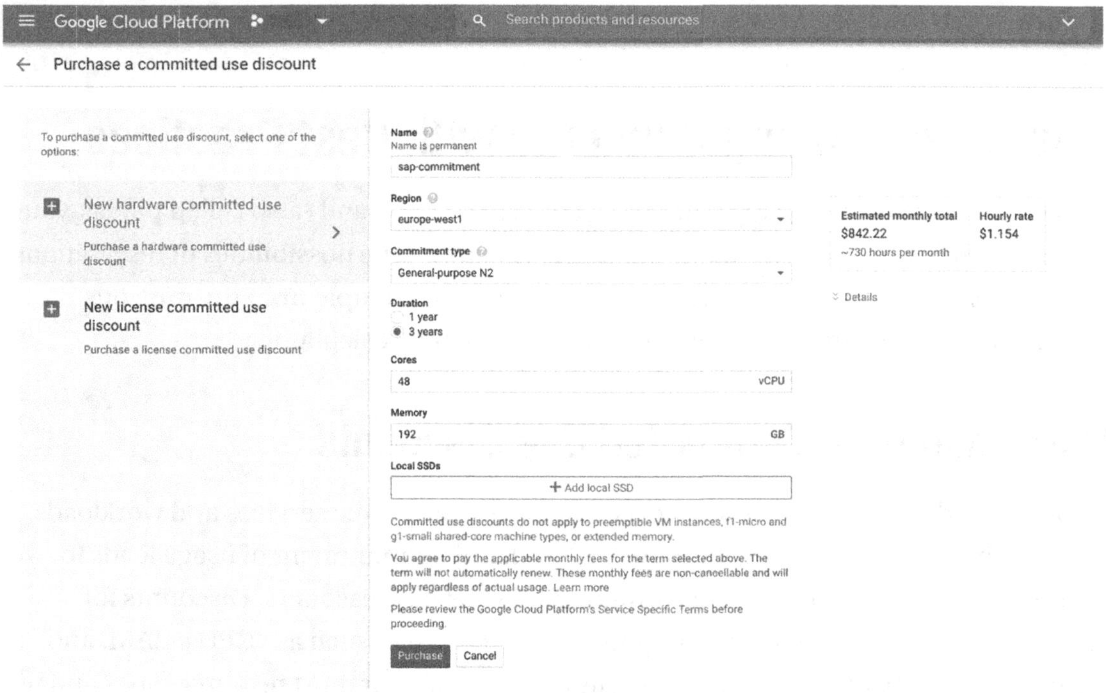

Figure 9-12. *Console screenshot: buy a committed use discount*

For all systems that are to be operated 24/7, which, for example, mostly applies to productive SAP systems, it is definitely recommended to purchase either a one-year or, for better discounts, a three-year committed use discount.

If you have sandbox or development systems in the landscape that do not need to run 24/7, then it may make sense for them to be paid for at the standard on-demand rate with no committed use. The hours per month at which the break-even point is exceeded varies by machine type and size. In many cases, this can be at around 200–250 hours per month. It is recommended to check this price ratio for your machines in the price calculator. A machine that is to run much less than 200–250 hours per month is definitely cheaper with the prices on demand and therefore much more flexible, as there is no commitment to a certain annual period. The same is also true for machines that are only needed for a short period of time, that is, only for a few weeks or months. This applies to migration machines, for example. These options should also be checked with the price calculator for your scenario, and one-year or three-year commitments should only be created from the profitability threshold.

Also, for operating system licenses like SLES for SAP, there is the possibility to buy discounts for committed use and thus achieve a cost saving of up to 57%. Saving and purchasing discounts is done in the same way as for the machine types in the menu for Compute Engine, but as can be seen in the figure via "New license committed use discount."

Another recommendation is that the purchase of the discounts is configured in the same project and in the same region in which they are to be used. This way, duplicate costs can be avoided. Discounts can be shared between projects, but not between regions. You should also remember that purchased discounts cannot be changed or deleted. Only additional, this means incremental, discounts can be purchased.

Committed use discounts are very flexible in the particular machine type group, and these discounts are not comparable to the concept of reservations. Committed use discounts are purchased on a total number of vCPU and RAM per machine type and can then be split into the possible VM sizes as desired. Thus, there is no commitment to specific machine size combinations.

To keep track of costs, cloud billing automatically provides many prebuilt reports on cost history, current cost trends, and forecast costs from Google Cloud.[23]

Reservations in Google Cloud

Reservations[24] in Google Cloud provide the ability to reserve resources so that you are ready for your Google Cloud projects in the future. This is recommended if you plan future growth, migrations or (un)planned peaks, disaster recovery, growth, or other activities. Reservations on Google Cloud are thus not comparable to reservations on other Hyperscalers. Once the reservation is created, that reserved instance is billed. The instance is available and reserved for you until you delete the reservation. This means reservations can be deleted at any time, unlike commitments (committed usage), which cannot be deleted before the end of the commitment period. Reservations are charged either via the on-demand price rate or, if discounts for committed use have been created, via these discounts.

---

[23] https://cloud.google.com/billing/docs/reports
[24] https://cloud.google.com/compute/docs/instances/reservations-overview

Main benefits of reservations

- Granted availability of resources when needed.

- No time constraints, can be created and also deleted at any time.

- Reservations qualify for all discounts (committed and sustained).

- Shared reservations can be shared between several projects which increases the flexibility in landscape planning and deployment.

Main limitations of reservations

- Not applicable to all services, only for Compute Engine, Google Kubernetes Engine, and Dataproc.

- 1000 VM instances per reservation can be reserved.

- Quota needs to be sufficient.

- Limited options for prioritizing the order in which reservations are consumed.

Google Cloud Quotas and Budgets

Quotas and budgets enable cost control in Google Cloud. *Quotas* restrict how much of a particular resource you can use. A quota is a specific quantifiable (countable) resource, for example, the maximum number of vCPUs or number of load balancers used in your project. There are two types of quotas: *rate quotas* (limiting the number of requests to the API or service) or *allocation quotas* (restricting the use of resources like the number of VMs used in a project at a given time). Some quotas are global and some quotas regional or even zonal.

Google Cloud is enforcing quotas to protect the community of Google Cloud users and prevent unforeseen spikes in usage, but also to help you manage resources to avoid unexpected costs and bills.

Quotas have to be managed and modified depending on the amount of resources you need; otherwise, you will run out of quota and receive a quota error during tasks like creating a new VM or a new project, calling an API, etc. Usually, quota increase requests are automatically evaluated and approved, but there can be exceptions in uncommon requests, and it can take up to two to three business days. Find more information about managing, monitoring, and increasing quota on the website.[25]

Budgets enable you to track your actual Google Cloud spend against a planned spend to avoid surprises on your bills by monitoring all charges. With budget alerts, you will receive email notifications and alerts, and from there on you can automate the cost control responses. All configuration possibilities and best practices are explained in the documentation.[26]

Pricing Calculation for the SAP S/4HANA on Google Cloud Architecture Example

To price a planned cloud landscape, Google Cloud provides a price calculator on the website.[27] In this section, the price calculator is explained, and a price for the landscape is determined based on the architecture, which was set up in the previous sections.

Most Google Cloud services can be calculated in the price calculator. To keep the complexity within bounds, the following example focuses only on the cost calculation of the Compute Engine instances for the SAP HANA and SAP application servers in both regions, as well as the associated required persistent disks and the SLES for SAP operating system licenses.

In a realistic price calculation, Google Cloud Storage for backups, the Cloud Load Balancer, IP address usage, network egress, Dedicated or Partner Interconnect or Cloud VPN, Cloud NAT, Cloud DNS, Cloud Operations, support, and, depending on usage, further services for NFS or backup tools from Google or third-party providers have to be added.

---

[25] https://cloud.google.com/docs/quota
[26] https://cloud.google.com/billing/docs/how-to/budgets
[27] https://cloud.google.com/products/calculator

The following systems of architecture were added in the price calculator:

- 2x n1-standard-4 for SAP HANA Studio and jumpbox, with SLES

- 3x n2-standard-4 with each 54 GB HDD, with SLES for SAP

- 3x n2-standard-16 with each 54 GB HDD, with SLES for SAP

- 3x n1-highmem-32 with each 843 GB SSD and 446 GB HDD, with SLES for SAP

- All with a three-year committed use discount (CUD)

The result is a list price (without enterprise discounts or the like – for these, contact your Google Cloud sales representative via the website). For the selected architecture, the costs are

USD 5344.11[28] per month (as of 22-September-2021)

This calculation can either be saved as a URL link or sent by email and further adapted and modified at future points in time.[29] Figures 9-13 through 9-15 show the complete price calculation in the calculator with the required VM instances in the regions, the operating system licenses, and the persistent disks per storage class and region.

---

[28] *The estimated fees provided by the Google Cloud Pricing Calculator are for discussion purposes only and are not binding on either you or Google. Your actual fees may be higher or lower than the estimate. A more detailed and specific list of fees will be provided at the time of sign-up. To sign up for Google Cloud and purchase services, please click one of the product links earlier.*

[29] https://cloud.google.com/products/calculator/#id=44aa2107-51c8-4
6ee-95a7-07c9bbeadc6d

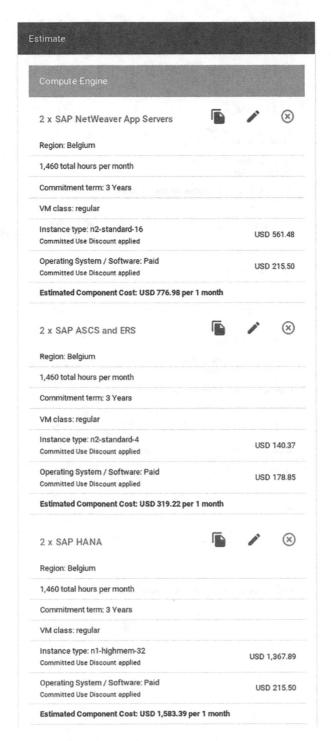

Figure 9-13. *Google Cloud Pricing Calculator – example calculation (part 1)*

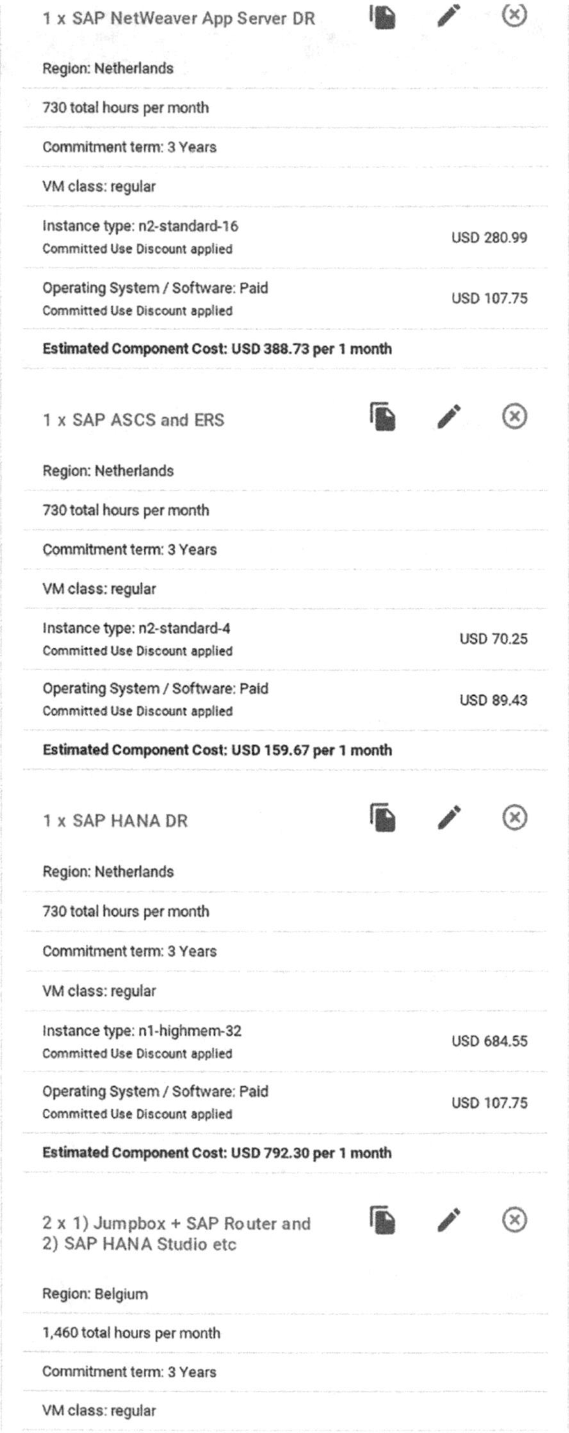

1 x SAP NetWeaver App Server DR

Region: Netherlands

730 total hours per month

Commitment term: 3 Years

VM class: regular

Instance type: n2-standard-16
Committed Use Discount applied

USD 280.99

Operating System / Software: Paid
Committed Use Discount applied

USD 107.75

Estimated Component Cost: USD 388.73 per 1 month

1 x SAP ASCS and ERS

Region: Netherlands

730 total hours per month

Commitment term: 3 Years

VM class: regular

Instance type: n2-standard-4
Committed Use Discount applied

USD 70.25

Operating System / Software: Paid
Committed Use Discount applied

USD 89.43

Estimated Component Cost: USD 159.67 per 1 month

1 x SAP HANA DR

Region: Netherlands

730 total hours per month

Commitment term: 3 Years

VM class: regular

Instance type: n1-highmem-32
Committed Use Discount applied

USD 684.55

Operating System / Software: Paid
Committed Use Discount applied

USD 107.75

Estimated Component Cost: USD 792.30 per 1 month

2 x 1) Jumpbox + SAP Router and
2) SAP HANA Studio etc

Region: Belgium

1,460 total hours per month

Commitment term: 3 Years

VM class: regular

Figure 9-14. *Google Cloud Pricing Calculator – example calculation (part 2)*

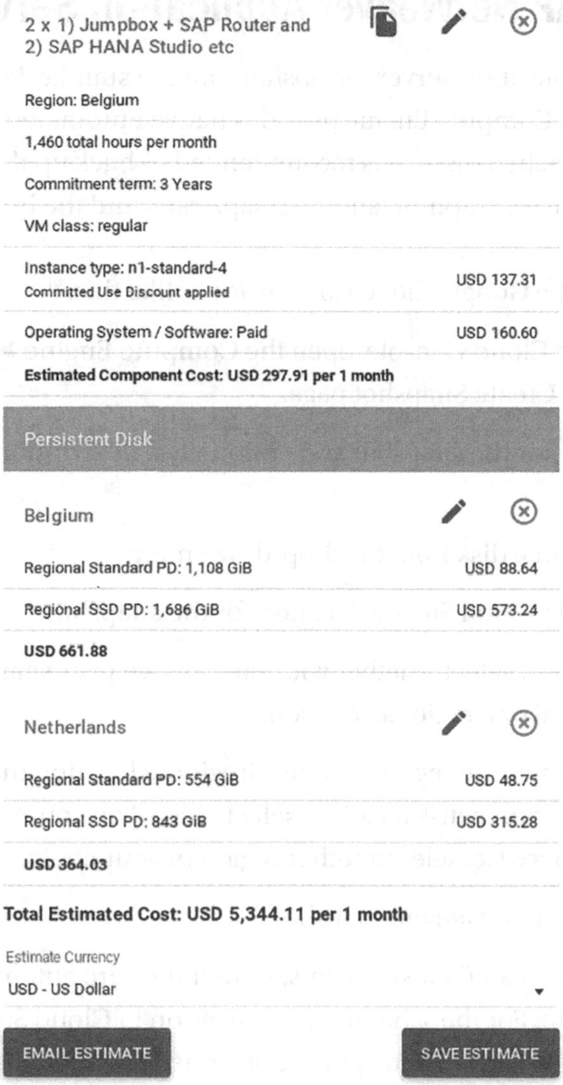

2 x 1) Jumpbox + SAP Router and
2) SAP HANA Studio etc

Region: Belgium

1,460 total hours per month

Commitment term: 3 Years

VM class: regular

Instance type: n1-standard-4
Committed Use Discount applied   USD 137.31

Operating System / Software: Paid   USD 160.60

Estimated Component Cost: USD 297.91 per 1 month

Persistent Disk

Belgium

Regional Standard PD: 1,108 GiB   USD 88.64

Regional SSD PD: 1,686 GiB   USD 573.24

USD 661.88

Netherlands

Regional Standard PD: 554 GiB   USD 48.75

Regional SSD PD: 843 GiB   USD 315.28

USD 364.03

Total Estimated Cost: USD 5,344.11 per 1 month

Estimate Currency

USD - US Dollar

EMAIL ESTIMATE   SAVE ESTIMATE

Figure 9-15. *Google Cloud Pricing Calculator – example calculation (part 3)*

Backup and Restore on Google Cloud

There are several ways to configure backup and restore on Google Cloud. These were already explained. This section looks at the configuration of the recommended native solutions.

Backups for SAP NetWeaver Application Server

For SAP NetWeaver application servers, snapshots are the standard option for creating backups. Google Cloud Compute Engine provides native automated snapshot functionality for the attached disks. It is recommended to back up the SAP NetWeaver file systems like /interfaces, /sapmnt, and /usr/sap/trans and the binaries like /exe and /boot with snapshots.

The operation via the Google Cloud Console looks like this:[30]

1. In the Google Cloud Console, open the Compute Engine ➤ Snapshots ➤ Create Snapshot page.

2. Enter a name for the snapshot and optionally a description of the snapshot.

3. Select the source disk from the drop-down menu.

4. Set the Google Cloud Storage location for the snapshot.

5. Under Location, select whether you want to save your snapshot to a multiregional or a regional location.

6. If you want to use the regional or multiregional location that is closest to the source disk location, select "based on source disk location"; otherwise, select another region of your choice.

7. Click "Create" to create the snapshot.

A schedule[31] can be created for snapshots, so that they are automatically created hourly, daily, weekly, etc. For the schedules, the location in Cloud Storage has to be configured, and deletion rules and application consistency can be defined. The configuration can be seen in Figure 9-16.

---

[30] https://cloud.google.com/compute/docs/disks/create-snapshots#create_zonal_snapshot

[31] https://cloud.google.com/compute/docs/disks/scheduled-snapshots

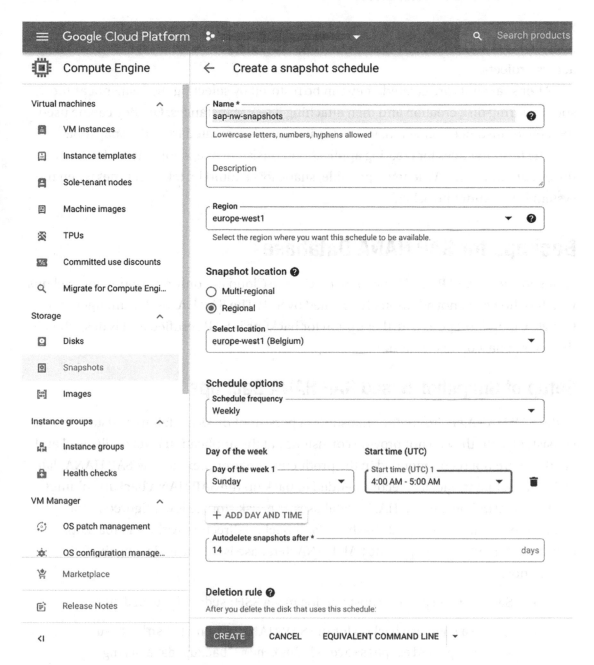

Figure 9-16. *Console screenshot: create a snapshot schedule*

After the snapshot schedule is created, they can be assigned to each drive respectively. Snapshot schedules can even be selected directly during a drive creation.

Snapshots associated with drives also continuously create system events that can be analyzed via Cloud Monitoring and audit logs. In general, snapshots can also be shared across projects.

After snapshots are created, they can be restored by selecting the snapshot as the source during disk creation and then attaching it to VM instances. Or, they can be used directly for instance recreation, where the instance is recreated from the snapshot.

The best practices for creating application-consistent snapshots can be found in the documentation.[32] Whenever possible, snapshots should be taken at times when the system is not under peak load.

Backups for SAP HANA Database

Snapshots for the SAP HANA database on Google Cloud are only one option for backups, which is, however, not additionally certified by SAP. The SAP HANA Backint Agent for Google Cloud Storage as a further option for backups is SAP certified and is described in the second part of this section.

Setup of Snapshot-Based SAP HANA Backups

In the SAP HANA environment, snapshots of persistent disks are failure resistant (crash consistent), but they do not provide consistency at the application level or file level and are therefore not recommended in the production environment for the SAP HANA data in /hana/data. Instead, it is recommended to back up the SAP HANA backup volumes.

When installing the SAP HANA databases, the disk storage is configured in the Deployment Manager template as the default backup directory with /hanabackup/data/SID. An initial backup of the SAP HANA database is performed using the following commands:[33]

- Switch to the primary host and log in via SSH: `sudo -i -u sid adm`

- Create a database backup for the SAP HANA system: `hdbsql -t -u system -p system-password -i inst-num "backup data using file ('full')"`

---

[32] https://cloud.google.com/compute/docs/disks/snapshot-best-practices

[33] https://cloud.google.com/solutions/sap/docs/sap-hana-ha-config-sles#back_up_the_databases

Configure the snapshots for each directory to be backed up. The configuration for snapshot creation with schedules is performed as already described in the previous section. For snapshots to be consistent, writes to the file system should be paused, and drive caches should be flushed so that the snapshot is consistent.[34]

Setup of SAP HANA Backint with Cloud Storage Backint Agent

If the SAP HANA Backint Agent for Google Cloud Storage is used, the SAP HANA database does not need a persistent disk for the /hanabackup, but the backups are stored directly in Google Cloud Storage. Before installing the SAP HANA Backint Agent and configuring backups, you should consider the following:

- Use SAP HANA DB administration tools to schedule backups.

- Use native OS compression because backups might not be efficiently compressed, but at the cost of CPU cycles and throughput.

- Unable to do deduplication even though it is an agent integrated to SAP HANA DB tools.

- But the application awareness is better than a volume snapshot.

- Take extra manual steps to do system copies using backups.

The following steps must be performed when installing and configuring backups with SAP HANA Backint:

1. The SAP HANA database that needs to be backed up has to be installed.

2. Create a Google Cloud Storage bucket for your backups. Choose the bucket location and bucket storage class.

3. Install the Backint agent on the SAP HANA host (in case a high availability cluster or a scale-out deployment installation on each node is required).

---

[34] https://cloud.google.com/solutions/sap/docs/sap-hana-operations-guide#creating_a_snapshot_of_sap_hana

4. Configure the Backint agent and SAP HANA in the parameters. txt file (configuration options can be found on the website[35]). The bucket name, service account, and more parameters can be configured like parallel_factor, rate_limit, threads, and more.

5. Test the configuration and if it is working as expected.

6. For troubleshooting and support topics, please see the official documentation.[36]

Scripting and Automation on Google Cloud

The following section provides an overview of the scripting and automation tools that can be used in the area of SAP systems on Google Cloud. In addition, three different use cases for automation scripts are shown in detail: the automated start and stop of instances and the autoscaling of SAP application servers. Finally, the SAP Landscape Manager Connector from Google Cloud is described.

Tools for Scripting and Automation on Google Cloud

There are different options and tools for automation in cloud environments. Commonly used options in Google Cloud are either with Google Cloud Deployment Manager or with other tools and open source projects such as Terraform, Ansible, Python, and more.

The benefit of Infrastructure as Code (IaC) or scripting is the automated creation of Google Cloud resources such as VM instances, disks, and so on. These are scripted once and then reused for the same or similar landscapes. This deployment path saves a lot of time in operations and is also less error-prone and risky.

The Google Cloud Deployment Manager service is used to deploy infrastructure. It automates the creation and management of Google Cloud resources. Flexible templates and configuration files can be created that deploy a range of Google Cloud services, including Cloud Storage, Compute Engine, and Cloud SQL.

---

[35] https://cloud.google.com/solutions/sap/docs/sap-hana-backint-guide#configuring_the_backint_agent_and_hana

[36] https://cloud.google.com/solutions/sap/docs/sap-hana-backint-guide

These IaC scripts are managed in a Google Cloud Source Repository, which is a fully managed and scalable service and is a private Git repository. Source code can be developed, tested, managed, and synchronized via version control. There is the ability to integrate with other Google Cloud tools such as Cloud Build, App Engine, Pub/Sub, and IT Operations Management products such as Cloud Monitoring and Cloud Logging.

Script examples and templates, as well as recommendations and troubleshooting procedures for Deployment Manager, are provided on the Google website[37] and for Terraform on GitHub.[38]

Use Case: Automated Start and Stop of Instances

Google Cloud Scheduler can be used to schedule many activities for automation, such as starting and stopping systems. Cloud Scheduler is a fully managed cron job scheduler that can schedule any job, including batch jobs and cloud infrastructure operations. You can automate everything, including retries during a failure, to reduce manual work and intervention. Cloud Scheduler serves as a single console interface to manage all automation tasks in one interface. To schedule backup tasks, Cloud Scheduler can also be used.

In SAP landscapes, automated start and stop can be useful for sandbox systems, or even for development and test systems, if they can be turned off during nights and weekends to save costs.

For such a configuration,[39] the Google Cloud Scheduler, Cloud Pub/Sub, and Cloud Functions services are required. Cloud Scheduler defines the exact schedule with the time specification and the day or repeat mode (e.g., Monday–Friday). These events triggered by Cloud Scheduler are received by Cloud Pub/Sub, Google's messaging-oriented middleware solution. Cloud Pub/Sub then triggers Cloud Functions, which executes snippets of code, such as launching instances and their attached startup scripts. The sequence is illustrated in Figure 9-17.

---

[37] https://cloud.google.com/solutions/sap/docs/dm-templates-for-sap

[38] https://github.com/terraform-google-modules/terraform-google-sap

[39] https://cloud.google.com/scheduler/docs/start-and-stop-compute-engine-instances-on-a-schedule

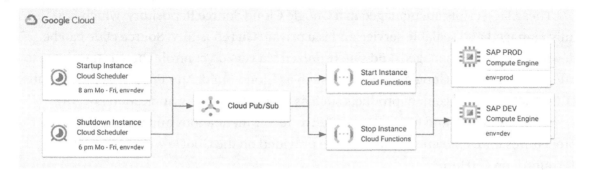

Figure 9-17. *Automated start and stop of instances*

Use Case: Autoscaling for SAP NetWeaver Application Servers

In most SAP landscapes, there is a varying but predictable usage of application servers. The predictability makes these systems good candidates to leverage the elasticity of the cloud, for example, with autoscaling, that is, shrinking and enlarging or adding and removing VM instances. Autoscaling for SAP application servers can be easily implemented and automated on Google Cloud. The main advantages of automatically scaling application servers are resource and cost savings. Two variants of autoscaling can be set up:

Scenario: Usage-based autoscaling

- Based on thresholds of the CPU, RAM, or other resource usage

- Implemented with the help of instance templates (or machine images), managed instance groups (MIG), and Google Operations

Scenario: Schedule-based autoscaling

- Based on a specific usage schedule with day and clock times

- Implemented with the help of Google Cloud Scheduler

More information, automation commands, and code examples can be found in the documentation.[40]

---

[40] https://cloud.google.com/blog/products/sap-google-cloud/best-practices-for-sap-app-server-autoscaling-on-google-cloud

Use Case: Simplification of Operations

Google Cloud and cloud-native capabilities simplify operations for SAP teams and system administrators. Requests from different projects and teams for urgent sandbox or project systems can be fulfilled quickly, with little effort and at low cost. Using instance templates (machine images), systems can be quickly copied and deployed in a new VM instance. On-demand billing also provides further flexibility here, as the systems can be deleted again after a few weeks or months and then no longer incur any costs. Cloning is possible for both the SAP HANA and SAP NetWeaver levels.[41]

SAP Landscape Management and Google Cloud

Another option for automating and managing the SAP landscape is the SAP Landscape Manager (SAP LaMa) with the Google Cloud Connector. Google provides this connector free of charge from the Google Cloud site, and the SAP LaMa license must be purchased from SAP. The following options for managing the SAP landscape via SAP LaMa are offered:

- SAP system/instance creation

- SAP system/instance move

- SAP system start and stop, also including virtual hosts

- Storage-based copy procedures based on Google Cloud disk snapshot technology for SAP system clones and system copies

- Storage-based copy procedures based on Google Cloud disk snapshot technology for SAP system update and database update

- Storage-based copy procedures based on Google Cloud disk snapshot technology for SAP HANA System Replication level creation

The system requirements, authentication and authorization requirements, possible scenarios,[42] and installation instructions[43] can be found in the documentation.

---

[41] https://cloud.google.com/solutions/sap/docs/
sap-hana-operations-guide#cloning_your_sap_hana_system

[42] https://cloud.google.com/solutions/sap/docs/sap-lama-connector-planning

[43] https://cloud.google.com/solutions/sap/docs/sap-lama-connector-deployment

Disaster Recovery on Google Cloud

To provide a disaster recovery system landscape, the desired disaster recovery option must be selected based on the RPO and RTO requirements. In this example scenario of the architecture, the full (hot) DR option was selected. This means that instances are replicated asynchronously at all levels of the system.

SAP HANA Disaster Recovery

At the SAP HANA database level, disaster recovery is also implemented with SAP HANA System Replication (HSR). For this purpose, a third SAP HANA instance must be provided, for which either manual or automated provisioning can also be selected. This is configured with asynchronous system replication starting from the secondary SAP HANA instance of the primary region. In the event of a disaster, it is recommended to trigger the takeover procedure of the SAP HANA instances manually according to the documentation.[44]

SAP NetWeaver Application Server Disaster Recovery

On the SAP application server level, disaster recovery is also provided with two VM instances: one instance for ASCS/ERS and one instance for the SAP NetWeaver application server. It is also recommended to trigger the takeover procedure manually in the application server area in the event of a disaster.

Recommendations for Disaster Recovery Planning

Depending on the choice of the disaster recovery method based on the desired RPO and RTO, the following points should be considered for all options:

Capacity planning: If a full disaster recovery option is not chosen, but a cost-optimized option, then capacity should be backed up with disaster recovery capacity planning.

---

[44]https://cloud.google.com/solutions/sap/docs/sap-hana-dr-planning-guide#triggering_a_takeover

Automation: Normally, a disaster recovery concept is initiated manually. This should be automated as completely as possible in the recovery from the backups and the start of the instances to ensure a fast (lowest possible RTO) and error-free recovery.

Documentation and test: Fully document your disaster recovery plan and ensure that documentation is available in the event of a disaster. Test your plan regularly and ensure that system administrators and the business are aware of the plan and trained in the process. Test this plan regularly using replica landscapes that can be copied and shut down quickly.

Summary

This chapter, after introducing a complete example architecture for SAP S/4HANA on Google Cloud, provided an overview of the general planning and deployment lists that can be used for any SAP deployments. A total of 25 steps were listed, which were split into general Google Cloud configurations for enterprises and SAP-specific steps on Google Cloud. These steps were then exemplified in the subsequent sections based on the introduced architecture.

The Google Identity Account, security, and network setup were followed by the provisioning of the Compute Engine VM instances for the entire SAP S/4HANA landscape, that is, the SAP HANA instances and the SAP NetWeaver application server instances in high availability mode. Here, manual and automated provisioning were addressed, respectively, and both ways were shown. Deployment based on automation with scripts is recommended.

This was followed by sections on the pricing and billing concept of the Google Cloud. The difference between on-demand billing and discounts for committed usage as well as reservations, quotas, and budgets was shown. The section concluded with an exemplary calculation based on the SAP S/4HANA on the Google Cloud example architecture introduced at the beginning of this chapter. This calculation was based on the public price calculator of the Google Cloud.

The next section gave an overview on the configurations for backup and recovery with snapshots and SAP HANA Backint for Google Cloud Storage.

The penultimate section gave an introduction to scripting and automation and the possible tools as well as use cases in the area of automatically starting and stopping instances, autoscaling for the application servers, and simplifying operations.

Finally, the setup for disaster recovery for this sample architecture was explained, and a brief overview of best practice recommendations was given.

Summary and Outlook

This chapter summarizes the key points from all previous chapters and provides an outlook on the future development of SAP S/4HANA systems in the public cloud.

Momentum of SAP S/4HANA

The end of traditional SAP systems has been set by SAP for 2025. This is when support for all non-HANA-based SAP systems is to end. Customers who have not yet switched to HANA or S/4HANA by then run the risk of handling their business processes with an ERP system that no longer has support. No company can afford this.

The momentum of SAP S/4HANA and the transformation to the cloud is now emerging from this deadline from SAP. Customers have little choice but to ignore the first of 2025. There are certainly companies that are currently more than satisfied with the ERP system they are using. Here, it makes little sense to switch to S/4HANA simply out of pressure.

Thus, companies are currently also looking around for alternatives to the transformation scenario. There are SAP customers who will deliberately not begin a transformation, but will continue to rely on the SAP ERP system. The decision is often driven by the low added value of SAP S/4HANA and HANA. The companies are very satisfied with their SAP systems, for example, ECC6.0 EhP 7 on Oracle, and the transformation to S/4 cannot generate the additional benefits as SAP propagates.

After 2025, SAP will no longer provide updates and patches for the systems. Support in the event of errors will also no longer be provided, and customers who have not converted the systems will be accepting a significant risk. Nevertheless, it would also be conceivable to ignore this deadline.

Even if there will be some customers who will not transform to SAP S/4HANA, it can be assumed that the majority have already taken this step, are currently doing so, or will do so in the future. With the large number of customers, every transformation to

© André Bögelsack, Utpal Chakraborty, Dhiraj Kumar, Johannes Rank, Jessica Tischbierek, Elena Wolz 2022
A. Bögelsack et al., *SAP S/4HANA Systems in Hyperscaler Clouds*, https://doi.org/10.1007/978-1-4842-8158-1_10

S/4HANA is also accompanied by a move to the cloud. This momentum will therefore persist for longer than 2025, as there will still be some stragglers converting systems after 2025.

Public Cloud Is an Established Trend

The public cloud is not a temporary trend, but it has already established itself so strongly that new business models are only being built on the basis of the public cloud. Be it the new Internet banks, which work exclusively on the basis of cloud computing, or start-ups, which can only generate business through the features of the public clouds. What they all have in common is that public cloud forms the backbone.

Nevertheless, some larger companies still show reservations when it comes to the question of "SAP in the cloud?". Here, companies are pursuing the strategy of least risk, which is absolutely right for critical SAP systems. Companies are very hesitant and start with the adaptation of the public cloud with noncritical applications, which do not have a significant impact on the business. A failure of these less important applications usually has no consequences. If an SAP system were to fail completely because of the public cloud, this would be tragic and would significantly affect the business and all processes of the company.

In this discussion and consideration, however, the facts should always be taken into account. These show that the public clouds, just like the private clouds, have hardware failures from time to time or that systems are affected by them. As with the recent failures of Facebook and WhatsApp, it is not uncommon for the employees to be responsible, while the hardware was working perfectly.

Currently, all larger companies are pursuing a strategy of using the public cloud as a target platform. Some companies have already used the public cloud at an early stage, such as Carlsberg, which strategically migrated all systems to the cloud at an early stage. Other companies are using the cloud as a new platform for the greenfield implementation of SAP S/4HANA systems. For those companies that do not yet have a footprint in the public cloud, there are two options:

1. The companies are already using the public cloud, but this has never really been made public, and the IT department in charge has no knowledge about it. This happens and happened again and again with very large corporations and must be explained by a lack of innovation in the IT department.

2. The companies do not use any public cloud because of security concerns. This scenario is not seen in large corporations, but rather in medium-sized businesses. Here, there are companies that process highly sensitive data, so outsourcing IT is out of the question.

All other companies and groups are already in the public cloud.

The three most important providers of public clouds, Amazon Web Services, Microsoft Azure, and Google Cloud, already have a long tradition, and the maturity of the services offered is very high. This is also the reason why SAP is also strategically pushing the cloud business. In addition to the SAP HANA Enterprise Cloud, SAP AG is constantly expanding the portfolio with new cloud services and new cloud offerings. This also includes RISE, which strategically relies on hyperscalers as a platform for operating SAP systems.

All these points show that the groups cannot avoid the public cloud and must adapt it as soon as possible. SAP systems will also move in that direction, as the advantages outweigh the (perceived) disadvantages.

Public Cloud As Innovation Driver

Hyperscalers are working hard to make public clouds and their resources as easy to use as possible. The aim is to keep the hurdle to entry into the world of public clouds as low as possible. However, this alone is not the most important reason for the strategic use of public clouds. Rather, companies and customers are focusing on using new features from the clouds.

In the previous chapters, you saw how easy it is to deploy new SAP S/4HANA systems in Hyperscaler Clouds. This showed not only simple environments but also highly complex environments. Creating a simple SAP S/4HANA system with high availability requires many components, like the cluster or the file shares. This can be deployed very easily in Hyperscaler Clouds. Of course, this requires some configuration steps, but customers can easily obtain all the necessary components from the cloud and do not need to acquire any additional hardware or software components.

The advantage of hyperscaler clouds is particularly evident when it comes to the issue of disaster recovery. All providers offer customers a variety of options for protection against a disaster. This can be through simple availability zones within a region; but this can also be through protection against the failure of a region (Dublin – Frankfurt). Thus, all customers can replicate common failure scenarios in the clouds as well. This also applies to data backup and data recovery. Here, the hyperscalers offer only the basic functionalities, but these are quite sufficient for some smaller system environments. However, for highly complex, productive, and highly critical SAP S/4HANA systems, an established backup/restore solution from a third-party provider should be used.

Automation is given a particularly high priority in the cloud. We have already looked at Terraform and Ansible to some extent in the previous chapters, but their potential is far from exhausted. Many companies already follow the principle of "immutable infrastructure," which is based on the fact that new infrastructure components can only be provisioned in a fully automated and tested manner. However, since SAP S/4HANA systems are very complex entities and have a high level of architectural complexity, it will still take some time before new SAP S/4HANA systems can be completely provisioned without administrator intervention. There are already options, such as the SAP Cloud Appliance Library, which addresses precisely this issue, but more can be expected here.

Digital decoupling decouples the additional functions from the core of SAP S/4HANA systems. In this way, the SAP S/4HANA systems can fulfill exactly those functions that are important. All additional functionalities and integration scenarios are provided by further supporting systems. In this way, the SAP S/4HANA systems have become future-proof. This means that new functions from the clouds can be easily configured to the existing systems. Companies are already going very far here and implementing the control of SAP via Amazon Alexa or using the large data stock from the SAP systems in Data Lakes to analyze the data afterward per Analytics.

The innovative power of public clouds is enormous, and it can be assumed that SAP will also use this power to implement and offer new features and new ways of working for the SAP S/4HANA systems.

Outlook

The previous chapters have introduced you to the idea, function, conceptual design, implementation, and use of Hyperscaler Clouds for SAP S/4HANA systems in detail. It is evident how easy it is to create such systems on the Hyperscaler Clouds and how easy it is to operate the systems on the clouds if the intrinsic advantages of the clouds are used.

We assume that in the foreseeable future there will be very few customers who do not operate SAP systems on the hyperscaler clouds. This trend is reinforced by the cost-effectiveness of the environments, the high level of security, the strong homogenization, and the simple control of the SAP landscapes. In this way, companies can no longer avoid it for long and will open up sooner or later.

SAP is strategically focusing on the cloud and will also make further investments here to make SAP S/4HANA systems fully cloud capable and, in particular, adapt the system architecture. This would significantly increase the reliability, availability, data security, and resilience of SAP S/4HANA systems. All customers will benefit from this.

The cloud market will remain highly dynamic. Nevertheless, it can be assumed that the balance of power will not change too much in the foreseeable future (three years). New entrants will have a hard time gaining a significant share of the market, even though the market still has a lot of potential. It is certainly not wrong for customers to rely on one of the three major vendors in the market, which have been described here in this book: Microsoft Azure, Amazon Web Services, and Google Cloud. All three hyperscalers continue to invest heavily in the future of public clouds, and all customers (small or large) will be able to benefit from this.

Index

A

ABAP Central Services (ASCS),
224, 377–381
Access control list (ACL), 222, 240, 242
Actifio Global Manager (AGM), 445–447
Active Directory Domain Service (ADDS)
architecture setup, 176
AWS resource, 179–181
components, 168, 169
directory-based services, 166
DNS name resolution, 175, 176
domain controller EC2s, 174
features, 167
forwarding rules, 177
GA, 166
implementation, 172, 173
managed service, 172
monitoring process, 180, 181
network elements, 176, 177
on-premise, 171, 172, 178, 179
prerequisite information, 174
replication setup, 173
Route 53 resolver, 176
scenarios, 177, 178
self managed deployment, 170, 171
Standard and Enterprise, 173
Additional application server (AAS),
216, 224, 381, 382
Advanced Business Application
Programming (ABAP), 30, 33

Alibaba cloud
IBM, 14, 15
Oracle, 14
private clouds, 15
specifications, 13
Amazon Elastic Compute Cloud
(Amazon EC2), 126
Amazon Machine Image (AMI), 126, 208
Amazon Web Services (AWS)
account credentials, 144, 145
active directory, 166–181
advantages, 122
availability zones, 134, 135
backup/restore
Backint agents, 244, 245
backup configuration, 250–255
centralized backup solution, 250
EC2 image backup, 249, 250
EC2 instance/EBS
volume, 245, 246
primary backup entities, 243
restore process, 255–257
snapshots, 246–249
benefits, 119
billing/cost management
service, 149, 150
browser support, 141, 142
business growth trend, 124, 125
calculator, 230
cloud framework, 263

© André Bögelsack, Utpal Chakraborty, Dhiraj Kumar, Johannes Rank, Jessica Tischbierek, Elena Wolz 2022
A. Bögelsack et al., *SAP S/4HANA Systems in Hyperscaler Clouds*, https://doi.org/10.1007/978-1-4842-8158-1

H

I, J

Printed in the United States
by Baker & Taylor Publisher Services